THE STRATEGIC IMPERATIVE

THE STRATEGIC IMPERATIVE:

New Policies for American Security

SAMUEL P. HUNTINGTON, Editor

Written under the auspices of the Center for
International Affairs, Harvard University.

BALLINGER PUBLISHING COMPANY
Cambridge, Massachusetts
A Subsidiary of Harper & Row, Publishers, Inc.

International Standard Book Number: 0-88410-895-3

Library of Congress Catalog Card Number: 82-8722

Printed in the United States of America

Library of Congress Cataloging in Publication Data
Main entry under title:

The Strategic imperative.

Includes index.
1. United States—National security—Addresses, essays, lectures.
2. United States—Military policy—Addresses, essays, lectures. I.
Huntington, Samuel P.
UA23.S8275 1982   355'.033073   82-8722
ISBN 0-88410-895-3   AACR2

CONTENTS

LIST OF FIGURES
AND TABLES

Figures

Tables

Preface

This volume is a product of the Program in National Security Studies at the Harvard Center for International Affairs, with which eight of the nine contributors were associated during the years 1979–1981. This program is designed to serve two major purposes: to promote the development and training of a new generation of strategic thinkers and to encourage the formulation of new approaches to the national security problems the United States will confront in the 1980s. In their work the participants in the program have generally attempted to get away from the scientific, technological, and systems-analytical approaches that have dominated American thinking on security issues. Instead they stress the historical, political, and cultural factors that shape strategy and security policy. They have also attempted to avoid the narrow focus on arms control that characterized much of American work in these areas in the late 1960s and early 1970s and instead to deal with arms control as only one of several components of security policy. These general approaches are reflected in the various publications the program has produced, including the essays in this volume.

This volume is also rooted in the widely shared belief among program participants that many of the key concepts that informed and shaped American strategy in the 1950s and 1960s no longer have the same relevance and usefulness in the 1980s. These include concepts of nuclear deterrence, mutually assured destruction, flexible response, escalation control, crisis stability, limited war, counterinsurgency, and others. The essays in this volume criticize some of these approaches and suggest alternatives. No effort is made, however, to provide either comprehensive or systematic treatment of the full range of strategic issues. Individual authors have not been assigned topics to cover or positions to argue in accordance with some master plan. Instead they were asked to write about topics on which they thought they might have something original and useful to say. Hence some subjects are dealt with more than once and others not treated at all. It is our belief and hope, however, that individually and collectively these essays will provide some new ideas as to how the United States should order its defenses during the coming decade.

Portions of the articles appearing in this volume have appeared previously as follows: Eliot A. Cohen, "Systems Paralysis," and Steven R. David, "Wielding Realignments: Adjusting to the Reality of the Third World," *American Spectator,* Volume 13, November 1980; Aaron L. Friedberg, "A History of U.S. Strategic 'Doctrine,'" *Journal of Strategic Studies,* Volume 3, December 1980; Michael I. Handel, "Numbers Do Count: The Question of Quality versus Quantity," *Journal of Strategic Studies,* Volume 4, September 1981.

The editor wishes to acknowledge his gratitude to National Affairs, Inc., for support of his work on the volume.

Samuel P. Huntington

THE STRATEGIC IMPERATIVE

1 THE RENEWAL OF STRATEGY

Samuel P. Huntington

REACTING TO CHANGE

The security of the United States was affected positively and negatively by several major developments during the 1970s: the decline in American economic strength compared to that of other countries; increasing U.S. dependence on foreign sources of oil, primarily from Africa and the Persian Gulf; the extension of Soviet influence in Angola, Ethiopia, Yemen, Afghanistan, and Central America; the American rapprochement with the People's Republic of China; the increased economic involvement of Soviet bloc countries with the West; the growing domestic problems within the Soviet Union; and the "Vietnam hangover" among the American public. As far as American strategy and national security policy are concerned, however, the most important change of the 1970s was the relative decline in American military power compared to that of the Soviet Union. From the mid-1960s through the 1970s Soviet military spending increased

The author is in debt to the participants in the Tuesday luncheon seminar of the Program in National Security Studies of the Harvard Center for International Affairs for the useful going over they gave this chapter, and is especially grateful to Joshua Epstein and Gary Samore for their thoughtful written comments on it.

1

3–4 percent annually in real terms. For seven years, from 1969 through 1975, American military spending decreased in real terms. As a result, in almost every category of military strength the Soviets were stronger vis-à-vis the United States in the late 1970s than they had been in the late 1960s. The development of Soviet military power was particularly manifest in: (1) the expansion and modernization of their forces and other Warsaw Pact forces in central Europe; (2) their deployment of modernized (SS-20s and Backfires) theater nuclear forces along their eastern and western frontiers; (3) the major increase (from fifteen to forty-four divisions) in their ground forces deployed along the Chinese frontier and in their air and naval forces based in eastern Siberia; (4) their continued development of a "blue water" navy, including aircraft carriers, and their more extensive deployment of that navy in distant waters, including the Indian Ocean; (5) the expansion and modernization of their strategic nuclear forces, including SS-18s, SS-19s, and submarine launched ballistic missiles (SLBMs), giving them at least parity with and, in some dimensions, superiority to the United States; (6) their sustained development of strategic defenses, including their air defense system, damage-limiting capability against U.S. land-based missiles, and civil defense system.

In the mid-1970s these developments stimulated a response in the United States, as executive officials, congressmen, and the public became increasingly alarmed about the Soviet build-up and increasingly wary of Soviet intentions. In its last year in office, the Ford Administration stopped the decline in military spending. Subsequently, the Carter and Reagan Administrations intensified the U.S. military response by: (1) deciding to develop and deploy cruise missiles, the MX missile, and a new strategic bomber; (2) launching a Long Term Defense Program for the strengthening of allied military forces in Europe; (3) agreeing with the NATO allies on theater nuclear force modernization and the simultaneous pursuit of negotiations with the Soviets on this issue; (4) inaugurating efforts to create a regional security framework for the Persian Gulf area, including the creation of a rapid deployment force and the permanent positioning of U.S. naval forces in the Indian Ocean; (5) expanding military and intelligence cooperation with the People's Republic of China; (6) taking steps to increase significantly the combat strength of the navy.

The rebuilding of American military power is clearly necessary for the security of the United States and its allies during the 1980s and 1990s. It is not, however, sufficient. Security is a matter of strategy as well as strength. At the end of the 1970s American strategic thinking was still in large part dominated by the ideas that had been developed during the very different circumstances of the 1950s and 1960s: nuclear deterrence; escalation control; mutual assured destruction; strategic stability; flexible response; counterinsurgency; limited war; arms control. These ideas were the product of an era when American military power—particularly nuclear power—was preeminent. No matter what efforts are made to expand U.S. military capabilities, that preeminence will not be restored. Consequently, many of the strategic ideas developed during that period of preeminence are of dubious relevance to the conditions of the 1980s. Americans are in danger of allowing their strategic concepts to become obsolete in a way that they would never allow their strategic weapons to become. American security in the 1980s requires not only a reconstitution of military strength but also a reformulation of military strategy.

THE ENVIRONMENT OF STRATEGY

Any reformulation will have to start with the critical changes in the strategic environment and the implications of those changes for American security. In addition to the change in the military balance, four trends of the 1970s could be of crucial significance for American strategy in the 1980s.

The Development of the Soviet Empire

American strategy obviously should be based on a realistic estimate of the most salient characteristics of its principal adversary. Those characteristics, and with them American images of Soviet reality, change over time. In the early years of the cold war the Soviet Union was perceived by Americans to be, and was in fact, the center of a global communist movement committed to world revolution. The "Soviet threat" at that time stemmed both from the strength of the Red Army in Europe and from the Communist parties and revolutionary movements around the world which the Soviet Union supported and which responded to its direction. This image of the Soviet Union predominated in National Security Council 68, drafted in the spring of 1950. Fifteen years later, Soviet reality and, to a much greater degree, American images of the Soviet Union had changed significantly. The Sino-Soviet split was a reality, and the Soviet Union was increasingly seen as a relatively conservative nation-state interested primarily in achieving strategic parity and in promoting its own economic development. As a result, detente, arms control agreements, and expanded East-West economic relations were in order. By the end of the 1970s this image of the Soviet Union had withered in the face of the sustained Soviet military build-up and the active attempts of the Soviet Union to expand militarily its control and influence directly and through proxies in various parts of the world. These developments make it accurate and useful to picture the Soviet Union now as primarily neither a revolutionary state nor a status-quo state, but rather as an imperial state.

The Soviet Union and the Soviet system constitute the last of the major nineteenth-century empires. Other continental empires—Hapsburg, Hohenzollern, and Ottoman—disappeared in the wake of World War I. The overseas empires—British, French, Dutch, Belgian, and Portuguese—evaporated in the decades following World War II. Perhaps the most important historical function of the Bolshevik Revolution was to enable the Tsarist empire to avoid the fate of its counterparts by providing it with new ruthlessly effective leadership, new institutions for rule, a new basis of legitimacy, and hence a new lease on life, extending its existence at least through the major part of the twentieth century. During this time the reconstituted empire grew to the point where it now consists of three major components: (1) the internal empire, dating from 1921, consisting of those peoples that have been formally incorporated into the Soviet state; (2) the contiguous empire, dating from 1945, consisting of the satellite countries adjacent to the Soviet Union (Eastern Europe, Mongolia, and, if the Soviets have their way, Afghanistan) and bound to the imperial power by political and economic controls and in many cases by the presence of Soviet troops; and (3) the overseas empire, dating from 1961, consisting of those countries at some distance from the Soviet Union and bound to it through political ties and high degrees of economic or military dependence (Cuba, Angola, Ethiopia, Yemen, Vietnam).

Like other empires in history, the Soviet empire is characterized by simultaneous processes of external expansion and internal decay. The logic of empire is such that enough is never enough; the dynamics of empire, if nothing else, demand the acquisition of additional territory to insure the security of existing territory. The process of expansion, in turn, creates internal stresses and strains, and encourages forces challenging imperial control within the empire at the same time that the empire itself is growing. The Soviet overseas empire in 1980 was more extensive than it had been in 1970. At the same time, Soviet control and influence in Eastern Europe was relatively weaker than it had been in 1970, and the two most momentous international developments in 1980—Afghanistan and Poland—testified to the problems the Soviets confronted in controlling their contiguous empire.

In the 1980s the development of the Soviet empire is likely to pose two major challenges to global peace and Western security. One challenge can come from that empire's impetus to expand; the other, from the processes within the empire working toward disintegration. Empires seldom decay peacefully, and imperial elites who feel threatened do not always act rationally. Soviet leaders are more likely to use more extreme forms of military force to maintain their empire than to expand it.

The Declining Effectiveness of
Nuclear Deterrence

In 1949 Winston Churchill (1949: 384) argued, "It is certain that Europe would have been communized and London under bombardment some time ago but for the deterrent of the atomic bomb in the hands of the United States." Five years later John Foster Dulles declared that as a result of the inability of the United States and its allies to mount effective conventional defenses throughout the world, the United States had decided "to depend primarily upon a great capacity to retaliate instantly by means and at places of our own choosing." The United States must rely on its own strengths, "especially air and naval power and atomic weapons which are now available in a wide range, suitable not only for strategic bombing but also for extensive tactical use . . . " (Kaufman 1956: 12–15). Effective U.S. monopoly (lasting into the mid-1950s) and overwhelming nuclear superiority (lasting well into the 1960s) enabled the United States to use the possibility of nuclear retaliation to protect the security both of itself and its allies against a variety of conventional military threats. In fact in some nineteen cases between 1946 and 1973 (fourteen of them involving the Soviet Union or China) the United States did employ its nuclear forces to deter hostile action or to achieve other political or diplomatic goals (Blechman and Kaplan 1978:47–49). The ability of the United States to use its nuclear forces in this way—at least against the Soviet Union—declined with the growth of Soviet nuclear capabilities in the middle and late 1960s. The last such use of the U.S. nuclear deterrent occurred in 1973, coincident with the emergence of nuclear parity, and involved an implied threat which, if called by the Soviets, would have been revealed as a bluff. The U.S. strategic nuclear deterrent, which had originally served to deter a conventional Soviet invasion of Western Europe, and had then been expanded to perform a variety of other functions, became in the 1970s increasingly limited to the deterrence of a nuclear attack on the United States or its closest allies.

Insofar as strategic nuclear forces contribute to deterrence elsewhere, their effectiveness depends upon the other military forces and the other means of deterrence to which they can be linked. "We now recognize," as Harold Brown observed (1979:76), "that the strategic nuclear forces can deter only a relatively narrow range of contingencies, much smaller in range than was foreseen only 20 or 30 years ago." In the 1950s extended nuclear deterrence was based on the rationality of the deterree; in the 1970s extended nuclear deterrence increasingly had to be based on the irrationality of the deterrer.

Multiplication of the Needs for Deterrence

The range of Soviet military actions that the United States needs to deter is a function of (1) Soviet military capabilities and (2) U.S. interests and purposes that might be threatened by those capabilities. During the 1970s both the former and the latter expanded significantly, making the problem of deterrence for the 1980s very different from what it had been previously.

Initially, as we have pointed out, the United States was primarily concerned with deterring a Soviet attack on Western Europe. In the 1950s, largely as a consequence of the Korean War, Japan and Korea were brought within the deterrence perimeter. The Communist conquest of mainland China also led to security agreements and military deployments to deter Chinese attacks against Taiwan (including the offshore islands) and Southeast Asia. As Soviet nuclear capabilities gradually developed in the late 1950s and 1960s, American policy became increasingly concerned with the deterrence first of a nuclear countervalue attack and then of a nuclear counterforce attack on the United States. Also in the 1960s, however, the deepening of the Sino-Soviet split plus the Cultural Revolution seemed to reduce the threat posed by Communist China, a shift formally recognized in 1969 with the abandonment of the planning assumption that the United States might simultaneously have to fight two major wars against the Soviet Union and China. Instead, U.S. military planning was directed toward a major war in Europe and a "half-war" in Korea. In this respect, the requirements of deterrence for the United States at the end of the 1960s were, in some measure, less than they had been earlier in that decade.

The following ten years, however, saw the emergence of three major new deterrent needs. First, the increasing dependence of the United States, as well as its allies, on Persian Gulf oil plus the enhanced capabilities of the Soviet Union to threaten that oil militarily inevitably directed American attention to the security of the Gulf region. The oil embargo of 1973–74 highlighted the vulnerability of the industrialized democracies to disruptions in the flow of oil. The fragility and instability of the political systems in many of the Gulf countries, the emergence of Islamic fundamentalism, the tensions between countries in the region, plus the unsettling effect of the Arab-Israeli conflict and the Palestinian presence in many Gulf countries, all underlined the opportunities which might develop for the expansion of Soviet influence. In early 1977 a major U.S. government study identified not Korea or Yugoslavia or Berlin but rather Iran as the most likely spot for U.S.-Soviet military confrontation in the short-run future. In the summer of 1977 a presidential directive officially elevated the Middle East and Persian Gulf to the level of Western Europe and East Asia as an area of vital interest to the United States. In effect the Carter Administration adopted a one-and-two-half-war military strategy. Soviet and Cuban intervention in the Horn of Africa, the coups in South Yemen and Afghanistan in 1978, the revolution in Iran, and finally the Soviet invasion of Afghanistan at the end of 1979 all reinforced the seeming threats to this region. Afghanistan also provided the opportunity for the public announcement of the conclusion reached two and one-half years earlier within the administration: "An attempt by any outside force to gain control of the Persian Gulf region will be regarded as an assault on the vital interests of the United States of America, and such an assault will be repelled by any means necessary, including military force.'' The ''Carter Doctrine'' thus officially committed the United States to deterring and, if necessary, defeating Soviet intervention in the Persian Gulf area.

Second, in 1969 the Soviet Union and China engaged in an intense war of words; Soviet and Chinese troops fought a series of border battles; and the Soviet Union asked the United States how it would view a Soviet attack on Chinese nuclear facilities. These events crystallized recognition within the government that, as President Nixon observed, it was not in American interests to let China be ''smashed.'' U.S. policymakers analyzed how the United States could prevent a Sino-Soviet war or, if that failed, influence its outcome. This policy, formulated even before the United States had any meaningful diplomatic contact with China, was ''based on a sober geopolitical assessment. If Moscow succeeded in humiliating Peking and reducing it to impotence, the whole weight of the Soviet military effort could be thrown against the West. Such a demonstration of Soviet ruthlessness and American impotence (or indifference—the result would be the same) would encourage accommodation to other Soviet demands from Japan to Western Europe, not to speak of the many smaller countries on the Soviet periphery'' (Kissinger 1979a:182–186, 764). As relations between China and the United States gradually improved through the 1970s, the extent of the American interest in deterring or defeating a Soviet attack on China correspondingly increased. By playing the China card, the United States gained a Chinese commitment.

Third, up to 1982, Soviet military attacks, with the debatable exception of Afghanistan, were directed against only their own allies, most notably Hungary in 1956 and Czechoslovakia in 1968. In neither case did the United States or other Western powers make significant efforts to deter the Soviets. When Soviet troops massed on the Czech border in August 1968, all the United States could do, according to Lyndon Johnson (1971:486), was to ''watch and worry.'' In some respects, even, steps were taken to reassure the Soviets that the NATO powers would not attempt to exploit the situation to loosen Soviet control in Eastern Europe. The United States, as Philip Windsor put it (1978:477–479), wanted ''to demonstrate to the USSR that, although it disapproved of the Soviet action, it would in no sense interfere in the Soviet sphere of influence. . . . At no time was *any* form of sanction discussed among Western European leaders.''

Contrast this with Poland in 1980–81. Top officials of both the Carter and Reagan Administrations repeatedly warned of the serious consequences that would follow if the Soviets interfered in "the Soviet sphere of influence." The NATO ministers declared that detente would be dead. Agreement was reached on a series of economic sanctions that would be applied. The U.S. secretary of defense spoke of the military sales to China that would inevitably follow. All involved predicted heightened defense preparations in the West. It is, of course, usually impossible to demonstrate that deterrence has succeeded; in this case, it is particularly difficult. From the summer of 1980 to the summer of 1981, the Soviets may have had good reasons of their own for not going into Poland on any of the five occasions when the crisis seemed to peak. In addition, whatever deterrent effect was provided by the United States and its NATO allies was undoubtedly secondary to that provided by the Poles themselves. It remains a fact, nonetheless, that for a year the Soviet leadership seriously considered taking a major military action to suppress what seemed to be highly threatening developments in an allied state—and did not take that action. When action was finally necessary, they arranged for it to be taken by the Polish military leadership, thereby softening considerably the sanctions that would have followed if they had acted themselves. If the West had not existed or if the West had adopted its 1968 posture, the probability would certainly have been much higher that the Soviets would have taken direct action against this threat to their vital interests.

Over the course of a decade American interests in deterring Soviet military action thus expanded to include the Persian Gulf area, the People's Republic of China, and, in at least some circumstances, Eastern European countries. These interests are real, but they differ significantly from those involving Western Europe, Japan, and Korea. These latter countries constitute what might be termed the "first zone of deterrence": the United States generally is highly involved with these countries politically and economically; the U.S. commitment to their defense is formalized in treaties and dates from the period of overwhelming U.S. nuclear superiority. Consequently, there is at least a residual possibility, even in the 1980s, that the United States might use nuclear weapons to defend these countries against conventional attack. The "second zone of deterrence," on the other hand, developed during the 1970s, years of nuclear parity or marginal Soviet advantage. U.S. interests in these countries are not as complex and deep as with first-zone countries, and U.S. commitments have not been embodied in formal treaties. There is no history of nuclear deterrence with respect to second-zone countries, and, as a result, primary reliance must be put on non-nuclear means of deterrence. Yet in the 1980s, Soviet military action against its Eastern European allies, against China, or in the Persian Gulf area seems far more likely than Soviet military action against Western Europe or Japan.

The Probability of Soviet-American War

One of the most remarkable phenomena of the twentieth century is that for three and one-half decades following World War II the United States and the Soviet Union engaged in an intense and multifaceted global rivalry and yet never during these years did American and Soviet forces directly engage each other militarily. That was a major achievement of both American and Soviet foreign policy. In the 1980s, however, at least three factors are likely to increase the probability of Soviet-American military conflict. First, as a result of the sustained Soviet military build-up during the 1960s and 1970s plus the U.S. reduction in its military effort during many of these years, the overall military balance will be more favorable to the Soviets during the early 1980s than at any other time since World War II, and it probably will be more favorable during these years than it will be in the late 1980s and in the 1990s. Thus is created the so-called "window of vulnerability." The significance of this window in Soviet calculations is difficult to evaluate. In the past, however, other powers (most notably Germany in 1939 and Japan in 1941) have gone to war to achieve objectives they believed important before the military balance, currently in their favor, turned against them. The Soviets themselves apparently considered taking military action against the Chinese in 1969 but did not, in part perhaps because of American opposition to such a move at a time when the Soviets had high hopes for what they could gain through detente. In the 1980s the very scope of the American defense build-up, particularly if it is intensely pursued, could increase the incentives for the Soviets to take immediate advantage of opportunities to expand their influence while the military balance remains relatively favorable.

Second, the area of potential overlap in conflicting interests and in the ability to apply military force has significantly increased. In the

1950s and 1960s the Soviet Union used military force primarily against its own allies, whom the United States did not wish to support by active intervention. As a result of the changes in East-West relations during the 1970s, the United States has come to perceive its interest in such situations rather differently in the 1980s. During the 1950s and 1960s, the United States intervened militarily in many parts of the world—East Asia, Southeast Asia, the Middle East, the Caribbean—where the Soviet Union lacked the interest, the capabilities, or both to respond in comparable fashion. This situation has also changed. The Soviet Union now defines its interests globally; it has actively supported military action by proxy forces in regions distant from itself; it has sent its own forces into Afghanistan. It has the navy and the airlift to project substantial forces into the Middle East, South Asia, and much of Africa. The "spheres of influence" that tacitly existed in the first decades of the Cold War have dissolved. Soviet and American political interests and military capabilities overlap, and as a result the probability has increased that the latter may be employed when the former conflict.

Third, political instability and upheaval is increasingly likely in areas of vital interest to the United States, the Soviet Union, or both. These areas include the Persian Gulf, Central America and the Caribbean, and Eastern Europe. In all these areas, social and economic change is creating forces that conflict with the inflexibility of rigid, authoritarian, and narrowly based political systems. In 1981 in El Salvador and Poland, as will be the case at some point in Saudi Arabia, political leaders confronted the problem of either adapting their political systems to the demands for participation by significant groups of their population or using military action to suppress the revolutionary forces at work among those groups. Each case, as would be true also with Saudi Arabia, involved the vital interest of a superpower. In each case also the opposing superpower had contrary interests: the Soviet Union and Cuba promoted revolution in Central America; the United States encouraged liberalization in Eastern Europe. At some point, these tendencies could provoke a military reaction when the neighboring superpower felt its vital interests threatened. In the Persian Gulf, the lines are less clearly drawn but the interests, at least of the United States and its allies, are no less crucial.

These circumstances increasing the likelihood of war between the United States and the Soviet Union clearly increase the importance of having an effective strategy for deterring Soviet actions that might make war more likely, of avoiding U.S. actions that would have the same effect without any compensating gain for U.S. interests, and of heightening the readiness of U.S. forces to fight a war if one should occur in the 1980s.

THE DIVERSIFICATION OF DETERRENCE

Basic U.S. national security policy and strategy in the 1980s will presumably continue to be directed to: (1) deterring Soviet military action against other societies; (2) if deterrence fails, defeating such military action; (3) minimizing the probability of war, particularly nuclear war, and limiting the damage to the United States and its allies, if war should occur; (4) encouraging the emergence of friendly regimes and democratic political systems in other societies; (5) countering other (that is, non-Soviet) threats to American vital interests.

The problem for U.S. strategy in the 1980s is to devise new ways of achieving these goals in the light of external expansion and internal decay of the Soviet empire, the new types of Soviet military action to be deterred, nuclear parity and the eroded nuclear deterrent, and the increased probability of Soviet-American military conflict.

In the 1950s the threat of nuclear retaliation was an effective deterrent because of the relative strength of U.S. nuclear forces and the relative vulnerability to nuclear attack of Soviet military forces and society. In the 1980s deterrence must similarly be based upon areas of relative Wesern strength and aimed at areas of relative Soviet vulnerability. A credible and effective deterrent must be directed at something which is valued by Soviet leaders at least as much as the physical survival of Soviet society and which constitutes a target peculiar to the Soviet Union, lacking an American counterpart against which they could threaten retaliation. The Soviet empire—the system of political, military, and economic controls that the Soviet leaders exercise over their internal, contiguous, and overseas domains—is clearly such a target. U.S. strategy consequently should be directed, in the event of Soviet aggression, primarily not to the physical destruction of the Soviet society but to the political destruction of the Soviet empire (Gray 1979). As compared to previous deterrent policy, such a strategy would: (1) pose a threat to the Soviets against which they could not retaliate in kind; (2) be morally justifiable in that it was directed toward the promotion of the liberty and national independence of the peoples under Soviet control instead of the nuclear devastation of the Soviet Union; and (3) be, in some sense, historically "progressive," in that the Soviet empire is becoming increasingly anachronistic, and the break-up of that empire would be in accordance with historical trends, much as the break-up of the Western colonial empires was after World War II.

The threat of retaliation against Soviet control of their empire is the means by which the West can capitalize on Soviet concern over the possible disintegration of their empire in order to contain Soviet drives toward expanding their empire. A secondary component in such a strategy should be directed toward the economic viability of the Soviet system. In the value hierarchy of the Soviet leaders, political control ranks far higher than economic well-being. The Soviet system is designed to sacrifice the latter in order to preserve the former. The Soviets do have an interest, however, in economic development and productivity, which manifested itself dramatically during the 1970s in their efforts to expand their economic relations with the West. Soviet economic problems are likely to increase in the 1980s. Soviet interest in securing technology, capital, and food from the West will hence remain substantial. Economics is an area of great Western comparative advantage, and it is, consequently, an area where the West can implement deterrence by threatening economic retaliation in response to Soviet aggression (as in the case of Poland in 1980–81) and holding forth the promise of economic benefits in return for Soviet restraint.

During the 1980s the most probable targets of Soviet military action are in zone two rather than zone one. U.S. strategy, consequently, must find ways to deter Soviet military action in these "new" areas as well as it has in the "old" areas since the 1950s. The threat of a nuclear response has, however, lost credibility with respect to Western Europe and has virtually none at all as a deterrent to Soviet action in China, Southwest Asia, or Eastern Europe. The multiplication of the needs for deterrence and the declining scope of nuclear deterrence thus require diversification of the means of deterrence.

Conventional deterrence and nonmilitary deterrence should supplement nuclear deterrence in Western strategy. Credible conventional deterrence in zone two, however, can rest only in part on local ability to resist Soviet military aggression. The central problem of U.S. strategy is to deter the Soviet military action against its neighbors when Soviet military superiority to any one neighbor is overwhelming and when the Soviets enjoy at least nuclear parity with the United States. Hence, the deterrents required for the 1980s should not only be diversified, they should also be interlinked and reinforcing. A strategy should be adopted that will make the chain of containment as strong as its strongest link rather than as weak as its weakest link. A strategy of diversified deterrence in the 1980s will necessarily tie Soviet military behavior in one area to the possibility of conventional military counteractions elsewhere and to nonmilitary political and economic sanctions aimed at the political stability and economic vitality of the Soviet empire. In contrast to previous American strategy, such a strategy would put new emphasis on nonmilitary deterrence, strengthen conventional deterrence by adopting a retaliatory strategy in Europe, and assure the counterdeterrent role of U.S. nuclear forces by bolstering strategic defenses.

NONMILITARY DETERRENCE

Strategists have generally focused on the role of military deterrence in preventing undesired military action by another state. But military actions may also be deterred through nonmilitary means, and the nonmilitary forms of deterrence—diplomatic, economic, and political—are normally subtler, cheaper, and less dangerous to apply than military means of deterrence. For these reasons they may also be less effective, and at times military deterrence may be indispensable. Military deterrence, however, normally involves increasing the prospective costs and risks of particular military actions by the other state. Nonmilitary deterrence may do this, but it also more easily can take a positive form in terms of providing inducements to the other state to refrain from undesired action.

In the past, nonmilitary deterrence did not play a significant role in American strategy. The areas where the United States wished to deter Soviet military action—Western Europe, Japan, Korea, and the United States itself—were too vital to rely simply on promises of nonmilitary rewards or penalties to induce the Soviets to refrain from attacking them. In addition, the military balance between the United States and the Soviet Union was such—particularly in the nuclear field—that military deterrence, particularly nuclear deterrence, was a very rational American choice. The United States also did not see it in its interest to attempt to deter in any serious way Soviet action against

Soviet allies, and the Soviet Union was not generally in a position to threaten militarily parts of the world of secondary interest to the United States, where nonmilitary deterrence might have been relevant.

Nonmilitary deterrence has a more significant role in American strategy in the 1980s than it had in the past for three reasons. First, the change in the military balance has increased the comparative advantage of the Soviet Union in the military field and hence narrowed the possibilities and increased the costs of military deterrence. Second, the desirability of deterring Soviet military action against zone-two countries, where U.S. interests are less central than in zone one, increases the need for less severe, more subtle, and more flexible means of deterrence. Third, two of the major developments of the 1970s— the expansion of the Soviet empire, particularly overseas, and the economic engagement of the Soviet Union with the West—open up new oportunities for using economic and political incentives and penalties for deterrent purposes.

Diplomacy normally is and should be the first line of deterrence. It can take the form of inducements, usually through concessions on other issues, or possible sanctions in the form of denunciations, curtailing or severing of diplomatic contacts, hardening of position or withdrawal of concessions on other issues, condemnation in the United Nations, and the like. In some instances, these may cause the deterree to cancel, modify, or postpone his proposed military action. If, however, that state views that military action as very much required by its national interest, it is unlikely to be deterred by diplomatic actions alone.

Economic inducements and penalties may be more effective. The Soviet economic system sets a ceiling on overall Soviet goals, its major weaknesses inherent in its institutional structure. The Soviets view that structure as inseparable from their entire political system. Any significant changes in it would, in their view, challenge their entire political-ideological system of control. Faced with this economic drag, the Soviet leaders at the end of the 1960s decided to bolster the operation of their economy, insofar as possible, through the import of Western capital and technology. For them, economic detente was a crutch to keep the system functioning as productively as possible without making fundamental changes in it. That crutch—in the form of technology, food, and capital investment—was made possible by Western credits and Soviet exports of oil, guns, and gold. It played a significant role in slowing the decline of the Soviet rate of growth.

In the 1980s the Soviets will confront considerably enhanced economic problems as a result of increasing oil and manpower shortages. The leveling off and probable decline in oil production will probably require a cutback in exports which have been responsible for more than 40 percent of their hard-currency earnings and which will be only partially compensated for by increased exports of natural gas. In this situation, the Soviets will have to choose either to acquiesce in an intensified slow-down of their economy, or to make fundamental structural reforms in that economy, or to increase the economic benefits they secure from the West.

As long as this third choice is, from their viewpoint, relatively cost-free, it is clearly the easier course for them to follow. Despite the unraveling of detente beginning with Angola in 1975, they were able through 1981 to maintain their economic involvement with the West, modified only by the economic countermeaures initiated by the United States in response to their invasion of Afghanistan and the imposition of martial law in Poland. Those measures imposed some economic penalties on the Soviet Union, and it seems likely that the prospect of more stringent and more widely supported economic sanctions by the West probably played some role in deterring a Soviet invasion of Poland in 1980 and 1981. The ability to apply economic deterrence is, however, dependent upon three conditions.

First, the deterring government has to have available to it inducements or penalties of the appropriate form and magnitude. There is normally a limited supply of both, and over time that supply can become exhausted. Once credits have been denied, grain embargoed, technology controlled, and capital equipment transfers prohibited, the United States has about used up the economic penalties it can apply to the Soviet Union. Similarly, in the reverse direction, once credits are granted, most-favored-nation status approved, and technology transfers opened up, there are relatively few additional benefits that can be offered to secure Soviet restraint, which may account in part for the intensification of Soviet expansive behavior in the middle 1970s. Within a narrow range, however, economic measures, particularly if applied in concert by the Western industrialized democracies generally, can have a major impact on Soviet economic development.

Second, the deterring government has to be able to apply the inducements and penalties flexibly so as to link them to the behavior to be deterred. This requires the government to have the legal authority, bureaucratic control and competence, and political power to take the actions required. With some notable exceptions, such as the Stevenson and Jackson-Vanik Amendments, the Export Administration Acts and other legislation generally give the American president sufficient legal authority to make effective use of economic measures for deterrent purposes. The federal bureaucracy has the competence to implement such measures, although the organizational structure for administering economic controls needs to be more centrally linked to foreign policy decisionmaking through the NSC system (Huntington 1978). The major problem comes, of course, from the political groups and politicians who see it in their interest either to promote or to eliminate particular economic relationships with the Soviet Union. The record of U.S. foreign economic policy, however, suggests that if there is some broad agreement between executive and congressional leaders on the goals of the policy, particularistic groups will not necessarily be able to dilute that policy significantly (Pastor 1980). Political leaders have also at times, as with President Carter and the grain embargo, defied the demands of major economic groups.

Third, unlike military deterrence which can often be applied by only one government, economic deterrence normally requires the cooperation of several states. Only in a few cases (for instance, the United States with respect to certain types of grain and technology) does one government exercise decisive control over a resource. Usually several possible suppliers exist, and some degree of intergovernmental cooperation is necessary. In terms of the economic deterrence of the Soviet Union, this obviously requires the participation of at least the seven major industrialized democracies represented at the economic summits. These countries accord different priority to Soviet actions to be deterred and have differing interests in economic relations with the Soviet Union. Agreement on economic measures becomes a complex diplomatic undertaking. The record of 1980–81 with respect to the application of economic measures against both the Soviet Union (regarding Afghanistan and Poland) and Iran shows the problems involved in attempting to secure agreement on some forms of common action. The ability of the United States to apply economic deterrence effectively with respect to zone-two countries during the 1980s will depend in large measure upon its ability to persuade its allies that the alternatives are either economic cooperation with the United States or military confrontation with the USSR.

Given the growing economic problems confronting the Soviet Union in the 1980s, economic diplomacy and economic deterrence have a crucial role to play in U.S. and Western policy toward the Soviet Union. The most obvious area for linking Soviet economic needs with Western security concerns involves the interests of both sides in adequate supplies of oil for the rest of this century. Western technology and capital can play a decisive role in the development of Soviet oil and gas reserves. Without this technology and capital the Soviets will not be able to develop those reserves to the same extent (and in some cases, not at all), and the initiation of new energy production will be substantially delayed. At the same time, the Soviets and their satellites have been expanding their military position and influence in Southwest Asia, the Arabian peninsula, and the Horn of Africa, thereby posing a major potential military threat to crucial sources of oil for the United States and its allies. This conjunction of needs and threats could provide the basis for trading Western economic help for the development of Soviet energy supplies in return for the elimination of the immediate Soviet military threat to Western energy supplies. Such an economic deterrent policy might involve proposing to the Soviets the following:

1. The Soviets should undertake to remove their own and to secure the removal of satellite military personnel from Afghanistan, Southwest Asia, the Arabian peninsula, and the Horn of Africa.

2. Western governments should undertake to promote the transfer of oil and gas technology to the Soviet Union, facilitate the construction of the natural gas pipeline to Western Europe, and encourage Western investment (possibly running into billions of dollars) in the development of the Yakutia, North Star, and other Soviet oil and gas reserves.

3. If the Soviets turn down this proposal or refuse to negotiate seriously concerning it, the Western governments will embargo the transfer of all oil and gas technology to the Soviet Union, prohibit all Western credits for or investment in Soviet energy development, and severely restrict technology transfers, credits, and trade in other economic areas.

A proposal of this sort should be a central element in U.S. and allied economic deterrence policy toward the Soviet Union in the early 1980s. It would clearly confront the Soviets with the choice between enhanced peaceful development of their own natural resources versus expansion of their military and political influence abroad. The United

States should give high priority to securing the agreement of its allies to a joint demarche to the Soviet Union, making clear that the current benefits the Soviets gather from economic engagement with the West will be lost unless they end their military presence in the Middle East. If, on the other hand, the Soviets are willing to undertake such a military withdrawal, the economic benefits that will be available to them from the West—particularly in the energy field—will be enormous.

The use of political means to contain Soviet expansion must necessarily focus on the Soviet system of control over the contiguous and overseas components of its empire. U.S. policy should obviously be directed toward promoting the dissolution of this empire in ways that do not threaten global peace and security. The amount of effort the United States devotes to this goal, however, is appropriately linked to the extent of Soviet efforts to expand their empire. By increasing the costs and risks of empire, the United States presumably can lessen Soviet incentives to expand it. Broadly speaking, there are two strategies the United States could follow in attempting to achieve this goal. It could attempt to loosen the bonds between the existing regimes and the Soviet Union, promoting economic, diplomatic, cultural engagement with Western societies, while recognizing that many countries, particularly those in Eastern Europe, have little choice but to maintain their security ties with the Soviet Union. Alternatively, the United States could attempt to weaken the existing regimes in the empire, encouraging opposition groups, promoting and supporting insurrection, and thus hoping to secure the overthrow of the current regime and its replacement with a new one less committed to the Soviet Union. The alternatives, in short, are to wean or to weaken the satellite governments.

The appropriate policy in any particular case will depend upon the strength of the dissatisfaction within the country with the current regime and the nature of that regime's ties to the Soviet Union. These can change over time. In some cases, such as Vietnam, Mongolia, and Bulgaria, both the regime and its ties to the Soviet Union may be so strong as to preclude much success for policies of either weaning or weakening (see Table 1-1).

In other cases, such as Cuba, Afghanistan, Cambodia, and Laos, the regime may be so heavily dependent upon the Soviets or on a Soviet satellite, Vietnam, that weaning the regime is not likely to succeed. In 1977-78, indeed, the Carter Administration tried a weaning approach to both Cuba and Vietnam and failed conclusively in both

Table 1-1.   Possible Policies Toward Soviet Empire
Regimes.

Weaken	Wean	
	Yes	No
Yes:	Ethiopia Yemen Angola	Cuba Afghanistan Cambodia Laos
No:	Poland Hungary Czechoslovakia East Germany Roumania	Vietnam Mongolia Bulgaria

cases. On the other hand, these four countries plus Ethiopia, Yemen, and Angola confront major domestic problems and various forms of domestic opposition to the incumbent regime. In four of the seven countries (Afghanistan, Angola, Cambodia, and Ethiopia) major insurrections were underway in 1982. Except for Afghanistan, these countries are also noncontiguous with the Soviet Union. All of these conditions make a weakening strategy appropriate.

In still other instances, most notably the Eastern European countries of Poland, Hungary, Czechoslovakia, East Germany, and Romania, substantial contacts already exist with the West, but there is, in most cases, a Soviet military presence and a demonstrated Soviet will to use military force if necessary to maintain the existing system. In these instances, a weaning strategy is clearly desirable. Both the Ford and Carter Administrations followed a discriminating policy with respect to these regimes, providing economic benefits to those countries that either liberalized their domestic economic or political system (Poland, Hungary) or established some degree of autonomy in their foreign policy (Romania). In the cases of Ethiopia, Angola, and, possibly, Yemen, it might be appropriate to apply a dual strategy of attempting to wean as well as to weaken the current regime. Ethiopia and Angola are economically dependent on ties with the West, and regimes in all three countries conceivably could dramatically change their political-ideological orientation. The probability of their being able to do this, however, is reduced substantially by the major Cuban troop presence in Angola and Ethiopia, and by the significant number of Soviet, East German, and Cuban personnel in Yemen.

In a sense, Eastern Europe and Mongolia constitute a Soviet zone one, that part of the empire which the Soviets clearly view as most essential to their own security. The other countries resemble a zone two, where in some cases Soviet involvement and commitment have reached high levels (for example, Cuba) but where underlying Soviet interests are less significant. In these cases, the interest may be as much a product of the involvement as vice versa. In dealing with the Soviet empire, consequently, the thrust of American policy, that is, to wean or to weaken, should be tailored to fit the particular conditions of each component of the empire, and the intensity with which that approach is followed should be linked to Soviet efforts to strengthen and expand their empire. The high probability of major political retaliation against the more vulnerable parts of their empire should help deter the Soviets from adventures in zone-two areas of crucial interest to the United States.

CONVENTIONAL DETERRENCE

Conventional forces can contribute to deterrence in three ways. First, by their presence in an area they can increase the uncertainties and the potential costs an aggressor must confront, even if—like the allied troops in Berlin—they could not conceivably mount a successful defense of the area. Second, conventional military forces can deter by raising the possibility of a successful defense and hence forcing the aggressor to risk defeat in his effort or to pay additional costs for success. This has been the traditional deterrent role of the NATO conventional forces in West Germany. Third, conventional military forces can deter by posing the threat of retaliation against the aggressor. This has, of course, been the classic deterrent role of strategic nuclear forces. In principle, there is no reason why conventional military forces cannot do likewise, provided there is something of value to the potential aggressor, like the Soviet empire in Eastern Europe, against which such forces can retaliate. A strategy of conventional retaliation in the form of a prompt offensive into Eastern Europe would help to deter Soviet military action against Western Europe and conceivably also in the second deterrent zone. Posing such a threat is central to a 1980s strategy that emphasizes conventional rather than nuclear deterrence.

A strategy of conventional retaliation would constitute a needed additional corrective to the decline in the credibility of the strategic nuclear deterrent with respect to Europe. It would round out the NATO deterrent posture in Europe, complementing the decisions on the build-up of NATO conventional strength in the Long Term Defense Program and on theater nuclear force modernization to counter Soviet Backfires and SS-20s. This strategy might require some modest changes in the character, deployment, and levels of NATO forces in Germany, but they would not necessarily be substantial. Implementing a conventional retaliation strategy requires more change in the NATO military mind-set than it does in NATO military forces. Since the beginning, NATO has thought about conventional war almost exclusively in defensive terms. NATO strategy, codified in its present form in MC-14/3, adopted in December 1967, stresses forward defense, flexible response, the NATO triad of conventional, theater nuclear, and strategic nuclear forces, and the eventual restoration of prewar boundaries. It posits, in short, a basically defensive strategy. There is, however, no reason why a defensive alliance should, once war breaks out, be limited to a defensive strategy. For thirty years U.S. nuclear strategy has served a defensive purpose by being offensively oriented. U.S. and NATO conventional strategy in Europe should also have a major offensive component.

Since the beginning of NATO Western planning has assumed that the major battles in a conflict on the central front would be fought in West Germany. As a result, West Germans decry the devastation to which their country would be subjected, even in a purely conventional war. They quite appropriately insist on a forward defense strategy, engaging the Soviets as far as possible from their population centers in Bavaria, the Rhine and Ruhr valleys, and the Hamburg area. Such a strategy, however, means that the allied forces have to be strung out more or less evenly along the entire eastern border of the Federal Republic. At any given point, therefore, they are vulnerable to an overpowering Soviet concentration of offensive forces. The logical extension of the forward defense concept is to move the locus of battle eastward into East Germany and Czechoslovakia. The result would be more effective deterrence and, if deterrence failed, less devastation in West Germany.

Current NATO strategy contemplates the possibility of eventually launching a counteroffensive. A major difference exists, however, between a conventional counteroffensive and a conventional retaliatory offensive. A counteroffensive occurs after the enemy's offensive has been brought to a halt and allied forces have been regrouped and prepared to drive the Warsaw Pact forces out of those portions of Western Europe they have occupied. A conventional retaliatory offensive, like a nuclear retaliatory offensive, would, on the other hand, be launched immediately whether or not the Soviet conventional offensive had been stopped. A counteroffensive, in short, sequentially follows the enemy's offensive; a retaliatory offensive occurs, as far as possible, simultaneously with the enemy's offensive.

This distinction is of fundamental importance in terms of the impact of these two strategies on Soviet military planning. To date the Soviets have been free to concentrate all their planning and forces on offensive moves into West Germany. A Western retaliatory strategy would compel them to reallocate forces and resources to the defense of their satellites and thus to weaken their offensive thrust. Most importantly, it is generally recognized that the extent of satellite participation in a war with NATO will depend upon the scope and speed of Soviet success in the conflict. As long as the Soviets are successful, they are likely to have complacent and cooperative allies. If, however, they are stalemated or turned back, disaffection is likely to appear within the Warsaw Pact. A prompt allied offensive into Eastern Europe would stimulate that disaffection at the very start of the conflict. Neither the Soviets nor, more importantly, the satellite governments could view with equanimity West German tanks on the road to Berlin and Leipzig and American divisions heading for Prague, Budapest, and Warsaw. From the viewpoint of deterrence, such a prospect would tremendously enhance the undesirability of war for the governments of the satellite countries. Those governments, which provide almost half of the Warsaw Pact ground forces on the central front, would lose more than anyone else in such a war and hence would become a puissant lobby urging their Soviet partner not to initiate war. The deterrent impact of a conventional retaliatory strategy on the Soviets could be further enhanced by allied assurances to Eastern European governments that their countries would not be invaded if they opted for neutrality and did not cooperate in the Soviet attack on the West.

Creating the conventional military forces that could, with a high degree of certainty, stop a substantial Soviet invasion of Western Europe appears to be beyond the political will of Western European statesmen and publics. Creating a conventional strategy and military force, however, for a prompt retaliatory invasion of Eastern Europe should not be beyond the ingenuity of Western military planners. For years Western deterrent strategy has assumed that a Soviet nuclear attack on the United States would produce a prompt retaliatory response in kind. Theater nuclear modernization in Europe assumes that Soviet use of theater nuclear weapons against Western Europe must also be met by a prompt retaliation in kind. Surely it is rather anomalous that plans do not exist to respond to a Soviet conventional attack on Western Europe with a prompt retaliatory attack in kind on Eastern Europe. Failure to have the plans and the capability for such action is a major—and potentially disastrous—gap in the overall structure of deterrence.

A strategy of conventional retaliation would help ease NATO's nuclear dilemma in at least two ways. First, as the demonstrations of 1981–82 against Theater Nuclear Force (TNF) modernization indicated, significant elements of public opinion in Western Europe and the United States are deeply concerned about a strategy that relies heavily on nuclear weapons. Shifting the emphasis in alliance strategy from the defensive use of nuclear weapons to the offensive use of conventional forces would moderate this source of opposition to NATO military planning. Second, if aggression does occur, the ability to implement a conventional retaliatory strategy would raise the NATO nuclear threshold and thereby make it more likely that NATO could avoid the "deepening trap" of an increasingly improbable "first nuclear use" that Iklé (1980) warned about. Surely it is politically more credible, militarily more desirable, and morally far more legitimate to have a strategy which, if war occurs, contemplates efforts to liberate Eastern Europe by conventional means rather than early recourse to weapons that make likely the slaughter of countless European, Russian, and, in all probability, American civilians.

Moreover, a conventional retaliatory strategy in Europe is relevant not only to the defense of Western Europe. By forcing the Soviets to face the possibility of a two-front war, it also contributes to second-zone deterrence. The Soviet Union is surrounded both by potentially hostile states and by potentially tempting opportunities to exploit its military capabilities for political advantage. Western strategy should capitalize on the former in order to limit the latter; Soviet strategy, just the reverse. A Soviet strategist can only see his country as encircled, and his perception would not be wrong. The classic response for a country in this position is to attempt to use the advantages it offers in terms of interior lines and the opportunities to divorce one area of action from another and thus to concentrate diplomatic attention and military force, if necessary, on one opponent or set of opponents at a time. The Soviet Union has a clear interest in attempting to separate its relations with Japan, China, Southwest Asia, Eastern Europe, Western Europe, and the United States into discrete packages, isolated, insofar as possible, one from the other. The logical corollary and preliminary to Soviet military action in China or the Persian Gulf is the fervent pursuit of detente in Europe; some rapprochement with China is a highly desirable prerequisite to military confrontation in Europe.

A striking parallel thus exists between the strategic position of the Soviet Union now and that occupied by Germany before World War I and between World Wars I and II. German policy was devoted to minimizing the likelihood of a two-front war or, if that proved impossible, to winning a quick victory on one front as early in the war as possible. The policy of Germany's opponents, on the other hand, should have been to insure that Germany could not take aggressive action in one direction without having to confront counteraction by other countries on the other front. The deterrent to German aggression was the high probability of concerted action by all of Germany's potential opponents. Such a collective policy required not only diplomatic agreement and understanding among the participating powers; it also required a military strategy which would make credible the threat of mutual, reinforcing action. Between the world wars, however, this was precisely what was lacking, most notably in the case of the French. France negotiated alliances with Poland and the states of the Little Entente (Czechoslovakia, Yugoslavia, and Romania) with a view to containing any German revanchism. To implement this foreign policy, France would have to be able to launch or to threaten to launch an offensive against Germany from the west if Germany moved against France's allies to the east. Hence, France presumably needed a professional, well-trained and -equipped standing army consisting largely of armored and mechanized divisions that could quickly move across the Rhine. This was, of course, precisely the army that Charles de Gaulle (1934) urged his country to have.

French military policy, however, was shaped not by French foreign policy requirements but rather by the presumed lessons of French military experience in World War I. Its key elements were the Maginot Line and the training through universal conscription of large numbers of reserves that could be mobilized to defend the country in the event of war. As a result, France was, as the postwar parliamentary inquiry put it, incapable of deploying even a modest expeditionary force to "chase three regiments of the Wehrmacht" out of the Rhineland in 1936. France was even more unable to impose any military restraint on Hitler as the Wehrmacht moved east in 1938 and 1939 (Challener 1955:264–265; Huntington 1961:9–10). French foreign policy was defensive in that its primary goal was to support the status quo and contain German expansionism. This defensive foreign policy could be effectively implemented only through an offensive military strategy. France instead pursued a purely defensive strategy, and the gap between foreign policy and strategy led to disaster.

A similar gap could well exist between American foreign policy and strategy in the 1980s. The ability to deter Soviet military action against China, Southwest Asia, or Eastern Europe cannot rest primarily on military forces in those areas. It will be many years, perhaps decades, before China is capable of repulsing a Soviet punitive incursion.[1] All the efforts to develop readily deployable U.S. forces for the Persian Gulf cannot remove Soviet geographical advantages or Soviet superiority to any indigenous forces that might oppose them. Nor could any satellite army in Eastern Europe by itself hope to hold the Soviet Army at bay for long. If deterrence is to be reasonably well assured, consequently, it must rest on the high probability that Soviet military action in any one area will also involve the Soviet Union in military hostilities in other areas. This can only happen if there exists a system of interlocking, reinforcing deterrents and if there is the military capability and strategy to take the offensive against Soviet vital interests in an area other than the one which the Soviets are threatening.

Nuclear retaliation from the United States in response to zone-two aggression is not credible. The Japanese are prevented by their constitution, capabilities, and psychology from offensive action, and U.S. air or naval offensive action against the Soviet Union from Japan would be incompatible with the U.S.-Japanese alliance unless it was directly related to an imminent military threat to Japan. China's military forces are and will be for several years capable of only the most limited offensive actions against Siberia or Mongolia. No capabilities, obviously, exist for offensive action from Southwest Asia or Eastern Europe. Only in Western Europe do military forces exist that could pose a significant and credible offensive threat to vital Soviet interests. A conventional retaliatory strategy in central Europe is thus desirable not only to compensate for the eroded credibility of the nuclear deterrent as far as Europe is concerned but also to help meet the new needs to deter Soviet aggression elsewhere.

A conventional retaliatory strategy in Europe would not be a substitute for the deployment of Western forces in the Persian Gulf and Indian Ocean areas or for the modernization of the Chinese armed forces. It would, however, supplement and reinforce these efforts and limit the resources that had to be devoted to them by providing an alternative means of securing an equal amount of deterrence. It is, for instance, in all likelihood politically impossible to deploy Western ground forces in the Persian Gulf area so as to provide deterrence-by-presence. Deterrence-by-defense will be possible under some circumstances, but it will be difficult and expensive; and if the Soviets were free to concentrate their forces on Southwest Asia, they clearly could overrun any force that the Western allies and Japan might deploy in a reasonable amount of time. It consequently makes great sense, as Secretary of Defense Weinberger put it (1981), for the United States, if forced into war, to "be prepared to launch counteroffensives in other regions and try to exploit the aggressor's weaknesses wherever they exist." In 1980 and 1981 the European allies of the United States expressed concern at times about the possible reorientation of American military planning, programs, and money from preparation for a European war to the development of the Rapid Deployment Force and other forces for the projection of American power into the Persian Gulf area (New York Times 1981:13). Clearly the United States needs to develop that capability rapidly. The extent of the resources reallocated to that purpose from European defense could be reduced, European worries assuaged, and the security of the Persian Gulf area equally well advanced if NATO adopted a retaliatory strategy in Europe. At present the Soviet Union is free to engage in military adventures in the Persian Gulf without concern about its security along the Elbe even as Hitler in the 1930s could move militarily into Eastern Europe without worrying about his security along the Rhine. A retaliatory strategy in Europe consequently should be particularly appealing to the European allies both because it would move at least some of the fighting eastward if deterrence failed and because it would limit the pressure to reallocate allied military resources from Europe to the Indian Ocean.

A somewhat parallel logic would apply to the deterrence of a Soviet attack on China. The provision of military equipment to China, including some forms of lethal equipment, is appropriate and desirable in terms of strengthening defensive deterrence along the Soviet border. At some point, however, the provision of weapons to China will run into problems of distinguishing between defensive weapons, which could only be used against the only power that might attack China (that is, the Soviet Union), and offensive weapons, which might give the Chinese some capacity for deterrence-by-retaliation against the Soviets but which might also give them the capability to attack Taiwan, to occupy portions of Vietnam, Cambodia, and Laos, and to threaten Thailand and other members of the Association of South East Asian Nations (ASEAN). China itself has recognized its interest in a strong NATO. A NATO strategy of conventional retaliation would reduce the importance of re-arming China beyond a certain point and would contribute to Chinese security by forcing the Soviets again to confront the possibility of a two-front war and potentially disastrous losses in the West if they launched an attack on their enemy in the East.

Finally, with respect to Eastern Europe itself, a NATO conventional retaliatory strategy can provide an additional deterrent to Soviet military action against a satellite government that is attempting to broaden its independence. It would, consequently, encourage satellite governments to see how far they could go in loosening Soviet controls. In 1950 the deployment of American troops to Europe significantly encouraged Tito in his resistance to the Soviets (Windsor 1978). An allied retaliatory strategy could well have a comparable effect in promoting the "Finlandization," if not the "Titoization," of Eastern Europe.

The central need in the containment of Soviet military aggression in the 1980s is thus to see the problem of deterrence as a whole and the ways in which the various geographical and functional components of strategy interlock with each other. It is erroneous to suggest, as some have (Aspin 1976), that the Soviet military build-up on the Chinese frontier does not increase the threat to the West or to believe, as the Chinese never would, that NATO strength and strategy have no relevance to the defense of China. In the 1980s geographical linkage is the essence of deterrence. If it is in the interest of world peace and Western security that the Soviets not go into Iran, China, or Poland, that certainty should be greatly reduced. A defensive posture does not require a purely defensive strategy and, indeed, may be undermined by such a strategy. Neither the United States, nor its major allies, nor China, nor regional powers can produce the conventional military forces to defeat those which the Soviets could mass at whatever place they might be tempted to invade. "It is impossible," as Secretary Dulles said in 1954 (Kaufman 1956:14–15), to match the "potential enemy at all points on a basis of man-for-man, gun-for-gun, and tank-for-tank." This is still the case. In 1954 deterrence could be provided by relying "primarily on our massive mobile retaliatory power which we could use in our discretion against the major sources of aggression at times and places that we chose." This is no longer the case. In the 1980s, allied capacity to launch a conventional retaliatory offensive into Eastern Europe is essential to narrowing the gap between foreign policy and strategy and to insuring against Soviet aggression into either the first or second deterrent zones.

The reasons for NATO putting much greater emphasis on deterrence-by-retaliation seem overwhelming. Yet in some circles there is an apparent reluctance to confront this need, and four arguments are often advanced against a NATO strategy of conventional retaliation.

First, it is argued that NATO military forces are too weak to support an offensive strategy. As we have seen, during the 1970s the conventional and theater nuclear force balances in Europe did shift significantly toward the Warsaw Pact. Every effort should be made to rectify this situation and to reestablish a balance of forces more comparable to that which existed in the mid-1960s. If NATO moves forward with its current plans, the military balance in Europe should be more satisfactory in the later 1980s than it was in the early 1980s. Even the 1982 balance, however, would not preclude NATO from adopting a conventional retaliatory strategy. In the first place, the Pact's advantage on the central front is significant but not necessarily decisive (Mearsheimer 1982). In 1981 the Pact had an advantage in divisional manpower of 1.2–1.36 to 1 and in overall manpower of 1.15–1.2 to 1. The Pact was greatly superior in numbers of tanks, but in terms of armored division equivalents, the Pact advantage was only 1.2 to 1, which could very likely be compensated for by NATO strength in airpower. Unlike the Pact, NATO's air strength is overwhelming in attack planes capable of carrying out the deep interdiction and ground-attack missions necessary to support a ground offensive. The introduction of the Leopard and M-1 tanks will also increase NATO's ground offensive capabilities. The crucial element in any offensive, moreover, is not the overall military balance between the two sides but rather the military balance at the point of attack. The great advantage of the offensive is that the attacker chooses that point and hence can concentrate his forces there. History is full of successful offensives by forces that lacked numerical superiority, including the German offensive in the West in 1940, the Japanese offensives in Southeast Asia in 1941–42, and the North Vietnamese offensive in 1975 (Stuart 1981). Nothing in the existing balance of forces in central Europe rules out a NATO offensive strategy, and that balance is more likely to become more favorable than less favorable during the course of the decade.

In addition, a NATO offensive strategy would pose serious military problems for the Soviet Union. It would, as we have pointed out, require a reallocation of some Pact forces from offensive to defensive purposes. It would also confront the Soviets with just exactly the situation their doctrine and strategy attempt to avoid: one in which they do not have control of developments and in which they face a high probability of uncertainty and surprise. It would put a premium on flexibility and adaptability, qualities in which the Soviets recognize themselves to be deficient. Furthermore, a prompt allied offensive into Eastern Europe would greatly increase the probability of a protracted war. Soviet planning, however, is in large part directed toward a short-war scenario in which the Soviets score a breakthrough, occupy a substantial portion of West Germany, and then negotiate a cease fire from a position of strength. With a retaliatory strategy, however, Soviet armies might be in West Germany but allied armies would also be in East Europe, and driving them out would require more time for mobilization and organization of a counteroffensive.

The basic point, moreover, is deterrence. The prospects for the sustained success of the allied offensive into Eastern Europe do not have to be 100 percent. They simply have to be sufficiently better than zero and to raise enough unpleasant uncertainties to increase significantly the potential costs and risks to the Soviets of starting a war.

Second, it is at times argued that an allied retaliatory strategy, duplicating in some sense Soviet offensive strategy, would create instability in crises, in which each side would be tempted to strike first.

Once implemented, however, this strategy should reduce the probability of crises in which either side seriously considers going to war. At present, assuming a lag of four to seven days in NATO mobilization, it is generally argued that Warsaw Pact numerical superiority would peak seven to twenty-one days after the Pact started mobilizing (Carnegie Endowment 1981). In any crisis, consequently, the Soviets would have substantial incentives to attack during this period before the mobilization and deployment of U.S. and West European reinforcements reduced their advantage. These incentives would decrease if they knew that such an attack would be met by an immediate Eastern European offensive by the on-line NATO forces. Similarly, in the absence of a planned NATO offensive, NATO success would depend entirely on its ability to blunt the Soviet offensive; NATO commanders would, consequently, be under greater incentive to launch preemptive "defensive" tactical air strikes against Soviet troop concentrations than they would be if NATO were itself prepared to launch a prompt retaliatory offensive.

Third, it is argued that instead of capitalizing upon the political weakness of the Soviet empire, a conventional retaliatory strategy would help to solidify the empire by enabling the Soviets to rally Eastern European governments and peoples to the defense of their homelands against Western imperialist aggressors. The Soviets, however, already make every effort to do this and consistently portray NATO as an aggressive alliance. It is not clear that they could say much more than they have been saying if NATO adopted a strategy of conventional retaliation. Again, it must be emphasized that the entire purpose of the strategy is deterrence: to create uncertainty in the minds of Soviet leaders as to what would happen in Eastern Europe. As has been argued, the adoption of this strategy should be accompanied with a clear invitation to Eastern European governments to avoid invasion by opting out of a Soviet-initiated war. At the very least, such an invitation would create uneasiness, uncertainty, and divisiveness within satellite governments, and hence arouse concerns among the Soviets as to their reliability. In practice, the allied offensive would have to be accompanied with carefully composed political-psychological warfare appeals to the peoples of East Europe stressing that the allies were not fighting them but the Soviets, and urging them to cooperate with the advancing forces and to rally to the liberation of their countries from Soviet military occupation and political control. A conventional retaliatory strategy is based on the assumption that the West German reserves, territorial army, and populace will put up a more unified, comprehensive, and determined resistance to Soviet armies than the East German, Czech, Polish, and Hungarian armies and peoples will to the advance of West German forces into East Germany and American forces into elsewhere in Eastern Europe. (If this assumption is unwarranted, the foundations of not only a conventional retaliatory strategy but also of NATO would be in question.)

Finally, the point is made that while a conventional retaliatory strategy may make military and even political sense in terms of the relations between NATO and the Warsaw Pact, opposition to it within NATO would be so great that any effort to adopt it would simply tear the alliance apart. Such is the usual reaction to any new idea, however, and the arguments and need for such a strategy are simply overwhelming. Its adoption would, moreover, reduce the intensity of debate over other NATO issues. Theater nuclear modernization would still be necessary, but adoption of conventional retaliation would clearly help to assuage some of the concerns that underlie the debate over NATO's use of nuclear weapons. As indicated earlier, such a strategy would also ease the tensions involved in allocating forces between the Persian Gulf and Western Europe. A coalition of sixteen democratic countries obviously cannot change its strategy without much soul-searching, discussion, and controversy. The need to strengthen deterrence, however, is compelling; debate on the recasting of NATO strategy to meet the conditions of the 1980s should be delayed no longer.

NUCLEAR DETERRENCE

Nuclear deterrence—that is, the implied or explicit threat to use nuclear weapons in response to an action by another state—has a role in American strategy in the 1980s, but that role is different from and less central than it was in previous decades. It will vary according to the types of actions to be deterred.

1. The threat of nuclear retaliation of some sort will remain indispensable to the deterrence of Soviet use of nuclear weapons against other countries.

2. Nuclear deterrence has a role, though a diminished one, along with conventional deterrence in deterring conventional attacks on Western Europe and Japan.

3. Nuclear deterrence has no role to play in deterring Soviet conventional aggression against second-zone countries, which is where aggression appears most likely in the 1980s. Here reliance must be placed on nonmilitary and conventional deterrence.

The credibility of some form of nuclear response to either a major conventional attack or a minor nuclear one against first-zone countries is enhanced by the development of limited nuclear options prescribed by National Security Decision Memorandum 242 in January 1974 and by the further elaboration of that strategy, including flexibility to alter preplanned options during crises, by Presidential Directive 59 in July 1980.

Under some circumstances the possibility of highly selective nuclear strikes against Soviet leadership and command and control facilities could also play a role in deterrent strategy that had the Soviet imperial system as its primary target. PD-59 gives high priority to such targets. Against this approach the argument is sometimes made that "killing the top Soviet leadership would leave no one for us to negotiate the end of the war with." By the same logic, however, it could also leave the U.S. no one to fight the war with. The destruction of the central political leadership of the Soviet Union and of the command and communications channels by which Moscow exercises control over its military forces and its satellites could well help precipitate the breakdown of Soviet authority that should be the wartime goal of American strategy. Nonetheless, in a counterimperial deterrent strategy, the overwhelming burden of deterrence will still have to be borne by conventional forces.

In the 1960s and 1970s discussions among strategists almost always implicitly assumed that nuclear deterrence was exclusively an American policy to be applied against other countries. That era is over. Nuclear deterrence is no longer a one-way street. The biggest changes in the role of nuclear deterrence in the 1980s are likely to come in Soviet rather than American strategy. For the Soviets nuclear deterrence will be far more important than it has been in the past. To date, Soviet nuclear deterrence has reflected the development of Soviet strategic nuclear forces to parity with those of the United States and hence has functioned almost entirely to limit the extent and credibility of American nuclear deterrence against Soviet conventional action. Colin Gray (1979:76) has suggested that this will continue to be its principal role. "It is very likely indeed that the Soviet Union sees its strategic forces largely in a counterdeterrent role—functioning to seal off local conflicts from influence by U.S. strategic forces.'' This is an unduly modest interpretation of the impact of Soviet strategic forces in the 1980s. American strategic forces are unlikely to play any significant role in zone-two conflicts; and the Soviet Union could never be sure that it could "seal off" zone-one conflicts, given past U.S. commitments and policy and the actual deployment in zone-one areas of American theater and battlefield nuclear weapons. Soviet nuclear deterrence in the 1980s is more likely to be aimed at another goal: "to seal off local conflicts [particularly in zone two] from influence by" U.S. and other Western *conventional* forces.

Such nuclear deterrence would fall squarely in the mainstream of Soviet strategic thinking. Occupying as they do, in Mackinder's terms, the heartland of Eurasia, the Soviets have always seen it as critical to their interests to dominate and, if possible, to control the rimland of Eurasia. To achieve this goal they need to minimize and, if possible, exclude American military forces and influence from that area. Consequently, it is very much in the Soviet interest to design their nuclear forces and strategy to deter the United States from projecting its military influence, by conventional or nuclear means, into the first- and second-zone countries of the rimland. Just as it was essential, as long as it was possible, for U.S. extended deterrence to extend to Western Europe, so is it also essential from the Soviet point of view for Soviet extended deterrence to extend to these areas adjoining and, in some cases, part of their empire. Under conditions of nuclear parity the extent of extended deterrence on each side will presumably be fairly limited. The advantages that the Soviets will possess in the strategic nuclear balance through the mid-1980s, however, make it possible that Soviet extended deterrence may extend further than American extended deterrence. In PD-18 in August 1977 President Carter declared it U.S. policy to maintain a strategic nuclear balance with the Soviet Union which would not deter the United States from taking conventional military action when its interests dictated. The question is: Is this standard being met?

Soviet extended deterrence could come into play in a variety of circumstances, ranging at the extremes from threatening vital American interests to defending vital Soviet interests. In a European crisis, for instance, the Soviets could use nuclear threats in an effort to deter the movement of U.S. reinforcements to Germany. The more probable cases, however, concern Soviet use of nuclear deterrents to persuade the United States not to employ conventional forces to defend U.S.

interests in second-zone countries. In the 1980s the October 1973 scenario could be played out in reverse. Consider, for instance, an insurrection in Saudi Arabia in which a radical revolutionary movement appears on the verge of overthrowing the Saudi monarchy, which then appeals to the United States for help. As Marines and the 82nd Airborne are being readied for transport to Riyadh, word comes that the Soviets have placed their nuclear forces on alert and announced that they would view U.S. military intervention in the Gulf as a hostile and provocative act. Would the United States go in to save the Saudis? It has been authoritatively stated that the U.S. nuclear alert in 1973 was a bluff, which would have been revealed as such if the Soviets had in fact transported their airborne divisions to Egypt. Would a comparable future Soviet action also be a bluff? What risks would an American president want to take to find out? How does one balance the imponderables on one side against those on the other? Would U.S. acceptance of the overthrow of the Saudi regime devastate U.S. credibility and influence in the Middle East? Would the United States be able to do business with a radical successor regime? Or would that regime use its control of a major portion of Western oil supplies to insist on a totally unacceptable solution to the Arab-Israeli dispute? On the other hand, if the United States did use military forces to suppress the rebellion, how would the Soviets react? Would they move in conventional military forces to help the rebels? Would they feel sufficiently assured by their marginal advantages in the strategic nuclear balance to take counteractions against Berlin or Israel? Would they bring the world to the brink and induce hysteria in the United States and Western Europe by evacuating their cities and threatening nuclear attacks on the vulnerable U.S. missiles?

In cases such as these, the Soviet Union would be using nuclear deterrence to support a conventional attack on U.S. vital interests. Another possible Soviet use of nuclear deterrence would be to deter American or other conventional assault on Soviet vital interests. By their very nature nuclear weapons are more useful as an instrument of deterrence than of compellance. The threat to use them is most credible when employed to deter nuclear or conventional assaults on targets that clearly are of overriding political and economic importance to the deterrer. Nuclear weapons are hence more useful to a country, like the United States in the 1950s and 1960s, which is defending the status quo rather than challenging it.[2] In the 1980s, the

Soviets will necessarily adopt the strategies of a status-quo power in attempting to maintain their empire against divisive forces from within and corrosive influences from without. Apart from the security of the Soviet Union itself, nothing is more crucial to the Soviet leaders than their hegemony in Eastern Europe, and if that hegemony seemed seriously threatened they surely would resort to nuclear deterrence if that seemed an appropriate tool for maintaining it. Nuclear deterrence which in the 1950s helped to prevent the expansion of the Soviet empire will in the 1980s help to preserve that empire.

This use of nuclear deterrence could occur in two situations. First, under some circumstances disaffected satellite governments or revolutionary movements within the empire could appeal to U.S. and other Western governments for direct or indirect military support. The Soviet Union would undoubtedly respond with a warning of the possible consequences, including nuclear ones, if the Western governents intervened militarily to support anti-Soviet forces in an area which it considers of vital importance to its own security. Second, if NATO adopted and threatened to implement a conventional retaliation strategy as a result of Soviet military action in China, the Persian Gulf, or central Europe, the Soviets would undoubtedly respond with the warning that they would use every means including nuclear weapons to repulse such an offensive. They would thus be setting forth, at least for deterrent purposes, a Soviet version of flexible response. The point at which the Soviets would actually use nuclear weapons to defend Eastern Europe would presumably depend upon how successful the Western conventional offensive was, how Eastern European governments and peoples reacted to that offensive, and what the Soviets saw as the probable American response to such use. The nature of that response, in turn, would depend upon the nature of the strategic nuclear balance at that time.

The changed role of nuclear deterrence in Soviet strategy thus has significant implications for its role in American strategy. In the 1950s and 1960s that role was primarily to deter Soviet use of conventional forces. In the 1980s that role has declined in importance, but U.S. nuclear forces must instead be able to play a counterdeterrent role and deter Soviet use of nuclear forces to deter American use of conventional forces, that is, they must be capable of meeting the criterion set forth by the Carter Administration's PD-18 in 1977. The development of a conventional deterrent against Soviet conventional attacks against either first-zone or second-zone countries does not free the United States from the need to maintain a nuclear deterrent against Soviet use of nuclear deterrence. Indeed, it makes it absolutely essential to do so. The effective carrying out of such a counter-deterrent strategy requires major changes in U.S. strategic programs so as to reduce the vulnerability of the United States to nuclear attack.

The ability of a country to use its nuclear forces for extended deterrence purposes depends upon its own vulnerability to a nuclear response. In effect, the effectiveness of extended deterrence varies inversely with the nuclear vulnerability of the deterrer. As U.S. vulnerability to Soviet nuclear attack increased, the scope and credibility of U.S. extended deterrence shrunk. Similarly, the ability of a country to use its nuclear forces in a counterdeterrent role is a function of its vulnerability compared to that of the country it wishes to deter. Thus, the relative effectiveness of Soviet extended deterrence and of U.S. counterdeterrence depends upon the relative vulnerability of their military forces, leadership, economy, and population to various types and levels of nuclear attack. At present the balance of vulnerablity is clearly against the United States. During the 1960s and 1970s, American military forces, leadership, and civilian economy and population became progressively more vulnerable to Soviet nuclear attack. In part this development could not be avoided. In part, however, it was the product of a strategic outlook—mutual assured destruction (MAD)—that saw a virtue in this condition. "It cannot have occurred often in history," as Henry Kissinger (1979b) later commented, "that it was considered an advantageous military doctrine to make your own country deliberately vulnerable." It certainly did not occur to the Soviets, who throughout this period consistently pursued a policy of attempting to insure that the destruction in a nuclear exchange would be anything but mutual. To protect themselves against the U.S. bomber force, they created an extraordinarily expensive and complex air defense system. To protect themselves against U.S. ICBMs (intercontinental ballistic missiles), they built their own ICBM force with a substantial hard-target kill capability against U.S. land-based missiles. To protect themselves against SLBMs, they significantly expanded their civil defense program in the early 1970s—precisely the time when, according to the MAD theory, they should have been abandoning it. For protection against both ICBMs and SLBMs, they continued to deploy the ABM (antiballistic missile) defenses permitted under the treaty and actively pursued research and development on more effective ABM systems. Soviet policy is, in short, clearly directed toward enhancing, as far as possible, the survival of Soviet leadership, forces, and society in any nuclear exchange. U.S. policy has not been directed toward this goal.

The result is a major survivability gap between the two countries. The Soviets provide protection in hardened or blast-resistant shelters for about 110,000 of their leaders. Nothing comparable exists in the United States. Soviet command and communications facilities are similarly hardened, while those of the United States are in many respects highly vulnerable. U.S. land-based missiles will be increasingly vulnerable to a Soviet first strike that in theory could destroy 80–90 percent of the U.S. ICBM force at the expense of a relatively small fraction of the Soviet ICBM force. U.S. bomber and missile submarine bases are similarly vulnerable. The United States possesses no comparable capability against Soviet strategic forces. U.S. theater nuclear weapons and tactical nuclear weapons in Europe are also highly vulnerable to surprise attack. Soviet civil defense (Director of Central Intelligence 1978) provides about 15,000 hardened or blast-resistant shelters (including those for the leadership) that could protect 12–24 percent of the total work force and 10–20 percent of the total urban population. Soviet civil defense planning provides for the evacuation of the remaining urban population to rural areas within two to seven days of warning. (How effective and feasible such evacuation would be in practice is, of course, impossible to say.) The United States has neither shelters nor meaningful evacuation planning. U.S. government agencies estimate that if a massive all-out nuclear exchange had occurred in 1978, 80–90 percent of the Soviet population could have survived the immediate effects of the attack, as against only 35–65 percent of the U.S. population (Huntington 1979:30). In any major nuclear exchange, great damage would be done to both sides' industrial facilities. Some evidence exists of Soviet attempts to provide some protection for industrial plants and machinery against nondirect hits, but it is impossible to say how extensive or meaningful these efforts are. During the 1970s the United States spent about $100 million a year on civil defense; it would have cost the United States about $2 billion a year to have duplicated the Soviet civil defense effort.

As this rundown suggests, after a nuclear exchange of almost any magnitude, the United States would be worse off vis-à-vis the Soviet Union than it was before. After an all-out exchange, the level of destruction on both sides would undoubtedly be so substantial that the differences which would exist—which might also be substantial—might not be terribly meaningful. Yet even after such an exchange, for the Soviet Union to end up with a population larger than that of the United States before the exchange and twice that of the United States after the exchange could be significant for the future of freedom in the world. In any event, as long as major asymmetries in survivability exist in so many dimensions, the United States is not in an effective position to use its nuclear forces as a counterdeterrent to Soviet use of their nuclear forces to deter U.S. conventional actions in defense of U.S. interests. From the Soviet viewpoint such a threat simply could not have high credibility. The restoration of something resembling equivalent survivability in the event of nuclear exchanges at any level must, consequently, be a major goal of U.S. policy in the 1980s.

The enhancement of U.S. survivability can be achieved through damage-limitation measures, civil defense, and active defense. To expand the currently rather limited U.S. damage-limitation capability against the Soviet nuclear forces requires the rapid deployment of the MX missile in some invulnerable basing mode and the intensification of the effort on the Trident II missile. These two programs will enhance both the payload and the accuracy of U.S. missiles and hence their hard-target kill capability. With such weapons the United States could conceivably destroy a large fraction of the Soviet missile and bomber force before they were launched.

Second, the United States needs to expand its ability to protect its leadership and population, which was virtually ignored for fifteen years. The beginnings of a change came in 1978 when President Carter approved PD-41 authorizing planning for the evacuation of U.S. cities in the event of a nuclear (or other comparable) emergency. The Carter Administration did not, however, provide the funds to implement this policy; those funds, which are almost invisibly modest beside the rest of the defense budget, should be rapidly made available. In addition, it would be wise for the administration to launch a serious study of the possibility of providing hardened shelters for a portion of the urban population, perhaps through a requirement that such shelter be included in all new residential or industrial-commercial construction within particular areas. In PD-53 and PD-58 the Carter Administration also directed that measures be taken to enhance the survivability of U.S. leadership, provide for the continuity of government, and protect U.S. command, control, and communications facilities.[3] Again, the achievement of equivalent survivability requires the prompt and full implementation of these directives.

Finally, the United States possesses no active defenses against incoming missiles and very little against enemy aircraft. At the moment, the latter vulnerability is not significant, but it quickly could become so if the Soviet Union acquired access to air fields in Central America or the Caribbean. The need to move ahead on ballistic missile defense, however, is urgent. Soviet missiles can destroy U.S. strategic forces, leadership, military facilities, industry, ports, and population. All the available evidence suggests that the Soviets themselves are rapidly moving ahead on ABM research and development and possibly the production of components for an ABM system. Given their strategic emphasis on protecting their homeland, it would be totally out of character for them not to do so. Developments in ABM-related technology suggest that the deployment of a site-protection ABM system to defend missile, bomber, and submarine bases, as well as other military facilities, could be feasible by sometime in the late 1980s. Serious potentialities exist for the development of laser-beam, space-based ABM satellites, which might provide broader coverage in the following decade. Even if it is simply to keep up with the Soviet Union, that is, not permit the survivability gap to widen significantly, the United States should give overriding priority to the development of these defensive systems. To the extent that such defenses enhance the survivability of U.S. nuclear forces, conventional forces, leadership, population, and economy, they will not only help to counter Soviet extended deterrence, but they could, conceivably, reverse in a small way the shrinkage in U.S. extended deterrence and thereby strengthen first-zone deterrence and reassure U.S. allies in Europe.

A heavy emphasis on defenses against nuclear weapons is often criticized on the grounds that it will launch a new phase in the arms race and thereby increase tensions and the probability of war. Such arguments are fallacious in two ways. First, it is quite clear from Soviet efforts that the defensive phase of the nuclear arms race is well underway, and the question for the United States is whether it will compete vigorously and successfully with the Soviets in developing its capacities for antinuclear warfare. If the United States does not do so, it will simply allow the Soviets to expand the advantages they already have in this area, which, in conjunction with advantages the Soviets also have in some aspects of nuclear offensive capabilities, could put the United States at a serious disadvantage in the event of a major crisis.

Second, and more important, is the fact that vigorous competition in the development and deployment of new weapons, which has been central to the Soviet-American arms race, does not increase the probability of war but instead does just the reverse. History shows rather conclusively that such qualitative arms races function as a substitute for war rather than as a stimulus to war (Huntington 1958). The thirty-five-year record of the Soviet-American arms race bears this out. If arms races inevitably lead to war, it is rather peculiar that this one has not done so by now; the proponents of the inevitability-of-war thesis surely have some explaining to do. In fact, however, the reason why their prognostications have not been borne out is that a qualitative arms race, if vigorously engaged in by both sides, tends to equalize military capabilities by leading to the virtually simultaneous introduction of new weapons by both sides and to restrict the economic burdens of the race by limiting the procurement of any particular generation of weapons. In a qualitative arms race the danger of war increases only when one side, without abandoning the race, also fails to compete vigorously in it, falls significantly behind in the competition, and then, discovering this, makes intense efforts to catch up. At that point the power that is ahead may be tempted to capitalize on its advantages.

A vigorously conducted qualitative arms race, on the other hand, acts to stabilize the relationship between the two competitors. It also focuses their attention on what the balance of military capabilities will be five to ten years in the future, and encourages them to direct their attention, effort, and investment to the development of weapons which will be important then. What is at stake is not who will win with today's military capabilities but who could win with tomorrow's. Such a perspective is, obviously, at odds with one which contemplates going to war in the immediate future. If both the Soviet and American governments concluded that war was inevitable during the next three to five years, they would immediately shift effort from the qualitative arms competition to the production of existing weapons.

During the era of U.S. strategic superiority and continuing into the 1970s, a central dichotomy existed in American strategy. U.S. nuclear strategy was almost entirely offensively oriented; virtually no attention was paid to active or passive defenses. Damage-limitation action against Soviet nuclear capabilities was stressed, but it played a role in U.S. planning primarily because it involved offensive action. In addition, U.S. ability to undertake damage limitation declined during the 1960s and 1970s as a result of the multiplication of Soviet launchers and warheads, the hardening of their silos, and their creation of an impressive air defense system. Conventional strategy, on the other hand, particularly in Europe, was entirely defensive in character. The possibility that a politically defensive alliance might have—and, indeed, might need—a militarily offensive strategy was apparently never seriously considered.

In a time of U.S. nuclear superiority, this offense-defense dichotomy between nuclear and conventional strategy was not necessarily inappropriate. The burden of deterrence rested upon the possibility of nuclear retaliation. If deterrence failed, the implementation of that threat could be delayed as long as an effective conventional defense could be mounted. In a time of strategic parity, however, almost the opposite relationship is true. The threat of nuclear retaliation is no longer credible as a deterrent to a conventional attack. The more effective deterrent of such an attack is the threat of conventional retaliation aimed at breaking up the Soviet empire. Conversely, nuclear defenses for U.S. forces, industry, and population are an essential counterdeterrent to enable the United States to use conventional forces to protect its interests. The assumptions of past strategy—that nuclear offense and conventional defense are stabilizing, but that nuclear defense and conventional offense are destabilizing—do not hold for the conditions of the 1980s. The United States should give top priority to eliminating the anomalies in the strategy that it has inherited from the 1960s and that simultaneously inhibit it from protecting itself and from taking war, if it should occur, into the Soviet empire in Europe. A balanced approach to deterrence in the 1980s requires that conventional strategy be diversified by giving greater weight to offensive action and that nuclear strategy be diversified by giving greater weight to defensive needs.

COPING WITH THIRD WORLD THREATS

The Soviet Union is the principal focus of U.S. strategic planning, and Soviet-American military conflict is more likely in the 1980s than in previous decades. The Soviet Union is not, however, the only conceivable source of threats to American vital interests, and the probability that American forces will engage Soviet forces is still less than the probability of their engaging other forces. Other governments or groups can threaten U.S. vital interests in three ways.

First, they can directly attack particular U.S. interests. A guerrilla force shooting rockets at ships going through the Panama Canal would pose a threat whether or not it had any affiliation with or support from the Soviet Union. An attack by the Iranian government or Islamic fundamentalist insurgents on Saudi oil facilities would pose a comparable threat whether or not those attacks had Soviet backing. The seizure of American embassies, planes, or citizens represents similar, if lower level, action to which the United States has to be prepared to respond militarily. The acquisition of nuclear weapons by a guerrilla group or, in some cases, by a government might also pose a direct challenge to American vital interests.

Second, some governments in the world are partial to the Soviets; others are partial to the West. A significant change in power between these two groups would have implications for U.S. security, even if the Soviet Union itself had not played any significant role in bringing that shift about. Coups d'etat in Saudi Arabia or in other Persian Gulf states or local wars in that area, Southeast Asia, the Middle East, or Africa could engage American interests if they threatened friendly governments.

Third, local conflicts and instability in the Third World can create opportunities for the direct expansion of Soviet or Soviet-proxy military influence and presence. American interests are clearly to minimize these opportunities. At times, however, they will exist; nonmilitary and conventional efforts at deterrence may fail; and the United States may find itself confronted with the need to respond to Soviet-bloc military actions in the Third World.

More specifically, the types of Third World military conflict that might pose threats to U.S. interests in the 1980s include: (1) coups d'etat against friendly governments; (2) insurrections or guerrilla insurgencies against friendly governments; (3) local conflicts in which a friendly government is invaded or in danger of being defeated by a less friendly one; (4) any of the above in which Soviet or Soviet-proxy forces play a significant role.[4]

The United States needs a strategy and the capabilities to deal with threats to its interests that arise from these types of conflicts. Declarations of American interest and deployments of American forces can help deter Soviet intervention and local aggression by regional powers. In some circumstances, they may also be able to reduce the likelihood of coups d'etat against friendly regimes. It is difficult, if not impossible, however, to deter those whom one cannot locate, identify, or be sure exist. The United States, as Steven David has persuasively argued (1982), undoubtedly should be prepared to help friendly governments suppress coups d'etat. The existence of some such U.S. capability—and knowledge of its existence—might have some deterrent effect on coup plotting in friendly countries. But these deterrent effects would be of a highly generalized nature, and the participants in any particular conspiracy or cabal might well have good reason for thinking that such an American capability would not be terribly relevant for their case. Hence a strategy for coping with Third World threats has to be directed to both deterring those challenges that are predictable and responding to those challenges that are not.

While there clearly may be some measure of overlap, the four types of contingencies just mentioned are listed in an order that generally reflects ascending levels of violence. From the 1950s into the 1970s, American strategic attention was largely focused upon the second and third types of contingencies. The Korean War was a clear Contingency Three case; the Vietnam War was a combination of Contingencies Two and Three. In connection with these involvements, American strategists developed theories of limited war and of counterinsurgency. Relatively little attention was paid to strategies for coping either with coups d'etat, which were frequent but seldom serious, or with Soviet military intervention in the Third World, which until the mid-1970s was relatively minimal.

Insurrections and local wars remain highly likely in the Third World in the 1980s. Many of these could directly affect major American interests. These could include insurgencies in the Gulf area, in Central America and the Caribbean, and conceivably in South Africa. Local wars that might raise the issue of direct American military intervention to support a friendly government could occur in Southeast Asia (Vietnam versus Thailand), the Persian Gulf (Iran, Iraq, or Yemen versus Saudi Arabia), North Africa (Libya versus Egypt, Tunisia, or the Sudan; Algeria versus Morocco), the Horn of Africa (Ethiopia versus Somalia, Kenya, or the Sudan), and quite possibly elsewhere.

The probability of direct participation by U.S. military forces in either prolonged insurgencies or local wars remains, however, relatively low, except in situations where that conflict might directly affect concrete American interests, such as Saudi oil production. The impact of Vietnam is strongest and most relevant with respect to U.S.

military involvement in counterinsurgency situations. The reluctance of any U.S. administration, Congress, and the public to countenance such involvement will undoubtedly remain high for most of the 1980s. The United States may often find it in its interests, as in El Salvador, to provide advice, training, money, and equipment to a friendly government fighting guerrillas. In the absence of a direct threat to concrete American interests or direct and overt involvement of Soviet or Soviet-proxy forces, the United States is not likely to find it militarily necessary, diplomatically desirable, or politically feasible to intervene with U.S. combat forces in such conflicts.

Fewer constraints exist on U.S. military involvement in a local interstate war. Major segments of the American establishment tend automatically to attribute legitimacy to revolutionary movements against Third World governments. They also tend almost automatically to attribute illegitimacy to any direct attack by one state on another across a recognized frontier. Consequently, there is likely to be greater public willingness to help a friendly government respond to an external attack than to an internal attack. In the absence of a simultaneous domestic insurgency or outside great power support, however, local interstate wars in the Third World do not generally lead to quick and decisive outcomes. The limited military capabilities of the combatants are more likely, as in the Iran-Iraq war, to lead to inconclusive stalemates, in which neither party is able to deal a death blow to the other. In this situation, the need for direct U.S. military involvement is also reduced.

During the 1970s the Persian Gulf assumed new importance as far as U.S. security is concerned. During the 1980s the probability of political instability in Saudi Arabia, Kuwait, Bahrein, the United Arab Emirates, and Oman is very high. Conceivably, a prolonged insurgency, a local interstate war, or direct Soviet military intervention could endanger oil supplies from this region to the United States and its allies. The most likely form of instability, however, is coups d'etat against one or more of these conservative Gulf regimes. The underlying causes of political instability are inherent in the rapid increases in wealth, rising expectations, social dislocation, conflicts between Western and Islamic values, and development of modern armed forces. In Saudi Arabia and the other Gulf states, there are at least four major possible sources of instability. First, conflicts within the established elite (for example, between the Sudairi and Jiluwi factions in Saudi Arabia) could get out of hand, leading to efforts by one group to exclude the other from power. Second, the military and other professional groups produced by modernization could be antagonized by the corruption of the existing regime and by their own failure to share adequately in the riches of oil and hence could attempt to overthrow the existing system through a coup d'etat. Third, Islamic fundamentalist groups (*ulemmas,* traditional tribal and local elites) could react against social and economic change, attempting a coup in order to stop such change. Fourth, Palestinian radical groups, alone or in conjunction with radical modernist or Islamic fundamentalist groups, could promote political upheaval so that less conservative regimes who are actively willing to support their cause against Israel could come into power.

All in all, the likelihood of the existing political elites in the Persian Gulf states surviving this decade is small. Even less likely is the survival of the existing political systems. It is difficult to predict the extent to which coups would bring to power regimes seriously hostile to U.S. interests. It is virtually certain, however, that *any* post-coup regime in a conservative Persian Gulf state will be less sympathetic to U.S. interests concerning oil and the Arab-Israeli dispute and more open to Soviet influence than the current regime in that state. In addition, a successful coup in one Gulf state could well trigger coup attempts in adjoining states. Coping with internal instability in Persian Gulf regimes is, consequently, a top priority for U.S. security policy in the 1980s. An overall strategy for dealing with these contingencies involves four elements.

First and most basic are efforts to conserve energy, to stockpile reserves, and to diversify energy sources so that the dependence of the United States and its allies on oil from this potentially unstable area will be reduced. While such efforts deserve top priority, they probably will not significantly reduce U.S. dependence on Persian Gulf oil before the end of the decade. The dependence of U.S. allies on this oil will continue even longer.

Second, the United States can encourage the existing Gulf regimes to take steps to postpone or reduce the likelihood of a coup. These would include measures: to moderate but sustain the pace of economic development; to distribute the fruits of development broadly among key groups in the population; to keep its military happy with money, promotions, and weapons; to divide the military establishment into two or more competing institutions; to limit corruption and distribute it widely; to negotiate the stationing of politically acceptable foreign forces in that country (for instance, Pakistani troops in Saudi Arabia) that could protect the regime; and to develop institutional channels so that those elements of the population which are mobilized through modernization can legitimately participate in politics.

Third, the United States can take measures in tacit cooperation with existing regimes to help them defeat coups if they should occur. In several instances in the recent past, outside assistance has played a significant role in defeating coups. The United States itself has acted to head off or defeat coups in Ethiopia, Venezuela, and elsewhere (David 1982). In a coup, communications play a vital role: the leaders of the coup have to convince the populace and, most importantly, potential supporters in the military and elsewhere that they have successfully deposed the previous regime and established themselves in power. The leader of the regime, on the other hand, has to demonstrate that he is still alive and functioning and able to appeal for support. The United States is fortunate that the Persian Gulf oil states are, indeed, located on the Persian Gulf. To assist in the defeat of coups in these states, the United States should provide radio transmitters and other communications facilities on ships off-shore, which could be used by government leaders to relay messages to their supporters and to appeal to their people. In addition, it would be wise for the United States to maintain a small specially trained, countercoup military force on U.S. ships in the region, equipped with helicopters and VSTOL (vertical short take-off and landing) aircraft, that could in in a matter of hours respond to the request of a threatened government for help.

Finally, the United States should position itself so that the damage to its interests is reduced if a coup succeeds. It is in the American interest, consequently, to expand and diversify its relations with the Persian Gulf countries—financially, developmentally, militarily, technologically—so that any successor regime will find it difficult and costly to attack American interests and sever connections with the United States. In addition, while it is difficult to predict who will lead a successor government, it is not so difficult to identify a small number of potential leaders for that government. In contrast to its behavior in Iran, the United States should attempt to develop and maintain friendly contacts with those individuals and groups likely to play leading roles in a successor regime.

The most serious sort of military contingency for the United States in the Third World would be direct Soviet or Soviet-proxy military participation in a coup, insurrection, or local war. The appropriate measures of nonmilitary and conventional deterrence can reduce significantly the probability of such involvement. Nonetheless, it still could happen, particularly in the Persian Gulf area. The likelihood of such intervention would be reduced if the United States were able to deploy ground forces in a deterrence-by-presence posture in the region. Such a deployment, however, would no doubt increase the already high probability of political instability in the region. To counter possible Soviet intervention, the United States needs to strengthen the Rapid Deployment Force authorized by President Carter in 1977, greatly expand and modernize its air and naval transport capabilities, pre-position equipment in the area where possible, maintain a respectable naval presence in the Arabian Sea, and negotiate agreements for access to local bases in emergencies. Although the Soviets probably could, if they wished, overwhelm local or allied forces in the northern Gulf area, the combination of these measures, plus a revision of NATO strategy to make them worry about their Eastern European flank, could provide fairly persuasive deterrence and then war-fighting capability if deterrence failed.

In the 1980s the United States may still have to come to the help of friendly governments fighting local interstate wars or combatting prolonged insurgencies, as it did in Korea and Vietnam. More than before, however, the United States will likely become involved in the other two contingencies located at opposing ends of the spectrum of violence: countercoup intervention, on the one hand, and counter-intervention against Soviet or proxy military forces, on the other. These two contingencies share one characteristic: they are unlikely to last long. A coup is a matter of hours or days at most. A Soviet military intervention to which the United States responded is also likely to be terminated quickly either because one side or the other has won what it wanted or because both sides react to the dangers of escalation by negotiating a cease-fire or disengagement. Because of their probable short duration, countercoup and counter-Soviet U.S. military interventions in the Third World are also likely to be more politically feasible than U.S. involvement in more prolonged civil and interstate wars. The theorists of limited war in the 1950s and 1960s discussed at length the ways in which war could be limited in terms of goals, targets, geographical areas, and forces and weapons employed. As the experiences of Korea and Vietnam make clear, however, the most significant limit on U.S. military action in a small-scale conflict is the limit of *time* (Huntington 1977). The American public simply will not permit its government to engage in long, drawn-out military actions to defend distant interests and to achieve ambiguous goals. Fortunately, the contingencies the United States is most likely to face during the 1980s are ones which will probably be of short duration. Thus, for both political and military reasons, U.S. strategy in Third World conflicts should be directed toward reacting promptly and achieving a quick decision.

CONCLUSION: FROM STRATEGY TO STRENGTH

The reconstitution of American military power is the first step in providing for American security in the 1980s. The weaker the United States is responding to the expansion of the Soviet empire, the greater the dangers it will face in dealing with the disintegration of that empire. The growth in the forces pushing for that disintegration can only reduce any inhibitions the Soviets may feel about using military force, including nuclear force, to maintain their empire. As an incomplete superpower, the Soviet Union must in the end rely primarily on military force to achieve its objectives. There is thus a need to deter the Soviets from taking military action to expand their empire and also a potentially even greater need to deter them from taking military action to prevent their empire's disintegration. These tendencies toward both the expansion and the disintegration leave the United States and its allies little alternative but to look to their defenses.

The reconstitution of American military power, however, has to be directed to the needs of the 1980s and shaped by ideas relevant to this decade. Americans tend to be ahistorical. They tend to think in terms of timeless truths or concrete cases, but not historical phases or eras. Yet each phase has its own distinctive characteristics and requirements, and as the Soviets have recognized, a new phase began about 1970 that is as distinctly different for them, and hence for the United States, as the phases that began in 1917 and 1945. The central concepts elaborated in American strategic thinking in the 1950s and 1960s can play only modestly useful roles in the military arenas of the 1980s. Times have changed; conditions are different; failure to weed out obsolete ideas can only invite disaster.

The current phase requires not only new strategic ideas but a new role for strategy itself. Throughout most of the nineteenth century the security of the United States rested on its isolation from any realistic threats. In the first half of the twentieth century, that isolation diminished, but its effects were reinforced by the extent to which its distance from Europe and Asia gave the United States time to capitalize upon its unmatched human and industrial resources and to mobilize the men, the machines, and the weapons to overpower its enemies—a process foreshadowed in World War I and then magnificently embodied in the fleets that Nimitz, Halsey, and Spruance led across the Pacific and in the armies that Eisenhower, Bradley, and Patton led across Europe in World War II. After World War II, American security rested primarily on its technological superiority and particularly its nuclear capabilities. These were used not only to prevent a direct attack on the United States but also to deter attacks on Western Europe, Japan, and other American vital interests. Over the years—from 1815 to 1970, in short—the key elements in American security posture were, successively, geographic isolation, industrial capacity, and technological superiority.

None of these is sufficient in the 1980s. Distance has been obliterated. Industrial capacity will be only marginally relevant for the conflicts the country is most likely to face. Nuclear superiority has been replaced by, at best, nuclear parity and perhaps marginal nuclear inferiority. Technology generally has come to be perceived as a double-edged weapon. At the same time, the overall military power of its principal rival has increased steadily over the past fifteen years, and the interests it has to defend have multiplied, most notably in the Middle East and Persian Gulf areas. All these developments clearly warrant the military build-up that the Carter Administration inaugurated and the Reagan Administration accelerated. But they also require something besides more money, more men, and more weapons. They require new strategic ideas and an entirely new emphasis on strategy and strategic thinking. In the past the security of the United States rested primarily on its superiority in physical factors. In the future, it will have to rest increasingly on a superiority in strategic insight, skill, and creativity, upon the ability of the United States to outwit its opponents instead of simply outproducing and outdeveloping them. The probability is high that the United States will go to war sometime in the 1980s. The task of American strategy is to determine how, given the constraints of the 1980s, the United States can win that war while at the same time deterring a worse one.

NOTES

1. The Chinese, of course, have a nuclear deterrent. If the Soviet military action against China was to be limited in both time and space, the Soviets might hope to avoid nuclear escalation by announcing their limited intentions in advance. If they had in mind a larger and longer term invasion of China, they presumably would start with a preemptive attack on Chinese nuclear forces and facilities.
2. This also explains why the consequences of nuclear proliferation, unsettling though they may be, are likely to be less unsettling than often anticipated. Those countries with the highest impetus to develop nuclear weapons are those like Israel, South Africa, Pakistan, or Taiwan which have reason to believe that at some point their very survival might be at stake.
3. The driving force behind the issuance of all three of these PDs, as well as PD-59 on nuclear targeting, was then Col. William E. Odom of the NSC, whom future historians may well identify as one of the major architects of whatever success the United States has in its next nuclear confrontation with the Soviet Union.
4. Here and in the following pages I draw on my remarks in the colloquium on "Vietnam Reappraised" (1981:3–26).

REFERENCES

Aspin, Les. 1976. "How to Look at the Soviet-American Balance." *Foreign Policy* no. 22 (Spring): 96–106.

Blechman, Barry M., and Stephen S. Kaplan. 1978. *Force Without War: U.S. Armed Forces as a Political Instrument.* Washington, D.C.: Brookings Institution.

Brown, Harold. 1979. *Department of Defense Annual Report Fiscal Year 1980.* Washington, D.C.: Department of Defense.

Carnegie Endowment for International Peace, Panel on U.S. Security and the Future of Arms Control. 1981. *Challenges for U.S. National Security. Assessing the Balance: Defense Spending and Conventional Forces.* A Preliminary Report, Part II. Washington, D.C.: Carnegie Endowment for International Peace.

Challenger, Richard D. 1955. *The French Theory of the Nation in Arms, 1866–1939.* New York: Columbia University Press.

Churchill, Winston. 1949. "United We Stand Secure." *Vital Speeches* 15 (April 1).

David, Steven. 1982. "Defending Third World Regimes Against Coups d'Etat." Unpublished manuscript, Center for International Affairs, Harvard University.

DeGaulle, Charles. 1934. *Vers l'Armée de Métiér.* Paris: Berger-Levrault.
Director of Central Intelligence. 1978. *Soviet Civil Defense.* Washington, D.C.: Government Printing Office.
Gray, Colin S. 1979. "Nuclear Strategy: A Case for a Theory of Victory." *International Security* 4 (Summer).
Huntington, Samuel P. 1958. "Arms Races: Prerequisites and Results." *Public Policy,* Yearbook of the Graduate School of Public Administration, Harvard University 8: 41–86.
———. 1961. *The Common Defense: Strategic Programs in National Politics.* New York: Columbia University Press.
———. 1977. "The Soldier and the State in the 1970s." In *Civil Military Relations,* edited by Andrew J. Goodpaster and Samuel P. Huntington, pp. 5–28. Washington, D.C.: American Enterprise Institute for Public Policy Research.
———. 1978. "Trade, Technology and Leverage: Economic Diplomacy." *Foreign Policy* no. 32 (Fall): 63–80.
———. 1979. "Civil Defense in the 1980s." In *Civil Defense,* Hearing before the Committee on Banking, Housing and Urban Affairs, United States Senate, 95th Congress, 2nd Sess., January 8: 24–35.
Iklé, Fred Charles. 1980. "NATO's 'First Nuclear Use': A Deepening Trap?" *Strategic Review* 8 (Winter).
Johnson, Lyndon B. 1971. *The Vantage Point.* New York: Holt, Rinehart and Winston.
Kaufman, William W. 1956. "The Requirements of Deterrence." In *Military Policy and National Security,* edited by William W. Kaufman. Princeton: Princeton University Press.
Kissinger, Henry. 1979a. *White House Years.* Boston: Little, Brown.
———. 1979b. "The Future of NATO." *The Washington Quarterly* 2 (Autumn).
Mearsheimer, John J. 1982. "The Conventional Balance on the European Central Front." *International Security* 7 (Summer).
New York Times. 1981. "U.S. and Distant Conflicts: Europe Fears Military Shift." June 11.
Pastor, Robert A. 1980. *Congress and the Politics of U.S. Foreign Economic Policy, 1929–1976.* Berkeley: University of California Press.
Stuart, Douglas B. 1981. "The Fall of Vietnam: A Soldier's Retrospection." *Parameters* 11 (June):28–36.
"Vietnam Reappraised." 1981. *International Security* 6 (Summer): 3–26.
Weinberger, Caspar W. 1981. "The Defense Policy of the Reagan Administration," Address, Council on Foreign Relations, New York, N.Y., June 17.
Windsor, Philip. 1978. "Yugoslavia, 1951, and Czechoslovakia, 1968." In *Force Without War,* edited by Barry M. Blechman and Stephen S. Kaplan, pp. 440–512. Washington, D.C.: Brookings Institution.

2 THE EVOLUTION OF U.S. STRATEGIC "DOCTRINE"— 1945 to 1981

Aaron L. Friedberg

INTRODUCTION

The United States has come to a conspicuous turning point in the evolution of its nuclear strategy. Over the next five years there will be changes in our force posture and employment policy as significant as those which occurred almost twenty years ago under John Kennedy and Robert McNamara. And the decisions made during the present period of transition will go an equally long way toward shaping the strategic environment in which we will have to live over the next twenty years, between now and the end of this century.

Change, especially when it is accompanied by a sense of urgency, inevitably produces turmoil, debate, and uncertainty. We sense that the concepts which have shaped our thinking are inadequate, but we have no ready substitutes with which to replace them. We feel the need to do something, but we are not at all sure what we should do.

Not surprisingly, the current debate over what weapons to buy, what targets to aim at, and what treaties to negotiate is cast largely in historical terms. Opposing camps warn against continuing to adhere to or daring to depart from the strictures of past policy. But what exactly

The views expressed here are those of the author. He wishes to thank Mr. Kurt Guthe for his advice and assistance.

53

has been our strategic nuclear doctrine over the last thirty-five years? What have been the character, structure, and purpose of U.S. plans for nuclear war and how have those plans evolved? Because the answers to these questions are so hard to find, the debate over future policy has become unnecessarily confused. Indeed, much of what today passes for informed discussion is really no more than noisy disagreement over opposing misconceptions.

A handful of mistaken notions tend to divide participants in the debate over nuclear strategy. There are those who believe that it would be a dramatic and dangerous innovation for the United States to aim its strategic nuclear weapons at the military forces (particulary the strategic nuclear forces) of the Soviet Union. In the past, it is argued, the United States has always relied almost exclusively on the threat of urban-industrial devastation to deter aggression. A change in policy would pose tremendous risks.

On the other hand, a growing number of analysts, critics, and observers claim that the United States has long lacked a strategy to conduct a nuclear war. In the event of a major conflict, it is argued, U.S. forces would be prepared to do little except execute massive nuclear attacks on Soviet cities. A change in policy is clearly essential.

These two contentions really form the opposite sides of a single, pervasive myth—that the United States has, does, and should (or should not, depending on one's view) adhere to the "doctrine of mutually assured destruction."[1] Over the years this myth has been perpetuated in a number of ways. In the writings of some highly regarded civilian analysts, descriptions of perceived reality have often been misinterpreted as prescriptions for planning and policy.[2] The statements of senior government officials with budgets to balance and axes to grind have sometimes encouraged the belief that U.S. war plans called exclusively for attacks on Soviet cities.[3] More recently, interested parties on both sides of an increasingly heated debate have often found it useful to defend or attack mythical past policies in order to resist certain military programs or to support calls for sweeping changes in strategy.[4]

At a somewhat deeper level, widespread belief in the myth of the doctrine of mutually assured destruction is symptomatic of several historical and conceptual confusions. For obvious reasons, detailed information about nuclear war plans is not readily available. Nevertheless, a good deal of authoritative commentary on the subject has appeared over the years. As declassification procedures go into effect, it will become easier to review actual planning documents. Indeed, this process has already begun (Rosenberg 1979). Using a variety of sources it should be possible to piece together a reasonably accurate, coherent picture of the evolution of official U.S. nuclear war planning. In the process, it should not be difficult to dispense with the two subsidiary myths mentioned above—that the United States has always avoided targeting Soviet military forces and that we have lacked a strategy to conduct nuclear war. The construction of a brief historical overview is the principal purpose of this chapter.

Lack of information is a problem, but it is not the only one. Even if it were possible to agree on facts, it might be extremely difficult to determine the level of analysis at which these facts should be interpreted. Thus, even if it can be proven that U.S. nuclear war plans and American strategic doctrine as a whole have not been governed by the dictates of an assured destruction philosophy, it could be argued that the world, in some larger sense, is still governed by those laws. In other words, even if U.S. war plans reveal a strong, traditional countermilitary tendency, it may still be the case that the threat of urban-industrial damage is the ultimate deterrent to war. I will have more to say about this question at the close of this chapter.

Finally, it seems clear that in the strategic debate, as in so many other areas, confusion is encouraged (and deeper disagreements concealed) by imprecision in language. In particular, the word "doctrine" is often used loosely and incorrectly.

Fritz Ermarth has suggested that strategic doctrine be defined as "a set of operative beliefs, values, and assertions that in a significant way guide official behavior with respect to strategic research and development (R&D), weapons choice, forces, operational plans, arms control, etc." (Ermarth 1978). If this is a good definition and if, over the last thirty-five years, the United States has truly adopted a "doctrine" of mutually assured destruction, an observer should expect to see evidence of adherence to an identifiable set of principles across a broad range of activities. Specifically, an astute analyst would expect to find a "strategy" which called only for massive retaliatory nuclear strikes against enemy cities, a force posture capable of executing such attacks but suitable for little else, a selection of weapons and an R&D process which reflected a complete lack of interest in defensive systems or offensive forces intended for countermilitary missions, and arms control and declaratory policies which stressed stability, equality and the importance of mutual vulnerability.

So much for theoretical prediction. Reality, of course, is rather different. Some of the things listed above are visible today, others are not. And some have been in evidence at various times but not at others.[5]

All this is an elaborate way of making a rather simple point. The United States has never adhered to a doctrine of mutually assured destruction. Indeed, by any reasonable definition of the word, this country has never *had* a strategic nuclear doctrine. Or, perhaps more precisely, the United States has had a strategic doctrine in the same way that a schizophrenic has a personality. Instead of a single integrated and integrating set of ideas, values, and beliefs, we have had a complex and sometimes contradictory melange of notions, principles, and policies.

At the risk of oversimplifying, it seems clear that U.S. strategic doctrine, such as it is, has always contained two different strands. One is "assured destructionist" in coloration and emphasizes the importance of the countervalue deterrent, the dangers of regarding nuclear forces as ordinary weapons of war, the risks of threatening the enemy's nuclear capabilities, the value of stability, and the necessity for indices of "sufficiency." The other strand is more traditional, arising as it does from some universal and time-honored principles of military action. It focuses on war outcomes, on the importance of preparing to achieve sensible objectives should deterrence fail, and therefore on the necessity for defeating the enemy by denying him his objectives and destroying his willingness and ability to wage war.[6] At times these two sets of ideas have come into open conflict. In certain areas one strain or the other has clearly been dominant. But often they have simply coexisted with one another.

The purpose of this chapter is threefold: (1) to recount the history of U.S. planning for intercontinental nuclear war between 1945 and the present; (2) to disprove two popular misconceptions about American nuclear targeting and strategy; and finally, (3) to demonstrate the strong and persistent presence of a traditional military element in official thinking and planning thereby discounting the myth that the United States has ever adhered to a doctrine of mutually assured destruction.

Current policy problems will not be extensively discussed. Nevertheless, it seems clear that a better understanding of the past can only improve our chances of acting wisely in the present. At the very least, exposing some old, widely accepted ideas to new scrutiny may help to improve the quality of debate on a number of very important issues.

TARGETING

Early Years, 1945-1950

The closest the United States has ever come to avoiding attacks on Soviet military installations was in the five years immediately following the close of World War II. During this period the American nuclear arsenal was extremely small—no more than a handful of atomic bombs were available, along with an equally small number of suitably equipped aircraft.[7] Specially trained personnel were also scarce—in early 1947 the Strategic Air Command (SAC) had twenty trained air crews and only six weapons assembly specialists (MacIsaac 1979:22).

Until 1949 the Soviets did not have nuclear weapons. Their military power was "conventional"—massive ground armies which remained largely intact after the United States had begun to disband its forces. The strategic bombing experience of the Second World War encouraged Western experts to believe that air power could be used most effectively to attack a conventionally armed opponent's war-supporting industrial base. The tremendous power of atomic weapons, demonstrated so effectively at the end of the war, reinforced this notion. In the words of a high-level Air Force report written in the fall of 1945 "[the atomic bomb] is primarily an offensive weapon for use against large urban and industrial targets" (MacIsaac 1979:22).

Thus shortages and an absence of extremely "time-urgent" targets (like Soviet nuclear weapons storage sites and delivery vehicles) combined with prevailing ideas about the utility of air power to shape early war plans. Cities were targeted because it was believed they could be found and hit from the air, because their destruction was thought the best way to weaken Soviet military might, and because no other logical target set existed.

Expanding Target Lists, 1950-1960

By the early fifties the situation had begun to change. The collapse of Nationalist China, the outbreak of war in Korea and the worsening of relations with the USSR seemed to increase the danger of a land war on the Eurasian periphery. Meanwhile, for the first time Soviet nuclear weapons tests raised the possibility of atomic attacks on the continental United States.

American planners began to become more actively concerned with the problems of defending Western Europe from a Russian invasion and preparing to disable Soviet long-range nuclear air power. As a result, the existing target lists were expanded and subdivided. Three general categories of target were identified. According to Henry Rowen, former deputy assistant secretary of defense for International Security Affairs and once president of the RAND Corporation, "The designated ground zeros were almost entirely (1) industrial facilities; (2) "retardation" targets, for example, transportation links whose destruction was intended to slow the westward movement of Soviet forces; and (3) counterforce targets, the bases of the small and concentrated Soviet long-range air force (Rowen 1975:222).

The counterforce target set, while it now clearly existed, was still quite small. In the words of one expert,

> . . . the counterforce target system, although a top priority, represented a lesser effort than the industrial/urban target system. The lack of urgency about counterforce targets may possibly be inferred from the fact that the Joint Chiefs did not agree on an approved counterforce target list until 1953 (Goldberg 1967:6).

As the decade progressed, both the U.S. and Soviet nuclear arsenals increased in size. In the mid-fifties the initial flights of the U-2 produced an increase in the quantity and quality of the target intelligence available to American military planners (Futrell 1971:551). As a result, Soviet nuclear installations undoubtedly began to make up a larger portion of the existing target lists.

During this period a debate over targeting policy began within the Air Force. One group argued that, as General Hoyt S. Vandenberg told a Senate subcommittee in June 1953, "The proper role of air forces is to destroy the enemy's industrial potential" (Futrell 1971:391). The other maintained, in the words of General Curtis LeMay, that growing Soviet nuclear power required the United States to ". . . go back to the rulebook and the principles of war and fight the air battle first, which means that we must as quickly as possible destroy their capability of doing damage to us (Futrell 1971:390).

In 1954 and 1955 a number of proposals for a shift to pure counterforce targeting began to appear. Ex-Secretary of the Air Force Thomas K. Finletter wrote in 1954 that "the old counter-industry concept. . . should be given up" in favor of plans emphasizing attacks on enemy nuclear and conventional forces, command control and communications systems and supply lines (Futrell 1971:391). In February of the same year General Nathan F. Twining declared, "We can now aim directly to disarm an enemy rather than to destroy him as was so often necessary in wars of the past" (Futrell 1971:390).

In theory, concentrating on promptly destroying Soviet forces-in-being offered the best means of achieving victory. This would be particularly true if, as was widely assumed, a future war turned out to be unrestrained, nuclear, and thus relatively brief. Avoiding unnecessary civilian casualties had considerable moral appeal. In addition, a declared U.S. intention to forego attacks on cities might encourage the Soviets to practice similar restraint (Leghorn 1955; Walkowicz 1955).

Despite its obvious attractions, the idea of "pure counterforce" or "counterforce no-cities" targeting failed to catch on within the Air Force. The principal reasons for this lack of enthusiasm seem to have been the operational and technical problems that such a change in plans would have created. Massive, accurate, and virtually simultaneous raids on all elements of the budding Soviet nuclear forces would have been required to guarantee the success of a pure counterforce strategy. And, while the U.S. Air Force certainly wanted more planes and better target information, in the period of 1954-56 they were simply not available. Nevertheless, Soviet military installations of all types were extensively targeted during these years (Goldberg 1967:10).

The First SIOP, 1960-1961

By the end of the fifties another debate over targeting had broken out, this one between the Air Force and the other services, primarily the Navy. With its Polaris ballistic missile submarine about to be deployed, some Navy officers began to argue that SAC had, in effect, outlived its usefulness. All that was required to deter the USSR from attacking the United States, it was claimed, was a secure force capable of destroying a finite number of Soviet cities (perhaps as many as 200) (Goldberg 1967:15). According to Navy spokesmen, additional forces directed at military installations represented wasteful "overkill" and could be eliminated. The Air Force counterattacked, calling the policy of "finite deterrence" a "bluff strategy" which did not "include the capability for military victory" (Futrell 1971:566–567). Moreover, the Air Force asserted that it should be given tighter operational control over all U.S. nuclear forces, including the Navy's new submarines.

A study completed in late 1959 resolved these issues. A Joint Strategic Target Planning Staff (JSTPS) was formed to facilitate interservice cooperation, draw up a National Strategic Target List (NSTL), and prepare a Single Integrated Operational Plan (SIOP) for the conduct of nuclear war (Ball 1974:11). An "optimum mix" of "high priority military, industrial, and government control targets" was designated for destruction in a single, massive attack (Rowen 1975:225).

The SIOP Revised, 1961–1974

In 1961 work on revising the first SIOP was begun. The principal purpose of this effort was to introduce some measure of flexibility into U.S. plans for all-out nuclear war.[8] To this end, in Henry Rowen's words,

> Basic U.S. options were developed that differentiated more clearly between attacks against military targets and against cities (Rowen 1975:227).

The new SIOP

> distinguished more clearly among . . . three tasks: . . . attack on (1) nuclear threat targets, (2) other military forces, and (3) urban-industrial targets. It also provided options for withholding attack by country and for withholding direct attack on cities (Rowen 1975:230).

The targeting of military installations thus continued under McNamara. In his often quoted Ann Arbor speech of June 1962, The Secretary of Defense said,

> . . . principal military objectives, in the event of a nuclear war stemming from a major attack on the Alliance, should be the destruction of the enemy's military forces, not his civilian population (Ball 1974:14).

McNamara reiterated this view in his fiscal year (FY) 1963 budget statement in which he argued, "A major mission of the strategic retaliatory forces is to deter war by their capability to destroy the enemy's war-making capabilities (Ball 1974:14).

Despite subsequent shifts in declaratory policy which encouraged the belief that only urban areas would be hit in an all-out war, in fact the targeting of military facilities continued throughout the sixties and into the seventies.[9] Henry Rowen notes that "from 1960 to 1974, the priority in the assignment of weapons was first, to the urban-industrial targets, and then to nuclear threat and other military forces." But he goes on to explain,

A high "priority" in this context means "most important." It does not mean first in time. Presumably the most time urgent targets would be military forces, especially nuclear threat ones. Highest priority also does not mean that the greatest *weight of effort* would have to be allocated against urban-industrial targets; rather that the *confidence* of being able to destroy these targets should be high (Rowen 1975:220; emphasis in the original).

It would appear then that McNamara's early thoughts on the utility of targeting Soviet military forces continued to be reflected in actual war plans for some time after official talk of counterforce attacks had virtually ceased. Desmond Ball, in his monograph *De'ja Vu: The Return to Counterforce in the Nixon Administration*, quotes an unnamed former assistant secretary of defense writing in 1971: "The SIOP remains essentially unchanged since then [McNamara's Ann Arbor speech of 16 June 1962]" (Ball 1974:16). Rowen confirms this view, saying,

> . . . the nuclear planning process experienced no important change from the early 1960s until 1974. The assignment of weapons to a growing target list went on in accordance with the political direction established in the early 1960s (Rowen 1975:232).

Moreover, he confirms the hints about the relative composition of actual nuclear war plans contained in the statement about target priorities just cited. "Most of our planned targets," he says, "were military forces" (Rowen 1975:232).

Targeting Options, 1974 to the Present

The changes in planning introduced in 1974 do not seem to have significantly altered the proportional makeup of U.S. war plans. Military installations were still targeted. Now, however, relatively small portions of the existing target lists, including military and nonmilitary targets, could be attacked without unleashing a full-scale nuclear assault.

Secretary of Defense James Schlesinger, in his annual report for FY 1975, explained the new policy with these words:

> (I)n addition to retaliatory targeting against urban and industrial centers, our war plans have always included military targets. . . . (I)f deterrence fails, the war plans provide the National Command Authorities . . . with a well thought-out, detailed sets of options. In the past, most of those options—whether the principal targets were cities, industrial facilities, or military installations—have involved relatively massive responses. Rather than massive options, we now want to provide the President with a wider set of much more selective targeting options (1974:4).

Schlesinger went on to say,

(T)argets for nuclear weapons may include not only cities and silos but also airfields, many other types of military installations, and a variety of other important assets not necessarily collocated with urban populations. We already have a long list of such possible targets; now we are grouping them into operational plans which would be more responsive to the range of challenges that might face us (1974:39).

A persistent interest in targeting military installations, including hardened Soviet intercontinental ballistic missile (ICBM) silos, is reflected in the public statements of high Defense Department officials from 1974 down to the most recent explication of U.S. doctrine— Presidential Directive (PD)-59. There is no reason to believe that military targets of all sorts have declined in significance over the last five years. If anything, they seem to have increased in importance.

In January 1976 Secretary of Defense Donald Rumsfeld stressed the value of targeting enemy submarine pens, command bunkers, and radar installations. He argued further that the United States should not "rule out coverage of some enemy silos, airfields, or submarine bases on a second strike." "Contrary to popular views," Rumsfeld asserted, "many of these targets would remain of interest after an enemy had struck, not only because some of the launch vehicles might have aborted or have been withheld but also because some of the launch points— bomber bases and certain ICBM silos, for example—could be used to reload and recycle offensive forces" (1977:47).

In January 1979 Secretary of Defense Harold Brown made similar arguments for retaining the capability to destroy at least some "hard targets"—missile silos, command bunkers, and nuclear weapons storage sites. "Attacks on these targets," Brown maintained, "would not disarm an enemy in a first-strike (because of his survivable non-ICBM forces), but on a second-strike could suppress his withheld missiles and recycling bombers." Brown argued further that enemy general purpose forces "can and should be targeted" along with "the command-control, war reserve stocks, and lines of communication necessary to the conduct of theater campaigns" (1979:77–78).

In a more general way, the Presidential Directive on nuclear strategy issued in the summer of 1980 stressed the deterrent value of counter-military targeting. Discussing PD-59 before the Naval War College in Newport, Rhode Island, Secretary Brown said, "It is our policy . . . to ensure that the Soviet leadership knows that if they chose some intermediate level of aggression, we could, by selective, large (but still less than maximum) nuclear attacks, exact an unacceptably high price in the things the Soviet leaders appear to value most—political and military control, military force both nuclear and conventional, and the industrial capacity to sustain a war." Brown went on to emphasize the "effective targeting of military forces" (1980b:7).

To summarize briefly, between the end of World War II and the first years of the fifties, the United States did not explicitly target Soviet miitary installations with its nuclear forces (although the targeting of urban-industrial areas during this period was intended to have an immediate effect on the war on the ground). From the early sixties to the present, Soviet military forces, and especially their "nuclear threat" forces, have apparently made up a majority of the designated targets against which American strategic nuclear weapons would be used in the event of war.

STRATEGY

It has become popular for critics of present American strategic policy to claim that the United States is not "serious" about the problem of nuclear war.[10] In its cruder form this criticism is usually directed at the "assured destruction" reasoning which is assumed to inform U.S. plans for the conduct of strategic nuclear war. Over the past twenty years numerous civilian analysts, politicans, and military men (some of them in a position to know better) have bewailed the inadequacy of a policy which, in the event of war, would leave the president no choice but to acquiesce to Soviet demands or unleash massive nuclear attacks on Soviet cities.

In fact, as our brief discussion of targeting should suggest, U.S. forces have long been prepared to do a good deal more than simply destroy large civilian targets. As the more sophisticated critics point out, however, target lists do not by themselves make a strategy. War plans must be directed at achieving some realistic political and military objectives or they will be empty, senseless, and dangerous.

The statement that the United States has never had a strategy for nuclear war is demonstrably false. To say that target lists have sometimes received a great deal more attention than war aims or to point out that existing forces have at times been inadequate to the tasks set them is to come closer to the truth. In other words, while the United

States has always had a nuclear strategy (a set of objectives, however crudely defined, and an accompanying plan containing detailed targeting and employment requirements), some strategies have probably been "better" than others. Nevertheless, it is important to remember that the question of what to do if deterrence fails has received a great deal of attention for a very long time. Suggesting that a little concentrated thought will "solve" the problem of nuclear war or produce a plausible "theory of victory" is both arrogant and misleading.

For purposes of discussion, the history of the last thirty-five years can usefully be divided into five distinct periods. From 1945 to 1950, U.S. planning for the conduct of nuclear war emphasized the prompt destruction of enemy urban-industrial areas. Between 1950 and 1960 American war plans called for simultaneous attacks on Soviet bloc economic and military targets. During the period of 1962–1974, the United States adhered to a strategy of "second-strike counterforce." Attacks on Soviet military installations were stressed, with strikes against economic targets to be held in reserve. From 1974 to 1977, official U.S. policy called for escalation control through limited strategic operations and attacks on enemy recovery resources if a war escalated out of control. Over the past three years American nuclear strategy has been undergoing a reexamination, and in August 1980 some changes in U.S. nuclear policy were officially announced.

City-Busting, 1945–1950

Strategic planning in the immediate postwar period was marked by confusion and disagreement. The likely character of a future war, the importance of air power in prosecuting such a conflict, and the effectiveness of atomic bombardment were all topics of considerable and unresolvable debate. At the same time, the shortages of weapons and delivery vehicles already cited rendered the early musings of the various military planning groups completely unrealistic. As David MacIsaac has noted, during the late forties "both the air staff and joint planners continued work on a whole series of so-called war plans whose only long-range significance would be to provide historians the problem of trying to sort them out. . . " It was not until 1948–49 that plans would emerge which, in MacIsaac's words, "would make any serious effort to make strategy conform to actual capabilities" (MacIsaac 1979:8).

Essentially, American military planners were looking for ways to defeat superior Soviet ground forces as quickly as possible. The best way seemed to be to hit at those cities containing the heart of the Russian war machine. As one observer notes,

> . . . the nuclear planning task was seen as an extension of strategic bombing in World War II. . . . It was principally the destruction of critical war supporting industries in order to affect Soviet battlefield operations, the longer term ability of its economy to support combat, and its will to continue the conflict (Rowen 1975:222).

Thus, in the event of war, the largest atomic air offensive feasible was to be unleashed against the USSR in the shortest possible period of time. Meanwhile American and allied ground and naval forces would conduct "a main offensive effort in Western Eurasia and a strategic defensive in the Far East."[11] Such operations might continue for some time, but it was hoped that massed atomic air attacks would quickly destroy the Soviet Union's willingness and ability to wage war.

In May 1948 the Joint Chiefs of Staff (JCS) ordered the Joint Emergency War Plan HALFMOON circulated for planning purposes. The Air Force portion of this plan called for the delivery of fifty atomic bombs against twenty Soviet cities with the intention of causing the "immediate paralysis of at least 50 percent of Soviet industry" (Rosenberg 1979:4). Although this particular document was not subsequently approved, it appears to have been more or less typical of the increasingly realistic war plans which began to emerge at around this time. In any case it reflects the central strategic idea of the period—that the Soviet Union could be defeated if its war-supporting industrial base could be shattered.

The Multilayered Threat, 1950-1960

The Air Force grew steadily more confident of its ability to knock Russia out of a future war with what General Curtis LeMay described in late 1948 as "a single massive attack" (Rosenberg 1979:5). At the end of the year Air Force Chief of Staff Hoyt S. Vandenberg predicted that execution of the then-current war plan (which called for delivery of 133 bombs against urban-industrial, government control, petroleum, transportation, and electric power targets in seventy cities) "could well lead to Soviet capitulation and in any event would destroy their overall capability for offensive operations" (Rosenberg 1979:6).

Others in the defense establishment were less sanguine. In mid-1949, at the request of Secretary of Defense Forrestal, the so-called "Harmon Committee" evaluated the impact of an atomic air offensive against the Soviet Union (Rosenberg 1979:6). The committee, an ad hoc group of Army, Navy, and Air Force officers, estimated that the projected attack on seventy Soviet cities would produce a 30 to 40 percent reduction in Soviet industrial capacity and as many as 2.7 million fatalities and 4 million casualties. In the words of the report, however, industrial losses "would not be permanent and could either be alleviated by Soviet recuperative action or augmented depending on the weighted effectiveness of follow-up attacks." More importantly from an immediate military standpoint, "the capability of Soviet armed forces to advance rapidly into selected areas of Western Europe, the Middle East, and the Far East would not be seriously impaired." The committee concluded that planned air attacks alone would not "destroy the roots of Communism, or critically weaken the power of Soviet leadership to dominate the people" (Rosenberg 1979:6). In short, a strategic air offensive against urban-industrial targets could not guarantee "victory" no matter how that crucial word might be defined.

Doubts over the prevailing Air Force strategic concept, fears about Soviet intentions in Europe, and the emergence of a Soviet nuclear threat combined to produce a shift in the U.S. strategy for nuclear war. As was discussed earlier, by the early fifties the target lists had been expanded to include "retardation" and counterforce (or "nuclear threat") installations in addition to the urban-industrial sites already targeted. These changes reflected the growing belief that nuclear forces would have to be used for immediate countermilitary purposes if an attack on Europe were to be halted and a Soviet long-range atomic air offensive prevented.

From this point until the end of the decade, as debates over targeting swirled in and around the military, the basic American strategy for nuclear war remained unchanged. If war came (probably as the result of Soviet aggression in Europe) U.S. nuclear-equipped forces—the long-range bombers of SAC, the Navy's carrier-based fighter bombers, and a growing number of nuclear-capable aircraft assigned to the European theater—were to carry out strikes against the full spectrum of targets within the Soviet bloc. War-supporting industrial, government control, nuclear threat and retardation targets were all to be hit simultaneously. War would be fast-paced, and it was assumed that the early stages of any all-out struggle would probably prove decisive.

The extent to which the nuclear air efforts of the various services would have been coordinated is unclear. Nor is it apparent what connection was assumed to exist between nuclear air and subsequent ground and naval operations. By the end of the fifties, however, the image of a "spasm war" seems to have dominated the planning process. It was assumed that a massive, multilayered, atomic air attack would prevent the Soviets from using their own steadily growing nuclear capability, slow or stop the Red Army's advance into Europe, destroy the Russian economy, and drain the Soviet state of its willingness to wage war. While ground and naval forces would undoubtedly participate in combat, the war would be won, and won quickly, with aerially delivered nuclear weapons.

The dominant concept of these years was embodied in "the strategy of the optimum mix" spelled out in planning papers prepared during 1959–1960.[12] It subsequently found its way into the first SIOP which, according to one observer, "contained only one plan under which the United States would launch all its strategic nuclear delivery vehicles immediately upon the initiation of nuclear war with the Soviet Union" (Ball 1974:11).

Second Strike Counterforce, 1962–1974

Initial Changes.   The election of John Kennedy in the fall of 1960 brought to power a group of men who had little or no vested interest in the policies of the previous fifteen years. Many of Secretary of Defense McNamara's aides and advisors came from the RAND Corporation where they had been instrumental in developing (and urging the Air Force to adopt) counterforce no-cities targeting strategies. These men believed that existing plans for the use of nuclear weapons were too massive and too inflexible. They argued that in its preparations for nuclear war the United States was committing itself to unnecessarily large and destructive attacks. The execution of such attacks might not completely disable a growing Soviet nuclear force, and a demonstrable lack of interest in anything short of all-out strikes would certainly do nothing to encourage Russian restraint in the event of war. Worst of all, the very size of the American nuclear threat might render it incredible, thus encouraging certain forms of limited aggression.

In early 1961 a review of the SIOP was begun. According to Desmond Ball, initial work on revising existing plans was completed by late summer, the Joint Chiefs of Staff gave their approval at the end of the year, and the proposed changes were adopted in January 1962 (Ball 1974:12). These alterations in the war plans were to shape U.S. strategy for the next twelve years.

As we have already seen, the revised SIOP grouped targets into three clusters—nuclear threat, other military, and urban-industrial (Rowen 1975:230). Attacks that differentiated among the three target categories were now feasible, and special preparations were made for withholding altogether strikes against cities (Rowen 1975:227 and 230). But what was the strategic purpose behind this change in war plans? What image of a nuclear war did the planners hold? And how did they believe it would be possible for the United States to achieve something resembling victory in such a war?

The answers to these questions were provided most clearly by McNamara himself in a series of speeches delivered during the course of 1962. In February, McNamara stressed the importance of forces capable of surviving an enemy surprise attack. Equally important, said the secretary, was the maintenance of the "machinery for the command and control of our forces which is itself able to survive an attack and to apply the surviving forces in consonance with national security objectives" (Ball 1974:14). McNamara went on to assert,

> With this protected command and control system, our forces can be used in several different ways. We may have to retaliate with a single massive attack. Or, we may be able to use our retaliatory forces to limit damage done to ourselves and our allies, by knocking out the enemy's bases before he has had time to launch his second salvos. We may seek to terminate a war on favorable terms by using our forces as a bargaining weapon—by threatening further attack. In any case, our large reserve of protected firepower would give an enemy an incentive to avoid our cities and to stop a war (Ball 1974:14).

These points were reiterated in the Ann Arbor speech. If forced into a war the United States would seek to destroy "the enemy's military forces, not . . . his civilian population." But, if necessary, the United States would "retain, even in the face of a massive surprise attack, sufficient reserve striking power to destroy an enemy society if driven to it." This structuring of U.S. forces and options would, in McNamara's words, give "a possible opponent the strongest imaginable incentive to refrain from striking our own cities" (Ball 1974:15).

The reasoning behind U.S. war plans was therefore clear and direct. In the event of war the primary U.S. objective would have been to strip away Soviet strategic nuclear power while minimizing civilian casualties and holding Russian cities hostage. Residual U.S. forces would have been used to extract a satisfactory political settlement from the Soviet leadership.

The emphasis in the thinking of high civilian officials and certainly in their public statements was on survivable second-strike forces. If the Soviets could not hope to destroy American forces in a surprise attack, there seemed little likelihood that they would ever use nuclear weapons against the United States. Strikes against cities would bring a devastating response. Ineffective attacks on U.S. forces would diminish the size of the Soviet arsenal and invite a counterforce second strike without severely weakening American nuclear might.

Despite the clear emphasis on retaliation, there appears to have been some thought given to the possibility of a preemptive U.S. first strike against Soviet forces. Such an attack would most likely have been carried out in support of North American Treaty Organization (NATO) forces in Europe. In the words of one author,

> The changes (in the SIOP) provided some preemptive counterforce options as part of graduated options, thereby codifying first-strike ideas that had inevitably been present in some form or other in the thinking of both military and civilian leaders (Goldberg 1967:25).

The Shift Toward "Assured Destruction."   Almost as soon as it was announced, the strategy of second strike counterforce began to come under heavy criticism from a number of different directions. Congressional "hawks" attacked the no-cities doctrine as weak and denounced its creators for lacking resolve. "Doves" worried that the new policy made it more likely that the United States would strike first with nuclear weapons. Soviet spokesmen denied the possibility that a nuclear conflict could be kept controlled, reaffirming their intention to strike simultaneously at all American civilian and military targets as soon as general hostilities began. Finally, the announced changes in U.S. strategy drew a mixed reaction from the European members of NATO. Some felt that McNamara's statements were designed to dissuade them from acquiring their own nuclear capabilities. Others feared that anything less than the threat of an all-out response would encourage Soviet aggression. Still others were concerned that a limited "strategic" war between Russian and the United States would leave the superpowers unscathed, while "tactical" nuclear weapons laid waste to Europe (Ball 1974:15).

All these criticisms undoubtedly had some impact on McNamara's thinking. More important in changing the direction of U.S. policy, however, were the increasingly apparent bureaucratic and budgetary consequences of a second strike counterforce strategy. SAC and the JSTPS had been skeptical of the move toward restrained attack planning, but the Air Force quickly saw an opportunity to increase its portion of the overall defense budget (Rowen 1975:231). Ball writes that by

> . . . late 1962, it was clear to McNamara that the Services, and particularly the Air Force, were using his declared policy of no-cities counterforce as a basis for requesting virtually open-ended strategic weapon programs— both more Minuteman missiles and procurements of a force of supersonic reconnaissance-strike (RS-70) bombers (Ball 1974:16).

In response to the perceived "missile gap" of 1960–61 the new administration had unleashed a surge of spending on strategic systems. Now the president and his secretary of defense wanted to control defense spending and channel a greater portion of the available dollars into conventional or nonnuclear forces. To do this they had to devise some means of measuring the adequacy of the U.S. strategic arsenal. And they had to find a way of using those force measurements to restrain service demands for further increases in spending on strategic forces.

Beginning in early 1963 the emphasis in McNamara's public statements began to shift away from problems of strategy toward issues of force sizing. In the defense program for fiscal years 1964 through 1968, McNamara repeated his assertion that the United States should have a secure second strike force able to—

> (1) Strike back decisively at the entire Soviet target system simultaneously or
> (2) Strike back first at the Soviet bomber bases, missile sites, and other military installations associated with their long-range nuclear forces to reduce the power of any follow-on attack—and then if necessary, strike back at the Soviet urban and industrial complex in a controlled and deliberate way (McNamara 1963:30).

The secretary went on to point out:

In planning our second strike force, we have provided, throughout the period under consideration, a capability to destroy virtually all of the "soft" and "semi-hard" military targets in the Soviet Union and a large number of their fully hardened missile sites, with an additional capability in the form of a protected force to be employed or held in reserve for use against urban and industrial areas (1963:30).

For the first time, however, McNamara began to raise questions about the future utility of a strategy which relied on large-scale counterforce attacks. He noted the continuing (although at this point still quite slow) growth of Soviet strategic forces, saying,

A very large increase in the number of fully hardened Soviet ICBMs and nuclear-powered ballistic missile launching submarines would considerably detract from our ability to destroy completely the Soviet strategic nuclear forces (1963:29).

Even if the United States had the offensive capability necessary to bring the majority of an expanded Soviet arsenal under attack,

. . . such a (U.S.) force would also have to be accompanied by an extensive missile defense program and a much more elaborate civil defense program than has thus far been contemplated. Even then we could not preclude casualties counted in the tens of millions (McNamara 1963:29).

In 1964 McNamara differentiated between the two missions which he said the strategic forces program, "comprising the offensive and defensive forces and civil defense," were designed to perform. The first was—

. . . to deter deliberate nuclear attack upon the United States and its allies by maintaining a highly reliable ability to inflict an unacceptable degree of damage upon any single aggressor, or combination of aggressors, even after absorbing a surprise first strike (McNamara 1964:12).

McNamara termed this the "assured-destruction" mission.

The second aggregate capability or mission (which McNamara dubbed "damage limitation") called for U.S. forces "in the event . . . (of) war . . . to limit damage to our population and industrial capacity" (McNamara 1964:12).

In early 1965 McNamara repeated this division and went on to stress that, of the two missions, assured destruction was the more important. The secretary suggested that "the destruction of, say, one-quarter to one-third of its population and about two-thirds of its industrial capacity would mean the elimination of the aggressor as a major power for many years" (McNamara 1965:39). A finite, identifiable system of targets would have to be hit in order to do this level of damage. Thus the requirements of the assured-destruction mission provided defense department planners with a useful force-sizing index.

Once an adequate capability had been acquired for the assured-destruction mission, additional forces would have to be justified in terms of their contribution to damage limitation. But, as McNamara hastened to point out, damage to the United States could only be limited through the successful application of a series of costly, interlocking offensive and defensive measures. The effectiveness of these measures seemed likely to decline as Soviet forces became larger and more capable. Moreover, as the Russians took steps to offset U.S. protective measures, the incremental costs of maintaining a given level of damage-limiting capacity would grow steadily. Unlike assured destruction, the concept of damage limitation was open-ended. It was therefore of little use to civilian officials searching for ways to control the growth of U.S. strategic forces (McNamara 1965:38–40).

By 1967 McNamara had taken his arguments a step further. In a statement accompanying the defense program for FY 1968–1972 and the 1968 defense budget, the secretary said,

> Damage limiting programs, no matter how much we spend on them, can never substitute for an Assured Destruction capability in the deterrent role. It is our ability to destroy an attacker as a viable 20th Century nation that provides the deterrent not our ability to partially limit damage to ourselves (McNamara 1967:38–39).

McNamara went on to argue that U.S. damage-limiting efforts were not only potentially wasteful but possibly counterproductive as well. He pointed out:

> If the general nuclear war policy of the Soviet Union also has as its objective the deterrence of a U.S. first strike (which I believe to be the case), then we must assume that any attempt on our part to reduce damage to ourselves (to what they would estimate we might consider an "acceptable level") would put pressure on them to strive for an offsetting improvement in their deterrent forces (McNamara 1967:39).

Similarly, an increase in Soviet damage-limiting capability would force the United States to "make greater investments in Assured Destruction" (McNamara 1967:39). Because of what he referred to as "this interaction between our strategic force programs and those of the Soviet Union," McNamara proposed that there was "a mutuality of interests in limiting the deployment of antiballistic missile systems (1967:40). He asserted that "in all probability all we would accomplish by deploying ABM systems against one another would be to increase greatly our respective defense expenditures without any gain in real security for either side" (1967:40).

Finally, in 1968, McNamara proclaimed the inevitability of "mutual deterrence." He pointed out that

> for a "Damage Limiting" posture to contribute significantly to the deterrent . . . it would have to be extremely effective, i.e., capable of reducing damage to truly nominal levels. . . . we now have no way to accomplish this (1968:47).

Neither the United States nor the Soviet Union could hope to limit damage to itself whether through the use of offensive or defensive means. "Under these circumstances," McNamara reasoned, "surely it makes sense for us both to try to halt the momentum of the arms race which is causing vast expenditures on both sides and promises no increase in security" (1968:53).

It is clear that between 1963 and 1968 the public statements of high Defense Department officials underwent a significant change. At the beginning of Kennedy's term, McNamara and his aides spoke of second-strike counterforce and reserve retaliatory forces. By the end of Johnson's term, civilian officials concentrated almost exclusively on defining the adequacy of U.S. strategic forces in terms of their ability to carry out the assured-destruction mission.[13]

The rhetorical shifts just catalogued were the outward manifestations of an internal debate over American strategic policy and, most importantly, over force size. McNamara and his aides were originally drawn to the strategy of second-strike counterforce because it seemed a more rational approach to the problem of nuclear war than the policy of indiscriminate retaliation they had inherited. Within the first year of McNamara's term two things quickly became apparent: first, that the United States enjoyed vast strategic superiority over the Russians; and second, that the strategy of second-strike counterforce provided no useful indicators of sufficiency.

The whole notion of assured destruction stemmed from McNamara's desire to establish some reasonable limits on the growth of U.S. strategic forces. He and his advisors believed that the United States would maintain a margin of quantitative and qualitative superiority well into the future. But their investigations of damage limitation quickly convinced them that before long, U.S. forces would not be able to suppress a Soviet attack to minimal levels at a reasonable cost. A form of "parity" in which both sides maintained secure, second-strike, assured-destruction forces was thus inevitable. Finally, McNamara and his aides became convinced that such a state of affairs was not only inevitable but desirable. Once parity had been achieved, neither side would have any incentive to increase further the size of its strategic forces. Negotiated agreements could then bring the arms race to a halt and ensure a stable strategic balance.

Acting on these apparently reasonable convictions, McNamara moved to limit the size and capabilities of U.S. strategic offensive forces. In addition, he discouraged the development of defensive systems and urged the initiation of arms control negotiations with the Soviets. The secretary of defense also issued a series of public statements that were to cloud and confuse the debate over U.S. strategic policy from the mid-sixties down to the present day.

Repeated discussions of the importance of maintaining assured-destruction forces left the unmistakable impression that U.S. war plans had been altered. It seemed obvious that American planners regarded the ability to attack Soviet urban-industrial areas as the *sine qua non* of deterrence. It seemed equally clear that U.S. forces were now directed solely against those targets. In the minds of many observers the U.S. strategy for nuclear war was now simply to blast away at Soviet cities once hostilities began. Victory had become impossible; mutual destruction was assured.

In fact, the evidence suggests that U.S. war plans changed little between 1962 and 1974 (Rowen 1975:232). The majority of designated targets were still military installations, and options for city-avoiding attacks were kept in the SIOP (Ball 1974:16). Contrary to increasingly widespread popular belief, U.S. operational plans continued to be guided by a strategy of second-strike counterforce.

The best explanation for the growing divergence between declaratory policy and actual employment plans during the 1960s is presented by Henry Rowen. He writes that

> the primary purpose of the Assured Destruction capabilities doctrine was to provide a metric for deciding how much force was enough: it provided a basis for denying service and Congressional claims for more money for strategic forces. . . . However, it was never proposed by McNamara or his staff that nuclear weapons actually be *used* in this way (Rowen 1975:227).

For the time being at least, there was no reason for any responsible officials to make such a proposal. U.S. forces were capable of destroying the full range of both urban-industrial and nuclear-threat targets within the Soviet Union. Under these circumstances it would hardly have made sense not to prepare options for comparatively small attacks aimed exclusively at the counterforce target set.

The Schlesinger Strategy, 1974–1977

Changes in the Balance. By the early seventies and perhaps as early as the late sixties these circumstances had begun to change. In 1966 the Soviets began to deploy large numbers of ICBMs in hardened underground silos. Between 1966 and 1970 the size of their land-based missile force grew by 1,007—from 292 to 1,299 ICBMs launchers. During this same period the Russian navy deployed twenty new ballistic missile submarines, increasing the number of submarine launched Ballistic Missiles (SLBMs) in its force from 107 to 304 (International Institute for Strategic Studies 1977:80, 90).

The Soviet strategic offensive arsenal was becoming larger and less vulnerable. At the same time, the number of U.S. ballistic missile launchers deployed had leveled off.[14] Because of decisions made in the early sixties, large numbers of warheads specifically designed to destroy hardened Soviet military installations were not procurred.[15] Inevitably, the capabilities of U.S. forces against Soviet nuclear threat targets began to decline. To quote Henry Rowen, "Increases in the number, hardness, and mobility of Soviet long-range nuclear forces . . . resulted in a decline in damage expectancies for this class of targets" (Rowen 1975:221).

By 1970 it would appear that the attack options available to a U.S. president had been significantly narrowed. In February, in his Foreign Policy Message to the Congress, President Nixon asked:

> Should a President, in the event of a nuclear attack, be left with the single option of ordering the mass destruction of enemy civilians, in the face of the certainty that it would be followed by the mass slaughter of Americans? Should the concept of assured destruction be narrowly defined and should it be the only measure of our ability to deter the variety of threats we may face? (Nixon 1970:122).

Although Nixon (or at least his advisors) certainly knew that existing plans did not contain only a single, counterurban-industrial option, the president's statement served to highlight an important fact. For the first time in several years the declaratory policy of the mid-sixties had begun to converge with real capabilities, if not with actual employment plans. Massive counterforce attacks could no longer be effectively executed. If he were to contemplate ordering a nuclear attack, the president would now be faced with three basic choices: (1) authorize strikes (preemptive or retaliatory) against Soviet forces that would probably weaken the United States more than the USSR; (2) unleash the massive assured-destruction strike on all targets, military and urban-industrial; or (3) do nothing.

In a sense the form of parity that McNamara had predicted in the early sixties had finally arrived. Neither the United States nor the Soviet Union could now hope to disarm the other in a preemptive first strike. Both sides had sufficient secure forces to do tremendous urban-industrial damage to the enemy, even after absorbing a surprise attack. But, as Nixon's statement indicates, the national political leadership was no longer certain that such a form of parity was desirable. At the very least, there was growing concern that because of changes in the strategic nuclear balance, U.S. war plans and the basic strategy they reflected were woefully inadequate.

The Search for a New Strategy.   During 1969 and 1970 a series of studies aimed at determining future U.S. military requirements was undertaken by the Nixon Administration. Particular attention was apparently paid to the strategic forces and to the problem of increasing the flexibility of existing nuclear war plans. In 1972, according to one observer, the Defense Department began to study possible revisions of the SIOP. Between 1972 and 1974, a full-scale interagency review was undertaken, resulting finally in the changes announced by Secretary Schlesinger in January 1974 (Davis 1976:3-4).

Schlesinger's public remarks during 1974 and 1975 and particularly in his annual reports to the U.S. Congress make clear the reasoning behind this fourth major change in American strategy. The shifts in the balance just mentioned had decreased the offensive damage-limiting capability of American strategic forces. Budgetary constraints and the force limits negotiated in the Strategic Arms Limitation Talks (SALT) made highly unlikely any considerable increases in the size of U.S. offensive forces. Moreover, as Secretary Schlesinger noted in 1974,

. . . the ratification of the ABM [antiballistic missile] treaty in 1972 . . . effectively removed the concept of defensive damage limitation (at least as it was defined in the 1960s) from contention as a major strategic option (Schlesinger 1974:37).

The United States could neither disarm the Soviet Union nor, through a combination of offensive and defensive means, significantly limit damage to itself in an all-out nuclear war. Yet existing war plans still consisted entirely of options for massive counterforce and combined counterforce-countervalue attacks. This fact caused concern on a number of counts.

First, there was fear that in the event of war a lack of flexibility would quickly lead to unnecessary and ultimately fruitless escalation. Given changes in the balance, the best hope of limiting damage in a nuclear war seemed to lie in finding a way to control the escalation process. Controlling escalation would in turn require that large-scale attacks be avoided as long as possible. Designing what Secretary Schlesinger called "selective response options—smaller and more precisely focused than in the past" was seen as a way of ensuring that if deterrence failed, the United States would be able to bring all but the largest nuclear conflicts to a rapid conclusion before cities are struck. "Damage may thus be limited and further escalation avoided" (Schlesinger 1974:38).

The character of existing war plans also raised questions about the American ability to deter certain types of threats. Since the early sixties the United States had relied on the threat of a disarming counterforce attack to deter limited Soviet strikes against targets on the North American continent. The probability of a Russian leader ordering attacks on one or two U.S. cities or on a handful of military installations seemed quite small, especially when the likely American response would have been to destroy all remaining Soviet strategic forces.

Now, however, the situation had changed. The United States could no longer threaten an effective, full-scale counterforce strike. And, according to Schlesinger, the Soviet Union had acquired "the capability in its missile forces to undertake selective attacks against targets other than cities." The secretary went on to assert that

this poses for us an obligation, if we are to ensure the credibility of our strategic deterrent, to be certain that we have a comparable capability in our strategic systems and in our targeting doctrine, and to be certain that the USSR has no misunderstanding on this point (Schlesinger 1974:4).

In other words, the United States needed options between inaction and very large attacks to deter the threat of controlled strikes against its territory.

There was another, more immediate problem. The U.S. counterforce threat had also been a central element in NATO strategy. In the event of a Soviet invasion of Europe which threatened to overwhelm conventional defenses, the United States was committed to use nuclear weapons. Such an attack might come before the Soviets initiated a nuclear offensive, or it could come in response to a Soviet theater nuclear strike. In theory an American nuclear response to Soviet aggression in Europe might be limited to the theater and might involve only those forces physically based there. In fact it seemed much more likely that U.S. strategic forces would be involved and that large counterforce strikes against Soviet intercontinental systems would be undertaken. With the American margin in counterforce capability now significantly diminished, threatening large attacks in response to theater aggression no longer seemed credible. Being forced to execute such attacks by the inflexibility of existing plans was an extremely worrisome prospect. Nevertheless, NATO in the early seventies seemed, if anything, to have grown weaker in the face of an ongoing build-up in Soviet conventional and theater nuclear capabilities. Some means of "extending deterrence," of "coupling" U.S. strategic forces with the European theater, continued to appear necessary.

Thus American planners were concerned with two central problems: how, in Schlesinger's words, "to shore up deterrence across the entire spectrum of risk" (Schlesinger 1974:5), and, if deterrence should fail, how to control the process of escalation in order to limit damage to the United States and its allies. The solution to both problems seemed to lie in the creation of smaller attack options that would increase the flexibility of existing strategic nuclear war plans. To quote Schlesinger again,

> What we need is a series of measured responses to aggression which bear some relation to the provocation, have prospects of terminating hostilities before general nuclear war breaks out, and leave some possibility for restoring deterrence. It has been this problem of not having sufficient options between massive response and doing nothing, as the Soviets built up their strategic forces, that has prompted the President's concerns and those of our Allies (Schlesinger 1974:38).

The grouping of targets into relatively small operational packages has already been discussed, and the concerns that lead to this restructuring of plans have been briefly reviewed. The purposes to be served by creation of these packages should be readily apparent. In the first instance, the existence of a wide range of options was assumed to increase the deterrent credibility of U.S. strategic forces. If deterrence failed in some less than all-out way, the new options would give the president the opportunity to respond in kind rather than unleashing a larger attack. In addition, some limited nuclear options (LNOs) were specifically designed to support theater forces. As Lynn Davis, a former deputy assitance secretary of defense for international security affairs, points out in her monograph *Limited Nuclear Options*, an LNO could serve a prompt military purpose by

> (1). . . stop(ping) the immediate aggression and creat(ing) a pause or hiatus in the enemy's military activities to allow time for diplomacy to work; and (2). . . chang(ing) an enemy leader's perceptions about the prospects for a quick, cheap victory (Davis 1976:7).

Finally, the existence of LNOs and the structuring of those options (relatively small attacks, mostly military targets, minimized collateral damage) was intended to facilitate escalation control (Schlesinger 1974:5). LNOs would provide a president with alternatives to a big, escalatory response to enemy aggression. And they would prevent the worsening of a military situation "on the ground," signalling U.S. resolve while at the same time indicating the American desire that an unfolding conflict be kept limited.

One final element in the thinking of U.S. strategists needs to be discussed. If escalation were to be controlled through the use of limited strategic operations, it would be essential that at each stage in an ongoing war, the enemy have no reason to raise dramatically the level of conflict. To ensure restraint the United States would always have to hold some of the enemy's most valued assets as "hostages." In essence, while executing one or a series of limited nuclear options the United States would have to continue to hold at least a counterurban-industrial assured-destruction force in reserve. To quote Secretary Schlesinger, "We shall rely into the wartime period upon reserving our 'assured destruction' force and persuading, through intrawar deterrence, any potential foe not to attack cities." That force, said Schlesinger, might have to be withheld "for an extended period of time" (Schlesinger 1974:5). Thus a central assumption behind the change in strategy announced in 1974 was that for the foreseeable future, Soviet forces would not be able to destroy U.S. forces being held in reserve.

A further change in U.S. nuclear strategy was announced in January 1977 by Schlesinger's successor, Secretary of Defense Donald Rumsfeld.[16] In his statement to the U.S. Congress, Rumsfeld compared two approaches to the assured-destruction—or, as he termed it, the "assured-retaliation"—mission. One, he said, was simply to "target major cities, assume that population and industry are strongly correlated with them, and measure effectiveness as a function of the number of people killed and cities destroyed." The other approach, in Rumsfeld's words,

. . . views assured retaliation as the effort to prevent or retard an enemy's military, political, and economic recovery from a nuclear exchange. . . . The effectiveness of the retaliation would be measured in two ways:
—by the size and composition of the enemy military capability surviving for postwar use;
—by his ability to recover politically and economically from the exchange.

Rumsfeld went on to advocate the second approach, announcing

The present planning objective of the Defense Department is clear. We believe that a substantial number of military forces and critical industries in the Soviet Union should be directly targeted, and that an important objective of the assured retaliation mission should be to retard significantly the ability of the USSR to recover from a nuclear exchange and regain the status of a 20th century military and industrial power more rapidly than the United States (Rumsfeld 1977:68).

Thus, by 1977 the publically declared U.S. strategy for nuclear war was as follows: In the event deterrence failed the primary U.S. objective was to control the process of escalation, bringing hostilities to an acceptable close at the lowest level of conflict possible, thereby limiting damage to the United States and its allies. If necessary, escalation control and thus damage limitation were to be achieved through the use of limited nuclear options. These options would serve both a military and a political purpose. If escalation control failed, the United States would seek to destroy Soviet military, political, and economic assets so as to retard the USSR's recovery in the postwar period. Such attacks would also be designed to limit the Soviet Union's ability to retard *U.S.* recovery.

Recent Developments, 1977–1980

In the summer of 1977 the Carter Administration began a review of U.S. nuclear targeting policy, the preliminary results of which appeared in the Defense Department Annual Reports for fiscal years 1980 and 1981. In June 1980 at Bodo, Norway, Secretary of Defense Brown briefed the NATO Nuclear Planning Group on the details of the "countervailing strategy." On July 25 President Carter signed Presidential Directive 59 which, in Secretary Brown's words, "codif[ied] our restated doctrine and [gave] guidance to further evolution in our planning and systems acquisition." One month later, in late August, Brown gave the first public explanation of the new policy in a speech at the Naval War College (Brown 1980c).

Carter Administration spokesmen went to some lengths to establish that the countervailing strategy was, in Secretary Brown's words, "a natural evolution of the conceptual foundations built over a generation by men like Robert McNamara and James Schlesinger" (Brown 1980c:3). Clearly there was a good deal of truth to this assertion. In the first instance, there was a continuing emphasis on the centrality of deterrence in the abstract and, more specifically, on the importance of maintaining a wide range of options in order to deter aggression. As Brown put it in early 1980,

> The most fundamental objective of our strategic policy is nuclear deterrence. . . . But our nuclear forces must be able to deter nuclear attacks not only on our own country but also on our forces overseas, as well as on our friends and allies. Nuclear forces also contribute to some degree, through justifiable concern about escalation, to deterrence of non-nuclear attacks. . . . [I]f deterrence is to be fully effective, the United States must be able to respond at a level appropriate to the type and scale of a Soviet attack (Brown 1980a:65–66).

If deterrence failed, Brown, like Schlesinger, argued that United States strategic nuclear strikes might be necessary to achieve U.S. military and political objectives while controlling escalation. In his August 1980 speech at Newport, Brown emphasized this point by saying, "Operationally, our countervailing strategy requires that our plans and capabilities be structured to put more stress on being able to employ strategic nuclear forces selectively, as well as by all-out retaliation in response to massive attacks on the United States" (Brown 1980d:7).

Finally, as a backdrop for limited strikes and as a last resort if escalation could not be controlled, Brown, like both Schlesinger and McNamara before him, emphasized the importance of a withheld threat against the Soviet economy and infrastructure. "[I]t is essential at all times to retain the option to attack urban-industrial targets—both as a deterrent to attacks on our own cities and as the final retaliation if that particular deterrent should fail" (Brown 1979:77).

Having noted these broad similarities, it is important to point out some rather striking differences between PD 59 and earlier strategic formulations. Instead of searching for absolute or "objective" indices of deterrent sufficiency, U.S. officials began to focus on Soviet views of nuclear war, on the "subjective" portion of the deterrent equation. As Secretary Brown said in his FY 1981 report,

> Our goal is to make a Soviet victory as improbable (seen through Soviet eyes) as we can make it, over the broadest plausible range of scenarios. . . . Deterrence, by definition, depends on shaping our adversary's prediction of the likely outcome of a war. Our surest deterrent is our capability to deny gains from aggression (by any measure of gain). . . .(Brown 1980a:66–67).

This formulation appears to have had important practical consequences, both in determining the types of targets selected for limited attacks and in shaping the emerging American image of a possible future war. The United States needed to be able to threaten and, if necessary, to destroy those facilities which the Soviet leadership deemed essential to a successful war effort. Thus Brown argued that

> (U.S.) plans should include options to attack the targets that comprise the Soviet military force structure and political power structure. . . . [W]e must be able to deter Soviet attacks of less than all-out scale by making it clear to the Kremlin that, after such an attack, we would not be forced to the stark choice of either making no effective military response or totally destroying the Soviet Union. We could instead attack, in a selective and measured way, a range of military, industrial, and political control targets, while retaining an assured destruction capacity in reserve (Brown 1980a:66).

Under the countervailing strategy there seemed to be a premium on designing "selective, large (but still less than maximum) nuclear attacks" intended to prevent the effective functioning of the Soviet war machine (Brown 1980b:7).

American officials also began to discuss the possibility that large but limited strikes might go on for some time. This possibility was not, as Brown and others took pains to point out, the result of an American belief that extended nuclear conflict was likely; rather, it was a reflection of concern over apparent Soviet attitudes toward such an eventuality. The secretary made this point in testimony before the Senate Foreign Relations Committee:

PD 59 does *not* assume that a nuclear war will necessarily be protracted over a period of many weeks or even months, because we are not at all convinced that it would be, or even could be. PD 59 *does* take into account Soviet literature which considers such a scenario to be a real possibility. As recently as last year [1979], Marshall Ogarkov (who is the counterpart of our chairman of the Joint Chiefs of Staff) wrote in the *Soviet Military Encyclopedia*: ". . . the possibility cannot be excluded that the war could also be protracted. Soviet military strategy proceeds from the fact that if a nuclear war is foisted upon the Soviet Union, then the Soviet people and their armed forces must be ready for the most severe and prolonged trials. In this case, the Soviet Union and the fraternal Socialist states . . . [have] objective possibilities for achieving victory." We must convince them—and PD 59 is a key part of that effort—that such beliefs are unfounded and dangerous (Brown 1980c:7).

There was very little detailed public discussion of what might happen if all efforts at restraint failed and an uncontrolled war broke out. As we have seen, U.S. officials underlined the importance of maintaining a last-ditch assured-destruction capability. But there was no description of how that exceedingly slippery term was to be defined. Measures of "industrial floor space" or "recovery retardation" were no longer bandied about as they had been in earlier years. In early 1979 there had been newspaper stories referring to the possibility of large-scale attacks designed to weaken the ability of the Soviet regime to control events within its "empire" and even within its own borders (Pincus 1979). If they were adopted, no such plans were announced in the latter part of 1980.

CONCLUSIONS

The preceding discussion of the history of U.S. nuclear targeting and strategy raises several interrelated analytical questions. How should we think about the problem of targeting Soviet military (and particularly long-range nuclear) installations? How should we evaluate past American strategies for nuclear conflict, and what can we learn from such an evaluation? What is it in our preparations, posture, and declaratory policy that has deterred Soviet aggression? Finally, can and should we seek a more unified strategic doctrine?

Counterforce Targeting

Much debate in the West presently centers on the presumed counterforce capability of proposed weapons systems. There is considerable concern expressed over the possibility of a shift from a policy of deterrence to preparations for "war-fighting."

Even at the strategic nuclear level it should be obvious that the distinctions between these two presumably antithetical conceptual approaches have always been clearer in theory than in practice. In any case it is apparent that U.S. war plans have always called for the widespread use of strategic nuclear weapons against Soviet military targets, including Soviet strategic forces. This last point is particularly important. Worry over the possible destabilizing consequences of targeting strategic forces is legitimate even (or perhaps especially) in a world in which the Soviets will soon possess an extremely potent counterforce capability of their own. However, any argument against improving the countermilitary effectiveness of U.S. forces must be based on a realistic consideration of present conditions, not on a harkening back to some mythical past state of affairs. The question is not, "Should we target Soviet conventional and nuclear military installations?" but, "Should we continue to do so? Why? Should we improve our capabilities for doing so? How? And if not, why not? What might be the consequences of not having an effective countermilitary capability (including a substantial capability against Soviet strategic forces)? And what should we target instead?"

Evaluating Past Strategies

The United States has always had a strategy for the use of its nuclear weapons. Having said this, it is important to ask if, at various times between 1945 and the present, existing war plans have made internal sense—if they have been supported adequately by existing capabilities, and, if executed, whether or not they could have been expected to achieve predefined objectives. Another more important set of questions will not be addressed here: Have U.S. war plans been built around the "right" military and political objectives? What alternative objectives would have made more sense? What overall wartime objectives should we be preparing to pursue today?

1945-1950.   Between 1945 and 1950 the United States lacked the resources for a pure city-busting strategy. Through most of that period the United States did not even have the weapons necessary to destroy a large number of Soviet cities. Even if the rather small attacks planned in the late forties could have been carried out, it seems unlikely that they would have achieved their intended objective—allowing the prompt defeat of Soviet ground forces by destroying Russian war support and political will.

1950–1960.   The growing size and destructive power of the U.S. arsenal coupled with expanded target coverage and the increasing precision of target location techniques probably made the war plans of the period of 1950 to 1960 more realistic than their predecessors. By the late fifties it would appear that the United States was well situated to devastate the Russian economy, disrupt Red Army operations, and disable the budding Soviet nuclear force. Whether planned strikes could actually have prevented Soviet nuclear attacks on the United States and its allies would have depended a great deal on unpredictable operational factors—warning time, alert rates, political willingness to launch a preemptive strike, and so on. Similarly, the outcome of any ongoing ground war would have depended on the ability of NATO forces to follow nuclear strikes with a decisive conventional thrust. It seems possible, however, that by some identifiable standard, the United States could have "won" a nuclear war during the 1950s.

1962–1974.   The strategy of second-strike counterforce (which, as we have seen, did not preclude the possibility of a counterforce first strike) made the most sense between 1962 and 1969 or 1970. During this period a U.S. preemptive attack could probably have disabled Soviet long-range nuclear forces while holding Russian cities hostage. Whether(as was intended) such an attack could have been accomplished without causing numerous Russian civilian casualties is unclear.

A Soviet preemptive attack on U.S. forces in the mid-sixties could have proved extremely disruptive, perhaps more so than was generally recognized at the time (Burt 1979). And the damage done to American urban-industrial areas in such an attack would likely have been substantial. Still, it would appear that American forces could have retaliated effectively against their Soviet counterparts without necessarily beginning an uncontrolled city-busting exchange.

Throughout this period, as during the fifties, the United States could have done very little to limit the damage done by an irrational surprise Soviet countervalue attack. However, U.S. retaliation would have been equally devastating and probably a good deal more so.

From the late sixties to the mid-seventies, U.S. war plans did not reflect real changes in the strategic balance that had rendered old targeting and employment concepts obsolete. The assured-destruction attacks which received so much public attention could undoubtedly have been carried out. (Whether their execution would, in fact, have assured the economic, political, and military destruction of the Soviet state is a matter for conjecture.) But full-scale counterforce strikes, whether preemptive or retaliatory, could not have disabled Soviet offensive forces.

1974–1980. The declining margin of U.S. advantage in counter-military capabilities gave rise to the strategy of escalation control through limited nuclear operations. This shift in doctrine reflected the belief that the United States was no longer in a good position to impose unsatisfactory war outcomes on the Soviets.

The new strategy rested on several sets of assumptions: (1) that the United States would be willing to execute limited strategic strikes of various sorts and that it would be able to do so, repeatedly if necessary; (2) that the Soviets would be willing to "play along"—to respond in a controlled way to limited U.S. attacks without escalating an ongoing conflict; and, even more important, (3) that the Soviets would lack realistic options between controlled response and all-out retaliation. In other words, the creators of the strategy of escalation control through limited nuclear options would appear to have relied on the continued existence of what might be called functional parity—a situation in which neither side could drastically alter the military balance by escalating to a higher level of hostilities.

Finally, it was assumed that LNOs would be accompanied by a range of other military and political measures. Escalation would have to be controlled and an intense war ended on favorable terms through a combination of sucessful local defense, withheld threats, and forceful diplomacy.

Could LNOs of the type discussed in the mid-seventies have been used to control escalation in the period 1974–1977? Could they be used for that purpose today? The best answers to these questions would appear to be "maybe" and "probably not." Although it is difficult to know with any certainty, there has never been much public evidence of elaborate preparations to coordinate limited-strategic, theater-nuclear, conventional, and diplomatic means in the event of war. It is not clear how much detailed thought has ever been given to the problem.

The United States has always had the theoretical capability to execute a range of limited strategic attacks, from the very large (McNamara's counterforce second strike) to the quite small (Schlesinger's proposed attack on Soviet petroleum refineries) (Senate Foreign Relations Committee 1974:11–12). Since the mid-seventies, much of the hardware needed to make more controlled strikes feasible has been developed and deployed (more accurate warheads, improved retargeting computers, and so on). It seems safe to assume that paper plans for limited attacks have also been prepared.

Nevertheless, the willingness of an American president to order an LNO has probably declined over the past five or six years. The political objections to such attacks—that they would encourage escalation rather than control it—remain the same. Military objections—that all but the largest LNOs would have no prompt effect on events in the theater of battle, and that the execution of LNOs would expose remaining American strategic forces to disruption and destruction while drawing down the U.S. nuclear arsenal—have undoubtedly become more intense. The principal reason for this change is that the Soviets seem to be improving their chances of benefiting from certain forms of intrawar escalation.

Growing countermilitary capabilities have not been accompanied by any visible change in Soviet doctrine. In their pronouncements on the subject, Russian military writers continue to discount the possibility of a controlled nuclear conflict. But as Fritz Ermarth has pointed out,

[Q]ualified acceptance in doctrine and posture of a non-nuclear scenario, or at least a non-nuclear phase, in theater conflict displays some Soviet willingness to embrace conflict limitation notions previously rejected. Soviet strategic nuclear force growth and modernization, in addition, have given Soviet operational planners a broader array of employment options than they had in the 1960s and may have imparted some confidence in the Soviet ability to *enforce* conflict limitations. It would not be surprising, therefore to find some Soviet contingency planning for various kinds of limited nuclear options at the theater and, perhaps, at the strategic level (Ermarth 1978:149).

In any case, growing concern over the possibility of a large and devastating Soviet LNO or counter-LNO directed at a wide range of allied military targets cannot help but feed doubts about the wisdom of relying on limited U.S. strategic attacks to control escalation.[17]

If a war fought in the mid- to late seventies had escalated out of control, could the United States have prevented the USSR from dominating the postwar period by destroying its recovery resources? Any large-scale nuclear attack on the Soviet urban-industrial base would obviously have enormous economic consequences. Proceeding from this simple statement to a more elaborate prediction of "recovery rates" (five years? ten years? twenty-five years? 1925 gross national product? 1950 GNP? 1980 GNP? Actual GNP or GNP per capita?) is virtually impossible. One has only to look at the econometricians' projections of U.S. industrial performance in *peacetime* to be convinced of that fact.

If the shift toward counterrecovery targeting produced a greater emphasis on attacking eocnomic choke points and centers of economic, military, and political control, then the post-Rumsfeld war plans were probably better designed to retard Soviet reconstitution than their predecessors.

Preventing enemy domination would have also required the destruction of Soviet capabilities for projecting all forms of military power and the protection of U.S. economic, military, and political assets. The American ability to do both of these things (and especially the latter) was and still is quite limited. In the late seventies the United States could probably have achieved its minimal war objective (preventing postwar Russian domination) only if massive nuclear attacks caused the permanent disintegration of the Soviet state.

1980–1981. The countervailing strategy emerged awkwardly (and perhaps somewhat prematurely) during a period of growing concern over the state of the strategic balance. The increasing capability of Soviet nuclear forces and the increasing Western awareness of worrisome Soviet attitudes toward the problem of nuclear war combined to produce a change in U.S. policy.

At the conceptual level PD-59 clearly represented a major advance over past guidance. By focusing attention on Soviet planning and, in a more general way, on the possible dynamics of a future nuclear war, the directive helped to redirect American planners toward central but often poorly understood problems.

In some sense however, PD-59 was too forward-looking. The danger of relying on sophisticated limited attacks when an increasing fraction of U.S. strategic forces are vulnerable to attack has already been mentioned. In the same way, discussing the possibility of protracted conflict when American command, control, communications, and intelligence facilities remain disturbingly fragile carries with it a certain risk of self-deception. There is a gap between concepts and capabilities which now needs to be filled.

Summary

Whatever its other faults, this attempt to evaluate U.S. strategies for nuclear war should point up two important facts. First, many nonstrategic (that is, other than central system nuclear), nonnuclear, and nonmilitary factors will affect war outcomes. Second, predicting outcomes and designing strategies to make the desirable appear to be possible is an extremely uncertain business. Everything from weapons effects, to operational military problems, to likely patterns of political decisionmaking in wartime is shrouded in doubt. Nevertheless prediction is an essential and unavoidable part of the strategic planning process at any level. If an attempt to evaluate past strategies for nuclear war makes us more humble about our ability to eliminate uncertainty in present planning, it will have served its purpose.

WHAT DETERS?

To focus on the traditional element in U.S. strategic doctrine, on war plans, and thus, implicitly, on deterrence failures is to risk the accusation that one lacks interest in the problem of preventing war in the first place. This is a milder second cousin to the claim that thinking about war makes it more likely. Neither is very enlightening or particularly fair.

In fact, deterrence may fail in a number of ways not the least likely of which is that one day, under the right circumstances, we and our opponents could have rather different images of how a conflict would turn out. For this reason alone we ought to be interested in war plans, estimates of war outcomes, and, more importantly, in the preparations and perceptions of our likely enemy.

Another more serious criticism of a history centered on war plans is that, in some substantial measure, it misses the point. Military planners always prepare for war; it is, after all, their job to do so. But, in the nuclear age, what prevents war is not the threat of military defeat but the spectre of societal devastation. This is true regardless of the doctrines, war plans, and capabilities of the nuclear superpowers. One plausible answer to the question, "What deters?" is thus, "the threat of massive civilian casualties and enormous economic losses."

This statement is neither false nor entirely true. It is worth remembering that a nuclear war of virtually any size or conceivable configuration would be destructive almost beyond belief. In the current cycle of nuclear revisionism, some of our more enthusiastic armchair strategists have tended to lose sight of those facts.

Moreover (although no such assertion about "negative causality" can ever be proven), it seems likely that the threat of societal devastation is still the primary deterrent to nuclear war. On any given day the leaders of both superpowers are aware that war could destroy them, and everything they have worked for and are presumably entrusted to protect. This is a generalized sensation rather than an entirely rational conclusion based on any elaborate set of calculations. But, like individual anxiety, it is a sensation that has important behavioral consequences. In large measure, then, the world has been and is likely to continue to be governed by the principles embodied in the notion of assured destruction.

For better or worse, however, things do not stop there. More traditional military considerations have always played a role in influencing the political and, of course, the military leaders of the United States and the Soviet Union. Calculations of relative advantage (or the lack of it) have been made during crises. Fears about vulnerability to effective countermilitary attack and the possibility of acquiring countermilitary advantages have, at various times, seemed to play a significant role in shaping the force-acquisition policies of both sides. In the case of the United States, and one can assume also the Soviet Union, military imperatives—the desire to destroy, disrupt, or disable the enemy's forces as quickly and efficiently as possible—have been pre-eminent in the design of operational war plans.

Day-to-day political reality may be dominated by the simple, horrible image of mass death and destruction. But another mechanism is at work beneath the surface. It is possible that under some circumstances, a nuclear war might *not* be an undifferentiated disaster. With a significant margin of military advantage (an effective offensive and defensive damage-limiting capability, for example) one side might be able to "win" even an all-out nuclear war. It certainly would stand a better chance of imposing an outcome on its weaker opponent short of total conflict. Apparently marginal advantages could also be significant—the ability to locate and destroy critical elements of the enemy's command and control system, for example. Finally, even the appearance or the perception of military advantage could have important political consequences in peacetime and crisis.

Military considerations matter. Even in the nuclear age they continue to play a role in determining the likelihood of any future war and its probable outcome.

As has been illustrated here, U.S. plans for nuclear war have always had a heavy countermilitary emphasis, even when (as in 1945–50) those plans called simply for strikes against Soviet cities. Our declaratory policy, especially during the last twenty years, has tended to emphasize the grim, human, economic, and social consequences of nuclear conflict. Saying that one or the other threat—defeat or devastation—was solely responsible for keeping the peace is clearly impossible. War has probably been prevented by a combination of counterforce and countervalue threats, by the seeming certainty of denial *and* punishment.

Perhaps we have been too intent in our thinking on finding the one "correct" answer to the question, "What deters?" A better question might be, "What kinds of threats deter what kinds of behavior and under what conditions?" Moreover, we might be wise to acknowledge the strong possibility that we will never be able to answer these vital questions with any high degree of certainty. What preparations should satisfy us in that event and what should we be ready to do if deterrence fails and we have no choice but to pursue our objectives by forceful means?

A MORE UNIFIED DOCTRINE?

We have seen that even during the sixties, when belief in the wisdom of such a policy was most widespread, the United States did not adhere to a doctrine of mutually assured destruction. Throughout that decade (as in the years before and after), U.S. policy was shaped by conflicting forces. Our "doctrine" contained two strands—one traditional and military, the other more modern and assured destructionist in tone.

It is probably no accident that the period in which (as the Soviets might say) the "contradictions" in U.S. doctrine were greatest was the time when the United States reached and then passed its broadest margin of strategic superiority. Notions of stability are likely to be particularly appealing to states which have exerted great effort, achieved significant military advantage over their principal opponents, and wish (or are forced) to turn their attention to other problems. The effects of the conflict between a desire for stability and the need to compete with a dynamic opponent tend to become obvious only as the previous margin of advantage begins to erode.

We are coming to the end of a ten-year interval during which neither superpower can reasonably claim to have possessed superior strategic nuclear capabilities. In the decade just past, our efforts to modernize the strategic forces and improve planning for nuclear war were, at best, only partly successful. At worst these efforts were sporadic, uncoordinated, and, at times, misdirected. With Soviet superiority looming on the horizon (Burt 1980), there must obviously be a premium on purposeful action and an efficient use of available resources. The function of doctrine is to provide direction to planning and to guide the making of difficult allocational decisions. Without a more unified and coherent doctrine it will be extremely difficult for us to make progress toward redressing an increasingly unfavorable strategic balance.

It seems clear that we are being forced to place greater emphasis on the traditional concerns which have always formed one portion of our ''doctrine.'' In the years ahead, we will have to pay a great deal of attention to the problems of preparing for war—persuading the Soviets that they cannot defeat us by using nuclear weapons and preparing to achieve rational military and political objectives if deterrence fails.

Progress in this direction will require that we first dispel some of the notions that have tended to underpin the other, more modern half of our ''doctrine''—that counterforce targeting and defensive systems are inherently dangerous, that nuclear weapons cannot have military and political utility, and that competition in the strategic nuclear arena is always undesirable.

In general, then, a more unified strategic doctrine will have to be more openly traditional in direction and tone. But it should be clear by now that the necessary changes really involve a shift in emphasis more than they do a dramatic intellectual counterrevolution in which all modern concepts are banished to the garbage heap of history.

Indeed (to mix metaphors) there is considerable danger that a number of worthwhile babies may be thrown out along with some tired bathwater. The assumptions that underlie the modern portion of our doctrine need to be reexamined, but much deserves to be retained. Nuclear weapons are qualitatively different from any others that mankind has previously possessed. Certain types of actions which a traditional approach would demand are risky and must be approached with great caution in a nuclear world—preparing to attack an enemy's forces and his command network, for example. On careful consideration, some such measures may seem necessary despite the dangers they pose. But they cannot be undertaken lightly. Finally, while such policies may have received excessive attention under the modern approach, efforts to steady the strategic competition through negotiated agreements are still worth pursuing (Friedberg 1978).

In a democracy, obtaining absolute unity of views on almost any issue is virtually impossible. Yet a defense establishment working at cross-purposes is unlikely to give adequate response to a rapidly changing and increasingly dangerous situation. We need a more unified strategic doctrine. To shape it we will have to first engage in an open and intelligent debate. But informed discussion and sensible change will be impossible if we do not first make a serious effort to understand the history of the last thirty-five years.

NOTES

1. If anyone doubts that belief in a U.S. doctrine of mutually assured destruction is widespread, let them consider the words of a congressman, a senator, a former cabinet official, and over one thousand high-ranking military officers.

   During recent Congressional hearings Representative Ronald Dellums referred to "the principle of mutual assured destruction" and to the targeting of "populations and industrial bases, which has been our historical targeting approach. . . . " He went on to ask if a shift toward "a primarily military target mode" would not represent "a significant point of departure" which might "put us into a potential hair trigger situation. . . " (House Armed Services Committee 1979:547).

   Senator Clayborne Pell, during hearings of the SALT II treaty, said, "Some years back, it was understood that the policy we had in the United States was a policy of mutually assured destruction (MAD)" (Senate Foreign Relations Committee 1979:381). .

   In his controversial Brussels speech in September 1979, former Secretary of State Henry Kissinger declared, ". . . I believe it is necessary that we develop a military purpose for our strategic forces and move away from the senseless and demoralizing strategy of massive civilian extermination. . ." (Kissinger 1979:267).

And, in a letter to Senator Frank Church, retired Admiral Thomas Moorer and 1,678 other retired general and flag officers from all the services decried the "concept of Mutual Assured Destruction (MAD) which has shaped U.S. policy since the 1960s. . . ." The officers went on to warn against "adherence to the obviously bankrupt doctrine of Mutual Assured Destruction (MAD)" (Senate Foreign Relations Committee 1979:61–63).

2.   Bernard Brodie is sometimes cited for his allegedly "assured destructionist" views. Brodie *did* argue that thermonuclear war would be "a catastrophe for which it is impossible to set upper limits very far short of the entire population of the nation." And he asserted that, having foresworn "preventive war," the United States was "henceforward committed to the strategy of deterrence." But he pointed out that "what looks like the most rational *deterrence* policy [threatening enemy cities] involves commitment to a strategy of response which, if we ever had to execute it, might then look very foolish. The strategy of deterrence ought always to envisage the possibility of deterrence failing."

     If deterrence failed, Brodie did *not* advocate the wholesale slaughter of enemy civilians. In fact, he argued that in the event of war, "the opponent's strategic bombardment power, insofar as it can be reached and destroyed is certainly the first and most important target system. There is in fact no other target system worth comparable consideration." Nor did he favor leaving American civilians exposed to Soviet attack. Writing in 1959, Brodie urged that "Provisions. . . be made for the saving of life on a vast scale."

     For Brodie assured destruction might have been an accurate description of the likely consequences of total nuclear war. It was certainly not an outcome he welcomed nor a "strategy" he favored (Brodie 1965:167, 393, 292, 402, 397).

3.   During the mid-sixties, Secretary of Defense McNamara's annual posture statements certainly contributed to this confusion. (See section entitled "The Shift Toward 'Assured Destruction.' ").

4.   To the list of notables in footnote 1 we can add:

     One-time Lockheed employee Robert C. Aldridge writes that "Deterrence is the strategic policy under which most of us believe the Pentagon is still operating." But he warns that in seeking to satisfy the requirements of its "clandestine military doctrine," the Pentagon is acquiring weapons suitable for "a knockout first strike" (Aldridge 1978: 1, 3, 63).

     Harvard history professor Richard Pipes, on the other hand, cautions that it is the Soviets who have devised a "fresh strategy" for nuclear war. He argues that "We are as oblivious to these staggering innovations in the art of war as the French and the British in their time had been to the German strategy of the armored Blitzkrieg."

According to Pipes, America's nuclear strategy (which "rests on the concept of deterrence") is largely the product of the postwar musings of "American intellectuals." These men believed that the use of nuclear weapons threatened all humanity, that no defense was possible against them, and that they therefore had no political utility.

Pipes closes with a call for "a military strategy to meet the Soviets" which, he says, ought to be designed by professional military men rather than professors of history, government, economics, or physics (Pipes 1978).

5. For example, since the early fifties U.S. nuclear strategy has called for a good deal more than the pure city-busting strikes which an assured-destruction doctrine would require. During the sixties procurement of ballistic missile defenses and hard target-killing warheads was constrained, in part because some high government officials believed that protecting populations and threatening enemy nuclear forces would be "destabilizing." There were no such constraints in the fifties. Some far less potent restraints still exist today.

6. This half of U.S. "doctrine" (the portion which has governed the formulation of operational war plans) bears a striking resemblance to the more unified Soviet doctrine about which so much has been written in the West.

7. In early 1948 there were only thirty-two modified B-29s capable of carrying the atomic bomb. In July of the same year there were apparently fifty bombs in the stockpile (Rosenberg 1979:64–65).

8. See the section entitled "The Multilayered Threat, 1950–1960" for a more detailed discussion.

9. See the section "The Shift Toward 'Assured Destruction' " for an explanation of the divergence between targeting and declaratory policy.

10. Colin Gray, for example, claims in a recent article that "Most Western strategic thinking, and even planning, betrays a basic lack of seriousness about the conduct of war" (Gray 1979:61). He goes on to assert (without any visible evidence) that "(I)t is unlikely that a U.S. retaliatory (second) strike in the mid-1980s with forces currently programmed would do as much damage as the Germans achieved in World War II." While this damage would be "highly concentrated in time" and accompanied by "residual radioactivity," Gray maintains that "neither of these factors need prove fatal, or even severely embarrassing, to a Soviet recovery effort" (Gray 1979:62). One wonders who is being less "serious" about the problems of nuclear war.

11. From Joint Emergency War Plan HALFMOON (May 19, 1948) (Rosenberg 1979:4).

12. See the section on "The First SIOP, 1960–1961" for a brief explanation of the origins of the optimum mix.

13. Throughout this period military officers still spoke openly, if cautiously, of their continued interest in the damage-limiting mission. Appearing before the Senate Armed Service Committee in 1968, General Earle G. Wheeler, then chairman of the Joint Chiefs of Staff, was asked if "our war plans do allocate weapons for damage limitation or counterforce." His response: "They certainly do" (Greenwood 1975:59).

14. In 1966 The United States had deployed 904 ICBM launchers. By 1967 the number had risen 150 to 1,054 where it remained from that point to the present (International Institute for Strategic Studies 1977:80).

15. Edward Luttwak refers to the cancellation in the early sixties of "a research program for large ICBMs (WS. 120)" (Luttwak 1976:22). More concretely, Ted Greenwood has detailed the rise and fall of the Mark 17, a hard target-killing warhead considered at one time as the primary multiple independently targetable reentry vehicle (MIRV) payload for upgraded U.S. ICBMs and SLBMs. Greenwood writes that the Mark 17 (which was finally cancelled in 1968) was "a prime target for cost-conscious budgeteers and was ultimately cancelled largely to save money. But, its strong identification in the services with the counterforce mission made its cancellation both a reflection and a symbol of the decreasing willingness of OSD to fund a program whose primary purpose was counterforce." As a result "neither Minuteman III nor Poseidon were optimized specifically for the counterforce mission" (Greenwood 1975:70–71).

16. There are indications that the modifications announced in early 1977 had been under consideration for some time, perhaps at the same time as the LNO concept was being discussed. Bernard Weinraub, in an article in the *New York Times*, has written that the policy of recovery retardation was "shaped under Secretary of Defense James R. Schlesinger and then publically outlined by his successor, Donald H. Rumsfeld" (Weinraub 1979).

17. Benjamin Lambeth discusses the Soviet image of a "limited nuclear operation" which, "if it exists, may very well envisage a massive and rapidly executed preemptive theater nuclear blitz against NATO, coupled with a simultaneous countermilitary attack against all interesting targets in CONUS [Continental United States], while holding U.S. cities as hostages with a large residual force to deter the United States from retaliating against the Soviet ZI [Zone of the Interior]" (Lambeth 1977:101).

REFERENCES

Aldridge, Robert C. 1978. *The Counterforce Syndrome.* Washington, D.C.: The Transnational Institute.

Ball, Desmond. 1974. *Déjà Vu: The Return to Counterforce in the Nixon Administration.* Santa Monica: The California Seminar on Arms Control and Foreign Policy.

Brodie, Bernard. 1965. *Strategy in the Missile Age.* Princeton: Princeton University Press.

Brown, Harold. 1979. *Annual Defense Department Report, Fiscal Year 1980.* Washington, D.C.: U.S. Government Printing Office.

_____. 1980a. *Annual Defense Department Report, Fiscal Year 1981.* Washington, D.C.: U.S. Government Printing Office.

_____. 1980b. Speech at the convocation ceremonies for the 97th Naval War College class, Newport, Rhode Island. Washington, D.C.: Defense Department press release, August 20.

_____. 1980c. Statement before Senate Foreign Relations Committee, September 16. Mimeo.

Burt, Richard. 1979. "Brown Says Soviets Long Sought Way to Knock Out U.S. Missiles." *New York Times* (May 31).

_____. 1980. "Soviet Nuclear Edge in Mid-80's is Envisioned by U.S. Intelligence." *New York Times* (May 13).

Davis, Lynn. 1976. *Limited Nuclear Options: Deterrence and the New American Doctrine, Adelphi Papers Number 121.* London: International Institute for Strategic Studies.

Ermarth, Fritz. 1978. "Contrasts in American and Soviet Strategic Thought." *International Security* 3, no. 2 (Fall):138–155.

Friedberg, Aaron. 1978. "What SALT Can (And Cannot) Do." *Foreign Policy* no. 33 (Winter 1978/79):92–100.

Futrell, Robert Frank. 1971. *Ideas, Concepts, Doctrine: A History of Basic Thinking in the United States Air Force 1907–1964*, vol. II. Maxwell Air Force Base, Alabama: Aerospace Studies Institute.

Goldberg, Alfred. 1967. *A Brief Survey of the Evolution of Ideas About Counterforce RM-5431-PR.* Santa Monica: The Rand Corporation.

Gray, Colin S. 1979. "Soviet Strategic Vulnerabilities." *Air Force Magazine* 66, no. 3 (March 1979):60–64.

Greenwood, Ted. 1975. *Making the MIRV.* Cambridge, Ma.: Ballinger Publishing Company.

House Armed Services Committee. 1979. *Hearings on Military Posture, 96: 1, part 1.* Washington, D.C.: U.S. Government Printing Office.

International Institute for Strategic Studies. 1977. *The Military Balance 1977–78.* London: IISS.

Kissinger, Henry A. 1979. "NATO: The Next Thirty Years." *Survival* 21, no. 6 (November/December 1979):264–268.

Lambeth, Benjamin S. 1977. "Selective Nuclear Operations and Soviet Strategy." In *Beyond Nuclear Deterrence,* edited by Johan J. Holst and Uwe Nerlich, pp. 79–104. New York: Crane Russak and Company.

Leghorn, Richard S. 1955. "No Need to Bomb Cities to Win War, A New Counterforce Strategy for Air Warfare." *U.S. News and World Report* 38, no. 4 (January 28): 78–94.

Luttwak, Edward. 1976. *Strategic Power: Military Capabilities and Political Utility.* Beverly Hills: Sage Publications.

MacIsaac, David. 1979. "The Air Force and Strategic Thought 1945–1951." Paper presented at a colloquium of the Woodrow Wilson International Center for Scholars, Washington, D.C., June 21.

McNamara, Robert S. 1963. *Fiscal Years 1964 to 1968 Defense Program and Defense Budget for Fiscal Year 1964.* Washington, D.C.: U.S. Government Printing Office.

_____. 1964. *Annual Defense Department Report, Fiscal Year 1965.* Washington, D.C.: U.S. Government Printing Office.

_____. 1965. *Fiscal Years 1966 to 1970 Defense Program and Defense Budget for Fiscal Year 1966.* Washington, D.C.: U.S. Government Printing Office..

_____. 1967. *Fiscal Years 1968 to 1972 Defense Program and Defense Budget for Fiscal Year 1968.* Washington, D.C.: U.S. Government Printing Office.

_____. 1968. *Fiscal Years 1969 to 1973 Defense Program and Defense Budget for Fiscal Year 1969.* Washington, D.C.: U.S. Government Printing Office.

Nixon, Richard M. 1970. *A Report to the Congress: U.S. Foreign Policy for the 1970s, A New Strategy for Peace* (February 18).

Pincus, Walter. 1979. "Thinking the Unthinkable: Studying New Approaches to a Nuclear War." *Washington Post* (February 11).

Pipes, Richard. 1978. "Rethinking Our Nuclear Strategy." *Wall Street Journal* (October 12).

Rosenberg, David Alan. 1979. "American Nuclear Strategy and the Hydrogen Bomb Decision." *Journal of American History* 66, no. 1 (June 1979): 62–86.

Rowen, Henry S. 1975. "Formulating Strategic Doctrine." In Commission on the Organization of the Government for the Conduct of Foreign Policy, Volume 4, Appendix K: *Adequacy of Current Organization: Defense and Arms Control,* pp. 219–234. Washington, D.C.: U.S. Government Printing Office.

Rumsfeld, Donald H. 1977. *Annual Defense Department Report, Fiscal Year 1975.* Washington, D.C.: U.S. Government Printing Office.

Schlesinger, James R. 1974. *Annual Defense Department Report, Fiscal Year 1975.* Washington, D.C.: U.S. Government Printing Office.

Senate Foreign Relations Committee. 1974. *Hearings on the U.S. and Soviet Strategic Doctrine and Military Policies, 93:2.* Washington, D.C.: U.S. Government Printing Office.

———. 1979. *Hearings on the SALT II Treaty, 96:1, part 4.* Washington, D.C.: U.S. Government Printing Office.

Walkowicz, T.F. 1955. "Counterforce Strategy, How We Can Exploit America's Atomic Advantage." *Air Force Magazine* 38, no. 2 (February): 25–29, 46, 51–52, 82.

Weinraub, Bernard. 1979. "Pentagon Seeking Shift in Nuclear Deterrent Policy." *New York Times* (January 5).

3 ELUSIVE EQUIVALENCE: THE POLITICAL AND MILITARY MEANING OF THE NUCLEAR BALANCE

Richard K. Betts

No quotation has been more widely used as grist on both sides of the strategic debate than Henry Kissinger's: "What in the name of God is strategic superiority? What is the significance of it politically, militarily, operationally, at these levels of numbers? What do you do with it?" (Kissinger 1974:215). Hawks believed the question demonstrated the dangerous nonchalance of arms control advocates who placed too much value on the Strategic Arms Limitation Talks (SALT) process as an end in itself. (Indeed, Kissinger later repudiated the views implicit in his own question.)[4] Doves noted the less frequently cited part of Kissinger's remarks—"If we have not reached an agreement well before 1977 . . . you will see an explosion of technology and an explosion of numbers. . . ., a world which will be extraordinarily complex, in which opportunities for nuclear warfare exist that were unimaginable 15 years ago" (Kissinger 1974:215) —to indicate the danger of subordinating treaty agreement to pusillanimous resistance to even a minor margin of Soviet advantage.

While the significance of nuclear superiority remained in dispute,

For helpful comments, thanks and more-than-normal absolution are due to Vaughn Altemus, Bruce Blair, Barry Blechman, Colin Gray, Samuel Huntington, Robert Jervis, Dennis Ross, and Kenneth Waltz.

both sides managed to reach grudging consensus on the desirability of parity or equivalence. (I use the terms interchangeably and explore definitions in more detail later.) Confusion continued because the consensus on principle did not translate into consensus on what distribution of forces constitutes equality or how precise the calculation need be. Consensus on principle was also superficial. On both sides it was more genuflection to reality constraints—the political infeasibility of achieving superiority or accepting inferiority—than genuine satisfaction with the criterion of parity. Two critical questions remain, and murkiness in the answers endures despite the huge volume of philosophical commentary and statistical gamesmanship unleashed in recent years. Why is equivalence important, and what is it? Before exploring either, it is necessary to appreciate why the conceptual basis for assessment is still unclear after decades of discussion.

THE NUCLEAR STRATEGY MUDDLE

There has been scant innovation in nuclear deterrence theory since the seminal works of Brodie, Wohlstetter, Kahn, Schelling, Kaufmann, and others in the 1950s. Yet debate persists, in exegetical variations on old themes, as the evolution of technology and politics make long-contending concepts fluctuate in salience.

Technological Rhythm and Conceptual Schizophrenia

Lumping sectarian differences over strategy into dichotomous camps risks oversimplification. For heuristic purposes two broad tendencies can be identified that have dominated theological disputes. (The disputes are theological because nuclear war is an untested abstraction about which judgments can only be made by theoretical inferences and leaps of faith [Betts 1979].) One school—for shorthand, called mutual assured destruction (MAD)—views nuclear weapons as so revolutionary that they render traditional strategy obsolete. Once both superpowers have large numbers, the only utility of nuclear weapons is for mutual deterrence; deterrence is best fortified by ensuring that nuclear war remains unthinkable because any attack will draw devastating retaliation against the other's population and

economy. The other school—for shorthand, called damage limitation—sees the nuclear revolution as raising the stakes and risks of
conflict dramatically, but without eliminating the strategic or
political utility of nuclear weapons. If full-scale war is unthinkable,
the side willing to take high risks by threatening or executing an attack that drastically reduces the victim's retaliatory options can
prevail by making clear that surrender is preferable to retaliation.
Deterrence is fragile and best fortified by counterforce capabilities
that match or exceed the enemy's, to deny him the option of
dominating a military exchange. The schism is highlighted by the fact
that both sides of the debate invoke the scriptural authority of
Clausewitz.[2]

The popularity of both approaches has varied with the vulnerability
of forces. Since the mid-1950s neither the United States nor the
Soviet Union has had high confidence in a disarming capability. Even
when the United States came closest to achieving such a posture in
the early 1960s it still faced the prospect of several million casualties
from Soviet retaliation in the best case, and the probability of
substantially higher damage. Even when critics attribute great
counterforce superiority to the USSR, few responsible hawks deny
that surviving American weapons would be capable of killing many
millions of Russians. (They argue, rather, that capability for
genocide is not a sufficient basis for strategy.) When changes in speed
or accuracy of weaponry increased the vulnerability of forces, the
balance of opinion shifted in favor of counterforce targeting; when
both sides had forces sufficiently invulnerable that either would
disarm itself more than its victim in a first strike (the situation around
the time of SALT I), persuasiveness of MAD was at its peak.

Another element of the context is that U.S. nuclear policy over the
past fifteen years has suffered and benefited from contradiction. On
one hand, every administration since Kennedy's has accepted mutual
vulnerability and foresworn efforts to achieve highly effective
damage-limiting capabilities. This was the prerequisite to SALT since
neither side could sensibly agree to codify unilateral vulnerability. On
this plane American policy has aimed for technical stability such that
a first strike would never be rational for either side. On the other
hand, the United States has never abandoned the policy of extended
deterrence and flexible response, which theoretically requires willingness to strike first if conventional or theater nuclear defenses fail
to halt a Soviet armored offensive into Western Europe. Persistence

of this contradiction is due to the demands of NATO allies, whose nuclear schizophrenia is even greater. European leaders are less willing to rely on conventional defense but also more insistent on the importance of arms control agreements.

There are rationales to modify the contradiction between policies that logically prohibit and require first-strike options. The concentration on development of selective or limited nuclear options since the early 1970s and the 1979 NATO decision to enhance long-range theater nuclear forces (LRTNF) have offered theoretically fuzzy but politically tenable intermediate alternatives between MAD and effective damage limitation. The size of the contradictions within policy, and between commitments and capabilities, has fluctuated, but the logical tensions have never disappeared.

Tension in policy has been reflected in operational doctrine. Contrary to popular assertions, the United States did not have a pure *strategy* of assured destruction after McNamara rhetorically abandoned the "no-cities" counterforce policy. He used assured destruction as a management tool to keep procurement under control once the requirements of *effective* damage limitation became prohibitively expensive. The error of many observers was in confusing *acquisition* policy with force *employment* doctrine, assuming that because disarming counterforce became impractical, the United States gave up counterforce targeting altogether. They mistook the floor for the ceiling. Assured destruction defined the *minimum* capabilities required, not the desirable level of forces. U.S. forces continued to exceed the requirements of assured destruction (which McNamara estimated at 400 megaton equivalents) by wide margins (Rowen 1975). Even in the late 1960s, administration spokesmen asserted that counterforce options were important, and were part of the reason for developing multiple independently targetable reentry vehicles (MIRVs). Although the Single Integrated Operations Plan (SIOP) and Nuclear Weapons Employment Policy for the U.S. strategic forces have been inaccessible to analysts, it is no secret that a majority of strategic weapons have been allocated to military targets even since U.S. leaders began stressing assured destruction (Ball 1981; Kahan 1975:108; Futrell 1971, vol. 1:390–399, vol. 2:548–572, 676–696). Hawkish dissatisfaction with rhetoric of assured destruction was muted as the 1970s approached because U.S. superiority, while declining, still provided a theoretical margin of escalation dominance. Doves who mistook rhetoric for operational plans remained unperturbed until James Schlesinger publicly emphasized targeting flexibility; this was misread as a reversion toward counter-force targeting, which in fact had never been abandoned. Actual U.S. strategy remained between two stools and only became con-troversial at times when the latent tensions became manifest.

Dialogue of the Deaf

Schizophrenia in strategy made the implications of strategic parity confusing. In the early 1970s parity was popular because detente, success of SALT I, and pervasive antidefense fallout from Vietnam put those who favored substantial damage limitation (thus placing a premium on nuclear superiority) on the defensive. By the end of the decade the tables had turned and proponents of MAD dwindled, as steady growth in Soviet forces raised the spectre of U.S. inferiority, and assertions that Soviet doctrine rejected mutual assured destruc-tion became conventional wisdom. While the balance of opinion shifted back and forth, however, debate about the significance of nuclear superiority made negligible progress.

First, despite refinement of arguments about prospective nuclear exchanges (facilitated by better data on the forces of both sides), debate remained theological because hypotheses about the psychology of nuclear deterrence remained immune to empiricism. Since deterrence has not failed, it is impossible to prove what could make it fail or how a victim would respond to the failure. MAD and counterforce advocates still argue past each other, relying on much the same terms and faiths as they did years ago. (The intellectual gulf is as large as that between Keynesians and monetarists, who at least have some means for testing their economic theories.)

Second, neither strand of thought has permanently triumphed because neither can close the circle of consistency, either in logic or between logic and feasibility. MAD is most persuasive on visceral grounds, relying on the implausibility of nuclear adventurism as long as the Soviets face survivable American retaliatory power sufficient to inflict unprecedented damage. The logic wavers when it comes to demonstrating the rationality of implementing countervalue retalia-tion if the Soviets are reckless enough to attack U.S. strategic forces while sparing large population centers which remain hostage to

Soviet reserve forces. In order to demonstrate why the same prewar logic of mutual vulnerability designed to deter the first counterforce strike does not also apply to deterring the first dedicated counter-value strike (that is, in second-strike retaliation), assured-destruction theorists fall back on the import of uncertainty, or "the rationality of irrationality": because the Russians cannot know that we would not lash back in fury even if doing so is suicidal, they cannot risk the possibility. It is reasonable to bank simultaneously on the aggressor's prudence and rationality, and the victim's unpredictability and potential irrationality. This belief that cold calculation of risks probably would apply more to one side than the other may be valid, and may cover most potential scenarios. But it is still a leap of faith and does not offer a hedge against some scenarios.[3]

Rather than rely on uncertainty, counterforce advocates prefer options that would be less irrational (even if still horribly unattractive) to implement if deterrence failed. Rather than make the first dedicated countervalue strikes, inviting reciprocal destruction of U.S. cities, a posture that facilitates counterforce second strikes is preferable since it would reduce Soviet escalation dominance, preserve mutual deterrence of mass murder of civilians, and leave the United States with bargaining power for termination of hostilities short of mutual annihilation. Given the impossibility of achieving a disarming capability, this position is transmuted into emphasis on flexibility and counterforce matching, and was called "countervailing strategy" in the Carter Administration.

This view gains in credibility by making more symmetrical assumptions about rationality, but it founders on feasibility. Operational requirements for such a strategy in a postattack environment are awesome since it requires maintaining integrity of command, control, and communications (C^3), as well as reconnaissance, damage assessment, and retargeting capabilities, which could all be crippled if not obliterated by initial Soviet attacks. The problems may not be beyond rectification (these concerns are the essence of PD-59, the controversial 1980 presidential directive on nuclear strategy), but the necessary measures are extremely challenging and expensive. Moreover, counterforce and countervalue targeting cannot easily be disentangled. Many military targets are co-located with population centers.[4] Counterforce matching is also criticized as destabilizing, nurturing reciprocal fear of surprise attack by raising anxieties about vulnerable forces: "to develop a posture based on the assumption that limited nuclear wars are possible is to increase the chance that they will occur" (Jervis 1979–80:629). But as long as matching does not reach the level of disarming capability, threatening assured-destruction reserves, this criticism is unpersuasive, or at least does not demonstrate that matching is more dangerous than conceding an edge to the adversary (Betts 1979:93–94).

Moderate variants of both schools of thought cope with logical weaknesses by considering limited nuclear options to control escalation. Counterforce advocates prefer limited options against military targets, to preserve the balance of forces and deny escalation dominance to the enemy. There are two problems with this position. First, it is questionable if used to rationalize first strikes in support of extended deterrence because there is negligible evidence that Soviet doctrine envisions limited exchanges at the intercontinental level. Second, if neither side has escalation dominance, neither has a clear reason to stop before the other, and the exchanges may reach the point of all-out expenditure of weapons more slowly, but completely nonetheless.

Assured-destruction proponents prefer limited options against countervalue targets; such a strategy facilitates limitation of the arms race in peacetime, and "since what matters in limited strategic wars . . . is each side's willingness to run high risks, it is the 'balance of resolve' rather than the 'balance of military power' that will most strongly influence their outcomes. . . . demonstration attacks would be more useful than attempts to reduce an opponent's military capabilities" (Jervis 1979–80:628). The problem with this rationale is the assumption that the balance of resolve is independent of the balance of forces (rather than determined or at least constrained by it) because a defender has larger stakes and is naturally more willing to suffer than an aggressor (Waltz 1981:16). While persuasive in general, the assumption does not cover all contingencies. It cannot account very well for German risk-taking in August 1914 or, especially, May 1940 and June 1941. It does not explain why the United States would launch nuclear attacks against the Soviet interior to "save" West Germany at a likely price of over 100 million dead Americans when the French in 1940 would not even pursue a scorched-earth policy or try to regroup near the Pyrennees rather than capitulate. Victims often prefer surrender to costs even much lower than suicide. Linking the deterrent to an aggressor's threats against "vital interests" does not solve the problem that an even *more* vital interest—physical survival of the American homeland—may be lost if nuclear weapons are unleashed. Most importantly, the axiom does not cover situations where *both* parties consider the *other* the aggressor (such as the four Arab-Israeli wars since 1948). Nuclear war is improbable under any circumstances, but it is least likely to flow from a simple Soviet lust for conquest. The more challenging and relevant scheme of deterrence is one that will work even in a messy situation where the Soviets' misperceptions lead them to see themselves as the ones who are most aggrieved and threatened. In this case it would be foolhardy to assume that the side with an edge in capabilities would be the first to retreat. The balance of resolve may be independent of the balance of forces or linked to it, depending on the nature of the crisis or the leaders involved, but the answer cannot be known in advance. The balance of forces, however, is an element that *is* more knowable. It is also more controllable in the peacetime planning process that establishes the strategic context of a future crisis.

WHY SUPERIORITY MATTERS

Even the compromises between pure theories of assured destruction and damage limitation have failed to overcome dilemmas that block a consistently rational nuclear employment doctrine to buttress deterrence. If MAD retaliation could be made unquestionably credible, or an effective damage-limiting posture of massive superiority could be achieved at acceptable cost, the dilemmas would recede, but neither alternative is plausible given the scope of Soviet power. Equivalence in strategic forces has no neat operational rationale: it provides more than necessary for assured destruction and less than necessary for substantial damage limitation. Why, then, should equivalence be sought? Nuclear parity is a nullity—the absence of overall advantage on either side. Therefore, the meaning of equivalence depends on the significance of the alternative—inequality.

In the most general sense nuclear equivalence exists when neither side can do more than the other can do to it, and superiority is the capacity, as perceived by national leaders, to inflict more damage, against a wider array of targets, than the adversary can inflict. While they offer little to theorists of the abstract logic of deterrence, these vague notions have probably affected policy decisions by U.S. and

Soviet leaders. In most cold war crises American leaders did not have confidence that they could wage a nuclear war that would limit damage to the United States to an "acceptable" level, but most of them still believed that the disparity in prospective damage to the USSR lent political utility to the U.S. advantage in forces. Whether or not they agreed what it meant or whether it existed, leaders have never been indifferent to the prospect of enemy nuclear superiority.

Strategic Stability: Technical versus Political

In the lore of deterrence theory, "stability" is one of the most loosely used terms, often denoting different things which may not be compatible. One usage is technical: an invulnerable configuration of forces such that the structure of the military balance itself precludes a rational decision by either side to strike first. Another category of stability is political. Though it receives less attention in deterrence literature, it is more important because it governs incentives to change the status quo by coercion. If neither superpower pursues revisionist aims, technical stability of forces is irrelevant. Technical stability may dampen political instability by discouraging provocative behavior, but it does not necessarily do so because the nuclear balance is only one element in the military balance as a whole. If strategic nuclear forces are so technically stable that they neutralize each other, imbalances in other forces may provide coercive bargaining chips to the side with non-nuclear advantages.

In the 1950s U.S. strategy aimed to preserve political stability in Europe (containment) by accepting a military balance of countervailing superiorities: U.S. nuclear superiority and threats of massive retaliation countered Warsaw Pact conventional superiority. In the late fifties, however, Khrushchev challenged political stability (with pressure on West Berlin) by asserting that Soviet missile developments had neutralized U.S. nuclear threats. "The Soviet political strategy based on bluff and deception was born of an unwillingness to incur serious risk of war and an unwillingness to forego gains that might be had without incurring such risk" (Horelick and Rush 1966: 110). As Soviet nuclear power appeared to grow, U.S. debate drifted toward consensus in favor of shrinking the conventional gap. The two gaps (nuclear and conventional) narrowed in the 1960s, but most

Western observers still believed that the Soviets retained a conventional advantage in Europe and the Americans, a nuclear advantage. By the 1970s the net balance appeared to shift toward the East, which kept the conventional edge while achieving nuclear parity.

This gradual tilting was not severely alarming early in the decade because the danger of potential military instability—Soviet exploitation of conventional military threats behind a nuclear shield that denied the West's capacity to threaten escalation—was dampened by the apparent growth of political stability: detente, SALT, agreements on European security, and mutual and balanced force reductions (MBFR) negotiations which held out the hope of achieving conventional equivalence. Declining political anxieties reduced concern about abstrusely defined weaknesses in technical military deterrence. Moreover, refined calculations of military balance are extremely contentious because imperfectly verifiable assumptions about certain variables—such as Soviet reinforcement rates or the likelihood of French commitment in the conventional battle, or Soviet intercontinental ballistic missile (ICBM) accuracy and U.S. antisubmarine warfare (ASW) capability in the nuclear battle—yield divergent net assessments. In the early 1970s skepticism spawned by the Vietnam trauma helped discredit alarmist assessments in the eyes of much of the American foreign policy elite, and in the late 1970s accumulated anxiety about Soviet initiatives in the Third World helped discredit benign assessments. The physical balance of military forces should logically be estimated independently from beliefs about adversary intentions, but pessimism about technical stability tends to vary directly with pessimism about political stability. Those who see the Soviet Union as aggressive also tend to see the military balance as unfavorable, while those who see the Soviets' intentions as less malevolent and their political gains as less impressive have more confidence in Western capabilities.

By 1980 anxiety about the shifting military balance muted in the prior decade was inflamed by continuing Soviet improvements in strategic forces. The extreme anxiety is that technical stability is declining and Soviet superiority might, in a crisis, tempt Moscow to strike U.S. strategic forces. This view sees *active* utility in superiority. The less extreme fear is that marginal Soviet superiority *reinforces* technical stability at the strategic nuclear level, giving Moscow more freedom to maneuver with conventional threats: theoretical military escalation dominance may yield practical political escalation dominance. This view emphasizes the *passive* utility of nuclear superiority. (Many argue that equivalence or even less provides the same shield to the Soviets against escalatory threats, but superiority makes the argument stronger.)

Those who denigrate these concerns counter with two arguments. First, since the danger is a conjectural matter of perception, it can be forestalled by staunch Western rhetoric and assertions that it does not exist. Second, nuclear superiority is a mythical political advantage. The West did not get anything positive out of superiority when it had it, and in any case the Soviet Union will not have the vast superiority that the United States had earlier in the cold war.

These counterarguments are only half true. They confuse the logical with the actual, assuming that what does not make sense will not be believed by others, forgetting that deterrence is in the eye of the beholder. Beliefs are rarely neutralized by exhortation. There is nothing objective about the logic of deterrence until it fails (in which case the outcome will prove one of the contending theories about the rationality of a first strike to have been correct). As long as the issue is how to preserve deterrence, the critical factors are subjective—what authorities *think* the outcome would be, and what they think the enemy might do, sensible or not. The simple fact that there is disagreement about this within policy elites indicates that the problem cannot be solved by assertion. It is a constitutional fact of life that debate in the West cannot be suppressed for the sake of presenting confident denials that the USSR has usable military advantages. Finally, the assertion that American superiority did not prove usable is questionable.

Nuclear Superiority: American Experience

Drawing lessons from history is dangerous because conditions are never the same. But if skeptics ask what the Russians could do with nuclear superiority, it is reasonable to raise the possibility that they might try to do what the United States did when *it* had superiority. Data on this question are murky and the conclusions debatable, but circumstantial evidence and tentative arguments are worth considering because at the least they inject doubt into theories that rest on denial of the utility of nuclear superiority.[5]

During much of the cold war the United States used nuclear superiority for leverage "on the cheap." The massive retaliation policy was the most general manifestation, but there were specific instances of tacit threats to initiate nuclear attacks. To demonstrate the relevance of superiority it is not necessary to argue that threats were rational. Indeed, it is striking that U.S. leaders would consider such initiatives even when they had reason to believe that the American homeland was vulnerable to devastating Soviet retaliation. Nor need one argue that the threats were credible. The fact that responsible authorities *believed* that brinkmanship could be effective, and that nuclear superiority was a crutch on which they could rely even to a small extent, is suggestive in itself. Finally, although no one can prove that such threats were effective, there is enough circumstantial evidence that Communist leaders took them seriously to invalidate confident dismissal of the utility of superiority.

There is also evidence, of course, to cast doubt on the efficacy of escalatory threats. U.S. atomic bombs did not deter China from intervening in Korea. When the Chinese acting chief of staff warned the Indian ambassador in Beijing that the People's Liberation Army would intervene if U.S. forces crossed the 38th Parallel, he said, "We know what we are in for. . . . The Americans can bomb us, they can destroy our industries, but they cannot defeat us on land." The ambassador recounted the general's reply when warned of the devastation that bombing might inflict:

> "We have calculated all that," he said. "They may even drop atom bombs on us. What then? They may kill a few million people. Without sacrifice a nation's independence cannot be upheld." He gave some calculations of the effectiveness of atom bombs and said: "After all, China lives on the farms. What can atom bombs do there? Yes, our economic development may be put back. We may have to wait for it" (Panikkar 1955:108).

In 1953, however, Eisenhower attempted to unfreeze the Panmujon negotiations by warning Beijing that unless a settlement were achieved, the United States could not be expected to refrain from using nuclear weapons against China (and nuclear missiles had just been moved to Okinawa). The two-year negotiating stalemate was promptly resolved. Eisenhower's principal assistant claims that the president later was certain that it was the warning that brought the Communists to terms, and Dulles suggested the same in public (Eisenhower 1963: 180–182; Adams 1961:48–49; Wells 1981:34). Subsequently, Dulles was certain that U.S. threats of nuclear retaliation were vital in ending the 1954–55 Taiwan Straits crisis, and nuclear contingency planning was central to the 1958 replay of the dispute (Kahan 1975:21–23). One observer believes nuclear threats were not influential in the first crisis but cites Eisenhower's statements that atomic munitions would be used against military targets in event of general war in Asia, and his later testimony that airfield and support targets had been picked for strikes if the Chinese pressed too hard (Kalicki 1975:84, 149–151). In the 1958 crisis the president and secretary of state indicated to field commanders that the United States was prepared to use nuclear weapons if conventional firepower failed to repel Chinese assaults on Quemoy, and movement of eight-inch nuclear howitzers to the island was expedited (Halperin 1966:112–114, 200). Furthermore, Khrushchev waited until after the crisis de-escalated to deny being frightened by U.S. "atomic blackmail" (Kalicki 1966:112–114, 200).

Nuclear superiority figured in the background of the three crises over Berlin. The least significant case was the 1948 blockade, when Truman dispatched additional B-29 bombers to Europe. It was uncertain that Stalin read this gesture as a nuclear threat, but American leaders saw the nuclear element as a fundamental part of the signal (Millis 1951:453–456, 491). At this time, however, the United States had nuclear monopoly, so the incident offers no direct lessons about the utility of superiority since then.

The next Berlin crisis occurred a decade later, after Khruschev claimed that Soviet ICBM development negated American nuclear superiority. "The Soviet leaders warned the United States that resistance to their demands by military means would mean world war" (Horelick and Rush 1966:121). Yet in a news conference on March 11, 1959, Eisenhower justified cutting the size of the army despite the Berlin crisis by implying that armed conflict in Europe would be nuclear.[6] Khrushchev's gambit failed because "although United States leaders constantly feared that the USSR might soon acquire a substantial ICBM force, at no time did they believe that the potential threat had become actual. Consequently, they . . . relied on the margin of United States superiority in intercontinental weapons (diminishing though they believed it to be) to maintain the West's position in Berlin" (Horelick and Rush 1966:121). In 1960 John Kennedy campaigned against the "missile gap," and Khrushchev renewed pressure on Berlin the following year. By late 1961 the advent of reliable reconnaissance assets had revealed that the USSR had deployed few

ICBMs, and U.S. officials pointedly informed the Soviets of our knowledge and our superior striking power (Ball 1980a:96–98). The third Berlin crisis ebbed early in 1962.

By the logic of simple versions of MAD, the U.S. government's reliance on nuclear superiority in these cases was reckless. The Russians certainly seemed to think so. Soviet analysts "often drew attention to what they regarded as an American lack of recognition of the consequences of Soviet retaliation in any attempted U.S. blitzkrieg by surprise nuclear attack" (Garthoff 1959:81). This point is often dismissed today on both sides of the strategic debate. Some hawks are so diverted by nostalgia for the golden age of U.S. superiority that they overemphasize its extent as well as the confidence that strategists had in actual operational capabilities for damage limitation. Some doves make the same mistake, except to argue that in the 1980s Soviet advantage will not be meaningful because it cannot be as overwhelming as that enjoyed by the United States in the first two cold-war decades.

Conventional wisdom holds that the United States was immune to Soviet attack before the mid-1950s. This may have been true, but certainly not in a worst-case analysis. As early as 1948 the Joint Intelligence Committee estimated that the USSR had 200 TU-4s capable of reaching the United States on one-way missions (which could hardly be written off since some U.S. bombers in the 1950s were programmed for one-way strikes). By late 1950 one government assessment warned that deficiencies in the hastily inaugurated "Lashup" air defense system made it possible that *all* Soviet bombers might penetrate. Testimony deleted from the public record of the 1951 MacArthur hearings cited Soviet capability to deliver severe nuclear damage against U.S. cities. A 1953 Massachusetts Institute of Technology report, *before* Soviet detonation of a hydrogen bomb, calculated that an attack on 100 North American urban areas would kill 19 million people.[7]

Soviet deployment of "real" intercontinental bombers by 1955 heightened concern about vulnerability, especially since U.S. interceptors deployed at that time could not reliably handle jet bombers. In 1957, public estimates by the Federal Civil Defense Administration that a Soviet attack would kill 82 million people were more optimistic than secret Joint Chiefs of Staff studies that, despite improved air defenses, calculated as many as 117 million dead (Jockel 1978:163–165).[8] Even if one assumes U.S. preemption and discounts these estimates by half or more, this could hardly have seemed at the time like a golden age of immunity to unacceptable damage.[9] Nevertheless, Eisenhower continued to rely on the threat of nuclear war to deter Soviet conventional military action.

Kennedy was not so confident, but the compensating buildup of U.S. conventional forces was only getting underway by the time of the 1961 Berlin crisis. In the 1962 Cuban missile crisis, on the other hand, U.S. conventional superiority in the Caribbean was overwhelming. Yet nuclear superiority was relevant in two respects. First, it was probably what provoked the risky Soviet decision to install missiles on the island, as a quick fix to diminish the imbalance.[10] Some maintain that the American advantage was so great that the Soviets feared the United States had a disarming capability, so that this situation in no way reflects the meaning of superiority when both powers had second strike capabilities. This counterargument has some merit, but missiles in Cuba would have been even more vulnerable to preemption than strategic forces in the Soviet interior, so they would not have bolstered second-strike capabilities. Moreover, few decision-makers in Washington really believed in U.S. ability to limit damage to "acceptable" levels. Optimistic assessments may have projected that surviving Soviet weapons would be too few to kill more than a few million Americans, but prudent estimates must have been higher. Even 10 million dead would probably have been "unacceptable damage" to U.S. leaders. McGeorge Bundy (1979:269) maintains that Kennedy believed that mutual nuclear deterrence existed at the time, and that rhetorical emphasis on the value of nuclear superiority was designed to reassure the American public.[11] But if the Soviets had the same view, it is less clear why they put the missiles in Cuba.[12]

The second aspect of nuclear superiority's relevance in the Cuban crisis is conjectural. The threat of deliberate U.S. nuclear escalation may partially explain why the Soviets did not counter the U.S. threat to invade Cuba by threatening Berlin, where *they* had conventional superiority (Nitze 1975:xi). This comparison raises again the question of whether the legitimacy or importance of interests at stake can make "the balance of resolve" independent from the balance of forces. If defenders really are necessarily more willing to escalate, despite risk of suicide—which would explain why Western nuclear threats could credibly protect Berlin—why would the Soviets back down from protecting Cuba in 1962? In both cases the superpowers were dealing with the security of allied territory, not homelands; both territories lay within the geographic sphere of influence of the opposing superpower; and in both cases the defender's legal rights in the territory at issue were unassailable. The comparison is imperfect, but some other element (beyond which side was the aggressor in either case, or which could lay claim to vital or legitimate interests in the disputed territory) must figure in explaining why threats to escalate for Berlin would have been more credible than threats to escalate for Cuba. The nuclear imbalance may be that element.

The last case of tacit nuclear threat was the U.S. worldwide alert during the 1973 Middle East war, to signal the seriousness of opposition to Soviet intervention to prevent destruction of Sadat's army by Israeli forces operating west of the Suez Canal (Kruzel 1977:91–93). This case is interesting because of its ambiguity. First, it occurred at a time of rough nuclear parity (slight net U.S. superiority in principal indices).[13] Second, it is uncertain that the signal "worked"; the Soviets may have refrained because they got what they wanted— halting of the Israeli offensive. According to Mohamed Heikal (1975: 255), "Brezhnev told Boumedienne and Asad that he thought it [the U.S. alert] was all a false alarm resulting from an American desire to overdramatize the crisis. If, he said, it was meant as a warning to the Soviet Union, the message had the wrong address on it." However, in the earlier 1967 war when the Soviets had *not* achieved their minimum aims, Brezhnev had responded to Boumedienne's complaints about Soviet restraint by asking, "What is your opinion of nuclear war?" (Quandt 1976:24).

The first point suggests that the balance of resolve and credibility of nuclear threats may indeed be independent of the balance of forces.[14] This does not contradict my argument in regard to Cuba and Berlin because the United States was no more clearly the defending party than the USSR in the 1973 encounter. The Soviets were not threatening to attack Israel or even to help the Egyptians regain territory conquered by Israel six years earlier. They were considering landing in unoccupied Egypt to separate the contending forces. Tacit nuclear threat may be a wild card, used as a crutch by any power willing to take high risks. Would the United States feel comfortable facing down such a threat by the Soviets in the future, simply because its imprudence made it appear to be a bluff? Analysts may take perverse comfort in the proposition that Soviet behavior is usually more cautious than American behavior. The USSR has seldom engaged in nuclear saber-rattling. One exception was the 1956 Suez crisis. The in-

direct threat in this case, however, was made from a position of nuclear superiority—against Britain and France, when Washington had
dissociated itself from their venture in Egypt (Speier 1957:318-322).[15]

None of these cases proves the coercive potential of nuclear superiority since we have no data on Soviets leaders' judgments in the
crises. The best reason to question the relevance of earlier cases is
that the much greater *absolute* number of survivable weapons on
both sides today may invalidate the applicability of past lessons because it is harder for either to contemplate a war that might leave
much of its society intact. The circumstantial evidence, though, suggests several points whose relevance to the future can be disputed but
not dismissed. First, the possession by one superpower (the USSR) of
second-strike capabilities sufficient to inflict damage at levels unacceptable in comparison to the stakes at issue did not dissuade the
other from relying on its margin of superiority to bolster its position
in crisis by invoking the possibility of initiating nuclear war if disputed territory were attacked by conventional forces. Second, if this
was a bluff, the Soviets never chose to force the issue and allowed the
crises to be settled on terms acceptable to Washington. Third, even in
the case where the balance of forces was least conducive to brinkmanship and the evidence is weakest that tacit nuclear threats affected
Soviet behavior (1973), U.S. leaders acted as though escalatory
threats could help them. In coercive diplomacy it is leaders' beliefs
that matter, not rationality according to detached analyses. If past
leaders risked nuclear threats, future leaders—on either side—might,
too.

Equivalence As a Goal

If superiority matters, why seek equivalence? Most simply, parity is
the only criterion on which political agreement—both internal and
external—can be built. Equivalence (as long as it does not give both
sides a first-strike capability) is a second best acceptable goal to most
contenders. For doves it is wasteful but unobjectionable; for hawks it
is less than ideal but preferable to inferiority. Between the superpowers, equivalence is the only logical basis for negotiating a mutually acceptable balance of forces. Between Washington and Western
European governments, the principle of nuclear equivalence straddles
the tension in alliance goals between extended deterrence based on

threats of first use and stabilization of detente based on reassurance of Moscow. The vague value of parity cushions the implications of scholastic differences over the logic of deterrence, broadening a consensus between governments and within elites on sufficiency and stability.

The question still remains as to why the United States should not seek superiority as long as the Soviet Union retains an advantage in conventional capabilities in Europe. In 1979 Kissinger argued,

> The change in the strategic situation that is produced by our limited vulnerability is more fundamental for the United States than even the total vulnerability would be for the Soviet Union because our strategic doctrine has relied extraordinarily, perhaps exclusively, on our superior strategic power. . . . Therefore, even an equivalence in destructive power, even assured destruction for both sides is a revolution in NATO doctrine as we have known it (1979:266).

Nuclear superiority, however, is not enough. The "limited vulnerability" existed over twenty years ago (and provoked the move toward conventional parity in the 1960s). All that has changed is the *degree* of doubt in extended deterrence. Parity has made the danger of deliberate escalation unmistakable rather than just probable. Helmut Schmidt (1978:3–4; emphasis added) recognized this in 1977:

> SALT codifies the strategic nuclear balance between the Soviet Union and the United States. . . . *SALT neutralizes their strategic nuclear capabilities.* In Europe this magnifies the significance of the disparities between East and West in nuclear tactical and conventional weapons. . . . *[T]he principle of parity.* . . . must be the aim of all arms-limitation and it *must apply to all categories of weapons.* . . . [S]trategic arms limitations confined to United States and the Soviet Union will inevitably impair the security of the West European members of the Alliance if we do not. . . . achieve a conventional equilibrium as well. . . . Today we need to recognize clearly the connection between SALT and MBFR.

Even if Washington managed to reestablish some margin of nuclear superiority it would be a risky crutch on which to rest. Evidence previously mentioned is ambiguous enough to question the supposition that nuclear threats can cover all bets. Fortifying the conventional balance would be a better investment. Nuclear threats may not be appropriate for any contingencies, but they are certainly not appropriate for contingencies beyond direct superpower confrontation (such as the Vietnam War). Eisenhower's massive retaliation doctrine was risky even if it worked in Europe, and re-establishing a nuclear advantage like that in the 1950s and '60s is not feasible. The Soviets' strategic build-up has created a baseline that makes it easier to match U.S. increases with incremental investments of their own. (For some reason a number of hawks who see Soviet leaders as ruthless in the international sphere believe that their domestic room for maneuver is so slight that they could not pay for more military investment by further squeezing civilian investment.) Were U.S. spending unconstrained, the Soviets could indeed be left in the dust. But the massive expenditures necessary to spurt far ahead without weakening other elements of military power are not in the cards unless there is a counterrevolution in domestic policy more ambitious than yet proposed by Reagan. One could argue that because a nuclear build-up would be cheaper than expansion of conventional forces, it is preferable. But the scale of effort (which realistically would have to be bought with reductions in general purpose forces) needed to establish an advantage large enough to give confidence in deliberate first use is tremendous, while the amount of conventional improvement to keep the Soviet conventional edge manageable is less than most assume.[16] Nuclear inferiority is too costly in strategic terms, but superiority is too costly in terms of domestic and alliance politics, budgetary demands, and conventional military power.

Even if equivalence is accepted as a goal, achieving it unilaterally is difficult if the Soviets remain proportionally more willing to sacrifice. Achieving it by negotiation is difficult because both sides have different conceptions of equivalence. A dozen years of SALT negotiations produced tenuous agreement on force levels (though not enough within the U.S. Senate to ratify SALT II) but did not bring Washington and Moscow to agreement on conceptual standards for parity. Indeed, SALT exacerbated the problem by focusing attention on arcane nuances of technical advantage. As long as parity did not exist, both sides seemed more concerned with the vaguely defined principle than with tying up every last thread of a complex balance.

WHAT IS EQUIVALENCE?

One reason the Carter Administration had trouble defending the fairness of the SALT II treaty was that there has never been an explicit U.S. consensus on the criteria for equivalence. Nor was there a consensus between the administration and Moscow. SALT focused on inputs, striking bargains over tradeoffs in elements of asymmetrical force structures, without specifying what the output should be in terms of operational capability. Equality was manifestly defined in terms of numbers of launchers, but only implicitly, at best, in terms of stability, hard-target kill capabilities, assured destruction, or other measures of what the asymmetrical weapon inventories could actually do to the opponent in a war. Ambiguity was not inadvertent. Technical inputs are easier to measure than hypothetical outputs. Both sides' different security concepts and priorities may preclude mutually acceptable clarity in the emergent balance. Similarly, conceptual dissension within the U.S. defense community may block agreement on the desirable operational implications of any nuclear balance. Precision is the enemy of any negotiation. Dean Rusk argued, "Once you involve yourself in a lot of detail, you are dead" (Newhouse 1973:45). If so, equivalence will remain elusive.

Prevalent Definitions and Statistical Combat

There are numerous concepts of parity, several of which I will discuss in ascending order of complexity. Judgment of the simpler formulations depends on one's theological position in traditional debates discussed earlier. Evaluation of more recondite variants is complicated by uncertainties in simulation of wartime force interactions; refined quantitative assessments mask unverified data, assumptions, or interrelationships.

The minimalist definition of strategic parity, advanced by Khrushchev in the late 1950s and accepted by some Western observers, identifies it with mutual second-strike capabilities, irrespective of differences in relative levels of destructive power; mutual assured destruction, even at unequal levels, constitutes parity. This may represent mutual deterrence, but not real equivalence; rather, it serves to discredit the importance of equality in forces.[17]

A trickier definition but still simpler than one based on exchange calculations is the Madison Avenue view. This emphasizes *perceived* advantage based on the simple images of untutored elites. In this argument perceptions depend on a few gross indices of striking power that are easily observable—numbers, size, and apparent modernity of delivery vehicles—which may not necessarily reflect the net capabilities apparent to professionals. Edward Luttwak concludes, therefore, that the Soviet Union won the battle of perceptions by deploying more and bigger ICBMs, whose advantage is not mitigated by the U.S. advantage in bombers because the untutored believe bombers are "old-fashioned" (Luttwak 1977:2, 4–7). This standard suggests that the United States should emphasize heavy ICBMs in its force structure, a change that might not be entirely desirable in terms of some conceptions of strategic stability or doctrinal flexibility. More dovish analysts, however, might use the Madison Avenue approach by emphasizing the American advantage in number of warheads (since the Soviet edge in yield per warhead is less easily appreciated), although this option is disappearing as Soviet proliferation of MIRVs narrows the gap.

There are two problems with a Madison Avenue approach. First, subjectivity of the standard is so compounded that it is impossible to translate it into procurement choices that do not seem surreal to many observers, and hence defeat the purpose of confidence-building. Translation depends on American perceptions of foreign perceptions; flimsiness of data on the latter tend to make the former an exercise in wishful thinking that projects the American perceiver's own instincts into judgment of what foreigners believe. Debate among American strategists would be aggravated rather than assuaged. Second, the notion is intellectually interesting but practically fanciful and strategically irresponsible. Budgetary politics and rational strategy preclude astronomical investments rationalized by public relations criteria that diverge from military logic. It is fine to have a force impressive to foreign leaders who lack serious understanding of nuclear strategy, but only if it is consistent with what impresses the important perceivers who are *not* untutored: the Soviet General Staff and Politburo. Operational effectiveness must be the prime criterion even if it does not coincide with the heftiest image that can be presented to nonspecialists. It is probable anyway that any balance enshrined in a formal treaty, whatever its component characteristics, would appear equivalent to ignorant observers by virtue of the agreement itself, which would carry more symbolic weight than pictorial differences between SS-18s and Minuteman IIIs.

The clearest elements of balance are static indices of destructive capacity: launcher numbers, throwweight, warhead numbers, circular error probable (CEP, a measure of accuracy), and equivalent megatonnage (EMT). Modern reconnaissance can count these with some confidence, and there is little dispute about figures. But the significance of static indices is uncertain when force structures are asymmetrical. The distribution of offsetting advantages that constitutes net equivalence depends on which indices seem most salient, and that depends on assumptions about their compound interaction.

This brings us to the most refined but trickiest level of assessment: dynamic calculations of wartime nuclear exchanges. This requires stipulation of which weapons are directed against which targets, which side strikes first, and variables such as the amount of strategic warning and consequent alert rates, weapon reliability, height of burst, effectiveness of active and passive defenses, scope and timing of attacks, performance of command, control and communications (C^3) systems, and depending on the level of analytic sophistication, factors such as atmospheric conditions. Unlike static force structure these variables are not observable and can only be extrapolated or simulated. This leaves ample room for judgment which can make strategic theories almost self-validating: within a substantial range almost any assessment of the balance can be proved by varying the premises of force interaction, or tilting estimates of system capabilities toward one end of the range of uncertainty. This does not imply intellectual dishonesty; it simply means that the impact of strategic preferences (and different views about how pessimistically uncertain variables should be treated) on appreciation of the strategic balance cannot be overcome by empirical analysis. Statistics become manipulable weapons in the strategic debate. Given the complexity of the factors involved in an exchange that cannot be tested, *any* model is Procrustean. A few examples illustrate the problem.

In 1974 Secretary of Defense Schlesinger presented the U.S. Congress with calculations of limited Soviet counterforce attacks meant to show that effective strikes could be mounted without inflicting massive collateral damage. The calculations indicated 800,000 fatalities (1.6 million total casualties) in a strike against ICBMs, and 300,000 dead (750,000 casualties) in a strike against bomber bases. Therefore, Schlesinger warned, imbalance in capacity for discriminating counterforce strikes could leave the United States vulnerable to "self-deterrence" from retaliation.

The Arms Control and Disarmament Agency (ACDA), however, challenged several assumptions in the Defense Department model (height of burst, wind conditions, fission content of weapons, and population protection), and estimated casualties at up to 50 million

(U.S. Senate Committee on Foreign Relations 1975:13–15, 25–26, 30–33). The Office of Technology Assessment (OTA) conducted another study which concluded fatalities could range up to about 18 million (Drell and von Hippel 1976:35). A later OTA assessment concluded, "The effects of a nuclear war that cannot be calculated are at least as important as those for which calculations are attempted" (U.S. Office of Technology Assessment, n.d.:3).

Another influential collection of calculations has been presented by Paul Nitze since the mid-1970s which project a marked imbalance in forces following a counterforce exchange, giving the Soviet Union escalation dominance in a crisis, Moscow would have more bargaining power since Washington would see only much greater losses as the alternative to accommodation (Nitze 1976, 1976–77). Jan Lodal (1976) rebutted this argument by changing the terms of reference, shifting the focus to from post*exchange* to post*attack* ratios and the impressive U.S. assured-destruction capabilities available after absorption of a Soviet first strike; he challenged the relevance of Nitze's calculations, but not the figures themselves.

Other analysts have challenged the data. Two note that fiscal year (FY)79 Defense Department calculations presented projections through 1987 more favorable to the United States. They also argue: (1) Nitze's data assumes that all U.S. bomber payload is expended against Backfire bases—lower priority targets even if the Backfires were caught on the ground—although official testimony has acknowledged that B-52s would be used against silos as well as other targets; (2) assuming that defenses prevent bombers from attacking silos, Nitze ignores the possibility of corridor-cutting; (3) Nitze's model, contradicting the Defense Department FY79 Annual Report, assumes minimal effectiveness of air-launched cruise missiles (ALCMs) against silos; and (4) since the Soviets normally deploy only four SSBNs near U.S. coasts, the transit of more submarines (to increase the threat to bomber bases) would give Washington time to surge alert and disperse bombers to additional inland bases, yet Nitze's model assumes that 30 percent of alert bombers as well as all those not on day-to-day alert are destroyed (Brewer and Blair 1979:20–22). In another paper Nitze's calculations yield alarming projections, but he assumes ALCM CEP is 300 feet and U.S. ICBMs have identical CEPs in 1977 and 1985 while comparable Soviet CEPs are cut in half during this period (Nitze 1979:25). The figure for ALCMs is higher than some other estimates in open literature, and it is hard to rationalize the lack of change in the U.S. ICBM CEP from 1977 to '85, given the intervening deployment of the new NS-20 guidance system. Nitze's basic conclusions may not be wildly incorrect. Estimates of the accuracy of Soviet SS-18s and SS-19s, revised since Nitze wrote, make the prospects grimmer than at the time of official FY79 projections. But Nitze's conclusions rest on combinations of assumptions about weapon-to-target allocations and system performance that are much more problematic than the apparent sophistication and clarity of his graphs suggest.

A final example of statistical warfare comes from the other side of the spectrum. In 1978 ACDA released a study that supposedly demonstrated a much more even balance of strategic capabilities than suggested by analyses such as Nitze's. ACDA, assuming that differences in Soviet and American target systems were not significant, evaluated effectiveness of both nations' forces against a hypothetical common set of 1,500 hard targets and 5,000 soft targets. The analysis also relied on the tradeoffs necessary to reach an "equal damage point" (EDP) against hard and soft targets (U.S. Arms Control and Disarmament Agency 1978:24–25). But neither abstraction is relevant. The USSR has many more hard targets than the United States, so the ACDA calculations exaggerate U.S. counterforce capabilities. And if the Soviets strike first there is no reason to believe they would seek to destroy as many soft targets as hard ones. Maximizing the butchery of civilians conceivably makes sense for a second strike, but offers no military payoff for the initiator of a nuclear war. (If desired, it could be accomplished in follow-up attacks with reloaded systems.) Stipulating the EDP as a goal, especially when the hypothetical number of soft targets is over three times greater than the hard, understates Soviet counterforce capabilities by draining them away for other missions. Also, the ACDA model apparently assumes that U.S. forces are fully generated and that the soft targets are point rather than area targets, which overrates the U.S. advantage in number of warheads and underrates the Soviet advantage in yield.[18]

Analyses can use similar physical inputs yet produce dissimilar conclusions about the balance because the studies are scenario-dependent, and vast uncertainties about circumstances of engagement govern the scenarios. Analysis can highlight important considerations but cannot transcend fundamental faiths about strategy. By the 1980s the definition of equivalence remained as elusive within the U.S. defense community as between U.S. and Soviet negotiators.

Preferred Definitions

The best simple norm for operational equivalence would be a distribution of forces that embodies no net advantage in either postattack counterforce capabilities or postexchange countervalue reserves. But as long as portions of American and Soviet weapons remain vulnerable, no definition of equivalent force structures can satisfy everyone. Because partial force vulnerability combined with the existence of MIRVs (which offer an exchange ratio favorable to an attacker) creates a "first-strike bonus," hawks like General Daniel Graham can argue that for the Soviets, "parity plus initiative is superiority" ("Documentation" 1977:178). Overcoming this problem would require (1) dismantling vulnerable forces on both sides; or (2) preattack superiority in counterforce capabilities by the nation striking second; or (3) a pre-attack asymmetry of forces capable of destroying hard targets that still did not give the favored side a meaningful advantage for a first strike.

The first solution is analytically ideal but politically fanciful. Massive sunk costs in ICBMs makes it hard for the Soviets to divest, especially when disparity in ASW capabilities favoring the United States makes sea-based elements less secure for them than for us. Were such a solution to free Washington from the huge costs of deploying a survivable ICBM, permitting funds to be rechanneled to air-breathing elements of the triad where U.S. developments are more advanced than the Russians'—or, in the longer term to the D-5 missile which could give the U.S. submarine force invulnerable fast counterforce capability—it could hardly seem equivalent to Moscow. The second solution would be obviously unequal by any "fair" standard—the possibility that *either* side could strike first. It might seem fair to Americans, but it would have to be achieved by unilateral effort in an expensive competition with Soviet deployments unconstrained by formal arms limitation based on capabilities rather than intentions.

The third solution may not be more practical but is worth exploring. It would balance ICBMs with *"time-urgent"* counterforce capability appropriate for preemption against *slow* counterforce systems (bombers and cruise missiles) which are less credibly threatening in terms of first-strike options. The Soviets would be allowed a small edge in the first, the United States a large edge in the second. Both could then capitalize on the force elements in which they have the most institutionalized vested interests and developmental momentum. This would, however, require agreement on limiting terminal air defenses of Soviet ICBM silos. (Defenders of Nitze's anlaysis debunk the significance of a second strike against Soviet silos with ALCMs by arguing that slow flight time precludes catching the missiles in the holes. But if the Soviets have decided to strike first, why would they not be as prepared to launch reserves on short warning of retaliatory ballistic missiles as they would be on longer warning of approaching ALCMs? The only rationale for counterforce targeting for second-strike retaliation is to preclude reloading of silos and retention of reserves. Both goals may just as well be served by slow counterforce.) Moreover, if the United States reduced ICBMs to expand air-breathing forces, it would reduce Soviet counterforce capability by trimming the target base against which ICBMs are uniquely useful.[19] (Massive Soviet throwweight becomes simple overkill if it can only be used effectively against countervalue targets.) Total counterforce capacity would be balanced, yet technical instability would be reduced since U.S. forces would be proportionally less vulnerable to a first strike, and slow counterforce capabilities should logically pose only a retaliatory threat, rather than a preemptive one, to the USSR.

The disadvantage would lie in movement toward a dyad, raising the risks from a technological breakthrough in ASW, air defense, or submarine-launched ballistic missile (SLBM) capabilities against bomber bases. Also, observers have come to more modest conclusions about how effective cruise missiles will actually be against hard targets (Bennett and Foster 1981). The problem for the Soviets is lack of agreement that air-breathing systems lack first-strike potential. Even if they admitted this about ALCMs, they view ground-launched cruise missiles (GLCMs) scheduled to be deployed in Western Europe as more threatening. This brings up the dimension of dispute about equivalence that rarely figures in American analyses but is central in discussions with Moscow: the role of U.S. LRTNF in the strategic balance. The Russians assessed the December 1979 NATO decision to modernize LRTNF with missiles capable of striking the Soviet interior as an attempt to circumvent SALT constraints and reestablish U.S. superiority. The U.S. position that LRTNF are balanced by Soviet SS-20s is rejected because they cannot reach U.S. territory; "equal security" in terms of homeland vulnerability rather than "essential equivalence" in force levels is the Soviet criterion for parity.

The logical U.S. counter is to define equal security in terms of the two collective alliances rather than the superpowers alone, so that Soviet weapons targeted on Western Europe must be compensated by weapons of comparable capability defined in terms of range rather than the countries in which they would land. Moscow would be allowed to counter the Chinese threat with intermediate-range systems in Far Eastern territory, where they could reach neither NATO nor American targets; negotiations on theater nuclear arms control would balance Soviet medium- and intermediate-range weapons capable of reaching Western Europe against U.S. LRTNF and British and French strategic forces. Mobility of the SS-20 raises problems but might be countered by the option to transfer medium-range nuclear-capable aircraft from the United States to Europe. Another problem with this formula is determining how dual-capable aircraft should be counted; the United States has steadfastly resisted incorporating such systems in negotiations. Moreover, NATO allies prefer not to seek full equivalence in LRTNF—which is why the 1979 decision was to deploy fewer than 600 GLCMs and Pershing IIs—for fear of decoupling U.S. intercontinental forces from European defense. Finally, the proposed standard of fairness would legitimize Soviet deployment of nuclear systems in Cuba—which Americans reject out of hand.

There are many other nuances or drawbacks to all these formulae, and many other potential schemes for defining equivalence. This is not the place for a full technical analysis. But definitional clarification, while needed for conceptual progress in the quest for equivalence, may complicate the problem as much as solve it. Perhaps equivalence must remain elusive because the closer we come to it, the more the approach dredges up contradictions underlying U.S. policy, alliance solidarity, and superpower conceptions of security requirements. The problem is further complicated by the growth of sensitivity to dimensions of strategy beyond the distribution of weapons themselves. This is due to the swing since the mid-1970s of U.S. opinion toward concern with flexibility and endurance in employment of nuclear forces for a long war, embodied at the end of the Carter Administration in the countervailing strategy. Richard Burt (1980:39, 51) suggests,

[I]t may become necessary to distinguish between two separate military balances: a *symbolic* balance based on static hardware counts and an *operational* balance reflecting the real capabilities of the two sides to engage in sustained nuclear conflict . . . a policy of reinvigorating American long-range nuclear forces would not be designed to once again attain "strategic superiority" . . . such a capability is beyond the reach of either superpower for the foreseeable future. However, . . . the United States could achieve a new form of nuclear advantage based not so much on static indices of nuclear capability or qualitative advantages in such areas as missile accuracy, but on the relative capacity to manage a nuclear conflict . . . "escalation agility" through preeminence in C³ offers the United States the best opportunity to offset the Soviet Union's crude preference for "escalation dominance."

Considerations such as survivability of C³ are indeed far more important than evening up marginal differences in force structures. Redressing the ICBM vulnerability problem is irrelevant if a decapitating attack could still paralyze the release of strategic retaliation, allowing time for the Soviets to reload and pare down surviving forces in waves of follow-up attacks. It is difficult, however, to conceive a definable or negotiable notion of equivalence in organizational and intelligence capabilities for nuclear war. U.S. debate as well as arms control negotiations have already been overloaded by the difficulties of assessing the balance of weaponry alone. Progress in conceiving and approaching equivalence in the latter dimension bilaterally, though an incomplete resolution, would facilitate unilateral adaptation in other dimensions.

POLICY, NEGOTIATION, AND THE
SCRAMBLE FOR EQUIVALENCE

Achieving nuclear equivalence in the 1980s will be extremely difficult because there is scant evidence that U.S. strategists can converge on a conception that is also acceptable to Mosow. Breakdown of SALT also indictes that parity or inequality will emerge more from competition than from negotiation. President Reagan's deferral of a meaningful basing solution for MX, and lead times for procuring new B-1s, indicate that the United States has to weather a "window" of tenuous parity at best and inferiority at worst until late 1980s. If the Soviets remain unrestrained by SALT or internal resource limitations, or if the U.S. ICBM basing dilemma is not resolved, the window might stay open indefinitely. U.S. disadvantage could be kept to a margin small enough so as not to cause alarm if improvements in conventional and theater nuclear forces reduce the need for extended deterrence. Dovish analysts' indifference to the prospect of limited Soviet superiority in strategic forces—on grounds that persisting U.S. second-strike capabilities render it unusable—is cavalier if the apparent influence of force imbalances in earlier crises is considered, unless parity is confirmed at the other levels of military competition. Hawkish analysts' fixation on negating any nuance of Soviet advantage in nuclear forces, on the other hand, is counterproductive if it exaggerates the problem, undermines confidence, distracts attention from other weaknesses (C^3) that are more dangerous than differences in force levels, or drains investments from conventional forces. Where ambiguities in the balance of nuclear force exist, analytical compromises are the only alternative to political neurosis.

Assessment

If simple assured destruction is the standard for force sufficiency, the analytical problem is easy because equivalence—a relative rather than absolute criterion—is not a requirement.[20] There would be few reasons to worry about either the balance or arms control (of offensive systems) because sufficient survivable forces could be preserved unilaterally irrespective of Soviet numerical superiority. Contrary to what some arms control advocates believe, it is the persistence of concern about asymmetries in counterforce capabilities, not the acceptance of mutual population vulnerability, that makes codification of equivalence through agreements important. But counterforce criteria are more complex and sensitive to uncertainty.

Prudent Soviet planners, like their Western counterparts, give the benefit of the doubt to their adversaries' capabilities and err on the side of caution in evaluating their own. If the Russians published their own assessments of the balance of forces, their graphs might appear more favorable to the United States than estimates such as Nitze's. (In this respect the Soviet penchant for secrecy, often admired by Americans disgusted with the porousness of the classification system in Washington, may have cost them significant debating points since they do not counter the apparent definitiveness of dynamic analyses that "prove" American inferiority.)

American leaders must rely on their own estimates and should demand that if Soviet denials of superiority are to be taken seriously, they be backed up by detailed data that give reason to doubt our own analyses, rather than just references to the few static indices that favor the United States. But two compromises in U.S. standards are reasonable if there is to be any hope of stabilizing equivalence for more than the fleeting moments when curves on the charts cross as cyclical surges and lapses in American investment match the more gradual and consistent pace of Soviet increases. One is to allow that a barely perceptible gap in capabilities reflected in dynamic calculations based on prudent American assumptions of system performance be considered equivalent since comparably prudent Soviet assumptions would make the gap disappear or favor the West. "Roughness" of parity, however, cannot be so broad that the Soviets have an advantage in most static indices, as projections suggest they will into the 1980s. The second compromise would be to reduce the salience of the distinction between time-urgent and total counterforce capability. If we are concerned with U.S. second-strike counterforce rather than preemptive options, it makes little sense to denigrate bombers and cruise missiles.

There should be no concession in discriminating LRTNF from central strategic forces. If the Soviets demand compensation for Western nuclear forces in Europe, it must be measured against their own theater forces. One compromise would be to allow Moscow to choose whichever of two negotiating pots—intercontinental or theater—into which they want to put elements of their forces. The *Backfire,* for example, would be covered in the agreed equivalent balance one way or the other, without forcing the Soviets to accept a worst-case U.S. assessment that the aircraft is an intercontinental bomber, unless they prefer to avoid giving the West better grounds for demanding that the USSR's regional forces be reduced to produce LRTNF equivalence. The two balances would have to be linked in one agreement. Another problem with SALT is that treaties have not been matched by MBFR agreements: nuclear parity subverts extended deterrence but is not balanced by conventional parity. Although this linkage may be infeasible, it is desirable.

Declaratory Policy and Military Doctrine

Official statements emphasizing the strength of U.S. forces may be useful in a crisis, but as long as the United States is an open society they are not a solution to achieving equivalence. Domestic debate is necessary for determining what criteria of balance should inform U.S. strategy and negotiating goals, but it handicaps ability to bargain externally. If the administration must satisfy dovish critics, it is hard to convince the Soviets that anxieties about parity are genuine; when hawkish critics are ascendant, the administration is constrained from accepting a view of equivalence—such as embodied in the SALT II treaty—that is acceptable to Moscow.

Using declaratory policy to clarify operational rationales behind the U.S. definitions of equivalence may help to pressure the Soviets into coming to terms with American anxieties. Rhetorical emphasis on mutual assured destruction, which a majority in the U.S. strategic debate favored ten years ago, exacerbated the latent tension between nuclear parity and NATO solidarity. Clarification of the countervailing strategy, however, coupled with the reasons Washington finds the Soviet throwweight advantage so threatening, might force the USSR either to admit its commitment to damage limitation (thus legitimizing a U.S. focus on dynamic counterforce calculations as a measure of equivalence) or to embrace the principle that weapons effective for preemption should be minimized on both sides (thus legitimizing U.S. schemes to reduce heavy ICBMs, the area of Soviet advantage). Otherwise, continuation of past patterns of negotiation focused on inputs and only marginal chipping away at planned force increases, rather than on outputs in terms of stability in operational options, will yield more of the same outcome—debilitating dissension in the U.S. defense community, and arms control pacts whose basis is ephemeral because force structures evolve faster than bargains can be struck.

Equivalence in any but the vaguest sense is hard to define in a manner that together satisfies such disparate groups as the U.S. defense community, allies, and the USSR. Political and intellectual obstacles are compounded by technological and budgetary ones. Evolution of weaponry makes equivalence a moving target; only a freeze on research, testing, and production would obviate this problem. Sunk investments in existing systems prevent the U.S. or Soviet governments from blithely scrapping major portions of their forces and procuring others just to accord with theoretical notions of stability even if notions could be mutually accepted.

Pure equivalence is a Platonic form which skillful policy can approach by honing down the rough edges of the balance, but the approach will be at best asymptotic and fluctuating. Letting the shifts tilt clearly over a long period toward Soviet advantage raises the danger of the political vulnerabilities suggested by cold war cases discussed previously. Overcoming both that danger and the intractability of definitional ambiguities by striving for recognizable superiority a la 1962, on the other hand, is as unrealistic as reliance on simple assured destruction. Given the commitments necessary to outstrip Soviet capabilities now deployed or deployable, marginal superiority would have to come at the expense of more important refurbishments of conventional forces. Conventional threats are far more immediate than Soviet attempts at nuclear blackmail, as long as the USSR has options at the conventional level and has more nuclear confidence than it did in the first two decades of the cold war. Rather than return to Eisenhower's massive retaliation policy (a golden age of brinkmanship that only seems appealing because we luckily faced Soviet leaders who lacked confidence in their own strategic deterrent) as a solution to guarding Europe or the Persian Gulf, better deterrence or defense could be acquired by allocating the resources to more global mobility, tactical airpower, and ground and naval forces. Nuclear equivalence should be pursued, despite inability to pinpoint it clearly, because it is safer than inferiority and more feasible than superiority. But as long as Washington wishes neither to reduce political commitments nor to continue accepting higher levels of risk, its price is complementary parities at other levels of force.

European allies need to move further toward reliance on conventional defense—a homily, but crucial. Disavowal of extended deterence is still taboo, but the first major movement in this direction—the Kennedy flexible response strategy—took several years of arm-twisting. Domestic pressures in Europe against LRTNF modernization might encourage responsible NATO governments' commitment to conventional options, although the odds will continue to be low. Coupling such a trend with MBFR negotiating initiatives could help to rationalize the commitment in allied eyes and make reasonable agreement on conventional reductions more attractive to Moscow. At the same time diplomacy should make clear that an American compromise in defining nuclear equivalence under SALT or theater nuclear arms limitations will vary inversely with Soviet intransigence in MBFR, so that the East cannot (while retaining a net edge in the overall military balance) guarantee restraint in U.S. investments that threaten ultimately to regain a margin of nuclear advantage.

Progress is also needed though admittedly unlikely in another respect. The superpowers need clearer agreement about the concept of stability expected to emerge from the configuration of forces blessed by a treaty. If they cannot agree on a functional notion of stability that is supposed to be reified in the balance of forces, then perhaps critics are right that the only stability Moscow wants is that which emerges from Soviet preponderance. But agreement would be a two-way street and would require more clarity in the U.S. position, in which admission that nuclear stability neutralizes nuclear threats would further undermine extended deterrence. Our own uncertainties and our allies' preferences stand in the way of stable equivalence as much as the Russians do. Nuclear equivalence has no value in a vacuum, but only in terms of the military calculus as a whole. If contradictions in U.S. strategic thinking and alliance diplomacy cannot be ameliorated, and if NATO allies cannot be spurred to pay for overall equivalence, parity may be a rhetorical sop rather than a real commitment. In that case even genuine Soviet cooperation will make equivalence, as ever, elusive.

NOTES

1. He said the remark was due to "fatigue and exasperation, not analysis" (U.S. Senate Committee on Foreign Relations 1979:169n).
2. Richard Pipes (1977:21) attributed Soviet devotion to nuclear warfighting concepts to belief in Clausewitz's dictum that war is the continuation of policy. Bernard Brodie (1978:72-73) countered with Clausewitz's point that war is meaningless except in pursuit of a political objective worth the price, a possibility foreclosed by the destruction an attacker would suffer in a nuclear exchange.
3. For arguments debunking concern with scenarios, see Waltz (1981: 20-21).
4. The problem varies inversely with the strength of the strikes. If the Soviets maximized effectiveness of a first strike by attacking U.S. C^3 as well as all bases for strategic forces, Washington and some other cities would be destroyed. According to McGeorge Bundy (1979:269), one declassified report said that a U.S. campaign against Soviet military targets, on the other hand, "would put some sixty warheads on Moscow . . . niceties of targeting doctrine do not make the weapons themselves discriminating." Desmond Ball (1980b:169-170) points out that "unlike the US, which has deployed her ICBMs generally in the centre of the country, the Soviet ICBMs extend across virtually

the entire USSR . . . Processing data on some 1,000 to 2,000 warheads and other objects such as penetration aids and booster fragments over this vast region might pose insuperable problems for the Soviet attack assessment system. This is especially the case *vis-a-vis* the three or four ICBM fields in the Moscow area.''

5.   Using an approach and measurements different from mine, one study reaches mixed conclusions on the relationship between nuclear superiority and favorable outcomes from U.S. shows of force. Barry Blechman and Stephen Kaplan (1978:49, 99–101, 128–129) conclude that success in shows of force did not vary directly with the degree of American superiority, and that nuclear saber-rattling was more effective when used to deter enemy actions than when used to compel changes in behavior. The short-term outcomes, nevertheless, were almost all favorable, and frequency of U.S. nuclear threats was greatest in the period of marked superiority.

6.   Eisenhower (1960:244–245, 249, 252) said, "We are certainly not going to fight a ground war in Europe." His comments on strategy were muddled, and he noted the self-defeating consequences of nuclear war. But when a questioner asked, "Does this mean that you are confident that the ground forces as they now exist are capable of handling . . . a brush fire situation that might break out?" he answered, "If we can't, then the war's gotten beyond a brush war, and you have got to think in much, much bigger terms." Secretary of Defense Neil McElroy also reiterated that any significant military conflict at the conventional level would probably lead to general war (Kahan 1975: 17–18). George Quester (1979:160–162) suggests that Eisenhower's confused rhetoric was purposeful, designed to convince the Politburo that he had no understanding of the danger of initiating nuclear war. But there is no evidence that the president's commitment was less firm in secret internal discussions than in public. In one National Security Council meeting as late as October 1960, Eisenhower insisted that in event of war with the USSR, nuclear weapons would have to be used from the outset and without restraint (Kistiakowsky 1976:400).

7.   The vulnerability estimates are drawn from declassified documents cited in Jockel (1978:18, 114, 157) and Wiltz (1975:3633). Ineffectiveness of air defenses was demonstrated by Operation TAILWIND in 1953. See the declassified "Memorandum Op-36C/jm, 18 March 1954," reprinted in *International Security* (1981–82:24).

8.   The FCDA study assumed a third of the Soviet attack was dedicated to military targets, while the JCS study assumed all weapons were targeted on population centers. The JCS study also made very optimistic assumptions about operational limitations on the Soviet attacking force.

9. Some analysts believe U.S. intelligence was so good that a disarming first strike against Soviet forces was possible in this period. Before the 1960s, however, U.S. reconnaissance was not extensive enough to ensure that all forces could be pinpointed, or that U.S. bombers would arrive before Soviet bombers were dispersed or launched. See the declassified 1955 "Briefing of WSEG Report No. 12," reprinted in *International Security* (1981–82:32). Some strategists today tend to forget the widespread sense of vulnerability in the late fifties. Consider the popularity of apocalyptic literature, some of it exaggerated, such as Shute (1957), Miller (1959), and Frank (1960). The latter novel ends a year after nuclear war, as remnants of authority begin to reestablish communication with surviving rural communities. An Air Force officer landing in a Florida town explains, "We're a second class power now. Tertiary would be more accurate. I doubt if we have the population of France—or rather as large as France used to be. . . ." Randy said, 'Paul there's one thing more. Who won the war?'

"Paul put his fists on his hips and his eyes narrowed. 'You're kidding! You mean you really don't know?'

"'No. . . . Nobody's told us.'"

"'We won it. We really clobbered 'em!' Hart's eyes lowered and his arms drooped. He said, 'Not that it matters.'"

"The engine started and Randy turned away to face the thousand-year night" (Frank 1960:278–279).

10. "Mikoyan confirmed this to a closed meeting of Communist ambassadors . . . as recounted later by the Hungarian charge present" (Brzezinski 1972:193).

11. Before the benefit of hindsight, Bundy (1964:355) asserted that all postwar presidents believed that U.S. nuclear superiority was very important (not just for fending off domestic critics) and aimed to preserve it. There is both a curious similarity and disparity in the way that Bundy and one of his successors have claimed that their beliefs while in office did not correspond with their public assertions. Whereas Bundy said later that he did not believe nuclear superiority was meaningful, yet extended deterrence is still viable, Henry Kissinger (1979: 264, 266) claimed that although he articulated this same combination of views while *in* office, neither was true.

12. Khrushchev (Talbott 1979:494) claimed two motives: to deter U.S. military action against Cuba and to equalize "what the West likes to call 'the balance of power.'" The first implies belief in the validity of extended deterrence—the threat to meet conventional attack with nuclear response—which, combined with the second, clearly suggests a belief that U.S. nuclear superiority was important and had to be neutralized.

13. In 1973 the United States had a small advantage in throwweight versus an even smaller Soviet advantage in number of delivery vehicles, and a large superiority in numbers of warheads versus a smaller Soviet edge in equivalent megatonnage (Rumsfeld 1977:20). Superior accuracy and reliability were also generally attributed to the United States in the early 1970s.

14. But Kissinger said later that he would not repeat the action under the conditions of strategic balance in the late 1970s.

15. Anthony Eden's public relations adviser said over twenty years later that the British Prime Minister had "dismissed threats of a Soviet missile attack as 'twaddle'" ("Briton Divulges Steps to '56 Decision to Seize Suez" 1979:6).

16. The Soviet edge in Europe is not overwhelming if one applies the same standards of risk and pessimism to both sides' capabilities. If French forces are counted, for example, the advantage in manpower shifts from the Warsaw Pact to NATO (Blaker and Hamilton 1977).

17. An astute exploration of what balances might yield equal capabilities to inflict casualties is presented by Schilling (1981).

18. Some of these points are made in Committee on the Present Danger (1978:3–4).

19. Even Colin Gray (1977:9) admits this, though he sees other considerations far outweighing the value of the solution.

20. This may not apply to more complex variations in countervalue targeting. Schlesinger's SIOP revision aimed to ensure that the Soviet economy would suffer no less damage and could recover from nuclear war no faster than the American. Quotations from the relevant directive, NSDM-242, can be found in Anderson (1980:C7).

REFERENCES

Adams, Sherman. 1961. *Firsthand Report.* New York: Harper & Row.

Anderson, Jack. 1980. "Not-So-New Nuclear Strategy." *Washington Post* (October 12).

Ball, Desmond. 1980a. *Politics and Force Levels: The Strategic Missile Program of the Kennedy Administration.* Berkeley: University of California Press.

_____. 1980b. "Soviet ICBM Deployment." *Survival* 22, no. 4 (July/August).

_____. 1981. "Counterforce Targeting: How New? How Viable?" *Arms Control Today* 11, no. 2 (February).

Bennett, Bruce, and James Foster. 1981. "Strategic Retaliation Against the Soviet Homeland." In *Cruise Missiles: Technology, Strategy, Politics,* edited by Richard K. Betts. Washington, D.C.: Brookings Institution.

Betts, Richard K. 1979. "Nuclear Peace: Mythology and Futurology." *Journal of Strategic Studies* 2, no. 1 (May).

Blaker, James, and Andrew Hamilton. 1977. *Assessing the NATO/Warsaw Pact Military Balance.* Washington, D.C.: Congressional Budget Office (December).

Blechman, Barry M., and Stephen S. Kaplan. 1978. *Force Without War: U.S. Armed Forces as a Political Instrument.* Washington, D.C.: Brookings Institution.

Brewer, Gary D., and Bruce G. Blair. 1979. "War Games and National Security With a Grain of SALT." *Bulletin of the Atomic Scientists* 35, no. 6 (June).

"Briefing of WSEG Report No. 12." 1981–82. *International Security* 6, no. 3 (Winter).

"Briton Divulges Steps to '56 Decision to Seize Suez." 1979. *New York Times* (November 25):6.

Brodie, Bernard. 1978. "The Development of Nuclear Strategy." *International Security* 2, no. 4 (Spring).

Brzezinski, Zbigniew. 1972. "How The Cold War Was Played." *Foreign Affairs* 51, no. 1 (October).

Bundy, McGeorge. 1964. "The Presidency and the Peace." *Foreign Affairs* 42, no. 3 (April).

_____. 1979. "The Future of Strategic Deterrence." *Survival* 21, no. 6 (November/December).

Burt, Richard. 1980. "Reassessing the Strategic Balance." *International Security,* 5, no. 1 (Summer).

Committee on the Present Danger. 1978. "An Evaluation of 'U.S. and Soviet Strategic Capability through the Mid-1980s: A Comparative Analysis.'" Press release, Washington, D.C., September.

"Documentation." 1977. *International Security* 2, no. 2 (Fall).

Drell, Sidney D., and Frank von Hippel. 1976. "Limited Nuclear War." *Scientific American* 235, no. 5 (November).

Eisenhower, Dwight D. 1960. *Public Papers of the Presidents of the United States: Dwight D. Eisenhower, 1959.* Washington, D.C.: U.S. Government Printing Office.

_____. 1963. *The White House Years,* vol. 1: *Mandate for Change: 1953–1956.* Garden City, N.J.: Doubleday.

Frank, Pat. 1960. *Alas, Babylon.* New York: Bantam.

Futrell, Frank. 1971. *Ideas, Concepts, Doctrine: A History of Basic Think-*

ing in the United States Air Force, 1907–1964. Maxwell AFB: Air University Aerospace Studies Institute (June). 2 vols.

Garthoff, Raymond. 1959. *The Soviet Image of Future War.* Washington, D.C.: Public Affairs Press.

Halperin, M.H. 1966 (portions declassified March 1975). *The 1958 Taiwan Straits Crisis: A Documented History (U),* RM-4900-ISA. Santa Monica: Rand Corporation.

Heikal, Mohammed. 1975. *The Road to Ramadan.* New York: Quadrangle.

Horelick, Arnold L., and Myron Rush. 1966. *Strategic Power and Soviet Foreign Policy.* Chicago: University of Chicago Press.

Jervis, Robert. 1979–80. "Why Nuclear Superiority Doesn't Matter." *Political Science Quarterly* 94, no. 4 (Winter).

Jockel, Joseph T. 1978. "The United States and Canadian Efforts at Continental Air Defense, 1945–1957." Ph.D. dissertation, Johns Hopkins University.

Kahan, Jerome H. 1975. *Security in the Nuclear Age.* Washington, D.C.: Brookings Institution.

Kalicki, J.H. 1975. *The Pattern of Sino-American Crises: Political-Military Interactions in the 1950s.* New York: Cambridge University Press.

Kissinger, Henry A. 1974. "Secretary Kissinger's News Conference at Brussels and Moscow." *Department of State Bulletin* 71, no. 1831 (July 29).

———. 1979. "NATO: the Next Thirty Years." *Survival* 21, no. 6 (November/December).

Kistiakowsky, George B. 1976. *A Scientist at the White House: The Private Diary of President Eisenhower's Special Assistant for Science and Technology.* Cambridge: Harvard University Press.

Kruzel, Joseph J. 1977. "Military Alerts and Diplomatic Signals." In *The Limits of Military Intervention,* edited by Ellen Stern. Beverly Hills: Sage.

Lodal, Jan. 1976. "Assuring Strategic Stability: An Alternative View." *Foreign Affairs* 54, no. 3 (April).

Luttwak, Edward N. 1977. "Perceptions of Military Force and US Defence Policy." *Survival* 19, no. 1 (January/February).

"Memorandum Op-36Cjm, 18 March 1954." 1981–82. *International Security* 6, no. 3 (Winter).

Miller, Walter M., Jr. 1959. *A Canticle for Leibowitz.* New York: Lippincott.

Millis, Walter M., ed., with collaboration of E.S. Duffield. 1951. *The Forrestal Diaries.* New York: Viking.

Newhouse, John. 1973. *Cold Dawn: The Story of SALT.* New York: Holt, Rinehart and Winston.

Nitze, Paul H. 1975. "Foreword: Vladivostok and Crisis Stability." In *Arms Treaties With Moscow: Unequal Terms Unevenly Applied?,* edited by Donald Brennan. Agenda Paper No. 3. New York: National Strategy Information Center.

_____. 1976. "Assuring Strategic Stability in an Era of Detente." *Foreign Affairs* 54, no. 2 (January).

_____. 1976-77. "Detering Our Deterrent." *Foreign Policy* no. 25 (Winter).

_____. 1979. "Current SALT II Negotiating Posture." Unpublished paper.

Panikkar, K.M. 1955. *In Two Chinas: Memoirs of a Diplomat.* London: Allen & Unwin.

Pipes, Richard. 1977. "Why the Soviet Union Thinks It Could Fight and Win a Nuclear War." *Commentary* 64, no. 1 (July).

Quandt, William. 1976. *Soviet Policy in the October 1973 War,* R-1846-ISA. Santa Monica: Rand Corporation.

Quester, George. 1979. "Was Eisenhower a Genius?" *International Security* 4, no. 2 (Fall).

Rowen, Henry S. 1975. "Formulating Strategic Doctrine." In *Appendices,* vol. 4, U.S. Commission on the Organization of the Government for the Conduct of Foreign Policy. Washington, D.C.: U.S. Government Printing Office.

Rumsfeld, Donald H. 1977. *Annual Defense Department Report FY 1978.* Washington, D.C.: Department of Defense.

Schilling, Warner R. 1981. "U.S. Strategic Nuclear Concepts in the 1970s: The Search for Sufficiently Equivalent Countervailing Parity." *International Security* 6, no. 2 (Fall).

Schmidt, Helmut. 1978. "The 1977 Alastair Buchan Memorial Lecture." *Survival* 20, no. 1 (January/February).

Shute, Nevil. 1957. *On the Beach.* New York: Morrow.

Speier, Hans. 1957. "Soviet Atomic Blackmail and the North Atlantic Alliance." *World Politics* 9, no. 3 (April).

Talbott, Strobe, ed. and trans. 1970. *Khrushchev Remembers,* vol. 1, Boston: Little, Brown.

Thomas, John R. 1962. "Soviet Behavior in the Quemoy Crisis of 1958." *Orbis* 6, no. 1 (Spring).

U.S. Office of Technology Assessment. n.d. *The Effects of Nuclear War.* Washington, D.C.: OTA.

U.S. Senate Committee on Foreign Relations. 1975. *Hearing, Briefing on Counterforce Attacks.* 93rd Cong., 2d sess.

_____. 1979. *Hearings, The SALT II Treaty.* 96th Cong., 1st. sess., Part 3.

Waltz, Kenneth N. 1981. *The Spread of Nuclear Weapons: More May Be Better,* Adelphi Paper No. 171. London: International Institute for Strategic Studies.

Wells, Samuel F., Jr. 1981. "The Origins of Massive Retaliation." *Political Science Quarterly* 96, no. 1 (Spring).

Wiltz, John. 1975. "The MacArthur Inquiry, 1951." In *Congress Investigates: A Documental History 1792-1974,* edited by Arthur Schlesinger, Jr. and Roger Bruns. New York: Chelsea House.

4 FOREIGN POLICY AND NUCLEAR WEAPONS: THE CASE FOR STRATEGIC DEFENSES

Stephen Peter Rosen

Before they possessed nuclear weapons, nations understood that shifts in foreign policy had to be accompanied by changes in the military strategy and force structure that would be called on to support that new policy. But no real discussion of nuclear doctrine accompanied the debate over the strategic arms limitation treaty, SALT II. The relationship between foreign policy and military strategy was totally ignored in favor of abstract discussions of "stability" and technical arguments over the Minuteman missile's vulnerability and the Backfire bomber's range. These questions were important, but as Michael Howard (1979) has pointed out, the United States has acted as if those were the only questions. In particular, American thinking about nuclear war has been dominated by a concern for stability and the ways in which new technologies or deployments could make war more or less likely. The nuclear balance had been stable, it was argued, and thirty-five years of peace had been the result, but arms races or strategic defenses could initiate war. The effort to reduce the damage that would be done by a nuclear war would make war more likely because it would reduce deterrence and hence threaten stability.

With our thinking about nuclear war paralyzed in this way, we have arrived at an excessively narrow and distorted view of the causes of war and peace. The balance of military power is obviously important, but within certain broad limits, war is now—as it was in the prenuclear age—the result of forceful, opposing national interests, and not simply the product of strategic instability. If the political objectives or policies of states shift so as to bring them into direct opposition, war is more likely even if the military balance remains stable. Conversely, strategic instability need not cause war if there is mutual political satisfaction among competing states.

Although there have been at least three periods of great strategic instability among nuclear powers since 1945, no war has resulted because there have been no grave political conflicts between the superpowers since the death of Stalin. Peace was not the result of "stability" but of the absence of large political conflict. Unfortunately, this is no longer the case. Current political factors make war more likely, and there is a need for a new strategic policy to deal with this danger. Specifically, the United States requires strategic defenses that will make nuclear war less terrible if it should come. Such measures have previously been rejected because they were thought to be destabilizing, but technical stability is only one part of the problem of peace and war. By overemphasizing technical stability, the United States has ignored the political aspects of nuclear war and peace, and has denied itself military means of protection. Technological means are now available to put active and passive defenses into operation.

THE HISTORY OF ARMS RACES

A long history lies behind the idea that arms races are destabilizing, that weapons gaps are destabilizing, and that either could lead to war. Yet when one looks over the period during which technology has made significant races or gaps possible, it is difficult to find even one war caused by instability. Arms races have certainly exacerbated international tensions, though they were always themselves the product of existing political tension. Technology has enabled states that had decided on wars to win them, and calculations of military balances have always entered into the decision to go to war. But what war was caused by instability that would not otherwise have occurred? The Napoleonic Wars? The American Civil War? Samuel Huntington (1958) has systematically studied the dynamics of twelve great-power arms races. Six end in peace. Three are terminated by World War II, but no one could claim that they were even a minor cause of the war with Hitler. Three end in World War I, and, in general, when it is argued that military instability can cause wars, the reference is to 1914. Military instability itself is the condition in which a government has a military incentive either to get in the first blow or to go to war immediately no matter who strikes the first blow. The first condition may be thought of as tactical instability, in which a first strike is crucial for victory; the second, as strategic instability, in which preventive war is the means to utilize a temporarily favorable overall military balance.

In what sense might instability have caused World War I? Technological competition in three areas might have done so. First, there was the naval armaments race between England and Germany. That race ended in an English victory in 1912, when the Germans gave up the effort to build a Dreadnaught fleet that could defeat the British. True, that race made relations between the two countries more tense, but that tension had a deeper political cause. England had sought closer relations with Germany since 1900. Each time, talks broke down because the price demanded by the Germans for their friendship was a free hand against France (Grenville 1964). England was to remain neutral in a war involving Germany, no matter how it started. No British government could accept this. In any case, there was no short- or long-term naval incentive for Germany to go to war in 1914 (Grey 1925:42).

Second, there was a military competition between Germany and Russia. German military superiority existed in 1914, but that "window of opportunity" was being shut by Russian military development. The German general staff certainly worried about that development. As Gerhard Ritter has pointed out, the largest window of opportunity open to the Germans was the result of the Russian military defeats and internal revolution in 1905. Yet Ritter found absolutely no sign that the architect of Germany's strategic plans, General Schlieffen, advocated a preventive war against Russia that would utilize this open window. Nor did Schlieffen's final memorandum, written in 1912, exhibit any anxiety about windows closing because of Russian military development (Ritter 1958).

Finally, it is argued that the plans for mobilizing armies in Europe, necessary because of the state of transportation technology, made first strikes decisive. Once one country mobilized, all would have to mobilize. Once mobilization began, the first side to finish mobilization and to strike would win. This ignores the fact that Austria and Russia did carry out partial mobilizations in 1912 without setting off general European mobilization (Albertini 1952:433). More important, it ignores the fact that from 1871 until 1900, Germany intended to mobilize the West but not to launch any large offensive. The elder Moltke wanted to fight a strategically defensive war against France. Mobilization and attack were not synonymous. They were only made so by the overconfidence of the new generation of German military men, who were intent on the total destruction of the French army. It was this ambition, not "instability," that linked mobilization and first strikes (Ritter 1958:18–20, 47).

But surely nuclear weapons created a world in which military-technological stability was much more important. This proposition rests on two claims: (1) that nuclear weapons and missile developments made possible sudden revolutionary changes in the balance of power that could destabilize the relationship between the superpowers and create incentives for war; (2) that the absence of war has been due to a stable balance of nuclear offensive power.

There is some truth to the conventional wisdom, but only some. The first claim is weakened by the fact that in the real world, friction slows down the process by which technical revolutions are turned into usable military equipment. This gives the opposing side time to adjust and makes it much less likely that it will go to war immediately to forestall its emerging inferiority. This is true of the initial nuclear revolution. We tend to think that the 1945 explosions were immediately followed by a Strategic Air Command springing full grown from the brow of Air Force General Curtis LeMay, but this was not the case.

Seven years after Hiroshima, the United States had 400 atomic bombs (Rosenberg 1979:65, 68). The net effect of the nuclear revolution was that by 1952 the United States was able to do in several weeks what had previously taken several months. The nuclear revolution was a real one, but it took many years to make a revolution within the operational capability of the American Air Force.

A revolutionary weapon requires the creation of a totally new industry. By definition, it makes older competing weapons obsolete. (Compare rapid-fire and single-shot rifles, aircraft carriers and battleships, jet-engined and piston-engined fighter aircraft.) However, it takes time to create this industry, build the new weapons, and phase out the old ones. Soviet intercontinental ballistic missiles (ICBMs) were first tested in 1957, but it was not until 1964 or so that any appreciable numbers of usable ICBMs were deployed in the Soviet Union. Work was begun on American multiple independently targetable reenty vehicles (MIRVs) in the early 1960s, but it was ten years before the United States had even a limited number in the field. This lag gives nations time to adjust, to develop their own capabilities. The now-or-never pressure to declare war does not develop.

The second claim, that peace has been the result of nuclear strategic stability, is not supported by historical experience. The world has passed through at least three periods of significant nuclear instability, without war. Nuclear instability exists when one country has the military incentive to launch a nuclear strike that will largely disarm its opponent. Instability is greatest when the incentive to launch first strike or to start a preemptive war becomes significant, which occurs when an enemy first acquires nuclear weapons. It recurs when the country begins to develop relatively invulnerable nuclear weapons and so begins to "close the window" of strategic opportunity. Such a moment first occurred in 1949, when the Soviet Union first detonated a nuclear weapon. Yet, despite calls from some scientists like Bertrand Russell, the United States did not launch a disarming first strike. This was a wise decision, but peace cannot be said to have been the result of nuclear stability, since stability did not exist.

The incentive to preempt recurred in the early 1960s. It is now generally known that in 1962 the United States had an impressive disarming capability compared to the Soviet Union. In particular, the only operational system capable of striking any large number of American targets was the Soviet submarine missile force. Soviet ICBMs were stored above ground, were not kept on alert, and were very vulnerable to American attack. So were the Soviet submarines, as the Soviets and Americans both found out during the Cuban missile crisis when the American Navy located the Soviet submarines operating off the U.S. coast and forced them to the surface where a close, armed guard could be kept on them. At the same time, the Soviet Union was in the process of designing and procuring systems that would not be so readily vulnerable to the U.S. military. The United States faced a now-or-never chance to go to war. Rather than doing so, high American defense officials applauded the emergence of secure Soviet second-strike forces. The world would be safer, they argued, when the United States could not preempt the Soviet Union. The closing window did not produce a war. While one can argue that American nuclear superiority kept the peace in the period of 1949 to 1969, it is impossible to maintain that peace was the result of stability.

Although the United States has not attempted to strike first, had positions been reversed, the Soviet Union might well have exploited its real but fleeting advantage. Its behavior toward China, however, indicates that its decisions to go to war are not driven by the presence or absence of this kind of stability. The third moment of instability occurred between the Soviets and the Chinese as the Chinese developed nuclear weapons. The facilities for the production of those weapons, and the weapons themselves, were vulnerable and became more so as the Soviet strategic force expanded. It is likely that the Soviet leaders thought seriously about preemption since they do differ from Americans in some crucial respects; yet they held back. Again, it is possible to imagine why they did not and to approve of their decision. But it is not possible to say that stability was responsible for peace.

Nuclear superiority may or may not be useful, but on balance it is better to have it than to face it. The argument here is simply that there is clear historical evidence that nuclear instability, of the kind that would be created by certain kinds of weapons systems, has existed and has not led inexorably to war.

Then why should we worry about nuclear war at all if instability has been so inconsequential? The answer: political factors produced peace for a generation, and political factors can make war possible now. War was not likely between 1950 and 1975 because each superpower had primary influence in the areas of the world most important to it, with no real desire to detach parts of the other's sphere of influence or control. This is no longer the case. The danger of a direct confrontation and war is greater, and so is the need for a strategy to reduce the damage done by that war. War will not become more likely because of the character of the two opposing nuclear forces, but the character of those forces will have considerable influence on how terrible the war may be.

THE SUPERPOWERS

The striking characteristic about the major source of tension between the United States and the Soviet Union from 1953 to 1961—the status of West Berlin—was the essential compatibility of American and Soviet interests in that area. The diplomacy, and more important, the military preparations that the Soviet Union did not, in fact, make, demonstrate that Soviet leaders did not believe that war was likely. The reason was clear. Dean Rusk and the American leadership were reluctantly willing to see the border between East and West Berlin sealed, ending the drain of Germans that threatened the viability of the Communist regime (Schick 1971). This is what the Soviets cared about, and this, the Americans were willing to give them.

If it is true that peace was the result of both superpowers' accepting each other's zone of influence, why did war not erupt when the American sphere of interest and influence was challenged by Krushchev in 1962? The right and left wings in America have come up with two opposing explanations of the outcome of the Cuban missile crisis. The right has argued that American nuclear supremacy, the ability to inflict far more damage on the Soviet Union than it could on the United States, forced Khrushchev to retreat and comply with U.S. demands. The left has interpreted the event quite differently. Khrushchev introduced missiles into Cuba, but both sides backed down in the crunch because of the fear of nuclear war. As Michael Mandelbaum (1979:142, 145, 147) put it, "Neither side dictated terms to the other. . . . this was the lesson of the missile crisis. The leaders of both countries acted on the presumption that a wide range of provocations might start a war between them, . . . and that it was therefore incumbent on them to avoid starting a war of any kind." Khrushchev withdrew the missiles, but "Kennedy understood from the beginning that he would have to pay a price to get what he wanted." The fear of escalation to a nuclear war forced Kennedy, as well as Khrushchev, to back down and to promise that the United States would not attack the Castro regime. Mandelbaum continues: "Kennedy made another concession. He agreed to dismantle the Jupiter missiles that the United States had stationed in Turkey."

The latter is a curious reading of history. At the time, most people realized that the American "concession" in Turkey was no concession at all. Kennedy dispatched the missile-carrying submarine, the *Sam Houston,* to Turkey in 1963 for no other reason than to show that we would base offensive missiles in Turkey if we chose to. The Soviet Union certainly did not seem happy with the compromise. Soviet First Deputy Foreign Minister Vaily Kuznetsov, negotiating the details, remarked to John J. McCloy, one of the U.S. representatives to the United Nations, "You Americans will never be able to do this to us again!" (Bohlen 1973:495–496).

Finally, the 1973 nuclear alert arising out of the Yom Kippur War is an example of how the superpowers carefully avoided threats to each other's sphere of interests. The resupply effort begun by the Soviet Union and later more than matched by the United States was no threat to the vital interests of either side. Two days after the Soviet resupply began, Kissinger commented that "if you compare their conduct in this crisis to their conduct in 1967, one has to say that Soviet behavior has been less provocative, less incendiary, and less geared to military threats than in the previous crisis" (Jabber and Kolkowicz 1979). When the Soviet Union did resort to military threat, it was to prevent the complete destruction of the Egyptian Third Army by the Israelis, an objective with which Kissinger was in complete sympathy, no matter how much he deplored the form of the Soviet diplomatic action. The "crisis" was resolved in a matter of hours because there was an obvious coincidence of American and Soviet interests, not because of the spectre of nuclear war.

Since the 1950s, challenges to each superpower's interests seldom have occurred, and when they have, it was quickly made clear that the challenger would lose the diplomatic contest because interference would be met with all means necessary. The pretexts and opportunities for fishing in troubled waters are always available. Yet there have been no superpower wars, partly as a result of Soviet inability to project power into the Western zones of influence, but mostly because steady military and diplomatic action made clear what the consequences of interference would be.

THE SITUATION TODAY

These safeguards no longer exist today. As U.S. Secretary of Defense Harold Brown pointed out in his 1979 posture statement, the inability of the United States to contain the Soviet Union militarily in Europe and in the Third World simultaneously was not a practical problem until recently, since the Soviet Union did not have the wherewithal to challenge the United States simultaneously in two areas. Now they do. More important, direct conflict between the superpowers is possible because there now exist areas important to both that are not clearly in one zone or the other and because it is by no means obvious what the consequences of intervention would be. The West's interest in the Persian Gulf is obvious, and the Soviet action in Afghanistan demonstrates that they, too, have a strong interest in that part of the world, for a number of reasons. After all, Russia was granted a zone of influence in northern Iran in 1907, and the Soviet Union occupied parts of Iran during the Second World War.

Wars did not start in these contested parts of the world, partly because of American nuclear strength, but more because of its clear and credible willingness to go to war. It should be recalled that Anglo-American pressure forced the evacuation of Soviet troops in northern Iran in 1946 at a time when America's strategic nuclear forces, for all practical purposes, were nonexistent and its conventional land capabilities in Iran were dwarfed by those of the Soviet Union. Can it be argued by anyone that Soviet leaders now understand that we would definitely go to war if they invaded northern Iran on some suitable pretext? Adviser-without-portfolio Marshall Shulman notes that as the American government observed the progressive build-up of Soviet forces on the Afghan border, it repeatedly warned the Soviet government not to intervene, with the observed results.

The peculiar problem facing the United States today involves reestablishing the policy of containment. Both the line around its spheres of interest and its willingness to fight to preserve those spheres have eroded over the last ten years. As a result, the Soviet Union may miscalculate and challenge the United States in an area where it expects no American response. The United States, however, may well feel compelled to respond.

This is the danger that makes a new nuclear strategy necessary. A doctrine making it abundantly visible that the United States is taking seriously the problems of limiting the damage resulting from a nuclear war would demonstrate to the Soviet Union that the United States would in fact take all steps necessary to stop Soviet advances. The present doctrinal confusion does not communicate any resolve to prevent war by communicating resolve. Equally useless is the doctrine that deliberately carries with it the risk of American nuclear suicide in the event of a general war. A doctrine of damage limitation would reduce the suffering if deterrence failed. Given the reality of political conditions today, the United States must not allow its nuclear strategy to be dominated by the problem of military instability. The concept of stability has been so enshrined that any measures to reduce the number of civilian deaths in a war is rejected out of hand.

Just how pernicious this fixation can be is shown by the current debate over urban evacuation as a means to limit fatalities in a nuclear war. There is serious disagreement about how quickly evacuations can be carried out and exactly how many lives it could save. The critics of evacuation within the U.S. Arms Control and Disarmament Agency agree, however, that 40 to 50 million American lives could be saved by the evacuation of American cities. The agency's objection was that reducing American casualties would make war more likely. Chief SALT negotiator Paul Warnke testified before a congressional committee that whereas "neither side could give serious consideration to initiating a strategic war," now because of the existing, stable balance, various measures that reduced the casualties one side would suffer could destabilize the balance. "If it were possible for either side to protect its people, its facilities, and its industry—whether by antiballistic missile systems and air defense or by sheltering its population or evacuating it, and hardening and dispersing the industry— *then adequate deterrence would no longer exist*" (Warnke 1979:4–5; emphasis added). Informed with this same understanding of stability, the analysts of Congress' Joint Committee on Defense Production developed scenarios to show how Soviet evacuation would invite an American first strike. Three options were involved:

1. Launch a nuclear attack while the crisis is escalating but prior to victim's directive to execute civil and industrial defense measures.
2. Launch a nuclear attack immediately upon notice that the intended victim has directed implementation of civil and industrial defense measures.
3. De-escalate the crisis, appear to give ground, and launch the nuclear attack as soon as the intended victim showed signs of relaxing any alert measures (Joint Committee on Defense Production 1977:4–5).

Nobody who had not immersed himself in the abstract logic of strategic stability to the exclusion of everything else could dream that an American or Soviet leader would contemplate these "three simple options" or that evacuation created a real danger of a preemptive war. What leaders could initiate a nuclear war because enemy civilians were leaving their cities, when even with adequate defenses of their own, they would suffer millions of dead in return?

Similarly, the deployment of ballistic missile defenses (BMDs) to shoot down attacking reentry vehicles (RVs) has been the cause of much concern. It is not reasonable on the basis of historical experience, to argue that either superpower would launch a first strike in cold blood to prevent the completion of an enemy antiballistic missile (ABM) system. Certainly, the superpowers would respond diplomatically, as the Soviets did in 1969 when the United States began to build an ABM system that promised to be far superior to their own. The Soviets also began making military preparations of their own.

If strategic defenses are not ruled out by international factors, are they realistic in terms of domestic politics? The lesson usually drawn from the civil defense efforts of the early 1960s is that Americans were very reluctant to accept war preparations that intruded directly into their personal lives. Mandelbaum writes in the 1961 Berlin crisis, "The American people, by failing to support civil defense, were, in effect, 'voting with their feet'—against nuclear war" (Mandelbaum 1979:123–124).

It is difficult to imagine anybody's voting for nuclear war with anything, but that is not the same thing as voting against defenses if war is thought likely. Mandelbaum points out that the July 1961 speech given by Kennedy raised the possibility of war and the need for civil defense. The reaction was not indifference toward or rejection of civil defense. On the contrary, Kennedy aide Theodore Sorenson, remembering that period, was worried that people had become altogether too interested in civil defense. The American people, he recalled, "got out of hand. People were talking about barring their neighbors from their shelters, do-it-yourself shelter kits were being sold and all kinds of articles speculat[ed] about how many or how few lives would be saved" (Mandelbaum 1979:122).

Public interest in civil defense should not be surprising. By and large, people will be willing to do all kinds of things to avoid being killed if they believe in the danger. In 1964 it was possible to remember a superpower crisis, and so support for civil defense was large. During the intervening years, the perceived danger of nuclear war declined, and with it went public support for civil defense measures like city evacuation. A 1979 survey of local civil defense organizations uncovered one predictable fact: the cities and states that regularly faced natural catastrophies took seriously the problem of evacuation and were reasonably good at it. The director of the Texas Department of Public Safety looked back on his experiences and concluded that "given a reasonable perception of a large-scale threat to their lives, people have reacted rationally in the past and have evacuated to areas of lower risk. We have no reason to believe that they would not do so in the event of a threat of nuclear attack, if they were properly informed and instructed on where to go and what to do" (Senate Committee on Banking, Housing, and Urban Affairs 1979:173–174).

There is, of course, one major domestic political obstacle to civil defense. Arms control and more costly national defense policies seem to be politically incompatible. In particular, it seems to be hard to convince people that there is a real danger that the United States will be at war with the Soviet Union and that Americans must be prepared but simultaneously should maintain a diplomatic and economic friendship with that nation. Logically, these ideas are not mutually exclusive; in terms of practical politics, they probably are.

Then would a system of BMD to protect cities be more feasible politically? The narrow margin by which funds for the Safeguard ABM system were passed in the Senate in 1969 suggests that political support was very thin even for a less ambitious ABM system. Safeguard was to defend Minuteman silos, a task with much less stringent technical criteria for success. Silos were "hard," unlike buildings, so attacking warheads could be allowed to get closer to the ground before being shot down. More important, the ABM system had only to assure that roughly one-third of the silos survived. That would leave the United States with enough missiles to destroy many Soviet cities. While an ABM system that saved only one-third of our cities would have accomplished something, it would also have left a great deal undone. This modest system was tepidly received even by hawks in the Congress. Senator Henry Jackson opposed an ABM site for his state of Washington; U.S. House Armed Services Committee Chairman Mendell Rivers wanted to cut the funding of the Safeguard in order to give more money to the Navy (Kissinger 1979). Why should a far more ambitious and expensive ABM system be politically feasible today?

One obvious reason is that the Safeguard system was the first American ABM system ever built, and like all first generation weapons systems, it had many problems. The larger question of reliability aside, there were flaws in the system that made it possible for a clever attacker to defeat Safeguard at a reasonable cost to himself. These flaws made it difficult for those otherwise sympathetic to the idea of active defenses to support wholeheartedly the expenditure of billions of dollars for Safeguard. We shall return to this subject, but for now it is enough to say that ten years of American work has solved many of the technical problems. With existing technology and without any exotic equipment like lasers or particle beams, it now seems possible to build an ABM system that, though not perfect, can shoot down large numbers of warheads. Moreover, additional defensive interceptors could be added to an updated ABM system more cheaply than additional offensive warheads could.

Second, the general political attitude toward defense spending is far away from what it was in 1969. All military spending was under attack in 1969 and 1970. A victim of this pressure, the defense budget underwent several years of real reductions. The *Washington Post* noted in 1970 that the long ABM debate had obscured a widespread assault on all kinds of military activities on Capitol Hill. Today the climate has changed. Congress added to the administration's defense budget in 1980, not subtracted from it. The political community that sees little need for increased defense spending still exists, but its attacks on various defense budgets no longer have the general political resonance that they did even five years ago.

This points to the third reason why BMD may be possible to fund. The threat that Safeguard was created to meet did not exist in 1969. Minuteman silos were not yet vulnerable, and there was no immediate prospect for a direct clash of Soviet and American arms. Those seemingly distant threats are now on top of us. The saving grace is that now, at least, the strategic need to limit damage to the United States in the event of war is a politically salient argument.

DAMAGE LIMITATION

If damage limitation is accepted as the basic objective of a new strategic doctrine, we must then ask which method offers the best and least costly hope of success. Damage can be limited by two methods: by shooting down attacking nuclear weapons and evacuating and sheltering the urban population or by developing an offensive force that can launch a preemptive strike to disarm the Soviet Union. The offensive alternative has the advantage of being based on ICBM technology that has been developed and deployed over the last twenty years. There are, however, three obstacles to an offensive damage-limitation strategy. First, such a strategy depends on an American first strike to disarm the Soviet Union before it launches its weapons. Many will point out that this creates an unstable situation, since the Soviet Union may feel it necessary to launch its weapons first in order to avoid their destruction on the ground. This is debatable, but it is unrealistic to assume that an American president could decide to unleash nuclear war deliberately if alternatives existed.

The second reason weighing against an offensive counterforce strategy is the ways in which the Soviet Union can evade it. As the Soviet Union watches the emergence of an American silo-busting

ICBM force, it is very likely that they will develop and deploy a mobile ICBM system of their own. They will have ten years to do so; they already have experience building the SS-16 and SS-20 mobile ICBMs. How useful will new accurate American warheads be against missiles whose locations the United States cannot ascertain? Unconcerned with the need to make their mobile ICBM compatible with an arms control agreement, the Soviets will find it easier to conceal the location of their missiles.

Finally, the counterforce strategy does nothing to deal with an attack launched from Soviet submarines. It will do the United States only limited good to build the capability to destroy Soviet ICBMs if the Soviets build more submarines that can have their way with American cities. Eliminating the Soviet ICBM capability is a good thing to do, but it would need to be supplemented by a successful antisubmarine warfare capability. Unclassified material that would enable us to evaluate such prospects is not available.

If there is a strategic requirement for damage limitation, does the technical capability to fulfill this requirement exist? The answer is a qualified yes, but one cannot overemphasize that damage can be limited but not eliminated. No system remotely plausible today will guarantee that 100 percent of all attacking weapons will be destroyed or that millions of people will not die.

There is general agreement that civil defense measures—in particular, urban evacuation and the preparation of factories to protect them against nuclear attack—can do some good. The debate has revolved around how much protection can be bought at what cost. The enormous imponderables involved in evaluating the effects of a large nuclear war make the merits of any civil defense plan relative. What is surprising is how narrow the range of difference is between those plans. Since 1976 T.K. Jones, a senior engineer working for the Boeing Aerospace Company, has been arguing two major points about Soviet civil defense (Jones 1976). First, by evacuating the inhabitants of Soviet cities over a period of days and sheltering them in the countryside, the Soviet Union could launch a first strike against a fully alert American nuclear force, take its retaliatory strike, and suffer fatalities amounting to about 5 percent of the total population. Evacuees would walk, if necessary, and dig the crude fallout shelters the Soviet civil defense manuals have described.

This is a startling proposition. More startling is the fact that the study which the United States Arms Control and Disarmament Agency turned out to refute the Jones report did not refute this position. If the Soviet Union evacuated its major cities, perhaps 10 to 15 percent of the population would be killed. The difference between 5 and 15 percent is a large amount: it is the difference between 13 and 40 million dead. But these figures are both closer to the fatalities suffered by the Soviet Union in World War II than they are to the total destruction of civilization which we ordinarily believe to be the outcome of nuclear war. This is not to suggest that the Soviet Union would initiate a nuclear war in cold blood or that it is confident of victory. But, if accurate, this analysis means that should nuclear war between the United States and the Soviet Union occur, the Soviet Union will be able to protect the lives of 85 to 95 percent of its people—no mean feat.

A second civil defense controversy, also spurred by Jones, concentrated on the question of protecting the economic infrastructure of advanced economies. In essence, Jones argued that cheap, simple measures could protect heavy machinery against blast pressures of thirty to forty pounds per square inch (psi). More elaborate but inexpensve measures could give about ten times as much protection and would guard against one-megaton and forty-kiloton explosions three-fourths and one-fourth of a mile away, respectively.

The most important conclusion to draw from all this arithmetic is the following: heavy industrial components, if not the building they are in, can be protected to the extent that a single megaton warhead could destroy only one large industrial park three-quarters of a mile in radius. The same warhead could destroy an unprotected industrial region with fifteen times the area. Devastation would be immense in both cases, but it would be possible to salvage a great deal more from the protected economy. The number of industrial targets would be reduced that the enemy could destroy with a given stock of warheads. Simultaneous attack on our military installations, our evacuated population, and our economy would be much less possible.

It is important to note what this kind of industrial preparation would not do. It would not protect people; evacuation and shelters would have to do that. It would not prevent the sudden, simultaneous disruption of the entire economy such as no nation has ever suffered. It would not deal with long-term radiation problems. It would not be able to protect industrial facilities like blast furnaces, long assembly lines, and oil refineries that cannot be cushioned and buried. If the bulk of the population can be protected and if important segments of the economy can be preserved, however, recovery will be easier. Elaborate preparations would buy more recovery capability but would require a greater change in our peacetime society. The measures proposed by Jones for population and industrial civil defense, however, are not expensive. Urban evacuation will depend on whether city agencies have planned basic evacuation routes and ways to distribute them, ways to keep public transportation running, and ways to use commercial food distribution networks to feed evacuees. Paper plans cost little, and the U.S. government has already begun work on the plans that, with a budget of less than $100 million, would help evacuate those cities vulnerable to fallout from an attack on our missile silos and bombers bases (Senate Committee on Banking, Housing, and Urban Affairs 1979:86). National preparations— analogous to Jones' plan—would involve $2.3 billion, not an inordinate amount to pay for some added ability to recover from a war (Joint Committee on Defense Production 1979:123).

There is no question that if $3 billion, and no more, were available, the most effective way to spend it in order to reduce the damage done to the United States would be to invest it on civil defense and not on an ABM system that would protect the urban-industrial areas of the United States. During the next few years, however, the United States will be setting aside tens of billions of dollars for strategic programs. It is likely that it will again spend 15 percent of the defense budget on its strategic nuclear programs, as was done in the early 1960s, instead of the 10 percent allocated in the 1970s. Paul Warnke spoke in 1979 of the need to spend $5–6 billion a year more on strategic offense in order to keep up with the number of Soviet strategic delivery vehicles that would be built if SALT II did not go into effect (Joint Committee on Defense Production 1976). Once the survivability of American ICBMs has been insured, that money will only buy more dead Soviets. If more money is available, how much BMD for American cities and industry could it buy, and how much would that defense be worth?

The Safeguard ABM system was intended as a defense of Minuteman silos, but it used the same missiles and radars, in approximately the same numbers, as did the Sentinel ABM system, which was to have provided a thin defense of American cities. Safeguard was budgeted at $6.2 billion (in 1969 dollars) for a twelve-base system, which might translate into roughly twice that many 1979 dollars. The main problem with Safeguard was not its budgeted cost, but the ease with which it could be defeated.

Many, though not all, of the objections that were valid in 1969 are much less valid now. To begin with, it was not and is not true that offensive warheads could be added more cheaply than defensive interceptors. A Soviet SS-9 costs roughly $30 million (in 1969 dollars) (Senate Armed Services 1970:224–225). Assume that an SS-18, a much more sophisticated missile, costs at least $30 million. Each warhead costs about $1 million, and if an SS-18 carries ten warheads, the cost of one extra offensive warhead is about $4 million. In 1969, a Sprint interceptor cost $1.1 million; a Spartan, $1.5 million (Senate Armed Services Committee 1970:224–225). Add $1 million each for warheads. Adding more interceptors was about twice as cheap a adding offensive warheads.

Many of the problems faced by Safeguard were caused by its reliance on radar to guide its missiles, radar that was expensive and that could be outsmarted by using chaff and other devices that have been available since World War II. But if the devices that can deceive radar have long been available, so has the countermeasure. Interceptors that use the target's infrared and optical characteristics, its "signature," to home in on it have been around for decades. The Army has used that idea to develop long-range interceptors that home in on RVs (Davis 1979). These homing interceptors have many advantages. First, they are inexpensive. They need rockets to propel them, a built-in computer to direct them, a sensor to find the target, and a warhead to blow it up. All of these components are also found in the Sidewinder air-to-air missile, the latest version costing less than $100,000 a copy. The infrared sensor used by the Stinger hand-held, ground-to-air missile is not terribly different from the one intended for the homing interceptor. The interceptor needs in addition a booster to get it into the general flight path of the attacking missiles, after which the built-in sensor and computers take over. But the interceptor is light, so that technically many of them could be put on one booster. And because it can continually refine its course by itself, it is a precision-guided munition that is very accurate and does not need a nuclear warhead. Decoys can be built that look like an RV to the interceptor, but because the interceptors are so cheap and because so many could be launched, a defender could realistically plan to go after all targets, decoy or real. The attacker would also have to give up space and weight devoted to real warheads if he used many decoys.

Second, these homing interceptors do not need ground-based radar-computer centers, which are complex and vulnerable to attack.

Initial warning of offensive missile launchers could be provided by satellites already in orbit. Additions to the satellite system would enable them to determine the flight path of the attacking missiles with some precision. Additional target information would be provided by small rockets launched to locate the targets and filter out warheads or warhead-like objects from the many objects that would also be approaching the United States. With that information, the interceptors can be launched and can guide themselves.

Homing interceptors are not a panacea. The lower layer of defense would use missiles much like the Sprint, developed during the 1960s and refined during the 1970s. One problem faced by the Sprint involved the complicated task of the computers. The cost of computer time has dropped dramatically since 1969, while processing speed and reliability have increased. The radar now being contemplated for this part of the system has been made much less costly by improved technology and by more realistic operating requirements. The problem of interceptor nuclear warheads blinding their own radars remains, though it is diminished by the fact that the first layer of defense will reduce the total number of nuclear interceptors required.

The two-layer ABM system is not perfect. Warheads obviously will penetrate, but the system will reduce the impact of the attack. If the Soviet Union responds to the construction of this system by building more offensive capability, it can be matched with more defenses for less money. Decoys, as far as we can see now, will not create an economically insurmountable problem. The system uses technology that has been available for many years. The interceptor system can protect targets that cannot be helped by civil defense, such as oil refineries and cities. It reduces the civil defense problem by reducing the amount of nuclear fallout that would hit the United States. Likewise, it is aided by civil defense: if people are less vulnerable, it is easier to think about protecting cities in addition to people.

With or without a complementary arms control agreement, civil defenses and ballistic missile defenses have the added advantage of being compatible with an arms control strategy that might be appealing to the Soviet Union. The leaders of that country have long shown a great deal of interest in limiting the damage done to their country in the event of war. They have seemed worried by the development of our offensive forces. In theory it is possible for us to offer them a package that would set limits to the offensive forces of both countries, but that would leave the Soviets free to build as much defense as they wanted. Defining and limiting the nature of the offensive threat would greatly ease the task of the defenses. U.S. ability to kill Soviet citizens would diminish, but that would be no cause for alarm as long as we could protect our citizens at least as well. America will be spending a sizeable amount of additional money on its strategic forces in the 1980s. It would be better to buy live Americans than dead Soviets. This strategy, unfortunately, is likely to fail, perhaps because the Soviets are aware that an American defensive system would probably be better than one they could build, perhaps because they would not be content with being able to inflict "only" as much damage on the United States as it could on them. Still, the approach should be made. In reviewing the 1972 ABM treaty, the United States should raise the issue of BMD for the defense of ICBM silos, a relatively uncontroversial issue of clear interest to both the Americans and the Soviets. The technology for a layered defense will be ready in the late 1980s. The 1982 treaty review is, therefore, well timed for a discussion on how to shift gradually from a strategic world dominated by offensive weapons to one emphasizing defenses.

With or without a complementary arms control agreement, civil defense and BMD will not stop nuclear war from being a catastrophe. Casualties will still be in the millions, though we could begin to hope that they would not be in the tens of millions. Even with strategic defenses, the vision of nuclear holocaust should still be so terrible as to deter statesmen from a deliberate attack in a less desperate crisis. But now, desperate crises are likely. In a Persian Gulf war, stakes will be high. The struggle will determine who will dominate world politics for the foreseeable future. In addition, the leaders of the Soviet Union may fear, with some justification, the domestic consequences of a major military defeat. The memory of how their own party rose to power may give them some cause to be desperate.

Given these circumstances, the need is urgent for an American strategic policy that tries to minimize, rather than maximize, the costs of a nuclear war. Analogies with 1914 are often made in order to suggest that the world may be heedlessly drifting into an unnecessary war now as European leaders allowed it to do then. It would be well to remember the lesson of 1916 and 1917: that even a necessary war can break the spirit of a nation if its conduct is militarily idiotic. For years, our nuclear policy has been based on deliberately inflicting and accepting tens of millions of civilian casualties. This was wrong, but war seemed distant and unlikely then. It is uncomfortably close now.

The major obstacle to developing a doctrine and a program of damage limitation is the fear of instability. The fear has been exaggerated and has distorted the U.S. view of the other real problems of war. The fixation with stability engendered the 1972 ABM treaty and now hinders U.S. withdrawal from it. Yet the ABM treaty has not succeeded in preventing arms competition, has not protected U.S. ICBMs, and has not protected its population. It may have helped to reduce tensions, though the absence of tensions ten years ago was for different reasons, and those reasons will now exacerbate tensions, with or without the treaty. In short, continued adherence to the ABM treaty brings no advantage to the United States and stands in the way of much that could be useful to its defenses. This country is not likely to survive a war for which it deliberately leaves itself unprepared. A nation can endure much in a war if the cause is widely embraced and people believe their lives are not being thrown away by their leaders. America must be defended—a task that must be taken as seriously as the nature of war and the level of destruction this country now faces.

REFERENCES

Albertini, Luigi. 1952. *The Origins of the War of 1941,* Vol. I. London: Oxford University Press.

Bohlen, Charles. 1973. *Witness to History.* New York: Norton.

Davis, William. 1979. "Current Technical Status of U.S. BMD Programs," Paper presented to the Conference on Ballistic Missile Defense sponsored by the Center for Science and International Affairs, Harvard University, November 1-2.

Grenville, J.A. 1964. *Lord Salisbury and Foreign Policy: The Close of the Nineteenth Century.* London.

Grey, Edward. 1925. *Twenty-five Years.* Vol. II. New York: Frederick Stokes.

Howard, Michael. 1979. "The Forgotten Dimensions of Strategy." *Foreign Affairs* (Summer).

Huntington, Samuel. 1958. "Arms Races: Prerequisites and Results." *Public Policy:*41-86.

Jabber, Paul, and Roman Kolkowicz. 1979. "The Arab-Israeli Wars of 1967 and 1973." In *Mailed Fist, Velvet Glove,* edited by Steven Kaplan. Washington, D.C.: Brookings Institution.

Joint Committee on Atomic Energy. 1969. "Scope, Magnitude and Implications of the U.S. ABM Program." 90th Congress. 1st Session, November 6-7.

Joint Committee on Defense Production. 1976. "Civil Preparedness Review, Part II, Industrial Defense and Nuclear Attack." 95th Congress, 2nd Session, April.

Jones, T.K. 1976. "Industrial Survival and Recovery after Nuclear Attack." Printed as Appendix II in hearings before the Joint Committee Production, "Defense Industrial Base: Industrial Preparedness and Nuclear War Survival." 94th Congress, 2nd Session, November 17.

Kissinger, Henry. 1979. *White House Years.* Boston: Little, Brown.

Mandelbaum, Michael. 1979. *The Nuclear Question: The United States and Nuclear Weapons, 1946-1976.* New York: Cambridge University Press.

Ritter, Gerhard. 1958. *The Schlieffen Plan: Critique of a Myth.* New York: Praeger.

Rosenberg, David Alan. 1979. "American Atomic Strategy and the Hydrogen Bomb Decision" (quoting the Harmon Report). *Journal of American History* (June).

Schick, Jack. 1971. *The Berlin Crisis: 1958-1962.* Philadelphia: University of Pennsylvania Press.

Senate Armed Services Committee. 1970. "Authorizations for Military Procurement FY 1970." 91st Cong., 1st sess, Part I, March 19-20, 25-27, April 1-3, 15-17.

Senate Committee on Banking, Housing, and Urban Affairs. 1979. "Civil Defense." 95th Cong., 2nd sess., January 8.

Warnke, Paul. 1979. Testimony before the Senate Committee on Banking and Housing and Urban Affairs, "Civil Defense." 95th Cong., 2nd sess., January 8.

5 GUESSING GAME: A REAPPRAISAL OF SYSTEMS ANALYSIS

Eliot A. Cohen

Robert McNamara once confessed that he considered the introduction of systems analysis to the Department of Defense to be his greatest legacy to American military policy. The Office of Systems Analysis—now the Office of Program Analysis and Evaluation—is no longer as powerful as once it was, but many defense experts, consciously or not, use the systems analysis approach when they discuss military problems as diverse as the acquisition of a new strategic bomber and the future of the tank in land warfare. The purpose of this chapter is to define systems analysis, examine its logic, describe the political and military consequences of its acceptance by the American defense community, and suggest a substitute for it.

After World War II American strategists concerned themselves with two subjects, strategic nuclear war and limited or counterinsurgency war. Both subjects were and remain controversial: academics, bureaucrats, and other members of the defense establishment take a variety of positions and disagree openly, often bitterly. The subjects were new, but at first the methods of studying them were not: students of strategy of the prenuclear era such as Bernard Brodie shifted their attention easily to the challenges of the nuclear age.

Systems analysis, however, which began in the late fifties and flowered during the 1960s, was a new type of strategic thought, a new way of approaching military problems of all kinds. After an initial flurry of controversy, it received little critical attention. Today, strategic thinkers may concede that systems analysis went too far, but they have not troubled to evaluate its effects or reexamine its premises and argument. As a result, the mindset fostered by systems analysis pervades the strategic community. A former undersecretary of the Navy has called it a way of looking at things that he could attribute to "no one all the time, but to lots of us some of the time, and some of us most of the time" (Woolsey 1978:21).

The systems analysts did encounter opposition, of course, from such men as S.L.A. Marshall, the combat historian of the American Army, Human Rickover, creator of the nuclear fleet, and Hanson Baldwin, the dean of American military correspondents. The criticism that these men offered was rarely thorough, however, because they dwelt on the arrogance of the practitioners of systems analysis and particular failures of their art, rather than flaws in the theory of systems analysis (LeMay 1968:x–xii; Rickover 1967:35–54; U.S. Congress, Senate Committee on Armed Services 1972:316–326). The analysts, in return, dismissed the opposition as the product of parochialism, intellectual sloth, and even cranky senility. In addition to a store of telling *ad hominem* invective, the systems analysts possessed two further defenses. The first was their willingness to denounce "bad analysis," even their own, a tactic which deflected theoretical arguments. In addition, the systems analysts were social scientists and benefited from the reputation of value-free social science. This ensured their popularity with those social and natural scientists who make up the bulk of this country's strategists and students of military affairs, because unlike other countries, the United States has few historians of war or military men of letters who could have replied cogently and publicly to this application of modern social science to the problems of war and war planning. Thus, for nearly two decades systems analysis has escaped the critical examination it deserves.

In order to understand what systems analysis is and what effects it has had on American strategic thought and defense planning, we must understand its roots. To begin with what systems analysis is *not*: systems analysis bears no theoretical relation to operations research, the mathematical study of particular military problems that began in England during World War I. Operations research became an accepted part of military planning and operations only during World War II, when operations researchers helped to direct bombing campaigns and to solve assorted tactical and logistical problems. Thus, the Royal Navy turned to operations research in order to devise the best tactics for a destroyer captain who had seen the point of origin of a torpedo trail but could not locate the fleeing submerged submarine that had fired it a minute or two earlier. The operations research bureaus acted as adjuncts to military staffs: senior officers assigned neatly defined problems, and the analysts applied the science of statistics to those problems. Nine out of ten times, according to the foremost English expert on operations research, the civilian recommendation was the same as the educated guess of trained and experienced officers (Blackett 1962:129). A similar case was made by Major-General Julian J. Ewell, commander of the 9th Infantry Division in the Mekong Delta during 1968–69. He distinguished between operations or combat analysis (which he applied extensively and successfully) and systems analysis. He, too, reached the conclusion that operations analysis was "a useful complementary technique," best done at a fairly low level of command, and by no means a substitute for military judgment (Ewell and Hunt 1974:5–6, 237–239).

The roots of systems analysis, unlike those of operations research, lie in economics and not in statistics or higher mathematics. The early systems analysts, including Charles Hitch, Roland McKean, and Alain Enthoven, were in fact economists, many of them from the RAND Corporation. According to them, "Choosing strategies and weapon systems is fundamentally an economic problem, using the term in its precise sense" (Tucker 1966:141). Systems analysis is therefore independent and far-reaching. "In the economists' world there are always alternatives, alternative ways of using resources or doing a job" (Tucker 1966:164). The systems analyst does not accept others' objectives: he defines his own. He is a critic and a policy entrepreneur, not a subordinate expert.

Thus, systems analysis does not necessarily, as its detractors sometimes claim, substitute incomprehensible mathematics for military calculation. It is, rather, a way of approaching military affairs (Hitch 1965:54). It is a school of strategic thought, not a scientific subdiscipline, and hence it can hold the allegiance of politicans, journalists, and professors who have long ago forgotten the substance of their college calculus courses. The application of mathematics and statistics to warfare dates back to the eighteenth century and before: artillerists used trigonometry in order to aim their cannon, and engineers studied geometry in order to construct defensible positions.

What was new in 1960 was not the use of numbers or equations to help solve military problems but rather the coronation of one social science—economics—as the rightful queen of war planning and strategy.

The most important tool of systems analysis is cost-effectiveness analysis, an economist's way of posing a problem and suggesting a proper solution. Cost-effectiveness (or cost-benefit analysis, as it is sometimes called) asks either "Given a fixed sum of money, how can we buy the most effectiveness (utility)?" or "Given a certain desired level of effectiveness, what is the cheapest method of achieving it?" If they phrase the question the first way, those who have the final say about buying weapons and devising strategy must make arbitrary and rigid decisions about how much money to spend, but do not need refined measures of benefit. The systems analysts do not, by and large, approve of such an irrational method of administration as fixing expenditure and then trying to buy the most one can within a given budget. They prefer the second approach, that is, to discover what is sufficient and then find the cheapest way of procuring it. Hence, their preoccupation with the question, "How much is enough?"—the title, in fact, of Alain Enthoven's and K. Wayne Smith's history of their experiences as two of McNamara's systems analysts.

Enthoven gives a good example of the cost-effectiveness approach by describing the logic of McNamara's preference (during the early 1960s) for a conventional aircraft carrier over a nuclear one—the *John F. Kennedy*, or CVA-67 (Tucker 1966:163). Enthoven put the problem this way: a conventional carrier costs $280 million, a nuclear carrier costs $400 million, and the four destroyer escorts needed to protect an aircraft carrier cost roughly $120 million. The systems analysts devised measures of effectiveness (sorties per time period, airplane bomb load, and so on) and attempted to discover the cheapest way of buying a certain level of effectiveness. They willingly reformulated the problem, however: given $400 million, which choice offered more effectiveness—the conventional carrier plus four escorts, or the nuclear carrier without? They rejected the notion that Congress could decide to buy the nuclear carrier because it believed it was worth the price, and then raise additional funds for four destroyers. The choice under such conditions, according to McNamara's advisers, would have to be between the effectiveness of a nuclear ship with four escorts and a conventional vessel with eight.

In both formulations, cost-effectiveness disregarded reality. First, if they used the fixed-cost-maximum-benefit method, the systems analysts disregarded political reality. Political choice is not economically rational: additional funds may have been available to enhance the power and prestige of the U.S. Navy by funding a nuclear aircraft carrier; these monies might not have been available to purchase four more destroyers. The choice from Congress's point of view was indeed between a nuclear carrier with four escorts and a conventional carrier with four escorts; annoyed legislators told the analysts as much. If they had adopted the second variant of cost effectiveness—fixed-effectiveness-least-cost—the systems analysts would have needed extraordinary, indeed unobtainable, measures of benefit, measures which could take into account all of the conceivable political and military contexts in which a carrier might be used, and the new and different kinds of tactics and strategy that a nuclear carrier could make possible. The systems analysts did not know what new tactics a CVN (Carrier Vessel Nuclear, as opposed to a CVA, or Carrier Vessel Attack) could take advantage of, or at least they did not attempt to find out. As a result, they wrongly assumed that it would operate the way a CVA did (U.S. Congress, Joint Committee on Atomic Energy 1963:41). They did not, because they could not, quantify the advantages of the CVN's difference from a CVA: a CVN can sustain high speeds almost indefinitely, can carry 50 to 100 percent more jet fuel and ammunition than a CVA, can carry fuel for her escort vessels, and carry more airplanes than a CVA. The airplanes a CVN carry require less care than those on a CVA because maintenance crews do not have to cope with the damage done by corrosive stack gases. More escorts are free for independent action because they do not have to protect a long train of tankers: the task force as a whole does not require vast quantities of oil. High sustainable speeds reduce the CVN's vulnerability to cruise missiles and torpedoes, and enhance its ability to patrol large areas. In short, by most accounts, McNamara and his men made the wrong choice (Roherty 1970:141–153).

McNamara's systems analysis-based opposition to the CVN-67 was not merely militarily incorrect; it demonstrated poor leadership and political ineptitude as well. The Navy was disgruntled after the rejection of such a powerful and prestigious piece of naval construction, and the Congress, bewildered by McNamara's opposition to the CVN, was angered by the recommendations and deportment of the systems analysts, by their rejection of the CVN on the cost-effectiveness grounds just described, and the arrogance with which they did so. In the interests of "rational" decisionmaking, McNamara had assured that future cooperation between Congress, the Office of the Secretary of Defense, and the armed services would be difficult. The use of systems analysis disrupted the easy human relations needed to sustain an endeavor as complicated as force planning and weapons acquisition must be (Trewhitt 1971:155).

The fixed-effectiveness-least-cost formulation narrows the focus of analysis: it prevents the strategist from appreciating the need for flexible weapons and tactics (Woolsey 1980:8). McNamara declared that he needed to know "the military effectiveness and the cost of a B-52 squadron as it relates to a Minuteman missile squadron and a Polaris submarine" (McNamara 1968:94). McNamara's need to define effectiveness—in this case, in terms of nuclear warheads delivered against Soviet targets—led him to disregard the multiple uses of weapons—in this case, the B-52. That strategic bomber was originally supposed to carry only nuclear weapons, but it served well as a conventional bomber in Vietnam, a use that was unforeseen and unintended when it was built.

Cost effectiveness requires simplification. The systems analyst divides up his studies by mission (for example, antitank warfare or interdiction of enemy logistics) or scenario (for instance, a sudden, massive Soviet invasion of West Germany). He defines a set of objectives, usually in the form of percentage attrition of enemy units, and considers different ways of achieving that objective. When a systems analyst defines the problem in terms of a mission, he artificially compartmentalizes war planning, neglecting the fact that weapons can do many different things: to take a minor example, during World War II the German eight-eight millimeter antiaircraft gun was discovered to be a superb antitank weapon and served as such. When the systems analyst works by scenario, he is particularly liable to disregard those elements of accident and unforeseeable enemy countermeasures which dominate real war and make nonsense of the best laid plans.

We have said that systems analysis usually defines success in terms of attrition of enemy targets. It does this because it needs straightforward indices of military effectiveness which can be varied in accordance with the application of different measures. One example is the casualties caused by air bombardment as compared with artillery barrage, an example used throughout Quade and Boucher's *Systems Analysis and Policy Planning: Applications in Defense*, one of the foremost systems analysis primers. Needless to say, this leaves out intangibles, in this case, the psychological effect of air attacks; it should be remembered that during the early stages of World War II the Luftwaffe did better service as a terror weapon than it did as a substitute for long-range artillery. Moreover, in wartime attrition varies according to the quality of troops and tactics on both sides: no weapon delivers a constant quantum of destruction per hundred rounds. A heavy machine gun that cut down hundreds of attackers in 1914 might have sucumbed later in the war to a dozen men skilled in infiltration tacts; Egyptian infantry equipped with antitank missiles were far less dangerous to Israeli tank crews on October 20, 1973, than they had been only two weeks earlier.

Such indices are difficult to construct and insufficiently informative, and therefore should not serve as measures of success because victory in war is not simply a function of attrition. Battles are won or lost when one side or the other surrenders, flees, or disintegrates; poor units can suffer few casualties and dissolve, and good units can lose many of their men and continue to fight (Marshall 1947). In real war an umpire does not award victory to the first side to disable 22 percent of its enemies.

To be sure, there are a few types of war and war planning that do lend themselves to such attrition analysis. For example, toward the end of World War II, loss rates in allied strategic bombing campaigns became more or less predictable. Such calculations may even serve a use in planning operations such as antisubmarine warfare in support of convoys, in order to ensure that a fixed amount of supplies and men cross from the United States to Europe safely. But even in such cases, technological or tactical surprise can nullify the most thorough and elaborate calculations, and developments in other theaters of war can make a level of attrition that was previously thought tolerable utterly unacceptable. Above all, if one customarily uses such measures one begins to think that war is far more predictable than it really is. One systems analyst attempted retrospectively to predict casualties in World War II, assuming full knowledge (unavailable, of course, at the time) of the weapons, tactics, and strength of all the contenders. His prediction was off the mark by a factor of between three and four (Quade and Boucher 1968:362).

Systems analysis means a way of approaching defense problems, a certain attitude, and thereby includes more than the techniques just described. The systems analysts themselves say as much (Enthoven and Smith 1971:61–65; Tucker 1966:7; Woolsey 1978:21). These attitudes or predispositions, however, are often necessary to make cost-effectiveness thinking work. The first and most important aspect of systems analysis as a mode of thought is quantification. McNamara defined systems analysis as "quantititative common sense," and his disciples declared that it is better to quantify than to use adjectives, even when numbers must be coaxed or coerced from uncooperative data. When the admirals who supported the nuclear aircraft carrier explained why nuclear power offered military advantages, McNamara asked, "Precisely what does this mean? Does it mean 10 percent better or 100 percent better?" Systems analysts do not need sophisticated computers or knowledge of abstruse higher mathematics, but they do need quantitative measures of military effectiveness, and they think they can devise them. Analysts concede that everything might not be quantifiable but, as James Schlesinger pointed out, "A ritualistic recitation of the danger of excessive quantification characteristically precedes the attempt to push quantitative analysis too far" (Kissinger 1965:97).

Systems analysis rests on the belief that rational analysis is always possible, and that calculated intervention based on such analysis can remold human institutions, no matter how huge and old, and redirect human behavior, no matter how seemingly persistent or perverse. Its intellectual roots are thus intertwined with those of the ambitious social engineering and economic fine-tuning projects of the 1960s. McNamara said in 1966:

> Poverty begets poverty, passing from generation to generation in a cruel cycle of near-inevitability. *It endures until carefully designed outer assistance intervenes and radically redirects its internal dynamics* (McNamara 1968:129; emphasis added).

Systems analysts believe in scientific method, and, therefore, in the superiority of their approach to the methods of procurement used until 1960. "Systems analysis extracts everything possible from scientific methods, and its virtues are the virtues of those methods. Furthermore, its limitations are shared by its alternatives" (Quade and Boucher 1968:427). To be sure, they admit that "analysis is necessarily incomplete" and "falls short of [natural] scientific research," but systems analysts are proud of this modest awareness of their imperfections—imperfections which they believe they share with researchers in the natural sciences. At least, as McNamara put it, they try to "establish a rational foundation as opposed to an emotional foundation" (Tucker 1966:34) for defense planning. Systems analysis is self-confident because it believes itself to be scientific. Its practitioners thereby overcome the natural diffidence civilians have before career officers who have both experience and the lien on respect due to those who lead men under fire.

The systems analyst claims that he makes no judgments about what policy ought to be; rather, he analyzes all that is analyzable and then leaves to the policymaker those questions which require a judgment based on political or moral considerations (Hitch 1965:76). This claim is ingenuous, because bureaucrats are notorious for deliberately framing questions in such a way as to predetermine the answers. Systems analysis, which depends so heavily on how a question is posed, is peculiarly susceptible to abuse of this sort.

The machinations of particular office-holders aside, systems analysis does have a principle of choice based on cost, as we discussed in our examination of cost effectiveness. The proponents of systems analysis maintain that it does not necessarily favor the cheaper of any two systems or alternatives, or less expenditure rather than more, but it is natural that a preoccupation with cost will lead to such a bias. In addition, systems analysis's emphasis on quantitative analysis, its affinity for numbers rather than adjectives, leads its adherents to concentrate on cost, for expense is eminently quantifiable.

Finally, we note that in practice, systems analysts have been highly partisan. This observation should lead us to ask whether in questions of defense policy—questions, after all, that affect men's lives, huge sums of money, and the welfare of an entire nation—value-free analysis is ever possible in the way that it is in such fields as inorganic chemistry (Storing 1962:307–327; Strauss 1953:35–80). Systems analysis encourages its practitioners to believe in their own objectivity and the bias of those who disagree, particularly officers in the armed forces. The result, especially during the McNamara years, was arrogance and condescension.

Because of systems analysis's roots in economics, the systems analyst assigns weight to arguments based on marginal utility. Accustomed to the notion that at a certain point large increases in marginal cost bring negligible increases in utility, he casts a jaundiced eye on the Navy's request for nuclear-powered aircraft carriers. He must be convinced that a 33 percent increase in marginal cost brings a 33 percent increase in utility. But because military utility is hard to measure, and because seemingly minor changes in speed or some other characteristic may add up to qualitative change, the systems analyst is prone to accuse services of "gold-plating" when, in fact, they are not. In 1964 Congressman Melvin Laird belabored McNamara for this sort of failure of systems analysis to account for the military significance of seemingly trivial technical advantages. Japanese air superiority at the beginning of World War II resulted in large part from the minor speed advantages of the *Zero* fighter. Laird argued that if the Japanese had bought the *Zero* according to cost effectiveness criteria, they might well have decided against an airplane engine capable of such efforts (McKean 1967:3-24; Tucker 1966:36, 142).

The systems analyst regards technology as the controlling element in war:

> The machine gun reduced to irrelevance much of the tactical planning preceding World War I. Armored warfare made a mockery of the assumption on which the Maginot Line was based. The development of naval aviation dealt battleships such a blow that their defenders became a symbol of adherence to outmoded thinking. But the problem is of greater proportion [today] than every before (Enthoven and Smith 1971:106).

According to him, technology dominates war. Thus, there is no point to the study of military history other than to impress upon ourselves the importance of understanding technological change. Technology today changes faster than ever; therefore, the experience of professional military men, who by nature are conservative and cling to outmoded methods of doing things, should not be given much weight. Furthermore, because technology rather than human nature is the most important element in war, the systems analyst can define success in terms of annihilating enemy targets ("attriting," in defense planners' jargon), not in terms of destroying the enemy's will to resist, disrupting the cohesion of his units, disabling his command structure, or outmaneuvering him.

The systems analyst applies his art primarily, although not exclusively, to problems of weapons acquisition. He exercises his ingenuity in devising objective measures for the outputs of military technology; thus, he believes that his voice should be the most important in defense planning. The technological determinism of the systems analyst and his preoccupation with indices of attrition lead the systems analyst to pay attention to logistics, the problems of delivering proper quantities of men and equipment to the front line.

These premises—the primacy of technology in war and the importance of logistics—mark systems analysis as a distinctive school of military thought. Other schools make differing claims about that which is decisive in war: for example, the skill in strategy of the commander (B.H. Liddell Hart), the cohesion of small units under fire (S.L.A. Marshall), tactical forms (Jean Colin and Cyril Falls), the nature of the regime behind the armies (Hans Delbrück and, in a very different way, Lenin and Mao Tse-tung). Systems analysis, however, does not resemble competing theories because, unlike them, it merely proclaims its premises; it does not examine or even attempt to prove them.

Military history does not bear out these extravagant claims for the preeminence of technology in war. To take two examples from the Enthoven and Smith quotation just given, the trench warfare of World War I had its precedents in the American Civil War, and the Maginot Line fell not simply because of the introduction of armored warfare, but because of the superiority of German armored doctrine and strategy to that of the French and British. Innovation in the means of war continues constantly: minor changes in technology and tactics, coupled with larger changes in politics or economics may add up to a revolution (Falls 1953:13–23). At the end of the eighteenth century minor improvements in military technology (particularly in standardized artillery), improved tactics (in the use of mobile artillery and infantry deployed in both column and line), and the forces unleashed by the French Revolution (changes which made possible total mobilization and suggested extreme political ends), made possible Napoleonic warfare—a type of war quite different from that of a generation before. Technology alone does not determine the nature of a particular war. If it did, why did the Western Front in World War I see only the static and squalid misery of trench warfare, while the Eastern and Levantine Fronts, where the same weapons were used and some of the same generals commanded, witness swift maneuver, spectacular advances, and sudden retreats?

Logistics does indeed deserve greater attention than it has traditionally received from military historians. Generals condemned for their timidity have often had prosaic yet compelling reasons for slow movement. Martin van Creveld's *Supplying War* (1977) examines the importance of logistics with admirable thoroughness. Yet frequently the most successful campaigns are those which take most risks with one's logistical support, as indicated by the history of the American Third Army under George Patton or the German Afrika Korps under Erwin Rommel. Conversely, simple sufficiency of means does not guarantee success, as the Arab armies demonstrated in 1967 and, to a lesser extent, in 1973 in their wars with Israel.

THREE PROPOSITIONS

If we accept systems analysis we must accept three of its fundamental—yet often hidden—propositions. First, *there is no distinct field of military or politicomilitary study and knowledge.* Defense planners would, according to the theory of systems analysis, benefit more from an advanced degree in economics than from combat or bureaucratic experience or knowledge of history. This is so because important measures of success can be reduced to numbers; attachment to a service distorts one's views; the essence of military assessment is evaluation of technology. The authors of the foremost systems analysis primer, *Systems Analysis and Policy Planning: Applications in Defense,* apply a general method to a particular set of problems, that is, defense planning. This and other primers use homely examples of housewives choosing washing machines, farmers pondering which crops to plant, and businessmen picking out limousines, to explain how strategists should select, procure, and deploy the armed forces of the United States.

The second proposition is that *we can know how much is enough. Fortune* magazine asked Secretary McNamara in 1965 whether the defense budget would be higher if the gross national product were $1 trillion rather than $660 billion. "Certainly not," he replied (Seligman 1965:246). The traditional view had been that limits on defense spending follow from the risks a country could accept and the price it was willing to pay for defense, but that because of the unpredictability of war, more intelligent spending would always be better than less.

Systems analysis tells us that we can in peacetime adequately determine our needs in war, yet war is intrinsically the most unpredictable of human activities. National security is not a commodity which a government can purchase at a known and stable market price, for it is a composite of intangibles and imponderables. No country enters war fully prepared for it.

In addition, the reduction of defense planning to the question, "How much is enough?" leads us to neglect larger political or philosophical issues. For example, a draft of one-quarter of all eighteen-year-old men might satisfy the manpower requirements of this country, but considerations of equity, or a certain understanding of the obligations of citizenship might mandate universal military service or none at all. In the long run these larger issues are of first order importance, yet the systems analysis mindset leads us to shun them.

Finally, the adoption of systems analysis leads us to believe that *systems analysis can ultimately direct not merely procurement but strategy as well.* Initially, the systems analysts claimed only to concern themselves with weapons procurement, not strategy or tactics. But, if we accept the systems analyst's technology-centered view of war, there is no reason why he should not plan and direct operations whose aim and method is simply calculable attrition. "The systems analyst is the fellow who is likely to be forced to deal with the problem in which the difficulty lies precisely in deciding what ought to be done, not simply in how to do it" (Quade and Boucher 1968:5, 428). Moreover, in practice one cannot design a weapon without predetermining its uses. For example, the armor, engine, and cannon of a tank will dictate in some measure whether one's tactics consists of rapid wheeling maneuvers by masses of vehicles or slower movement conducted by infantry, artillery, and armor operating together. A decision to buy a small aircraft carrier may force the Navy to conduct war according to a defensive strategy, to protect lines of communication rather than attack the enemy. Thus, even if systems analysts did not wish to shape strategy and tactics, they would do so nonetheless.

THE INFLUENCE ON POLITICS

The spread of systems analysis did not merely shape the way we think about military problems; it affected the distribution of political power in Washington as well. Even before McNamara came to the Pentagon, civilian secretaries of defense were consolidating and increasing their control over the armed services. American statesmen had realized that the postwar military establishment, huge by comparison with its pre-1940 predecessor, needed central civilian control. This began, of course, with the unification of the War and Navy departments, and the creation of the Joint Chiefs of Staff and the Office of the Secretary of Defense during the late 1940s. In the latter years of the Eisenhower Administration new agencies were created, whose writ ran throughout the defense establishment—the Defense Atomic Support Agency, the Defense Communications Agency, and Defense Research and Engineering, for example; and regional commands were established that cut across service lines.

McNamara, however, moved faster and further in extending civilian control than previous secretaries had done. This sometimes took absurdly petty forms, as when he proudly announced the "consolidation of eighteen different types and sizes of butcher smocks, four kinds of belt buckles, and six kinds of women's exercise bloomers" (McNamara 1968:98–99). McNamara increased his control of the Defense Department by his own diligent study and investigation, by increasing the size and responsibilities of the Office of the Secretary of Defense, and by introducing program budgeting and systems analysis. The Office of Systems Analysis served McNamara faithfully. Its members were loyal to him alone, and largely because of this, he soon became "the basic force planners in the whole system" (Murdock 1974:84). The Office of Systems Analysis administered the Planning-Programming-Budgeting-System (PPBS), the master key to McNamara's Defense Department. Requests for funds or new projects went through that office and thereby enhanced its power.

The introduction of systems analysis, however, had an effect that extended beyond increasing the bureaucratic power of a particular office. Because systems analysis rejected prudential military knowledge, it enabled young civilian analysts to contradict and oppose their military rivals with clean consciences. Their self-confidence came not from superior knowledge or intuition, but from possession of superior analytic tools. Previously, statesmen who coerced military services into choosing certain weapons, tactics, or strategies did so either on the basis of political considerations or because they had studied and thought through a particular military problem. Winston Churchill and David Lloyd George, for example, imposed innovations on the British Navy (oil-fired engines and the convoy system, respectively) but not on the basis of arcane analytic techniques.

The bureaucratic potency of systems analysis made it attractive even to those civilians who knew its failings. Henry Kissinger, for example, condemned McNamara's methods and his subordinates:

He overemphasized the quantitative aspects of defense planning; by neglecting intangible psychological and political components he aimed for a predictability that was illusory and caused needless strains to our alliances. His eager young associates hid their moral convictions behind a seemingly objective method of analysis which obscured that their questions too often predetermined the answers and that these answers led to a long-term stagnation in our military technology (Kissinger 1979:296).

Despite such trenchant criticism, however, Kissinger brought K. Wayne Smith, one of the foremost systems analysts, to his national security staff. He used this small systems analysis office to conduct bureaucratic guerrilla warfare against Secretary of Defense Melvin Laird who had reduced the power of the systems analysts.

At first the armed services fought systems analysis. In part, of course, they did so because the increased power of the Office of the Secretary of Defense (OSD) decreased their own freedom of choice and discretion about the running of the American defense establishment. More galling, however, was the demeanour of the systems analysts. The generals of the early 1960s, men who had had high rank during World War II and the Korean War, did not take kindly to the schoolmasterish condecension of such lectures as the following:

> Although inevitably some people will resent the application of dispassionate, cold analysis to something as rich in meaning and tradition as warfare and strategy, there is no sensible alternative in the nuclear age (Tucker 1966:148).

One story is told of Alain Enthoven, one of McNamara's top assistants still in his early thirties. When Enthoven visited U.S. Air Force headquarters in Germany, an officer began to give him a briefing schedule. Enthoven testily interrupted, "General, I don't think you understand. I didn't come for a briefing. I came to tell you what we have decided" (Trewhitt 1971:13).

After the initial struggle, the American military made its peace with systems analysis. It did so at first in order to parry the thrusts of the systems analysts working for McNamara. The services created their *own* systems analysis offices, whose assessments rarely concurred with those of McNamara's men but favored instead the services' pet projects. After a while the most abrasive analysts left office, and perhaps those who remained became less irritating if only because they became more familiar. Under Melvin Laird, who had opposed systems analysis as a congressman during the 1960s, the services regained a considerable portion of their discretion. Laird did not appoint a replacement for the assistant secretary of defense for systems analysis for a year, and in the meanwhile he reduced the role of that office in defense planning (Korb 1979:85–96). Furthermore, he fended off Kissinger's systems analysts with a skill that even won the grudging admiration of the national security advisor.

Systems analysis did exert a genuine attraction on some parts of the armed forces. The technological branches of the armed services, particularly the Air Force, were favorably impressed by systems analysts' treatment of technology as the prime determinant of war. The engineering, problem-solving approach long taught at West Point was compatible with systems analysis. More important, however, the attrition mentality of systems analysis struck a responsive chord in other segments of the military, particularly in the Army. The dominant tradition of the U.S. Army dates back to Ulysses S. Grant and extends through William Westmoreland. It relies on the aggressive application of numerical strength and, above all, firepower to grind into oblivion an economically inferior opponent. This strategy was successful in World War II, substantially so in Korea, and partially so in Vietnam. Insofar as it hopes to substitute tons of bullets and bombs for American casualties, it reflects the value American society puts on the lives of its citizens. Under certain conditions—protracted conventional war—it may even make sense, for it is the natural if inelegant strategy of a large and wealthy nation. Finally, and not least important, the military accepted the dominant civilian view of military affairs because most armies sooner or later adopt the opinions of the society they fight for. Since World War II the American armed forces have been particularly sensitive to shifts in domestic opinion. Thus, many younger officers have accepted, often enthusiastically, the jargon and frame of mind created by systems analysis, to the dismay of more traditional senior officers. In 1978 Vice Admiral J.B. Stockdale darkly observed:

> Today's ranks are filled with officers who have been weaned on slogans and fads of the sort preached in the better business school of the country. . . . The loss of that war Vietnam demonstrated that we cannot adopt the methodology of business without adopting its language, its style, its tactics, and above all its ethics (Stockdale 1978:2).

The systems analysis approach under McNamara produced two beneficial effects. First, the systems analysts urged, and the services endorsed, greater investment in logistical facilities, specifically cargo ships and long-range transport aircraft. Systems analysis does, as we know, pay heed to problems of logistics. It was natural, therefore, that the systems analysts would concentrate on that part of the American defense establishment. They proposed unusual solutions to old problems. New vessels such as the so-called RO-RO ships (cargo ships that could easily load and unload assorted military hardware at primitive ports over the world), Fast Deployment Logistics ships, and floating storehouses of weapons—pre-positioning, as it was then called. The controversial C-5A, the largest transport aircraft in the world, was supported by the systems analysts who were subsequently chagrined by the huge cost overruns that it incurred.

Those branches of the armed services that handled logistics had not previously been bureaucratically powerful primarily because their tasks were far from glamorous. Perhaps the systems analysts exaggerated the magnitude of the problem. After all, the American logistical system functioned well enough during World War II, the European crises of the later 1940s, and the Korean war; historically, logistical support can be improvised from new production and the existing stock of merchant vessels and today, the commercial air fleet. It should also be noted that the Joint Chiefs of Staff supported the expansion of logistical facilities, although admittedly at a time of expanding budgets when the purchase of a new transport did not mean one fighter-bomber foregone. All this notwithstanding, the systems analysts did good work; their success was demonstrated by the smoothness and rapidity of the Vietnam build-up.

Secondly, systems analysis had other long-term effects that extended beyond the reinforcement of civilian control and increased attention to logistics and nuclear weaponry. To begin with, the introduction of systems analysis slowed down the acquisition of new weapons (Head 1978; Knorr and Morgenstern 1965; Mansfield 1968:62–78; Roherty 1970:109–110; Woolsey 1980:5). Many of the new weapons associated with the McNamara period were developed during the 1950s—for example, *Polaris, Minuteman*, the F-111, and the AR-15 rifle.

Systems analysis requires, of course, analysis, the description of a mission and various ways of achieving it, lengthy studies of comparative effectiveness, and so forth. Systems analysis suggests that there is one best or cheapest way of solving a problem: if that is so, it makes sense to take the time figure it out. Such delays have military and monetary costs, however. The continual reevaluation of nuclear versus conventional power added years onto the acquisition of the *Kennedy*; prolonged systems analysis killed the B-1 bomber (until the Reagan Administration resurrected it); a new main battle tank did not appear until 1980—over two decades after the introduction of the

M-60. Melvin Laird's reforms speeded up procurement by introducing the "fly before you buy" program, which involved the purchase of prototypes of a desired type of weapon (for instance, a tank or a fighter plane) and then comparing the differing prototypes to discover which would be best. This allowed defense companies to exercise their ingenuity and have the product tested before a decision to buy was made. It also reduced the amount of unproven or state-of-the-art technology that had to be built into new weapons. Although these reforms ameliorated the problem, they did not solve it. In some ways the Soviet system for acquiring weapons technology—continual prototyping and improvement by competing design bureaus—delivers more consistent improvement in technology, despite the USSR's generally lower level of technical development (Alexander 1978; Head 1978:555–557).

Systems analysis opposes innovation when the changes involved seem to take the form of an expensive version of the current, basic design. According to systems analysis, "The problem of justifying a modification is essentially the same as that of justifying a new development" (Quade and Boucher 1968:103). Thus, systems analysts argued that a nuclear carrier merely performs the same missions that a conventional carrier could carry out more cheaply, that the B-52 could take the place of a new strategic bomber, that a modified M-60 could delay the need for a new tank. Now, in each case the military changes involved were considerable; in each case technological improvement offered a hedge against increases in enemy strength. Throughout history improvement in military technology has required an open mind and a willingness to risk a leap in the dark. The rewards can never be entirely foreseen, but they may be substantial and may become fully apparent only after a long period of operational deployment or during a war (Churchill 1924:124–148).

In evaluating new technology of the sort under discussion, systems analysis takes the narrow view. An article by a systems analyst opposing the B-1 and favoring retention of the B-52 (a bomber over twenty years old) assumed that the Soviets would not develop a capacity to shoot down low-flying aircraft on the basis of the rather bizarre argument that this country would not be willing to spend the money necessary for similar capacity on our side. The article did not mention the relationship of B-1 procurement to the American negotiating position at the Strategic Arms Limitation Talks, it dismissed the possibility that procurement of a new manned bomber might have symbolic and therefore political value; it did not discuss the possibility that the new bomber might be needed for conventional bombardment missions, as the B-52 was (Wood 1976).

Systems analysts favor technological innovation, however, if they believe that a new (usually inexpensive) weapon can fill an old mission. The best and most recent example of this phenomenon is the claim of the systems analysts for precision-guided munitions (PGMs), in particular, infantry-carried, wire-guided antitank missiles. Their calculations of exchange ratios (for example, an antitank missile costing some tens of thousands of dollars can destroy a half-million-dollar tank) suggest that the tank is obsolete: they urge the acquisition of large numbers of such weapons to replace current tank-heavy units. Their recommendations pay little heed to two things: first, the possibility of countermeasures (for instance, formations that use artillery and mechanized infantry to flush out and destroy the PGM crews, or improved armor design); second, the difference between results scored on a test range by a healthy, relaxed, and safe test engineer and what actually happens when a missile is fired on the battlefield by a debilitated, nervous, and frightened soldier. The love affair of the systems analyst with precision-guided munitions extends to naval cruise missiles as well. It is now argued that large vessels (such as aircraft carriers) are fatally vulnerable to such weapons and that therefore the Navy should buy smaller vessels instead (Hart 1978; Woolsey 1978). Here again, systems analysts view warfare as a sort of one-move chess problem, rather than as a game in which the fortunes of the two sides surge back and forth. Various countermeasures (electronic and others) can nullify or reduce the dangers posed by cruise missiles; large vessels, particularly large aircraft carriers, can absorb far more punishment and destroy potential assailants earlier and at greater distances than smaller ones. The technological determinism of systems analysis leads its proponents to exaggerate the importance of such inventions as cruise missiles and PGMs generally. In addition, the political implications of the systems analysts' recommendations—for example, building only small aircraft carriers equipped with small numbers of short-range airplanes—are rarely brought up. In this case, the consequence of such changes would mean the abandonment of a fleet capable of exerting its power for long periods of time in remote parts of the world.

Systems analysis is particularly prone to advocate single weapon solutions to complicated problems because it seeks the optimal weapon, rather than a flexible mix.

> Simply put, building and maintaining a tactical cruise missile force to destroy some prescribed set of ground targets which figure in contingency plans should render both sea-based and land-based tactical air forces noncompetitive (Garwin 1978:61).

Yet one of the few lessons of military history is the superiority of forces trained and equipped for combined arms operations to those which rely on one type of weapon alone. From the Roman legion, which used javelin and short sword to defeat the Macedonian phalanx, to the Mideast war of 1973, those forces that could attack their opponents in various ways, that could match their tactics to their enemies' weaknesses, or that could quickly devise new expedients to counter enemy superiority in one arm—they have held the upper hand. The dangers of reliance on one type of weapon can be seen in the opening phase of the 1973 Yom Kippur War. The Israelis after 1967 had shifted to single weapon tactics—the use of large formations of unsupported tanks. They suffered defeat during the first few days of the war because their enemy had devised a force that could counter that one weapon, a force composed of antitank missile armed infantry. Later the Israelis returned to the combined arms formations which had been so successful in 1967, and deployed infantry and artillery to nullify the advantage of the Egyptian missileers (Herzog 1975:270–271; Schiff 1974:1–77).

Systems analysis discourages the study of one's opponents: the language, politics, culture, tactics, and leadership. The unit of analysis is the mission or the object, and the enemy is therefore often regarded as a passive collection of targets. As Edward Luttwak has pointed out, the attitude of the systems analyst is like the engineer building a bridge across a river, who does not for a moment think that the river will act deliberately in order to thwart him. Alternatively, systems analysis assumes that the enemy resembles us. McNamara suggested that the Air Force train its pilots in combat squadrons, the way the Soviets do. He said, "If it is not viable for us, one would conclude that it is not viable for the Soviets" (Enthoven and Smith 1971:143). This ignores, of course, the difference in equipment, organization, doctrine, and culture of the two sides. Similarly, military analyses performed by Enthoven of the conventional balance in Central Europe argued that NATO and Warsaw Pact forces were "equal" because both sides had equal numbers of soldiers and artillery tubes. Again, his analysis did not account for all those factors that have traditionally shaped the outcome of war (Enthoven and Smith 1969).

Finally, systems analysis leads its practitioners to neglect the importance of politics in the largest sense. During the early stages of the Vietnam war, the Office of Systems Analysis did not directly manage the Vietnam war, but the mindset of systems analysis led McNamara to think in terms of "making the costs exceed the benefits" for the North Vietnamese, rather than in terms of breaking the enemy's will and ability to fight or arranging a political solution to the problem. Moreover, the systems analysts put pressure on the American commanders in the field to produce numerical measures of success (Thompson and Frizzell 1977:194; Westmoreland 1976:273). The measures—body counts, the hamlet evaluation system, and so on—gave the American high command no real sense of how the war was going.

> "Ah, les statistiques!" one of the Vietnamese generals exclaimed to an American friend. "Your Secretary of Defense loves statistics. We Vietnamese can give him all he wants. If you want them to go up, they will go up. If you want them to go down, they will go down" (Hilsman 1967:523).

The numerical indices corroded the honor of the officer corps by providing the corps with a powerful incentive—indeed, at times a compulsion—to lie.

Henry Kissinger describes how in July 1970, when the Egyptians, under Soviet guidance, began to move surface-to-air missiles (SAMs) to the Suez Canal, systems analysts argued that Israel would make a more cost-effective choice if it bought weapons to repel a cross-Canal attack rather than use expensive *Phantom* jets to destroy the SAMs. Kissinger commented, "These arguments overlooked that a defensive strategy implies a war of attrition, a prospect fundamentally intolerable for a country outnumbered by around thirty to one" (Kissinger 1979:581). In 1971 Kissinger's systems analysts suggested that Vietnamese troops from the Mekong Delta be moved north to participate in operations near the Demilitarized Zone (DMZ). Their plans took no notice of the fact that troops who fought well to defend their homes in the south would desert rather than fight in Laos (Kissinger 1979:987).

CRITICISM OF SYSTEMS ANALYSIS

Systems analysts are willing and even eager to condemn defective analysis but not reexamine the premises of the whole approach, yet we must ask whether a method that consistently makes the same mistakes is not inherently flawed. Our main criticism of systems analysis, one that embraces all the others, is that it does not treat war as a unique phenomenon which requires application and experience—real or vicarious—in order to be understood.

We do not argue here against civilian control of the military, nor even against civilian intervention in questions of armament, tactics, and strategy. Such intervention is legitimate and necessary; more than once has it saved a great nation from defeat. But control and direction must come from an understanding of war as a complicated and difficult art, not from overweening confidence in the lore of economics. An art critic need not be an artist, but he must appreciate the difficulties of painting and sculpting.

Carl von Clausewitz, the greatest (perhaps the only) philosopher of war knew of approaches that resemble systems analysis. He described, for example, the relative merits of a squadron of cavalry, a battery of artillery, and a battalion of infantry:

> If we could compare the cost of raising and maintaining the various arms with the service each performs in time of war, one would end up with a definite figure that would express the optimum equation in abstract terms. But this is a guessing game . . . (1976:286).

This, of course, at a time when the technology of war was much simpler than it is today and therefore theoretically more amenable to systems analysis. Clausewitz continued by assuming that the squadron, battery, and battalion cost the same amount of money. Could we then calculate the optimal cost-effective solution of our military problems?

> It might conceivably be possible if destructiveness were all that had to be measured; but each branch has its own particular use and thus a different sphere of effective action. But the spheres are by no means fixed; they could be expanded or contracted . . . (Clausewitz 1976:286).

Clausewitz, therefore, decisively rejected systems analysis.

The administrative reforms of the Laird and Packard years at the Defense Department undid some of the damage done by systems analysis. It is not, however, in administrative reforms that the answer to systems analysis will be found. What we need instead is to reschool ourselves in the study of war.

We should begin by accepting the Clausewitzian analysis of war, which holds that war is partly a science but largely an art, an art that "includes all activities that exist for the sake of war, such as the creation of the fighting forces, their raising, armament, equipment, and training'' (Clausewitz 1976:127). War is a whole: we should reject, therefore, an artificial separation of the art of procurement from the operational arts of strategy and tactics; we should also reject the reductionism of the mission or scenario. War is an activity that should always be guided by political intelligence—even, when necessary, in the planning of battles. Nonetheless, war is an activity dominated in practice by moral and psychological forces because of the dangers it involves and the pressures it engenders. War is intrinsically unpredictable, primarily because of the problem of enemy reaction to our measures at the technical, tactical, strategic, and political levels.

Our study of war and our planning for it should include intensive study of our Soviet opponents or, indeed, any other adversary we may face. Rather than planning for attrition as systems analysis would have us do, we should discover our enemy's political and military weaknesses and match our strategy to them. Thus it might be better, as Samuel Huntington has suggested, to deter Soviet aggression in Europe by designing forces capable of breaking the Soviet grip on its East European empire, rather than attempting to increase an attrition level by 1 or 2 percent. As S.L.A. Marshall put it in his discussion of the reasons for the brilliant Israeli victories against the Arabs in 1956 and 1967:

> The basic study in all warfare is the mind and nature of the probable enemy, compared to which a technical competence in the handling of weapons and engines of destruction is of minor importance. Failing in the first, we will most likely fail in everything (Marshall 1958:6).

Israeli victories, particularly that of 1967, stemmed in part from an understanding of the political and even culturally based military weaknesses of their enemy, on an entire spectrum from disjointed alliance politics to a disinclination for night fighting. In 1973 the situation was reversed: the Israelis failed to understand their opponents and, worse, held them in contempt. The Egyptians, in particular, made use of their own primary strength—the solidity of peasant soldiers defending static positions with simple weapons—and took advantage of the rashness and overconfidence of their enemy, whose impulsive and uncoordinated tank charges on the first few days of the war played into their hands (Haykal 1975; Herzog 1975; Luttwak and Horowitz 1975; Schiff 1974). On both sides, therefore, an understanding of the enemy's mind, his culture, and his character was crucial to military success. As we have just argued, systems analysis leaves such intangibles out of its calculations and indeed would seem to deny their importance.

We must study past wars, for it is only through real or vicarious experience that one can acquire an understanding of the nature of war. A study of military history will not, to be sure, provide recipes for behavior in any given instance. It will, however, give us a feel for what works and what does not, much as a novelist's knowledge of literature and society helps him produce a coherent and believable tale.

Problems of war and preparation for it lie along a spectrum from politics (the purposes of war and the constraints on its conduct) through strategy (the coordination of battles), tactics (the direction of actual fighting), technology, and psychology (the motivation of soldiers or the selection of commanders). Systems analysis leads us to believe that only one part of the spectrum is important—technology. Even then, the choices it points to are suspect because technology should be chosen only after a consideration of other factors as well.

Systems analysis has led us to concentrate on the wrong problems, even to define them incorrectly. For example, the long and generally fruitless attempt to achieve standardization of weapons in NATO resulted from the belief that it was militarily dangerous and economically inefficient for an alliance not to deploy uniform weapons. The solution proposed was economic: a "free market" in weapons, each country specializing in the weapon it produced best, or all purchasing the single best type of weapon. Such a free market was impossible for political reasons, although advocates of standardization saw only the machinations of dogmatic or corrupt cliques, rather than the natural consequences of national independence and egoism. Moreover, the entire project rested on unproven and dubious assertions about the military value of standardization, assertions not matched against a historical study of similar problems (Cohen 1978a).

The NATO standardization question reveals the failure of systems analysis thinking to consider politics; the question of women in combat reveals the failure of systems analysis at the psychological end of the spectrum as well. The systems analyst views the problem in terms of physical capacity, arguing that if a woman can operate a fork lift she can operate a tank. Our new model analyst would view that as beside the point, saying that we must study individual behavior and unit cohesion under fire, and asking whether the psychological requirements of combat (and the unforeseeable physical ones) do not mandate masculine characteristics and relationships (Cropsey 1980; Gilder 1979; Webb 1979). He would ask whether this society intends to preserve women from combat for other moral or social reasons. He would study the experience of other countries which have incorporated large numbers of women, Israel in particular.

We must realize that we will find no simple alternative to systems analysis, for one of systems analysis's worst flaws is its penchant for terrible simplification. We cannot turn to a different, ready-made school of American strategists because the methods of systems analysis have spread throughout the strategic studies community and are no longer confined to a few adepts. We cannot merely reject a technique; we must change a way of thought.

We are not well prepared to begin a Clausewitzian study of war. The war colleges of this country are, for the most part, mere one-year way stations for Army and Air Force colonels or Navy captains on the way to higher ranks (Bletz 1972; Cohen 1978b; Korb 1976; Turner 1972). Our higher officer corps may be better educated than ever before, if we simply count postgraduate degrees in business administration, but there is reason to wonder whether the corps' affection for management has not weakened its ability to understand—and fight—war (Ginsburgh 1964). Our civilian institutions either concern themselves with narrow technical studies or, in the case of our best universities, slight military history as a subject unworthy of academic study. The abundant literature on military affairs that does exist often takes a narrow view: writers cleave to subfields within rigidly demarcated specialties such as sociology or political science, or preoccupy themselves with one set of problems such as arms control. We find few writers who possess a broad knowledge of history and politics, resist the cumbrances of a mechanistic social science, and, while keeping a larger view, are nonetheless willing to immerse themselves in technical detail (Ermarth 1978; Howard 1979).

At the very least we must change the national war colleges into institutions for the higher study of war. A good start would be their transformation into two-year institutions and an improvement in the quality of instruction. There and at leading universities we should stimulate interest in military history, strategic theory, and war studies in general. Civilians in the Defense Department should be particularly required to study war from a theoretical and historical point of view.

One of the larger consequences of systems analysis's critique of war as a unique activity has been a change in the self-conception of the officer corps. Civilians should curtail the pressure they exert, whether it is deliberate or not, on officers to look and sound more like IBM executives than the aloof or even disagreeable generals who won the world wars. Those men, such as George Patton, were traditional soldiers who nonetheless were well educated in the liberal arts, in their profession, and in the history of war. They did not lose sight of the crucial fact that their entire professional lives were, out of necessity, devoted to preparation for war, an activity utterly different from business. Henry Kissinger describes in his memoirs the replacement of that generation of officers by "a new breed, skilled in jargon and better bureaucrats." He observes,

> On some levels it eased civilian military relationships; on a deeper level it deprived the policy process of the simpler, cruder, but perhaps more relevant assessments which in the final analysis are needed when issues are reduced to a test of arms (1979:35).

Systems analysis raises the wrong questions and often delivers the wrong answers. If, as seems likely, this country will face military challenges in the next decade, we must prepare ourselves for uncertainty and sacrifice, and we cannot do so by means of methods that promise predictability and technological fixes. Our technical and numerical superiority did not prevent us from losing the Vietnam war. We may fight our next battle under far less propitious circumstances than in Vietnam, which is all the more reason, then, to turn away from the study of economics and toward the study of war.

REFERENCES

Alexander, Arthur J., 1978. "Decision-Making in Soviet Weapons Procurement." Adelphi Papers 147/148. London: International Institute for Strategic Studies.

Blackett, P.M.S. 1962. *Studies of War Nuclear and Conventional.* New York: Hill and Wang.

Bletz, Donald Ferree. 1972. *The Role of the Military Professional in U.S. Foreign Policy.* New York: Praeger.

Churchill, Winston S. 1924. *The World Crisis,* vol. I. New York: Charles Scribner's Sons.

von Clausewitz, Carl. 1976. *On War,* trans. by Michael Howard and Peter Paret. Princeton: Princeton University Press.

Cohen, Eliot A. 1978a. "NATO Standardization: The Perils of Common Sense." *Foreign Policy* 31 (Summer):72–90.

_____. 1978b. "Army War College Educational Policy Study." Report to the Director of Academic Affairs, U.S. Army War College, Carlisle, Pennsylvania.

van Creveld, Martin. 1977. *Supplying War: Logistics from Patton to Wallenstein.* London: Cambridge University Press.

Cropsey, Seth. 1980. "Women in Combat?" *The Public Interest* 61 (Fall): 58–89.

Enthoven, Alain C., and K. Wayne Smith. 1969. "What Forces for NATO? And from Whom?" *Foreign Affairs* 48, no. 1 (October):80–90.

_____. 1971. *How Much is Enough? Shaping the Defense Program 1961–1969.* New York: Harper and Row.

Ermarth, Fritz. 1978. "Contrasts in American and Soviet Strategic Thought." *International Security* 3, no. 2 (Fall):138–155.

Ewell, Julian J., and Ira A. Hunt. 1974. *Sharpening the Combat Edge: The Use of Analysis to Reinforce Military Judgment.* Washington, D.C.: U.S. Department of the Army.

Falls, Cyril. 1953. *A Hundred Years of War.* New York: Collier.

Garwin, Richard L. 1978. "Effective Military Technology for the 1980s." *International Security* 1, no. 2 (Fall):50–77.

Gilder, George. 1979. "The Case Against Women in Combat." *Parameters* 9, no. 3:81–86.

Ginsburgh, Robert N. 1964. "The Challenge to Military Professionalism." *Foreign Affairs* 42, no. 2 (1964).

Hart, Gary. 1978. "The U.S. Senate and the Future of the Navy." *International Security* 2, no. 4 (Spring):175–184.

Haykal, Mohamed. 1975. *Road to Ramadan.* New York: Quadrangle.

Head, Richard G. 1978. "Technology and the Military Balance." *Foreign Affairs* 56, no. 3 (April):544–563.

Herzog, Chaim. 1975. *War of Atonement.* Boston: Little, Brown.

Hilsman, Roger. 1967. *To Move A Nation: The Politics of Foreign Policy in the Administration of John F. Kennedy.* New York: Doubleday.

Hitch, Charles. 1965. *Decision-Making for Defense.* Berkeley: University of California Press.

Howard, Michael. 1979. "Forgotten Dimensions of Strategy." *Foreign Affairs* 57, no. 5 (Summer): 975–986.

Kissinger, Henry, ed. 1965. *Problems of National Strategy.* New York: Praeger.

_____. 1979. *White House Years.* Boston: Little, Brown.

Knorr, Klaus, and Oskar Morgenstern. 1965. "Science and Defense: Some Critical Thoughts on Military Research and Development." Policy Memorandum no. 32. Princeton: Center for International Studies.

Korb, Lawrence J., ed. 1976. *The System for Educating Military Officers in the U.S.* Pittsburgh: University of Pittsburgh, Center for International Studies.

————. 1979. *The Fall and Rise of the Pentagon: American Defense Policies in the 1970s.* Westport, Ct.: Greenwood Press.

LeMay, Curtis. 1968. *America Is in Danger.* New York: Funk and Wagnall.

Luttwak, Edward, and Dan Horowitz. 1975. *The Israeli Army.* New York: Harper and Row.

McKean, Roland N., ed. 1967. *Issues in Defense Economics.* New York: Cambridge University Press.

McNamara, Robert S. 1968. *The Essence of Security: Reflections in Office.* New York: Harper and Row.

Mansfield, Edwin, ed. 1968. *Defense, Science, and Public Policy.* New York: W.W. Norton.

Marshall, S.L.A. 1947. *Men Against Fire.* Washington, D.C.: Combat Press.

————. 1958. *Sinai Victory.* New York: William Morrow.

Murdock, Charles A. 1974. *Defense Policy Formulation: A Comparative Analysis of the McNamara Era.* Albany: State University of New York Press.

Quade, E.S., and W.I. Boucher, eds. 1968. *Systems Analysis and Policy Planning: Applications in Defense.* New York: American Elsevier.

Rickover, Hyman. 1967. "Cost-Effectiveness Studies." In U.S. Congress, Senate Committee on Government Operations. *Planning-Programming Budgeting: Selected Comment.* Washington, D.C.: U.S. Government Printing Office.

Roherty, James M. 1970. *Decisions of Robert S. McNamara: A Study of the Role of the Secretary of Defense.* Coral Gables: University of Miami Press.

Schiff, Zeev. 1974. *October Earthquake: Yom Kippur 1973,* trans. by Louis Williams. Tel Aviv: University Publishing Projects.

Seligman, Daniel. 1965. "McNamara's Management Resolution." *Fortune* 72, no. 1 (July):177 et seq.

Stockdale, J.B. 1978. "Taking Stock." *Naval War College Review* 31, no. 2 (Fall):2.

Storing, Herbert, ed. 1962. *Essays in the Scientific Study of Politics.* New York: Holt, Rinehart and Winston.

Strauss, Leo. 1953. *Natural Right and History.* Chicago: University of Chicago Press.

Thompson, W. Scott, and Donaldson D. Frizzell, eds. 1977. *The Lessons of Vietnam.* New York: Crane and Russak.

Trewhitt, Henry L. 1971. *McNamara.* New York: Harper and Row.

Tucker, Samuel A., ed. 1966. *Modern Design for Defense Decision: A McNamara-Hitch-Enthoven Anthology.* Washington, D.C.: Industrial College of the Armed Forces.

Turner, Stansfield. 1972. "Challenge: A New Approach to Professional Education." *Naval War College Review* 25, no. 2 (November/December):2–3.

U.S. Congress, Joint Committee on Atomic Energy. 1963. *Nuclear Propulsion for Naval Surface Vessels. Hearings before a subcommittee of the Joint Committee on Atomic Energy.* 88th Cong., 1st Sess.

U.S. Congress, Senate Committee on Armed Services. 1972. *Weapons Systems Acquisition Process Hearing: Before the Senate Committee on Armed Services.* 92nd Cong., 2nd Sess.

Webb, James. 1979. "Women Can't Fight." *The Washingtonian* (November).

Westmoreland, William. 1976. *A Soldier Reports.* New York: Doubleday.

Wood, Archie L. 1976. "Modernizing the Strategic Bomber Force Without Really Trying—A Case Against the B-1 Bomber." *International Security* 1, no. 2 (Fall):98–116.

Woolsey, James R. 1978. "Planning A Navy: The Risks of Conventional Wisdom." *International Security* 3, no. 1 (Summer):17–29.

_____ . 1980. *The Uses and Abuses of Analysis in the Defense Environment.* Washington, D.C.: American Enterprise Institute.

6 NUMBERS DO COUNT: THE QUESTION OF QUALITY VERSUS QUANTITY

Michael I. Handel

Quality is more important than quantity—but is best in large numbers.

Israeli Proverb

Wars, battles, and campaigns can be won by various types of armed forces, based on different combinations of *quantitative* and *qualitative* components. The choice of a particular force posture is determined by many considerations, among which are found historical traditions, political attitudes, military doctrine, economic, industrial, and budgetary constraints, and the availability of manpower.

The quantitative elements are relatively easy to identify and measure (that is, the number of aircraft, ships, tanks, artillery pieces, divisions, stocks of ammunition, oil). The concept of quality, however, must be divided into two major categories: (1) material aspects and (2) nonmaterial aspects. Material quality stands for the quality and performance of weapons which can be measured by their speed, range, firepower, reliability, and durability. Many of these specifications can be measured, but the trade-offs between them cannot: the amount of emphasis to assign to reliability instead of to state-of-the-art performance, the suitability of a certain weapons system to the quality of manpower available, and its performance in comparison with the enemy's weapons—all are very difficult to estimate, despite claims to the contrary. The second, nonmaterial qualitative dimension includes the quality of manpower, level of training, motivation and morale, the quality of the military doctrine chosen, military organization, staff work, planning, and political leadership; these factors cannot be readily measured. On the whole, therefore, the qualitative dimension, especially the nonmaterial element, is more elusive and difficult to define—let alone to measure precisely.

The total military power available to any given state can be schematically be presented as follows:

$$\text{TOTAL MILITARY POWER} = \text{QUANTITY} \times \text{MATERIAL}$$
$$\text{QUALITY} \times \text{NONMATERIAL QUALITY}$$

Within certain contraints, each country can choose between a number of possible combinations of the quantitative and qualitative elements in constructing its military force posture. Ideally, each country wants to strike the optimum balance between the two elements, thus providing the necessary level of security and the power to meet its goals and needs. Nevertheless, such a choice is far from easy, since the synergistic qualities of various combinations are difficult to evaluate; and new, different weapons, doctrines, and adversaries appear in every war.

The question of whether a war was won primarily because of quantitative superiority or was decided by a qualitative edge is not simple to answer even in retrospect. *History is full of contradictory examples even within the same war.* Only in extreme cases is it relatively easy to point to the decisive impact of one element. For example, given the ratio of forces and the roughly equal material quality available to the British and French allies and their German adversaries, it can be argued that the decisive German victory in the West in 1940 was achieved as a result of the better quality of the invading German army. Similarly, in light of the overwhelming Arab quantitative superiority and the roughly equal material quality of weapons technology possessed by Israel and its Arab neighbors, it can be argued that the superior quality of the Israeli Army has been the decisive factor in the five Middle Eastern wars fought so far.

On the other hand, Nazi Germany, which was not qualitatively inferior, as we have mentioned, finally succumbed to the overwhelming quantitative superiority of the allies, as did Japan. Likewise, Finland, which was initially successful in defending itself and in proving its qualitative superiority, was quickly crushed by the Soviet Union's quantitative superiority.

There are a few lessons that can be drawn from the examples mentioned:

1. In the cases where quality was the decisive factor, it was the nonmaterial elements of quality (that is, a superior doctrine, superior planning and staff work, high morale and an offensive spirit, and leadership) which proved to be decisive. *No important modern war has been won by the technological superiority of weapons alone.* It is therefore impossible to accept Major-General Fuller's statement that "tools, or weapons, if only the right ones can be discovered, form ninety-nine percent of victory. . . . Strategy, command, leadership, courage, discipline, supply organisation and all the moral and physical paraphernalia of war are as nothing to high superiority weapons—at the most they go to form the one percent which makes the whole possible" (Fuller 1943:61–62). If anything it is the conclusion of this research that the qualitative nonmaterial elements *are the most decisive in war.* The United States won World War II *primarily* because of its material superiority, while all of its technological excellence could not help it in Vietnam.

2. Qualitative elements, particularly the nonmaterial ones, appear to be the most decisive in quick and short wars, while quantitative superiority normally yields results only in a prolonged conflict, since not all of the superior quantity of military power available to a state can normally be brought into action from the outset. The outcome of wars is relatively indifferent to material technological quality.[1] Thus, the two most important factors are nonmaterial quality in short wars, and superior quantities in prolonged wars. The United States has neglected both of these vital factors during the last decade.

THE AMERICAN APPROACH

From a historical perspective, the possibility of more heavily emphasizing *material* or *technological* weapons in structuring a specific force posture is a fairly new phenomenon. Since the middle of the nineteenth century, warfare has become more and more *capital-intensive.*[2] After World War I, and even more so since World War II, war became not only more capital-intensive but also more technologically oriented. Until the end of World War I, military technology, while very important, offered a limited array of weapons. In today's world, revolutionary advances in technology offer many meaningfully different types of weapons, all of which are designed to accomplish similar military missions. For example, a tank can be knocked out by a variety of hand-held weapons, antitank missiles, air-to-ground munitions, other tanks, conventional artillery, guided artillery, and specially designed mines. Although all of these weapons have the ultimate task of destroying a tank, they vary enormously in cost, reliability, performance characteristics, and operational requirements. Given adequate budgetary support, creative imagination is the most important limit to the choice, design, and production of weapons in the present technological environment. The tremendous increase in the variety of weapons designs has not made purchasing and production decisions any easier.

Nowhere has material quality been emphasized as much as in the United states; technological excellence was and is seen as the panacea for pressing military problems, and technical-engineering solutions seem to offer a "quick fix." This not-so-new trend in the American approach to war has reached exaggerated proportions during the last decade and a half, particularly since the end of the war in Vietnam (despite the failure of U.S. superior technology to achieve a victory in that war).

A few reasons for this attitude are:

1. American society in general depends more heavily on automation and technology than any other society. The attitude that perpetuated the never-ending process of acquiring the latest model cars, television sets, stereos, and home appliances also found its way to weapons acquisition.

2. Technology is seen as the area in which the United States has a considerable edge, which will compensate for other weaknesses and give the necessary margin of advantage over any adversary. Perceived as the main potential opponents of the United States, the Soviet Union and China had a substantial quantitative advantage over the United States for which the United States could compensate by producing better military equipment. Moreover, since the end of the Vietnam war and with the establishment of its all-volunteer force, the American manpower pool has decreased, touching off a frantic search for superior technology to compensate for the further quantitative decline of the U.S. armed forces.[3]

3. In the Western world, the high value attached to the life of each individual, each soldier, has led to the desire to minimize the loss of human lives in war. Great efforts have been made to obtain the very

best weapons for the American soldier. This may paradoxically *reduce* the capacity of American society in general to maintain its strength and increase its total national power vis-à-vis its adversaries. The assumption that the overall power of the United States will increase the most if each soldier or pilot gets the best weapon or aircraft is not true, if too few of these weapons can be purchased. The emphasis on material quality will only be justified under the following circumstances.

First, if both adversaries are approximately on a similar quantitative and nonmaterial qualitative level, then improvements in material quality may give one of the states a military advantage. In other words, when all other things are equal, qualitative improvements in materiel *will* augment a country's total strength. (As we shall see shortly, however, all other things are normally *not* equal.)

Second, if a country has developed, to the extent of its ability, its quantitative and nonmaterial qualitative elements, then the only way left to increase its power is by developing better weapons.

Third, if and when the development of the qualitative material element *does not* lead to the neglect of the other two dimensions of national power or to *overreliance* on technical solutions to solve non- or only partly technical problems, an increase in material quality will then create no imbalance among the three elements of power.

WEAPONS TECHNOLOGY

The trend toward greater reliance on material-technological quality in the power equation has led to the development of increasingly sophisticated and complicated weapons systems which have inevitably emphasized quality over quantity; absolute performance levels over considerations of cost; gadgetry over reliability; "clean" experimental and laboratory conditions over the "messy" environment of the battlefield, and in the final analysis, the state-of-the-art technology for its own sake over war-fighting capabilities.

Superior weapons technology is not always more reliable and better suited for combat, and better technology carried to extremes can have some serious disadvantages that may actually *reduce* the total military power of the United States. Consider these points:

1. Generally, the more sophisticated and technologically advanced weapons systems become, the more they cost in absolute terms, meaning that fewer of these systems and their spare parts can be purchased.

2. There is always better technology in the near future, and too many weapons systems are produced only in smaller quantities, in anticipation of better things to come. Many weapons systems become conceptually (if not practically) obsolete before they are produced, but no substitute systems are being prepared to take their places. This develops into a never-ending race in which the best is the ever-present enemy of the good. Thus, large-scale weapons production is constantly deferred to a later date, while experiments and development continue, and sufficient weapons and munitions are available when they are needed.

3. An exaggerated emphasis on technology often also leads to the overreliance on technical performance and firepower instead of on doctrinal and nonmaterial solutions, thereby inhibiting creative military thinking. It results in an emphasis on the material aspects of war and in neglect of critical nonmaterial dimensions such as careful strategic planning, the development of better tactics, improved training, the use of surprise and deception, and other factors related to the human element in war.[4]

4. Finally, more sophisticated and complex major weapons systems usually require better and more intelligent manpower to operate them. Such higher quality manpower for operation and maintenance is not always available in adequate numbers, particularly not for the all-volunteer U.S. armed forces. In such cases, high technology is mismatched with the quality of manpower available.

The cost of modern complex weapons systems, weapons platforms, and all types of guided and unguided ammunition produced in the United States has skyrocketed. "To counter an increasingly dangerous perceived threat, or to gain advantage over potential adversaries, each new generation of weapons has been driven to the 'state of the art' in performance. The result has been rising unit production costs . . . in almost all classes of weapons. Thus keeping a constant-strength military force (in size, age, and capability relative to assumed increases in potential adversaries' performance) requires additional defense procurements on the order of 5 percent each year (excluding inflation)" (Gansler 1980:15). At the same time, the reliability of many of the weapons produced may have declined. A few examples will demonstrate this trend.[5]

The cost of the latest U.S. Main Battle Tank (MBT), the M-1, the first newly designed tank to be produced in the United States in more than two decades, is now estimated at $1.8 to $2.0 million per unit by the mid-1980s. At this price, the United States would be able to purchase a much smaller number of tanks and will have to maintain older models in service for a longer time.

Despite the high cost—and because of the high technology and advanced design—the M-1 is beset by many problems. To begin with, it suffers from a serious case of excess weight (close to sixty-two tons!), which means that only a single tank can be transported by the largest U.S. long-range military cargo airplane, the C-5A. No other cargo aircraft can carry the M-1. This is, of course, a serious drawback; in contrast to the Soviet Union, *The United States does not have any modern light tank available in large numbers that can be transported by air.*

The M-1 is equipped with a modern turbine engine that was used in the past only in helicopters.[6] In tests the engine proved to be unreliable. Dust—the normal environment of tanks—is apt to interfere with its functioning, rendering it especially unsuitable for desert warfare, one of the most likely areas it will operate in the future. In addition, the engine uses 20 percent *more* fuel than a regular diesel tank engine. This will certainly increase the operational costs of the tank and also increase the need for logistical support in time of war. The M-1 can operate only ten instead of twenty-four hours without refueling; and although it was designed to have a cruising range of 275 miles, it has demonstrated a range of about 140 miles in field tests. It requires much more maintenance than the older, simpler tanks; it was designed to operate "320 mean miles between failures," but field tests have so far indicated that a breakdown would occur at about half that number. Finally, it has been argued that the turret design of the M-1 is highly vulnerable to a well-placed shot; it is referred to as a "perfect shot trap."

The M-1 is not without its advantages: it is faster (it can go from zero to twenty miles per hour in 6.1 seconds); it boasts better survivability (despite the vulnerability of the turret); it has better "first-hit" capability, range-finding, and night-fighting equipment than its predecessors. Many of its "bugs" will gradually be ironed out. Still, the new German Leopard and the Soviet T-72 and T-80 tanks now in service will be equipped with better guns for a long while. Altogether, in light of its cost, its excessive weight, engine performance and maintenance problems, and fuel consumption, and in light of the quality of the Soviet tanks and the latest innovations in, and abundance of, antitank weapons of all types, the M-1 appears to be a poor choice.

In all probability, an upgraded version of the M-60A3 or a new, less sophisticated tank would be only marginally inferior in performance to the M-1—but could be more reliable, simpler, and more economical to operate and maintain, and could be produced in larger numbers. (Between 1977 and 1979, the United States produced, on the average, 650 M-60A3 tanks per year as compared to more than 2,500 in the USSR. The United States now produces 10 M-1 tanks per month or 120 per year; but when the production lines of the M-60A3 are closed down in 1982, the production of the M-1 is expected to rise to 60 per month or 720 per year in two plants.) This is a very low rate of production when the Soviet tank production is taken into account, with the high rate of tank attrition expected in any future war, and when we consider that the United States also has to reequip some of its allies' armies.[7]

The cost increases of high technology, "gold-plating" practices combined with a considerable decline in reliability and combat readiness, is even more apparent in the American military aircraft industry. The current production costs of three of the four fighter aircraft that constitute the backbone of American air power have escalated to around $20 million per unit. The U.S. Navy F-14 (Tomcat), one of the most sophisticated and expensive fighters, will cost $28.8 million per unit in fiscal year (FY) 1981, and $36.4 million per unit in FY 1982. The U.S. Air Force F-15 (Eagle) now costs approximately $20 million per unit. In the late 1960s and early 1970s, the U.S. Navy and Air Force had decided to compensate for the expected high costs of the F-15 and F-14 by procuring also larger numbers of cheaper aircraft such as the F-16 and F-18. But the Hi-Lo Mix (as it is called) turned out to be a Hi-Hi Mix.[8] The F-18 (Hornet), originally designed as a small, *light* fighter-bomber, a *low-cost* complement to the expensive F-14, turned out to be neither light nor cheap; its cost is put at $30.2 million for FY 1981, and at a staggering $36.4 million for FY 1982. The original price expected by the Navy for purchasing the F-18 between 1981 and 1986 was around $21 million per unit. In 1979, the F-18 program was 29.3 percent of the U.S. Navy's aircraft procurement program; this figure rose to 36.9 percent in 1980, and will probably be as high as 44.1 percent by 1982. The total price tag for the complete F-18 program is now calculated to be around $30 billion—or larger than the Trident program and not far behind the MX missile program. The F-16, which was supposed to be the mass-produced light fighter of the 1980s at $6 million per unit, now costs at least $15 million.[9]

While there is no doubt that on a one-to-one basis, these technological marvels can outperform all other aircraft presently in use, they are all plagued by serious problems. The state of the art has, on the whole, not resulted in more reliability and battleworthiness. Quite to the contrary, it has led to the procurement of fewer planes, fewer of which are mission-ready.

The latest inventory of U.S. war planes has recently been referred to as "a giant fleet of elite lemons." As it turns out, newer and better aircraft are not more mission-capable than older aircraft. The U.S. Navy front-line interceptor-fighter, the F-14A, was not ready to perform its missions nearly half of the time, and the Air Force's F-15 was not capable of performing its mission 44 percent of the time during FY 1979. The U.S. Air Force had originally tried to attain 70 percent mission-readiness for F-15s in peacetime. (Serious maintenance problems have afflicted not only the U.S. tactical fighter-bomber airfleet but also the giant C-5A cargo planes, only 45 percent of which are usable at any given time, while the rest are grounded for maintenance or shortage of spare parts.)[10] Because of the growing cost per plane, fewer can be purchased each year, thus generating powerful pressure to invest a larger percentage of the funds available in purchasing as many planes as possible, while relatively reducing the investment in purchasing spare parts and ammunition. As a result, fewer of these more expensive aircraft are airworthy, and in wartime they will have to fly more sorties per aircraft per day; and the pressure to achive a higher turnaround rate naturally puts a heavier than expected burden on maintenance. This may have created a situation in which the United States does not have sufficient aircraft available to perform the necessary number of missions in a high-attrition combat environment.

In some ways, not unlike many underdeveloped countries, the United States has for some time followed a policy that emphasizes purchasing the largest possible number of major costly weapons platforms, but has neglected to pursue an adequate policy of spare-parts acquisition and a reliable maintenance level. Experience has shown that a smaller number of better maintained aircraft and better trained pilots can be (depending on the adversary) much more effective than a large number of poorly maintained aircraft, helicopters, or tanks.

One way in which American designers of modern fighter aircraft (the F-15, in this case) had hoped to reduce the maintenance load was by designing a special computer to test the complex avionics system;

yet the diagnostic instrument has no less than 40,000 parts which are subject to frequent failure (it is out of order 50 percent of the time) (*Aviation Week and Space Technology* 1981:90). Thus, instead of alleviating the maintenance load, a new problem has been created. Another attempted solution was to design modular boxes that could easily be removed from the aircraft, be replaced by similar "boxes," and be sent to the producing factory for repairs. The U.S. Air Force now depends on factory manpower for a good deal of the maintenance of its ultrasophisticated equipment. To rely on remote factories for maintenance in wartime is, of course, a somewhat chimerical scheme; the factories themselves often have great difficulties and require a lot of time to repair the equipment. The backlog of repairs and the high cost of these modules do not allow them to stock enough to keep the aircraft operational at all times. Spare parts become too expensive to stock in the quantities needed to support the black box concept properly. (The accumulated shortage of spare parts for the Air Force alone is in the order of close to $3 billion.) In some cases, the shortage of spare parts for the F-14 and F-15 was so acute that some aircraft had to be cannibalized in order to keep others in operational condition. Current shortages, combined with the fact that the industrial base is unable to produce enough spare parts for both civilian and military aircraft and can only be expanded very slowly, means that the shortage in spare parts for military aircraft will be carried over well into the mid-1980s.

But even without a shortage of spare parts, the newly designed, state-of-the-art aircraft in the U.S. inventory are beset by myriad problems, only a few of which will be mentioned here. Touted as the engine that would open "a whole new realm of fighter techniques," the F-100 engine, which powers the F-15 and F-16, stalls under certain conditions in midflight, and requires excessive maintenance and spare parts (especially the turbine blades). Over $400 million have been invested additionally in order to improve the performance of this engine, and the end is not in sight. Serious problems have also developed with the Navy's F-14 engines, which must virtually be rebuilt at a cost of $640 million during the next five to six years. Again, there is a good chance that many of these problems will eventually be worked out, but in the future, *durability,* not performance, should be the hallmark of power plant design.

The habit of cramming state-of-the-art technology into each aircraft has also resulted in oversized and overweight aircraft. Because the size of both the F-14 and F-15 has been considerably increased, these planes are easier to detect at longer ranges by radar and easier to identify in dogfights. While both types of aircraft could probably outmaneuver any other single aircraft and engage in battle at longer distances (which is often of more theoretical than practical significance under the confused conditions of air battle), smaller aircraft such as the MiG-21 or the F-5E have distinct advantages. The lessons of the air war over North Vietnam taught U.S. fighter pilots that they needed a lighter, faster-turning aircraft (Sprey 1980). They may have gotten such a plane with the F-16, but the problem with the F-16, quite apart from what has been noted about its engine, is that it is not an all-weather plane suitable, for example, for central Europe.[11] Moreover, extensive air combat exercises conducted by the U.S. Air Force in Nevada in 1977 demonstrated that in one-on-one engagements, the performance of the latest generation aircraft (such as the F-15) was superior to that of the older and simpler F-5E (a plane similar to the Soviet MiG-21). The kill ratio achieved was in the order of eighteen to one (and not as an earlier Air Force computer model showed—that an F-15 armed with the *unreliable* long-range Sparrow air-to-air missile [at $108,000 apiece] would achieve an absurdly high kill ratio of seventy-eight to one). In the larger and more realistic dogfight configuration (four-on-four or larger), the kill ratio between the superior F-15 and the F-5E "plummetted" to about two to one. Statistics of air-to-air engagements between the Israelis and Egyptians during the 1973 war show that around 50 percent of the dogfights involved eight or more aircraft.[12] It can be expected that the Soviet Union in Europe, for example, would be able to send a relatively much larger number of aircraft into battle than the Arabs were able to, and hence the average size air battle involving the USSR would be even larger than the battles in the Middle East in 1973. Moreover, the latest generation of Soviet fighter aircraft such as the MiG-21 bis, the MiG-23, and the SU-24 are better aircraft than the F-5E; in fact, the latest models of the MiG-21 bis come close in performance to matching the F-16. All of the newer Soviet aircraft are produced in large numbers.[13]

These experiments and experiences indicate that in air-to-air combat, *the number* of aircraft is more important than the sophistication of their design and theoretically superior performance. (According to Sprey [1980], most air battles are conducted well below the maximum speeds and performance limits of modern fighters.) If this is the case, it is certainly wise to invest in many cheaper, more reliable fighter aircraft armed with proven and improved air-to-air missiles to compensate for any limits in their performance. It appears that less sophisticated, less costly weapons platforms produced in larger numbers and equipped with better precision-guided munitions will be a better investment than a small number of weapons platforms equipped with mediocre missiles.

Two other problems related to the quantities and costs of modern weapons platforms and munitions can be mentioned briefly. Primarily related to weapons platforms (particularly aircraft), the first problem consists of cost-benefit and psychological elements. There is a limit to the amount of national resources that any country can invest in a war without going bankrupt, even if it ultimately wins. The costs of modern high technology aircraft have escalated to the point where endangering them in battle is highly undesirable.[14] Few targets can justify risking a $20 to $30 million aircraft. Aircraft have become progressively more vulnerable to many relatively cheap guided and unguided antiaircraft weapons systems (an area in which the Soviet Union, as we shall see shortly, has a relative advantage over the United States and NATO).

Attempts to reduce aircraft attrition to fire from the ground by the use of counterelectronic measures or by the development of stand-off weapons (that is, weapons that can fire at targets while staying outside their defensive perimeter) all have their limits. In the final analysis, the only solution to the cost-effectiveness dilemma of expensive aircraft is to design and produce larger numbers of cheaper aircraft.

The psychological dimension of this problem is that the *growing* costs of aircraft and their *shrinking* number will undoubtedly make commanders reluctant to commit such aircraft into action. The threshold of committing these aircraft into battle may be raised, and the decisions to send them into combat will have to be made somewhat higher in the hierarchy of command (Boyd 1973). The time may not be far off when aircraft, like mercenary armies in the eighteenth century, will become too expensive to be risked in war. The conclusion is inevitable: more expensive aircraft in smaller numbers buy *less* security. The same is, of course, true of many other expensive major weapons systems such as tanks, ships, or even precision-guided munitions. (It can easily be seen why a tank commander will be more reluctant to commit M-1 tanks than M-60s to a battlefield saturated with cheap and effective antitank weapons.)

The second point concerns the escalating costs of modern munitions, particularly the latest types of precision-guided munitions (PGMs). It is very difficult to obtain an accurate estimate of the cost of many of the PGMs purchased by the U.S. government; their prices vary widely in different budget years according to the number ordered, the different makes or models of each weapon, and whether the research and development (R&D) costs are included (see Gervasi [1977] for example). But one thing is clear: their soaring costs allow for purchasing and stocking smaller quantities, while the small production lines lead to increased costs. The TOW (tube-launched optically-tracked wire-guided) antitank missile, the main antitank weapon of the U.S. Army, costs around $4,000 per unit. The TOW is a good example of a missile whose large-scale production (over 275,000 so far) has actually reduced their cost in real terms.[15]

Such munitions have even become too expensive for practice. Simulators must be used instead of live fire, certainly reducing the effectiveness of the operators, who have had no opportunity to get the "feel" of the weapons actually used in combat. "An Air Force pilot often goes through his whole fighter plane career without firing a real missile, while his Navy counterpart fires one every two years" (Wilson 1980:2).[16]

The U.S. Air Force and Navy currently suffer from a severe shortage of air-to-air missiles. A number of reports claim that both services have enough air-to-missiles available for only a day or two (at the most a week) of intense fighting. This would leave the United States in an extremely serious predicament in a prolonged war, since the slow rate of production and the lack of surge capability in the production of such highly complex missiles could not make up for the numbers expended. To expand the production lines would take many months, perhaps even a year.

A cautionary note is in place here. Although the accuracy and kill probability of PGMs is much higher than that of many unguided munitions, it is not as high as predicted by those who are not familiar with their limitations and their performance under actual combat conditions. In laboratory-type simulations and testing, almost all PGMs will achieve a 0.9 (or 90 percent) probability kill (P_k)—for example, for tests of the TOW, Maverick, and so on. Under battle conditions, against moving targets using active and passive countermeasures, the real probability kill will be much lower. Even according to the often accepted definition of PGMs (which is, according to

Digby [1975:1], "a guided munition whose probability of making a direct hit at full range when unopposed . . . is greater than a half"), seven or eight missiles are required to secure a 99 percent kill. When the probability kill in actual battle is closer to 0.1 (10 percent), many more missiles will be needed to knock out one target. (Close to forty-four missiles will be required to achieve a 99 percent kill if the P_k is 0.1, and close to ninety if the P_k is 0.05 [5 percent].) Unlike unguided munitions, which are less accurate but are immune to external interference and countermeasures once they have been fired, sophisticated munitions are *always* vulnerable. Moreover, once a sophisticated adversary has had the time to become familiar with the performance characteristics and weaknesses of the munitions in use, he will develop effective technical and tactical countermeasures. Therefore, it can be expected that in a prolonged war, the effectiveness of some PGMs may sharply decline rather than increase. If American military planners have purchased the *already small* numbers of sophisticated munitions on the basis of their theoretical—not practical—precision, their real number will be in even shorter supply.[17] In addition, it must be remembered that the Russians also have (particularly in surface-to-air and antitank missiles) a large number of PGMs. Attrition will surely work both ways.

THE FALLACY OF THE PASSIVE ENEMY

The problem of striking the correct balance between quantity and quality always has another side to it—that of the opponent. No force posture can be planned in a vacuum, independent of an evaluation of the weapons and material available to its major adversary. When it is said that quality compensates for lack of quantity, it is assumed that the quality weapons of one side are clearly superior to the weapons of the adversary who emphasizes quantity. If this assumption is incorrect, that is, if there is no meaningful margin of quality over the weapons systems and manpower of the adversary, then, in the absence of larger quantities of weapons systems, the adversary will obviously have the advantage.

Many Americans take it for granted that the quality of major American weapons systems is superior to that of the USSR, and therefore conclude that the United States can afford to produce fewer weapons systems while still effectively defending its interests against the USSR. But this assumption is unwarranted.[18]

The following is a typical statement frequently made by Defense Department officials, senior military officers, and other defense experts: "We have a high technology obsession. . . . It's the old question of quantity versus quality. *The Soviets have opted for quantity and we've opted for quality.* But for all we spend, things too often end up overdesigned and just don't work" (my emphasis). The latter part of this statement is indeed often true; the problem lies with the first part of the statement. Does the evidence indicate that the Soviets have opted for quantity and not for quality? The answer appears to be that the Soviet Union has chosen both—and has ended up with a better balanced force posture. While the Russians have modern high technology weapons that are not the final word in the state of the art and that often do not equal *some* of the American major weapons systems on a one-to-one basis, most of their major weapons systems are excellent and fairly reliable. Indeed, if the combination of technology and reliability is taken into account, the major Soviet weapons systems may well be at least as battleworthy as those produced in the United States. The Soviet Union's computer and electronic industries are not as sophisticated as those of the United States, and the Soviets have not yet landed a man on the moon; but by deciding to put most of their industrial and engineering efforts into the weapons industry, they have done very well. (The Soviet Union has *not* landed a man on the moon, but its research and activity in space is currently much more enterprising than that of the United States.) One thing is clear—even if, in some cases, Soviet technology still lags behind that of the United States, the technological gap in weapons design between the two countries has narrowed considerably. Recent American intelligence reports indicate, for example, that the Soviet Union has already closed the quality gap in the production of precision-guided munitions—an area in which the United States was supposed to hold a substantial and important lead.[19]

An examination of certain important weapons systems shows that the USSR is ahead of the United States technologically as well as in the overall quality of these weapons. For example, the T-72 tank produced by the USSR in large quantities is better than the best American tank now in operation, the M-60A3. The T-72 has better protection, a more efficient shape and silhouette, and above all, a better gun than that of the *future* M-1! (In addition, Soviet tanks are built to operate in a gas warfare environment; the M-1 is not.) By the time the United States finally unveils its technological marvel, the M-1 protected by

Chobham armor, the USSR will already be producing a better and probably more reliable tank, the T-80 (Middleton 1980; see also Cooley 1980). The M-1 is the first new American tank to be produced in twenty-two years; the T-80 will be the fourth new Soviet tank produced in twenty years.

In addition to having more tanks, the Soviets also have a much larger number of *much better* armored personnel carriers, particularly of their Infantry Fighting Vehicle (IFV), the BMP (Aversach 1980). Altogether, the Soviets are estimated to have some 55,000 modern APCs and IFVs; the United States has some 10,000 M-113s, all of them of older design. The Soviets have excellent heavy and medium artillery (some 19,000 pieces), though it is still less mobile than that of the United States. They also have a much better antiaircraft defense system, which includes the largest variety of antiaircraft missiles (the SA-3, SA-4, SA-6, SA-8, SA-9, and the new SA-10 and SA-11); in all they have over 150,000 missiles (Cobb 1979). They also have a large number of mobile antiaircraft radar-guided guns (the ZSU-23-4), whose great effectiveness was demonstrated in the Middle East war of 1973. Not only does the Soviet Union produce advanced weapons—it also produces them in large quantities, while the American R&D establishment has many problems in moving from research to massive weapons production.

Since the early 1960s, the Soviet Union has made great progress in modernizing and expanding its navy. The United States has lost its long-held naval superiority, and the two navies are now estimated to be at about the same strength.[20] The Soviets have recently put into service a new heavy cruiser, the largest to be built by any country since the end of World War II. The 22,000-ton Sovremenny carries, in addition to conventional guns, an array of surface-to-surface missiles (up to 200 SSN-X-19 as well as 12 surface-to-air launchers). The Soviets are now also constructing four large antisubmarine warfare ships and three new missile-cruisers. Recent U.S. intelligence reports indicate that the Soviet Union has already (and suprisingly) launched a new cruise-missile-firing titanium-built submarine of over 13,000 tons which, according to these reports, will make American aircraft carriers ten times more vulnerable. The range of their anticarrier missiles extends the threat to U.S. carriers from 20 miles to as much as 200 miles (Middleton 1981; Wilson 1981).

The different doctrines behind the American and Soviet navies demonstrate some of the problems involved in comparing the quantity and quality of different weapons designs. Such comparisons may be fairly easy where aircraft or tanks are concerned, but there is no clear way to compare a large surface navy (as the United States had in the 1950s) and a huge submarine fleet (as the Soviets had in the 1950s). Today, the bulk of the U.S. Navy is concentrated around thirteen large aircraft carriers; the Soviet navy has a powerful submarine fleet and a larger variety of surface vessels, with a considerable anticarrier missile capability. Which fleet is more powerful to do what against whom is a complicated question. It appears that the U.S. Navy, with its larger supercarrier fleet, is better equipped for long-range intervention and limited war operations (such as in the Persian Gulf), while the Soviet navy is primarily designed for an all-out war over control of the sea lanes and communications lines of the Western world. As long as the U.S. Navy does not have to engage the Soviet navy directly, it is more useful as a political and limited war instrument; in an all-out war, however, American supercarriers might prove to be extremely vulnerable to Soviet conventional and nuclear missile attacks. Despite the greater suitability of U.S. carriers for long-range intervention, the United States has, over the years, developed a highly unbalanced navy; it has invested too much in the more vulnerable supercarriers, their defense systems and their aircraft, while neglecting the development of other surface vessels, particularly transport and landing capabilities (which are also essential for intervention and limited war) as well as other areas in which the Soviets excel, such as sea-to-sea missiles and conventional submarines.

It is perhaps less well known that the Soviet air force underwent an intensive process of modernization. Not only do the Russians now have 8,800 planes of all types as compared with 6,400 for the United States but they have also introduced better, longer range tactical aircraft which carry heavier payloads. Most of the aircraft now being added to the Soviet air force in large numbers are only half a generation behind the latest American modern aircraft. These planes include the Sukhoi-15, Su-17, Su-20, the Sukhoi-24, and the MiG-23 and -27. The Soviets are now about to introduce three new fighters: an interceptor mission variable-geometry-wing air-superiority fighter (referred to as Model K) similar to the U.S. Navy F-14; a single-seat fighter (Model L) similar to the U.S. F-18; and a small, ground-attack aircraft (Model J) designed for close air support with an antitank gun system similar to the U.S. A-10 ("Soviets to Field Three New Fighters" 1979). It seems as though the Soviets are emulating the United States in trying to produce more sophisticated types of aircraft, including the latest avionics such as terrain-avoidance radar,

Doppler navigation equipment, Gatling-type guns mounted in pods, side-looking airborne radar (SLAR); real-time electro-optical (television) surveillance for reconnaissance; laser-guided weapons; and new families of antiair and air-to-surface missiles. They will not be far behind in the development of sophisticated air-to-surface stand-off precision-munitions of all types (*Aviation Week and Space Technology* 1980:13). In addition, they have made great strides in an area in which the United States held a tremendous advantage only a few years ago—that of helicopter gunships. They are now producing large quantities of the Mi-24 "Hind" gunship, considered to be the most advanced of its kind in the world (Hansen 1978).

Of particular concern to Western observers is the fact that the tremendous qualitative progress made by the Soviet Union during the last two decades was, unlike the American weapons procurement program, accompanied by a considerable increase in the number of major weapons platforms. This may be explained by the larger Soviet military expenditures as well as by the fact that the Soviet Union was not involved in an expensive and prolonged war as the United States was in Vietnam. But the Soviet weapons design philosophy, large production lines, and lower production costs also explain the simultaneous qualitative and quantitative expansion of the Soviet force posture.

A 1976 study comparing the costs of American and Soviet jet engines of similar performance found that Soviet engines were inherently less costly (between one-third and one-half the cost of the comparable American engine); they would have been cheaper even if they had been built by American workers, in American factories, with American materials. The reasons for the far lower cost of the Soviet engines were "design differences, maintenance philosophy differences, and specification differences" (Gansler 1980:83). The Soviets emphasize the development of weapons systems that are *more producible* (although Soviet designs are made to lower standards of tolerances and materials). An example of a very high-performance, low-cost system design is the Soviet MiG-25 aircraft:

> It does not require advanced electronics, exotic materials, precise manufacturing techniques, or complex structure. Similarly, it used stainless steel and aluminum as the primary airframe materials, instead of synthetic materials, as used by the U.S. Rivets were left unground (except in aerodynamically critical areas), and welding was said to be crude, but adequate. Larger engines were used to overcome the drag penalties. The

radar, though based on technology that is out of date by American standards, is one of the most powerful ever seen in an aircraft, and therefore less vulnerable to jamming. The overall MiG-25 has been described by American aerospace analysts as "unsurpassed in the ease of maintenance and servicing," "a masterpiece of standardization" and "one of the most cost-effective combat investments in history" (Gansler 1980:251–252).[21]

Similar statements can be made concerning Soviet tanks, antiaircraft missiles, and radar.

Frequently, the American research and development effort acquires a momentum of its own. Instead of producing large quantities of reliable and battle-proven weapons systems as the Russians do, the American R&D establishment usually prefers to keep developing and improving prototypes. As a result, the United States may have the latest state-of-the-art weapons on paper but only has limited numbers of not-necessarily-battle-proven weapons for the troops in the field.

The Russians, for example, have been producing night-seeing devices that are cheap and reliable though by no means as advanced as their American counterparts, but the Russian devices are supplied to the troops in adequate numbers. The U.S. Army, on the other hand,

. . . has done extensive development work on night-seeing devices, but has bought or ordered only 20 percent of the goggles it needs—30,000 sets at $6,000 each. . . . Instead, the Army intends to wait for the next, better generation of the goggles—ones that will permit troops to see by starlight what they now can view only under at least one quarter moon—to fill the order. Those devices will not be ready until 1985 (Toth and Kempster).

This is typical of the problems involved in the development of other major weapons systems such as a light air mobile tank or an infantry-fighting vehicle.

The explanation for the delay in the large-scale production of sophisticated weapons is that the best is the enemy of the good in a never-ending process of improvement.

Once the facilitating technology is available or can be foreseen, the eventual appearance of new weapon system program ideas is almost inevitable. . . . As long as major and minor advances in basic physical concepts and specific component performance continue to appear, new ideas for the development of weapon systems and major subsystems will be forthcoming in quantity. Defense firms in particular are prolific sources of evolutionary ideas (Peck and Scherer 1962:236).[22]

This continuous process can be highly counterproductive; it resembles the frame of mind of the student who constantly improves on his dissertation without ever completing it. This attitude also reflects, no doubt, the different historical experiences as well as the ideologies of both states. For the Soviet Union and for the Marxist ideology, conflict and war are an ever-present and unavoidable reality—and peace is the exception. For the United States, despite its direct participation in more prolonged wars than the Soviet Union since the end of World War II, psychologically peace is the rule and war is the exception; following every war, the United States temporarily withdraws into isolationism. Due to geopolitical considerations, the Soviet Union cannot afford to withdraw from the affairs of the world and therefore has a continuous program of massive weapons production and of more incremental changes in its weapons design. The American weapons design and production effort tends to vacillate between the extremes of involvement and resignation. The Soviet Union normally has the edge in the number of troops and weapons available for immediate action; the United States may have the advantage of starting a war with the most advanced weapons. The danger with the American policy is that the expansion of American forces requires *time*. Given the nature of modern war—its speed, growing rates of attrition, and the growing complexity of the weapons produced (which require much longer production lead times)—it is not clear at all that the United States will have the necessary time available to build up its forces before it is too late in a time of national emergency.

To claim that the USSR is emphasizing quantity over quality in military equipment is to foster a *dangerous misconception*. It may have been true in the 1950s or even the 1960s, but it is certainly not true in the 1970s and the 1980s. When it comes to military equipment, the Russians are second to none. They may have different designs and different types of weapons which do not lend themselves to a simple comparison with Western weapons, but they are certainly *not inferior*. In fact, the Russians appear to have the best of both worlds—they have quantity *and* quality.

Even if the United States had, overall, better weapons systems than the USSR, its qualitative edge would not be so overwhelming as the difference in the quantities of weapons produced by the two countries. (In other words, suppose that on the average, the U.S. weapons systems are two to three times better than those of the Soviet Union—which is doubtful—the Soviet Union still produces four to five times as many weapons.) In other words, the "quantity gap" between the United States and the USSR is much greater than the "quality gap" between them. Quality is not, however, limited to weapons systems and technology. The demand for quality must also apply to the soldiers who operate the weapons.

THE QUALITY OF MANPOWER

The quality of weapons systems discussed so far cannot be analyzed without considering another qualitative dimension—the manpower available to operate the weapons. Obviously, the higher the quality of manpower—in terms of intelligence, education, training, morale, and motivation—the better they can operate complicated weapons systems in the highly confusing environment of the modern battlefield. In this context, only a limited discussion of this question will be possible.

Contemporary weapons systems can be classified in two ways: (1) according to their complexity and the number of functions they can fulfill, and (2) according to the battlefield environment for which they are designed. Two "ideal types" of weapons emerge from such an analysis: on the other hand, we find simple single-purpose weapons operated in a simple environment (for instance, bazookas, rifles, antitank missiles) and, on the other hand, complex multipurpose weapons systems operated in a complex environment (for instance, fighters, tanks, electronic warfare systems). Frequently, the more complicated weapons systems become, the more purposes they can serve; that is, a fighter-bomber can be used for interception, bombing missions, air-to-ground support, and reconnaissance. The more operations they have to carry out simultaneously (such as fire missiles, monitor radar screen, head-on display, speed, level of fuel, and monitor instruments), the higher the quality of manpower required to operate such a system. Complicated weapons systems tend to break down more frequently in operation; and when they do, they require high-quality logistical support, in terms of routine and base maintenance as well as in immediate repairs under battlefield conditions. This puts increased demands on finding higher quality manpower for support operations. The growing demand for higher quality manpower also extends to command and control functions on all levels, especially the lower and middle-range echelons.

A battle between two tanks or between infantry is obviously a simpler affair than a battle involving many fast-moving tanks, assault and antitank helicopters, and self-propelled artillery, combined and coordinated with attacks from the air. This takes place in an environment where great attention must be paid to countermeasures of all types or to the possibility of operations in a chemical warfare environment. In the last decade, the complexity of the battlefield and of newly designed, latest generation weapons systems has increased exponentially. (Compare, for example, the World War II M-3 Sherman tank and the Mustang P-51 fighter-bomber with today's M-1 or the F-14.) There is evidence that during World War II, as well as in the war in Vietnam, some weapons systems had already become too complicated for the average American soldier (Milward 1977:192–193).

There is little doubt that American weapons systems have become too sophisticated to be efficiently operated in case of malfunction by the caliber of manpower available to the All-Volunteer Force (AVF). (This situation may be compared to the overall decline in the quality of secondary school education. Now, every child is capable of making much more complicated calculations with the aid of a hand calculator or computer, but he knows less about the mathematical principles and logic behind their operation, and will remain helpless when the batteries run out. Similarly, the M-1 can do everything faster and better, but if things should go wrong in its fire computer or range finder, its crew will be helpless.)

Currently, as Figure 6–1 shows, the quality of U.S. manpower and its weapons design philosophy seem to work at cross-purposes. In recent years, the salary incentives and a variety of social problems and attitudes have reduced the quality of manpower available to the AVF; since it was established, a larger percentage of new recruits come from the lowest socioeconomic and underprivileged groups in the United States than ever before. Some 42 percent of the Army ranks are now black, and perhaps an additional 10 percent belong to other minorities, primarily Hispanics. (The Marine Corps is 26 percent black.) The percentage of blacks and other minorities in *combat units* is even higher—as high as 60 percent in certain infantry divisions. In addition, given their lower chances of finding satisfactory employment outside the Army, the rate of black reenlistment is higher than that of whites. The percentage of blacks in the U.S. Army is over three times higher than their percentage in the overall population (Cameron 1980; Moskos 1980; Webb 1980).[23] Many of the white enlistees have lower levels of education than the blacks.

Figure 6-1. Manpower Quality and Weapon Suitability in Relation to Facility of Operation and Diversity of Weapons Systems.

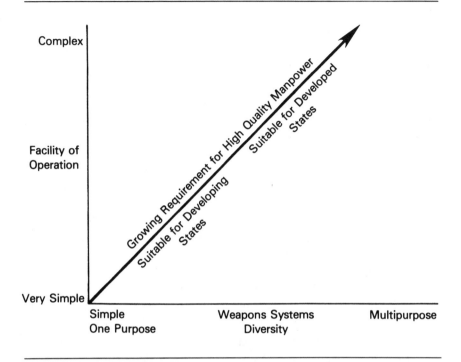

This shift in the socioeconomic background of enlisted men is, of course, reflected in their aptitude and intelligence as well as discipline. In 1979, 46 percent of the Army recruits belonged to what is called "Category Four"; that is, the lowest intelligence level from which the armed forces are allowed to recruit. The average percentage of Category Four recruits throughout the armed forces was 30: the Marines have 26 percent; the Navy has 18 percent; and the Air Force has 8 percent. (The lowest IQ level accepted in this classification is 80; these recruits have a fifth grade reading level and are marginally trainable.) As a matter of policy, the percentage of soldiers of this group should never exceed 10. (If the armed forces had a choice, they would try not to recruit any soldiers from this group at all.) If we include in this calculation soldiers belonging to "Category Three," well over 60 percent of the U.S. Army belongs to the two lowest intelligence groups that qualify for the service.[24]

The number of high school graduates in the U.S. armed forces continues to decline. A full 25 percent of the nonhigh-school graduates read at the sixth or seventh grade level. Many of the Army's maintenance manuals cannot be understood by the new recruits and must be rewritten on a simpler level—or as has been suggested, on the "comic book level."[25] In a national emergency, the U.S. armed forces would have to expand quickly, but the level of noncommissioned officers (NCOs) necessary for the training of new soldiers would be very low. Thus, the capacity of the United States to expand its armed forces in time of war is further restricted. This decline in the level of intelligence and education is, in turn, reflected in the competence level—or rather, incompetence level—of American soldiers. Recent Skill Qualification Test (SQT) scores were unusually low, and very few of those tested managed to pass (Fialka 1980a:12). According to Senator Sam Nunn, a recent army training study revealed that 21 percent of American tank gunners serving on NATO duty in Germany did not know how to aim their battle sights.

People in the lowest intelligence categories had great difficulty operating the Army's air defense weapons, including the shoulder-fixed Redeye missile, because they could not remember a complex firing sequence, and could not recall the differences between silhouettes of American and enemy aircraft. They also had trouble reading instruction manuals. Tank crews were found to average 40 to 50 percent below the skill level required by Army standards for combat readiness. Tank repairmen fared no better. When 666 repairmen were tested, they correctly diagnosed the mechanical problem from 15 to 33 percent of the time. The chance that they would correctly repair the tank once they found the problem was between 33 and 58 percent (Fialka 1980b:10).

Furthermore, the rising cost of fuel and ammunition, difficulties in maintenance, shortages of spare parts, and the decline in available budgets have all caused a decrease in the amount of training at a time when it is needed the most. This has been reflected in the lower performance level of American troops in NATO exercises, when compared to the other NATO forces (Fialka 1980c:1). The AVF also suffers from a manpower shortage; and while the absolute number of soldiers needed is small (about 4 percent), the major shortages are primarily in the higher quality technical professions (for example, doctors, engineers, pilots [who prefer the more lucrative civilian market] and many NCOs and petty officers). This results in a further decline of combat readiness of aircraft, tanks, ships, and other major weapons systems which require considerable maintenance work.

Approximately 40 percent of the enlistees in today's military fail to complete their period of obligation. This high "turbulence" or turnover rate is an alienating experience that ultimately reduces battlefield effectiveness.[26] Continuity in terms of soldiers working and training together for extended periods of time is crucial for teamwork. Tank crews, maintenance crews, or any other kind of crew cannot function properly unless their members know each other. Teamwork is essential not only for improving technical efficiency and skills but also for the creation of an *esprit de corps*—a sense of comradeship and social cohesion.

The United States, a modern and advanced industrial nation with armed forces possessing the most sophisticated weapons in existence, has gradually been reduced to recruiting soldiers on the level of an underdeveloped society.

As Figure 6–2 indicates, the continued existence of the gap between the quality of American weapons systems and the quality of soldiers to operate them will contribute to the further decline of American military power and may force a war on the United States when it is least ready to defend itself. A credible level of national security comprises an effective conventional military force posture, requiring not only financial, scientific, and technological support but also a sub-

Figure 6-2.   Men-Material Gap.

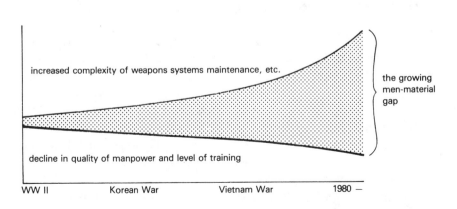

stantial investment in human talent, intelligence, and motivation. One cannot function without the other.

The solution to the current predicament cannot be quick or simple. It will require a new policy simplifying weapons systems procured by the United States together with an all-out effort to increase the recruitment of better qualified manpower. This will necessitate a new recruitment policy—perhaps a return to the universal draft or, alternatively, an improved set of financial and other incentives.

All of this is not meant to imply that the Soviet Union does not have its own difficulties and weaknesses; it, too, has a serious problem in obtaining the high-quality manpower needed for modern warfare. The Soviet situation, however, is somewhat easier to deal with because they have universal conscription as well as a heavier emphasis on the design of simpler weapons systems that require less training to operate.[27]

CONCLUSIONS

The current combination of qualitative and quantitative elements in the American force posture is highly imbalanced. It is imbalanced both from within (that is, the sophistication of its weapons is not ideally suited to the decline in the quality of manpower; spare parts necessary for the maintenance of its major weapons systems are in short supply) and from without (that is, in comparison to the Soviet arsenals).

Most important of all, the American force posture has declined *quantitatively well below the minimum* necessary to protect its global interests vis-a-vis the Soviet Union. Overemphasis of technological excellence has actually weakened the United States. Weapons, ammunitions, and spare parts were purchased in considerably lower numbers; they became less reliable, require more maintenance, and require more sophisticated soldiers to maintain and operate them—all this while the quality of manpower available has been declining for a considerable length of time.

Meanwhile, the Soviet Union has been steadily improving the quality of its weapons and munitions while producing them in increased numbers. Technology is not a panacea; and when carried to the extreme, it creates more problems than it solves. It cannot be decisive against an adversary who has comparable high-performance technology in greater amounts.

Achieving a more realistic balance in the United States will require basic changes in the traditional approach to national security, preparations for war, and war itself. It will necessitate major adjustments in weapons design philosophy, self-criticism, and a continuing debate on these issues. It will take time and agonizing decisions, as well as changes in attitude similar to those involved: for example, in the reluctant transition from eight-cylinder gas-guzzlers to small economy cars. But it can be done.

In this context, some of the conditions that will facilitate such changes are mentioned here on a general level.

1. It must be realized that the U.S. conventional force posture requires as much attention and careful study as the nuclear force posture.

2. There has been a steady decline, in absolute and relative terms, of the conventional force posture since the war in Vietnam; and the current level of forces and preparedness is inadequate to protect the national goals of the United States.

3. Conflict is an ever-present reality, not a remote, abstract contingency.

4. An increased level of preparedness, a more powerful force posture, and the readiness to use force are necessary to back up day-to-day policymaking and to promote American interests. Such a force must *always* be ready and available for use, not only a continually deferred promise for the future.

5. Improvements and expansion will entail sacrifices for the American people. The constant expansion of Soviet power certainly extracts heavy sacrifices from the Soviet population. For Americans, the sacrifices will include a greater readiness to serve their country in addition to financial support. To expand the U.S. armed forces as is needed and at the same time to improve the quality of manpower will require the reintroduction of the draft in the United States.

6. War and national security involve much more than technology, procurement, and material quality, and wars cannot be won by superior technology.

What are some remedies for the current weaknesses of the American force posture?

There must be radical changes in weapons design philosophies. Among other things, more ideas and specifications for the design should emanate from the military itself (for example, pilots, tank corps, field commands) and less from the R&D people and the industry.

Emphasis must be shifted from the state-of-the-art, expensive weapons systems to simpler, more reliable, and more easily maintained weapons systems. The latter type of weapons will be cheaper to produce and hence can be made in larger numbers. Given the much higher rates of attrition that can be expected in a future war, larger quantities of major weapons systems, spare parts, and ammunition must be produced. Weapons designers must learn to think small, not only in terms of F-15s, M-1 tanks, or supercarriers but also concerning smaller A-4 or F-5 types of tactical aircraft, air-mobile tanks, AFV and IFVs, new mortars, cheaper night-sight equipment, trucks, and the like. A greater effort should be invested in the production of precision-guided and other types of munitions. The most sophisticated weapons platforms are only as good as the weapons they carry; less sophisticated platforms with more versatile, accurate munitions will probably be cheaper and more effective. All types of weapons must be better tailored to meet the quality of manpower available, even while the military is trying to attract more highly qualified manpower. Finally, reference must be made to another qualitative point not discussed in this article, which is nevertheless of the greatest importance: more effort must be put into reexamining the U.S. military doctrine, its relevance to modern warfare, and its suitability for different types of war in different regions of the world. Certainly, the heavy use of tactical air support, strategic bombardments, counterguerrilla tactics, and the incredible emphasis on firepower and technology all failed to yield positive results in the Vietnam war. Furthermore, the foregoing suggestions for improvement will be of limited value unless the United States is able to develop a more creative and innovative military doctrine. While the role and development of the qualitative, nonmaterial dimensions in warfare—particularly that of military doctrine—were not discussed in this chapter, my ultimate conclusion is that they constitute the most critical and decisive dimension. This dimension will require more attention and the investment of much greater mental efforts during the 1980s.

NOTES

1. Concerning the difference in quality between the European colonial states and the colonized nations in the nineteenth century, Michael Howard emphasizes that it was much more than Western material

and technological advancement which determined their superiority: "European artillery, breech-loading rifles, and machine-guns made the outcome of any fighting almost a foregone conclusion." But as an afterthought he adds: "Almost, but not quite . . . as the British survivors of the Zulu victory at Isandhlwana in 1879 and the Italian survivors of the Ethiopian victory at Adowa in 1896 would have been able to testify. Even superior weapons, if deployed without tactical skill and used against forces superior in leadership and courage, did not necessarily guarantee victory. Colonial conquest still owed at least as much to the superior cohesion, organization, and above all self-confidence of the Europeans as it did to their weapons" (Howard 1979:121n–122n).

2.   "The tendency of modern fighting is to become increasingly capital-intensive. One measurement of this is the amount of capital expended on killing one enemy; this has been estimated as roughly ten times as much in the Korean War as in the Second World War" (Milward 1977:170).

In the war in Vietnam, for example, 340 artillery shells were required to achieve one enemy casualty and 1,200 shells to effect one kill (Marriott 1977:115). According to Jack Merrit and Pierre Sprey (1979:9), "Combining cost and kills, munitions cost per air-to-air kill has gone up by a factor of 8,000 since the Korean War (to Vietnam)." The same trend, although to a lesser extent, has recently developed in the Soviet Union.

This development is illustrated for the United States at war since World War II in this very instructive table:

The Trend in U.S. Battle Inputs, Manpower versus Firepower

Item	World War II (1941–45)	Korea (1950–53)	Southeast Asia (Fiscal 1966–71)
Scale of war effort (millions of man-years)	31.4	6.0	9.7
Combat exposure (millions of man-years)	6.2	0.4	0.5
Munitions expended (millions of tons)	6.96	3.13	12.92
Surface-delivered	3.94	2.11	6.59
Air-delivered	3.02	1.02	6.33
Rate of munitions expenditure (tons per man-year of war effort)	0.2	0.5	1.3
Rate of battle inputs (tons of munitions to man-years of combat exposure)	1.1	8.1	26.1

Source: White (1974:6).

3. Perhaps the best example of the attempt to compensate for the quantitative decline in manpower through sophisticated technology is the extensive research effort invested in the development of multiple independently targetable reentry vehicles (MIRVED) PGMs: for example, the WAAM program in which one precision-guided missile, bomb, or artillery shell carries many smaller precision-guided warheads, each of which can independently home in on a different target (in this case, armored vehicles). Therefore, one shot by *fewer soldiers* can achieve numerous kills. See, for example, Furlong (1978:1378–1379).

4. For example, according to a senior Israeli armaments expert, most of the research teams that the United States sent to Israel after the 1973 war were only interested in weapons performance, and the effectiveness of different types of American and Soviet munitions; almost no one showed interest in tactical problems, doctrinal improvisations under pressure and the like.

5. For the need to produce more reliable weapons, see Moore, (1980: 23, 25).

6. On the problems of the XM-1 (now referred to as M-1) see, for example, Patton (1980:28–38, 80–83) and Custance (1980:60–62, 88).

7. Small as it is, American tank production comes under further pressure because of the need to supply friendly countries such as Israel and Egypt, which have an insatiable appetite for modern tanks. This has been mentioned as having an adverse impact on the United States' own combat readiness. The United States currently produces, at the most, around 600 tanks per year as compared with the close to 2,700 tanks produced in the Soviet Union. *The Economist* reports that the Soviet Union produced in 1979 no less than 40,000 antiaircraft missiles, 1,800 combat aircraft (including combat helicopters), 3,000 tanks, and 4,000 armored personnel carriers. See also the Pentagon (1981).

8. See Collins (1980:229); also Myers n.d. 48–52. Myers contends that the primary motive behind the Hi/Lo mix concept was not so much the wish to produce larger quantities of cheaper aircraft as much as it was to produce less complex and less sophisticated fighters, since the experience of the 1960s demonstrated the "inverse relationship between sophisticated equipment and a quality combat force" (Myers n.d.:48). The F-18 can hardly be referred to as an unsophisticated aircraft.

9. The European (West German-British-Italian) Tornado multirole combat aircraft has also run into very serious cost over-runs (*The Economist* 1981:40). During World War II, fighter aircraft were produced in very large series (the P-51 Mustang over 14,000; the P-47 over 15,000; the F-4U over 12,000). During the early 1950s, the F-86 was produced in numbers over 6,000, and by the late 1950s and 1960s,

the F-4 Phantom was produced in quantities over 5,000. The F-5 Freedom Fighter, the most widely deployed in the non-Communist world, has also been produced in large numbers. Over 3,450 have been produced so far at about $4.0 million in current prices. Today's supersophisticated aircraft are produced in the order of the high-hundreds to lower thousands: 521 of the F-14 were ordered; 729 of the F-15; 1,366 of the F-16; and 1,377 (1,030) of the F-18 (see White 1974:47). This, of course, means that fewer missions can be flown and that fewer planes can attack fewer targets. See also Deitchman (1979: 29–63).

10.   It would be interesting to compare the maintenance level of other modern air forces, such as those of Sweden, West Germany, Israel, or even the Soviet Union, to that of the United States. The data for other countries are, however, highly classified and cannot be obtained. It does appear, though, that *other* Western countries maintain higher standards of maintenance. See also Spinney (1980:30).

11.   General Dynamics' F-16 air combat fighter is being viewed within both the Defense Department and Congress as an incomplete system at a time when increased emphasis is being placed on all-weather, beyond-visual range, air-to-air systems.

12.   This was the well-known AIMVAL/ACEVAL air-to-air exercise designed to evaluate U.S. air-to-air fighter tactics, as well as the performance of different types of weapons and aircraft. The exercise demonstrated that (1) force ratios are important, (2) the presence of "a crowd" severely reduces the effectiveness of sophisticated weapons systems, and (3) the relative size and signature of the contending aircraft is very significant.

    The importance of force ratios is also as true for other major weapons systems such as in tank battles. This is demonstrated by the two Lanchester Laws. See *Models, Data and War: A Critique of the Foundation for Defense Analyses* (1980:66–69).

13.   According to an article in the authoritative *International Defense Review,* new models of the old mid-1950s MIG-21 will be able to match the new ultrasophisticated and expensive F-16 in almost all respects. See Danyalev (1978:1429–1434). Even in its newest versions, the MIG-21 will of course be much cheaper than the comparable F-16.

14.   In his article, Myers (n.d.) goes even further by suggesting that high technology, inexpensive, surface-to-surface missiles can undermine the basis for a separate tactical fighter-bomber air force. Many of the air-to-ground attacks can, in his opinion, be accomplished by surface-to-surface missiles for 20 percent of the cost and without the loss of valuable pilots (Myers n.d.:51–52). This proposition is highly questionable. Against relatively small and very mobile targets (such as

tanks), surface-to-surface missiles cannot be as accurate or effective. Assuming a reasonable rate of attrition (below half a percent), aircraft can be used again and again, whereas missiles can be used only once.

15. The TOW antitank missile is an exception in that its price has been cut by 25 percent since the first missiles were produced in 1969. There is, however, some doubt that the TOW missile would be able to penetrate the new armor of the T-64, T-72, and T-80. See *International Defense Review* (1978:1373); also Middleton (1980:7).

16. Yet another reason given for this situation is an "embarrassing shortage" of missiles. (For example, only a third of the necessary Sparrow AIM7 are in stock for the F-15.) The higher costs of air-to-air missiles reduced the number being purchased. The Air Force and Navy have air-to-air missiles sufficient for only a day or two of intense fighting. See Barnard (1980:1).

17. According to Secretary of Defense Brown, it was assumed before the war in Vietnam that the kill reliability of the Navy AIM-7E would be 0.5. Yet in Vietnam, it demonstrated a kill probability of only 0.11. In his own words, "If the implied four or fivefold improvement is not realized in a future, the penalty will be much greater because of the difficulty of surging production of such complex weapons" (cited in "Secretary of Defense Brown's Memo on Tac Air Readiness" 1980: 34).

18. It is important to recall that the Soviet Union's technological capability has more than once been seriously underestimated by the United States. In the late 1940s, the United States underestimated by a few years the USSR's ability to produce an A-bomb and later an H-bomb. In both instances, the USSR produced these weapons way ahead of the schedule computed by the Americans. Later, in the mid-1950s, U.S. scientists and engineers refused to believe that the USSR would be able to orbit a satellite before the United States. Despite all preceding Soviet announcements, U.S. political leaders and scientists were completely taken by surprise when the USSR launched its first Sputnik. Yet many Americans still perpetuate the myth of the Soviet Union's technological backwardness and its alleged emphasis on quantity at the expense of quality.

19. According to John Collins, the U.S. technological military superiority (that is, the American qualitative edge) is tenuous at best. The USSR has the edge in no less than twelve important areas of military technology; the United States has a similar lead in only eleven. Although the United States is catching up in four areas of advanced technology, the Soviet Union is closing the gap in eleven. See Collins (1980:101–114).

20. This is the evidence of U.S. Navy leaders. See "U.S. Has Lost Naval Superiority Over Soviets, Leaders Tell Hill Panel" (1981:10).

21. Former Under-Secretary of Defense William J. Perry suggests that Soviet fighter aircraft built in the last decade are in general more complex, and more expensive than comparative U.S. aircraft (see *Washington Post* 1981:C1).

22. See also Fox (1974:10).

23. Despite their growing proportion in the armed services, blacks make up only 4.7 percent of the officers in all branches of the armed services. The Navy has the lowest proportion of black officers, 2.3 percent of its total of 62,127; that is, approximately 1,400 black officers.

24. Category Four recruits require one and a half times as much training, both in time and frequency of repetition, as Category Three recruits. The cost of training material, such as ammunition, was 40 percent more. Performance decay was significantly greater among lower mental groups. See "Doubts Mounting About All-Volunteer Force" (1980:1095); see also Fialka (1980:10).

25. A check at Fort Benning in 1976 revealed that 53 percent of the enlistees had a fifth grade or lower reading ability.

26. The high turnover and "personnel turbulence" between military units weakens morale and cohesion of primary groups and considerably reduces combat effectiveness. It has been observed that "the American Army since World War II has experienced a progressive reduction of primary-group cohesion until the Vietnam war, when it may be argued, it almost ceased to exist. The major thrust of our argument is that the performance of the American Army during the Vietnam War indicates a military system which failed to maintain cohesion under conditions of combat stress. Our data suggest that the Army in the field exhibited a low degree of unit cohesion at initially all levels of command and staff, but principally at the covert squad, platoon and company level. . . . It seems evident that to the extent that cohesion is a major factor in maintaining an effective fighting force, the Army in Vietnam had ceased to be effective. Indeed, the Army began to border on an undisciplined, ineffective, almost anomic mass of individuals who collectively had no goals and who, individually, only sought to survive the length of their tours" (Gabriel and Savage 1978: 8-9, 13, 31). The Army is trying to improve this situation. See Fialka (1980a:1).

27. The Soviets appear to do a little better, although they have their own problems. See "Soviet Armed Services Showing Weaknesses In Several Key Areas" (1980:1, A-10).

REFERENCES

Aversach, Stuart. 1980. "Soviet Forces Under Test: Superior Machines, Slow Reaction." *Washington Post* (August 12):1.

Aviation Week and Space Technology. 1980. (December 15):13.

_____ . 1981. (February 16):90.

Barnard, Richard. 1980. "A Short War: Navy, Air Force Face Severe Missile Shortage." *Defense Week* (May 19):1.

Boyd, John. 1973. Quoted in Stuart H. Loory, *Defeated: Inside America's Military Machine.* New York: Random House.

Brown, Harold. 1980. "Memo on Tac Air Readiness." *Armed Forces Journal* (May):34.

Cameron, Juan. 1980. "It's Time To Bite the Bullet on the Draft." *Fortune* (April 7):54.

Cobb, Tyrus W. 1979. "Tactical Air Defense: A Soviet-U.S. Net Assessment." *Air University Review* 30 (March-April):18–39.

Collins, John M. 1980. *U.S.-Soviet Military Balance: Concepts and Capabilities, 1960–1980.* New York: McGraw-Hill.

Cooley, John K. 1980. "How American-Russian Capabilities Match Up." *Christian Science Monitor* (March 5):12.

Custance, George. 1980. "Is the XM-1 Tank Obsolete?" *National Defense* (October):60–62, 88.

Danyalev, Georg. 1978. "MIG-21 bis and F-16A Air Combat Potential: A Comparison." *International Defense Review 11,* no. 9:1429–1434.

Deitchman, Seymour J. 1979. *New Technology and Military Power: General Purpose Military Forces for the 1980s and Beyond.* Boulder, Colo.: Westview Press.

Digby, James. 1975. *Precision-Guided Weapons,* Adelphi Papers, no. 118. London: International Institute for Strategic Studies.

"Doubts Mounting About All-Volunteer Force." 1980. *Science* (September 5):1095.

The Economist. 1980. (August):36.

_____ . 1981. (February 21):40.

Fialka, John J. 1980a. "Army Views Manpower Situation as a Crisis." *Washington Star* (March):12.

_____ . 1980b. "25% of Recruits in Low-Intelligence Category." *Washington Star* (March 11):10.

_____ .1980c. "U.S. Posts Dismal Record in NATO Competitions." *Washington Star* (December 16):1.

_____ . 1980d. "Army Plans Reforms To Make Fighting Units More Cohesive." *Washington Star* (September 6):1.

Fox, Ronald J. 1974. *Arming America: How the U.S. Buys Weapons.* Boston: Harvard Business School.

Fuller, John F.C. 1943. *Machine Warfare: An Inquiry into the Influence of Mechanics on the Art of War.* Washington, D.C.: The Infantry Journal.

Furlong, R.D.M. 1978. "WAAM, The U.S. Air Force's Next Generation of Anti-Armor Weapons." *International Defense Review* 9:1378–1379.

Gabriel, Richard A., and Paul L. Savage. 1978. *Crisis in Command: Mismanagement in the Army.* New York: Hill and Wang.

Gansler, Jacques S. 1980. *The Defense Industry.* Cambridge, MA.: The MIT Press.

Gervasi, Tom. 1977. *Arsenal of Democracy: American Weapons Available for Export.* New York: Grove Press.

Griffiths, David R. n.d. "F-16 Questioned in Defense Dept., Congress." *Aviation Week and Space Technology* (August 18):92–93.

Hansen, Lynn M. 1978. "Soviet Combat Helicopters." *International Defense Review* 11, no. 8:1292–1246.

Howard, Michael. 1979. *War in European History.* London: Oxford University Press.

International Defense Review. 1978. 11, no. 9:1373.

Marriott, John. 1977. "Precision-Guided Munitions." *NATO's Fifteen Nations* 22 no. 5 (October-November):115.

Merrit, Jack, and Pierre Sprey. 1979. "Quality, Quantity, or Training." *USAF Fighter Weapons Review* 79 (Summer):9.

Middleton, Drew. 1980. "Soviets Introducing New Tank in Europe." *New York Times* (March 16):7.

———. 1981. "Soviets at Sea: New Ships for Distant Bases." *New York Times* (January 25):3.

Milward, Alan S. 1977. *War, Economy and Society, 1939–1945.* Berkeley: University of California Press.

Models, Data and War: A Critique of the Foundation for Defense Analyses, PAD-80-21. 1980. Washington, D.C.: General Accounting Office.

Moore, Robert A. 1980. "Tactical Warfare Developments into the 1980s." *National Defense* (August):23–25.

Moskos, Charles C. 1980. "How To Save the All-Volunteer Force." *The Public Interest* (Fall):74–89.

Myers, Chuck. n.d. "Hi/Lo What?" *Military Science and Technology* 1:48–52.

Patton, Phil. 1980. "Battle Over the U.S. Tank." *New York Times Magazine* (June 1):28–38, 80–83.

Peck, Merton J., and Frederick M. Scherer. 1962. *The Weapons Acquisition Process: An Economic Analysis.* Boston: Harvard Business School.

Pentagon. 1981. *Soviet Military Power.* Washington, D.C.: U.S. Government Printing Office.

"Soviet Armed Services Showing Weaknesses in Several Key Areas." 1980. *New York Times* (December 9):1, A-10.

"Soviets To Field Three New Fighters." 1979. *Aviation Week and Space Technology* (March 26):14–16.

Spinney, Franklin. 1980. "Defense Facts of Life." Paper presented to the Subcommittee on Manpower and Personnel of the Senate Armed Services Committee, May.

Sprey, Pierre. 1980. "Mach 2, Reality or Myth?" *International Defense Review* 8:1209–1212.

Toth, Robert C., and Norman Kempster. 1980. "U.S. Pushing Weaponry Technology to the Limit." *Los Angeles Times* (September 10).

"U.S. Has Lost Naval Superiority Over Soviets, Leaders Tell Hill Panel." 1981. *Washington Post* (February 6):10.

Washington Post. 1981. (February 22):C1.

Webb, James. 1980. "The Draft: Why the Army Needs It." *Atlantic Monthly* (April).

White, William D. 1974. *U.S. Tactical Air Power: Missions, Forces and Costs.* Washington, D.C.: The Brookings Institution.

Wilson, George C. 1980. "Missiles Too Costly for Practice by Pilots." *Washington Post* (June 23):2.

———. 1981. "Soviets Launch Huge New Attack Submarine." *Washington Post* (January 9):1.

7 THE SUPERPOWER COMPETITION FOR INFLUENCE IN THE THIRD WORLD

Steven R. David

The coming years are virtually certain to bring increased American-Soviet competition for influence in the Third World. The demand for scarce resources, decline of detente, and instability in the Third World itself will all contribute to an environment dominated by superpower confrontation. The high costs of American and Soviet intervention (as illustrated by the Vietnam and Afghanistan experiences) will insure that direct, protracted military actions against Third World states will continue to be a rare feature of the superpower struggle for influence. Rather, the success of the United States or the Soviet Union will increasingly be determined by their respective abilities to persuade Third World regimes that they should adopt a pro-American or pro-Soviet alignment.

The process of convincing Third World states to adopt a particular foreign policy orientation is, in one respect, very complex. Issues of ideology, economic development, and security are all factors that sway countries from one side to the other. From the American perspective, however, this process of persuasion is much simpler. If the United States seeks to compete successfully with the Soviet Union for influence in the Third World, it must demonstrate its ability and willingness to protect the leadership of those regimes which it seeks to attract; this will be possible only if the United States can convince these select individuals that political alignment with the West is in their best *personal* interest.

The need for American policymakers to insure the survival of friendly leaders follows from the nature of the Third World itself. Despite the rise of Third World nationalism, the level of political participation in most Third World states remains very low. The most important reason for this is the relatively brief existence of the vast majority of Third World countries as independent entities (frustrating the development of a state consciousness) and the arbitrarily drawn colonial borders (creating linguistic, ethnic, and cultural divisions within states). The result is the absence of a sense of political community with its system of shared values and traditions that has evolved in the developed states of the West.

A lack of meaningful political participation by the general population has created a situation whereby most Third World states are run by dictatorial regimes in which the significant foreign policy questions are decided by a single individual or, at most, a small group. When one speaks of a Third World state aligned with a superpower, one is really referring to the chosen orientation of a certain individual or group of individuals. Therefore, to secure a pro-American alignment it is reasonable that the United States meet the needs of this small but critical elite.

For these elites no need is greater or more pressing than the need to stay in power—not because Third World leaders are any more ambitious or megalomaniac than their Western counterparts, but because the threats they face carry much graver consequences. Confronted with a situation in which conflict or the threat of conflict is endemic, where institutional means of succession are often lacking, and were loss of power can mean loss of life, it is not surprising that Third World leaders are intensely concerned with defending their position. In a sense, then, the success of the United States in the Third World will depend on how well it can manipulate and satisfy two of the most basic human desires—the drive for power and the fear of death.

The need for American policy to focus on the security concerns of Third World leaders does not mean that other factors do not play a role in the alignment decision or that remaining in power is always the predominant preoccupation of the ruling elite. Rather, it is in American interests to concentrate on this area because it provides the Soviets with the best opportunity to extend their influence throughout the Third World. By making short-term security considerations paramount (something well within Soviet capabilities) the Russians are able to prevent the competition for influence in the Third World from moving into other areas where the United States could capitalize on its strengths. The Soviet need to deny the United States the opportunity to exploit its assets can best be appreciated through a brief examination of the relative appeal of the superpowers to Third World leaders in the areas of ideology and economics.

IDEOLOGY AND ECONOMICS

With the Soviet Union as the superpower with a "revolutionary" ideology, one would expect that nation in particular to benefit from the ideological considerations of determining foreign policy orientations in the Third World. This was indeed the case during the decolonization period of the late 1950s and early 1960s when many Third World countries turned to the Soviet Union in the belief that Marxism was the answer to their needs. For the leaders who emerged (such as Sukarno in Indonesia and Nkrumah in Ghana) ideology played an essential legitimating role in their regimes. By identifying goals and defining enemies, ideology was necessary to mobilize the popular support to tear down old political institutions while justifying the excesses required to create new ones (Huntington 1970). Given these needs, the appeal of Marxist ideology over the tenets of capitalism or liberal democracy is obvious.

Once the destruction of the old order is completed, however, the appeal of ideology and its contribution to the alignment decision diminishes rapidly. The new regime finds that its institutions cannot possibly live up to the demands of the ideology it professes (especially if it is Marxism), making the presence of ideological concerns a threat to the very consensus it helped to create. Rather than seeking to raise the salience of ideology in governing, a new leader would more likely seek to downgrade its impact, depriving his enemies of the use of the ideological tool used so effectively in achieving power in the first place (Huntington 1970). Thus, while the process of deciding foreign policy orientation may initially contain within it a significant ideological element, once a regime is confronted with the problems of governing, its role declines markedly. With decolonization largely completed in the Third World, it is reasonable to expect that ideology will no longer be a major factor in determining alignments.

Furthermore, even in those situations where the importance of ideological considerations appears to remain high, the benefits to the Soviet Union are dubious. It is now difficult to find any Third World regime whose pro-Soviet orientation has largely been determined by ideological affinity with the Soviet Union. Regimes that do profess socialist or Marxist leanings (such as in Zimbabwe and Tanzania) take great pains to assert that they are not copying the Soviet model but are tempering their ideologically driven direction with the "objective" conditions they are confronting in their respective countries. Similarly, one would be hard-pressed to find *any* revolutionary movement that looks to the Soviet Union for its ideological inspiration. While economic and military assistance are sought, when it comes to searching for a model to follow, the gray, listless, plodding bureaucrats of the Kremlin lack the revolutionary fervor that any radical group must instill to attract followers.

Unlike ideological considerations, economic concerns have the potential to become increasingly important in the development of relations between Third World states and the superpowers. While the extent to which economic issues will determine foreign policy orientations will vary greatly among Third World leaders, it is safe to predict that the greater their influence, the more likely it is that they will act to produce a pro-American foreign policy. The fact remains that the United States enjoys a clear superiority over the Soviet Union in meeting the economic aid and trade needs of the Third World.

The American edge in economic aid is demonstrated by the fact that from the end of World War II to 1979, the United States has extended loans and grants to the Third World amounting to over $107 billion as compared to approximately $18 billion by the Soviet Union (Central Intelligence Agency 1978a, 1980). Furthermore, Soviet economic aid had been generally less well received than aid from the United States. At a time when Third World countries are becoming increasingly vocal about the need for aid to their economies, assistance from the Soviet Union (to a greater extent than from the United States) has tended to be directed toward developing export-oriented industries whose purpose is to serve the requirements of the Russian economy rather than helping Third World countries meet their own market needs. In addition, repaying Soviet aid frequently involves a double disadvantage for the recipient because the latter is forced to purchase Soviet goods of inferior quality at prices 20 percent or more above the world market, using artificial exchange rates which are beneficial to the Russians (International Institute for Strategic Studies 1978). Although the Soviets have attempted to cope with some of these problems by paying above-world market prices for goods from favored countries (for instance, sugar from Cuba) and by devising jointly managed, public-sector development plans for Third World countries (Central Intelligence Agency 1979), their aid programs must still be judged inferior to that of the United States.

In a similar fashion, Soviet trade cannot match American trade as an instrument of influence. In total volume, American trade with the Third World has consistently been many times that of the Soviet Union, even excluding oil. Taken together, Third World countries tend to earn trade surpluses with the United States while suffering trade deficits with the Soviet Union (Central Intelligence Agency 1980). Much of the Soviet trade carried out is bilateral with Russian manufactured goods, being exchanged for raw materials and thus perpetuating the "dependent" nature of the Third World economies (International Institute for Strategical Studies 1978). Moreover, the same complaints raised by Third World countries regarding the low quality of Soviet aid are raised in connection with Soviet goods.

The Soviet inability to match the United States in either the quantity or quality of its economic assistance and trade accounts for the fact that economic factors have not played a major role in any Third World leader's deciding to turn to the Russians. Realizing that they are operating in a realm of inferiority, the Soviets in most cases have not even made a serious attempt to provide large-scale economic aid to regimes seeking its support. In situations where massive assistance was given (for example, Egypt) its effectiveness—both in terms of alleviating economic problems and in drawing the regime closer to the Soviets—has left much to be desired.

American policymakers, recognizing the Soviet weakness and confident of their own strength, have long sought to translate the economic concerns of Third World states into political influence. Throughout the 1950s and 1960s the United States promoted policies leading to long-term development in the Third World. It was hoped that such development would lead to the establishment of liberal democracies which in turn would insure the creation of pro-Western regimes. More recently, American economic superiority has been invoked to justify optimism about the future of the U.S.-Soviet competition for influence in the Third World. This view is best typified by former Ambassador to the United Nations Andrew Young's statement, "We don't have to fear communism in the area of economic competition. The sooner the fighting stops and the trading starts, the quicker we (the United States) win" (*New York Times* 1978).

While both of these views maintain elements of truth, they are nevertheless fatally flawed. First, given the fact that it took the West several centuries to develop liberal democratic governments, there is no reason to abandon hopes for the Third World tò follow a similar path—in the long run. With the United States and its allies so increasingly dependent on raw materials such as oil, however, it can no longer afford to wait for the Saudi Arabia's of the world to transform themselves into functioning democracies. Similarly, Andrew Young is correct to assert that as long as the American-Soviet competition remains economic, the advantage will lie with the United States. What he (and others who share his view) fail to perceive, however, is that this conclusion is equally clear to the Soviets. Consequently, they will do all in their power to make certain that the "fighting" (or the threats thereof) will never stop in areas where they seek to extend their influence.

The Soviet strategy of focusing on security concerns to compensate for ideological and economic weakness demands an American response. Clearly, if the United States cannot meet the basic security requirements of Third World leaders, it will attract precious few of those leaders no matter its long-term strengths might be. This does not mean that the United States should simply back any anti-Soviet or pro-Western leadership without first considering the character of the regime, its importance to American interests, and the type of support demanded. Moreover, in most cases, it would be unrealistic to expect American support to require direct U.S. intervention whenever a regime faced trouble. The United States must, however, demonstrate that it will act effectively within the limits of its commitment to make certain that the leadership it chooses to support remains in power. Admittedly this appears to be a short-term solution, but it must be remembered that such "short-term leaders" as President Sadat of Egypt and King Hussein of Jordan, stayed in power years longer than most observers thought possible. Moreover, as already stated, long-term stability cannot be reached in the face of short-term insecurity.

CAUSES OF EXTRALEGAL REGIME CHANGE

The overwhelming importance that leaders in the Third World place on remaining in power focuses attention on the various ways they can be overthrown. Although it is impossible to delineate all the reasons for extralegal regime change and because such change is often due to a complex mix of factors, there are still four basic ways that regimes are forcibly removed from power: social revolution, internal rebellion, external invasion, and coup d'etat.

Social revolution, which can be defined as a massive upheaval for radical change, has been the most studied cause of the fall of Third World regimes. In part, this has been due to its sheer drama. Because social revolutions involve and affect so many people, they are a distinctly observable and electrifying event. Furthermore, unlike other changes in regimes revolutions, almost by definition they produce an abrupt departure from the direction of the previous leadership. Thus, while countries like Bolivia can experience some two hundred coups without attracting much attention (even in Bolivia itself), it is difficult to ignore the protracted struggles leading to the enormously significant triumphs of such revolutionary leaders as Mao Tse-tung and the Ayatollah Khomeini.

Despite the attention lavished on social revolutions, that avenue is perhaps the least promising one for the United States to focus on in its competition for influence with the Soviet Union. One reason is that despite their considerable importance, social revolutions are nevertheless a relatively rare occurrence in the Third World. Furthermore, reversing a true social revolution when it does occur is a most difficult task, especially for a country such as the United States where direct support for a counterrevolutionary role would often be lacking. Finally, social revolutions are an enormously complex phenomenon requiring an examination and analysis extending beyond the confines of this chapter. All of this does not mean that the United States can or should ignore the impact of social revolutions when they take place. What it does mean is that failure to cope with social revolutions should not paralyze the United States from acting against other threats to Third World leaders which are more frequent, easier to control, and more readily understood.

One of the more significant threats faced by Third World leaders is that of invasion by one or more of their neighbors. Clearly, any leadership which cannot perform the most basic duties of protecting its population from foreign aggression or preserving the sanctity of its borders is not likely to remain in office very long. It is not surprising, therefore, that a foreign state wishing to remove a regime from power might launch an invasion in the hopes of either forcefully eliminating the offending leadership or exposing its weakness to the extent that indigenous forces make its continued tenure in power impossible. Vietnam's invasion of Cambodia and Tanzania's invasion of Uganda are recent examples of one nation overthrowing the regime of another through armed attack. Significantly, if the postdecolonization norms against infringing on sovereignty continue to erode, as appears likely, similar interstate conflicts to bring about regime changes will undoubtedly increase.

The threat of armed conflict, however, need not come from outside the state. Internal rebellions caused by a multiplicity of factors (especially religious, ethnic, and tribal differences) have been persistent in many Third World countries and are likely to intensify in the future. That many of these groups have more limited aims (for instance, greater autonomy) than those of revolutionary movements should not obscure the fact that their struggle often results in the collapse of the central regime they are contronting. This has already occurred in Ethiopia where the Eritrean rebellion helped bring about the downfall of Emperor Haile Selassie, as well as several of his successors. Other threats to leaders from disgruntled groups include the Polisario in Morocco, the Kurds in Iraq and Iran, and the Moslem rebels in the Phillipines. In addition, while not engaging in any active rebellion at present, the 300,000 Shi'ites on Saudi Arabia's eastern coast represent a potential threat to the royal family.

By far the most common threat to a regime's survival comes from the coup d'etat—the sudden forcible overthrow of a government by a small group. Since World War II there have been approximately 100 successful coups and about an equal number of unsuccessful attempts. (Exact totals are difficult to determine because of variations in the defining of coups by different sources.) The reasons why coups are so prominent in Third World regime changes are found in the previously mentioned characteristics of these countries: the concentration of power in a narrow elite (often the military), the relative political apathy of the great majority of the population, the lack of a democratic tradition, and the absence of any institutionalized procedures for succession. Since these conditions are likely to continue in most Third World countries for the forseeable future, so, too, will coups persist in playing a central role in regime change.

In order to compete successfully for influence in the Third World, therefore, the United States and the Soviet Union must convince leadership elites that they can and will provide the assistance necessary to help cope with the threats of outside invasion, internal rebellion, and coup d'etats. Defending against external threats and internal rebellion requires that the superpowers demonstrate a willingness and capability to implement effective military assistance policies to Third World states. Forstalling coup d'etats requires policies focusing on the personal protection of the leadership elite. The comparative effectiveness of the superpowers in these two broad areas (as perceived by the Third World leaders) will determine their success or failure in the Third World.

MILITARY ASSISTANCE

In assessing the relative strengths and weaknesses of American and Soviet military assistance policies and capabilities, it becomes clear that one can no longer take American superiority for granted. Although the United States still retains some important advantages, the Soviets have improved their position to the point where they maintain an edge over the United States in several key areas. This is especially true regarding the less than vital countries (e.g., Kenya, Morocco, and Sudan) which make up the vast majority of the Third World and though important, are not critical enough to justify direct Soviet or American intervention. Among these states the Soviet assets have already proved instrumental in securing pro-Russian alignments (for example, Ethiopia and Angola) and have the potential (when combined with other actions) of increasing the attractiveness of the Soviet Union for regimes throughout the Third World which face severe security problems.

One of the most prominent advantages of the Soviet Union in the military assistance area lies in its position as the world's leading producer of conventional arms. In a given year the Russians produce approximately six times as many tanks, three times as many armored personnel carriers, eight times the artillery pieces, and twice the combat aircraft as the United States (Department of Defense 1977). The huge pool of weapons this creates is enhanced by the Soviet proclivity (duplicated in their nuclear weapons programs) to stockpile virtually everything produced regardless of age. The Russians are thus able to transfer massive amounts of arms without drawing on stocks used by the Soviet forces. American military personnel are still resentful about the stripping of combat forces in Europe to resupply Israel in 1973. For a less than vital country, this type of action would be unthinkable.

The huge quantities of arms produced and stockpiled by the Soviet Union has enabled it to play the leading role in the transfer of weapons to Third World countries. This development warrants emphasis due to statements by American policymakers (most notably former President Carter) quoting figures that indicate the United States overwhelmingly dominates the arms trade, and should therefore assume the responsibility for its reduction. While it is true that in certain years the United States has indeed accounted for more arms sales to the Third World than has the Soviet Union, such figures are misleading for several reasons (Central Intelligence Agency 1978b). They ignore the difficulties inherent in calculating dollar-ruble exchange rates, in determining the actual costs of Soviet programs, and in allowing for the different compositions of American and Soviet arms packages. (For example, American arms sales include a much higher proportion of support and services than do Soviet sales as illustrated by the fact that major combat equipment makes up approximately 75 percent of Soviet sales and only 40 percent of American sales [Department of Civil Defense 1979].) Furthermore, by focusing on arms sales, cancellation of contracts (such as occurred in Iran) are not always reflected in current figures.

The result is that the Soviets, while behind in sales, *deliver* greater amounts of actual weapons to Third World states than does the United States (Central Intelligence Agency 1978b). Moreover, the Soviets lead in the transfer of weapons which are most important in resolving Third World conflicts: tanks, artillery, surface-to-air missiles, and supersonic aircraft (U.S. Congress 1981). Finally, this trend toward increased Soviet arms transfers shows no signs of slackening; Soviet arms deliveries to the Third World (even measured by the misleading dollar terms) substantially exceeded U.S. arms deliveries in 1979 and 1980 (U.S. Congress 1981).

Even though the Soviets have in recent years widened their lead in arms transfers to the Third World, it has been suggested that the higher quality of American arms still leaves the United States as the preferred security patron. Indeed, when one examines the upper reaches of technology, U.S. weapons with their sophisticated electronics and computers generally outperform their Soviet counterparts. Unfortunately, since most Third World conflicts are fought with older, "obsolescent" equipment, this American advantage often proves illusory, especially since most Third World forces lack the requisite training and expertise to operate sophisticated weaponry (particularly aircraft). In Third World conflicts the levels of weaponry most commonly used—the assault rifles, artillery, armored personnel carriers, antitank arms, and even tanks—give a qualitative edge to the Soviets who often produce weapons more effective under battlefield conditions than those from the United States. For the armed forces of the Third World, what is critical is not whether the American F-15 jet and XM-1 tank are superior to the Soviet MiG-25 and T-80 but whether reliable, usable weapons exist in the field and which side has more of them.

The Soviet capability and willingness to transfer large amounts of appropriate arms to the Third World becomes even more attractive when one considers price. Generally, Soviet weapons cost much less than their Western equivalents. For example, on the average a regime can purchase five MiG-21s for the price of a single F-5. (Variation in models and equipment can move the ratio up or down.) Furthermore, the Russians have demonstrated a greater willingness than the United States has to discount prices for political purposes. In addition, American demands for payment in hard currency have left some regimes (for instance, Ethiopia) without the arms they needed and have alienated others (for instance, Sudan and North Yemen) by forcing them to turn to an uncooperative Saudi Arabia for financing.

While the Soviet advantages in arms production, quality, and price are certainly attractive to regimes considering a pro-Soviet alignment (and chilling to those who are not), it is the speed with which the Soviet Union can respond to immediate crises faced by Third World leaders that ultimately makes it such an attractive patron. On the average the Russians deliver their arms in one-half the time of the United States (Central Intelligence Agency 1978b). Their huge stockpiles enable them to draw from existing supplies, while the United States must frequently delay arms shipments (as it did with an Ethiopian request for Phantom aircraft) until the requested arms can be manufactured. Furthermore, the Russians enjoy a relatively unfettered political process of arms transfer, which allows them to implement decisions rapidly and massively. The United States, on the other hand, must normally confront a bewildering array of executive and congressional committees before an arms deal can be completed. By the time a favorable decision is reached (if indeed it ever is), it could very well be too late.

The Russians also maintain a significant edge over the United States because of their greater skill in using proxies. Because political and other factors have precluded direct Western and Soviet interventions in most Third World conflicts, the capacity to project force into those conflicts through well-trained, disciplined proxy troops has become highly significant (David 1979). This becomes particularly clear when one bears in mind that most Third World forces are often ill prepared to fight a major engagement with modern weapons.

The Soviet use of Cuban troops in Angola and Ethiopia amply demonstrates the power of competent proxies to decide the outcome of a conflict. One does not have to view the Cubans as Soviet puppets to realize that the congruence of Cuban and Russian interests, whether forced or not, is rapidly producing a situation whereby Soviet support is perceived as being tantamount to victory. Small wonder, then, that a high-ranking African official remarked that no leadership in Africa is now prepared to defy the Russians openly.

Aside from the overall benefits proxies can provide to a threatened regime, they have proved absolutely essential for any leadership seeking to change military suppliers in the midst of a conflict. It takes approximately nine months for trained Third World pilots to adapt to new aircraft and about six months to retrain tank crews. Maintenance personnel for new equipment take even longer to train. These lead times make it impossible for a leadership to turn to a new supplier when war is imminent or underway unless the new patron can provide the manpower to operate the new arms. An examination of the Ethiopian conflict of the late 1970s illustrates the importance of proxies and the Soviet superiority in this area.

Beginning in 1953, Ethiopia's military depended on the United States as its main source of weapons. This relationship began to unravel when the Emperor Haile Selassie was deposed in a military coup in 1974. The new Ethiopian leaders resented the United States for having allowed their archenemy Somalia to achieve with Soviet help what they regarded as military superiority. In part due to this resentment, they turned to the Russians for aid in coping with Somalia as well as with other threats. In the summer of 1977, the Somalis, realizing that the Ethiopians were now caught between suppliers and fearing for their own long-term security in the wake of the new Russian preference for Ethiopia, seized the opportunity to strike at the Ethiopians to settle their long-standing irredentist claims in the Ethiopian province of the Ogaden. The invasion proved to be a stunning success as the Somalis by September nearly captured the ancient Ethiopian provincial capital of Harrar. If Harrar had fallen, the Ethiopian leadership—and the Soviet position in Ethiopia—might well have collapsed.

The Russians reacted with a huge shipment of arms to Ethiopia (amounting to approximately $1 billion or three times what the Ethiopians received from the United States in twenty-five years) which, although impressive, was virtually useless to the American-trained Ethiopian forces. With a Somali victory imminent, it was clear that weaponry alone would not be enough. In this context the Cuban intervention proved decisive. Transported directly to the battlefront by the Soviets (who also served as commanders), the Cuban troops, who eventually numbered over 17,000, stemmed the Somali advance and, in time, along with the newly trained Ethiopian forces, rolled the Somalis back and ended the threat to the Ethiopian regime.

There is little doubt that the manner in which the Soviets replaced American influence in Ethiopia carried implications that transcended the limited boundaries of the Horn of Africa. By rescuing a beleaguered, American-trained Ethiopian army through the rapid transfer of massive quantities of sophisticated weaponry and the introduction of large amounts of Cuban troops who could use those weapons right away, the Soviets demonstrated the capability to defend a newly realigned client in the midst of a war without the direct intervention of Soviet combat personnel. One wonders what the outcome of events would have been if a Soviet-trained Ethiopian army had turned to the United States in the midst of a conflict. Would the United States have sent arms quickly enough? Would they have made a difference in the absence of direct American intervention?

As impressive as these Soviet strengths are, the United States also maintains advantages in providing military assistance to protect the Third World states it chooses to support. In the area of training, American programs are virtually always judged more thorough and effective than those run by the Soviets. This is due largely to the efforts of U.S. advisors who, despite the "ugly American" reputation, often are much better received than their Soviet counterparts. In addition, many Third World nationals (after enduring bitter experiences in the Soviet Union) have expressed a preference for training in the more open and less inhibiting atmosphere of the United States (Heikal 1975).

Once the weapons arrive in a Third World country, American support and services usually prove to be far superior to that of the Soviets. While the Russians excel at delivering large amounts of weapons very quickly, they rarely show much concern with how the arms will be kept in fighting condition. American maintenance programs, on the other hand, are considered among the best in the world. The

American advantage in support and services is enhanced by the Soviet practice of demanding that inoperable equipment be replaced as opposed to the more efficient and less expensive American emphasis on simple repairs. Furthermore, the United States provides an adequate supply of spare parts when it transfers weapons to another country (as witnessed by Iran's persistent defense against the Iraqi invasion in the fall of 1980 despite an American arms embargo). The Soviets, in contrast, are known for keeping spare parts at very low levels, thus forcing their clients to cannibalize equipment and maintain a precarious dependence on continued Soviet supplies (Central Intelligence Agency 1978b). It is small wonder that in at least two Third World countries (Egypt and the Sudan) problems with the Soviet military assistance effort were cited as a contributing factor to the Russians' eventual expulsion.

In the field of military assistance, therefore, both the Soviets and the Americans possess advantages and disadvantages. Generally, the Soviets excel in short-term crisis interventions, while the United States is superior in the long-term development of an effective fighting force. The extent to which military assistance concerns will benefit one superpower or the other depends then on the urgency in which a regime requires assistance in order to survive. Regimes facing no existing or imminent military threat would normally (all other factors being equal) be best served by turning to the United States, while regimes (which are not of vital American interest) facing a pressing military threat might be best advised to turn to the Soviets. The latter recourse is especially valid if the pressing military threat is Soviet-backed.

SUPERPOWER PROTECTION AGAINST COUPS

The difficulties inherent in protecting regimes from the consequences of large-scale military threats pale in comparison to the problems involved in devising strategies for the protection of leaderships from indigenously created coups d'etat. Military bases in the country, foreign aid, and influence with key groups do not ensure the safety of any government (nor allow the cultivation of a friendly successor) as the United States learned in Libya and Ethiopia and the Soviet Union found in Egypt and Somalia. In the past the United States has demonstrated some skill in protecting regimes from internal challenges. As is now well known, the United States helped to restore the Shah to his throne in Iran in 1953, and in 1960 rapid American action succeeded in preserving Haile Selassie's position in Ethiopia in the face of an attempted coup. This type of action, however, has been rare and is likely to remain so. Furthermore, the United States lacks a strong capability to influence the elite politics in which most coups originate. In this crucial area the Soviets are developing the more effective policies.

In reaction to recent setbacks in the Third World, current Soviet policies are designed not merely to protect a Third World leader but also to utilize that leader's concern for his survival to prevent him from straying from a pro-Soviet path. Again, the skilled use of proxies is crucial to this process. By employing Cuban and East German security personnel, this cocoon-like strategy ensures effectiveness and loyalty to Soviet goals without incurring the political costs that direct Soviet involvement would bring. For the most part the Cubans are playing a subordinate role to the East Germans in this area, with most of their activities restricted to providing bodyguards for individual leaders (such as Mengistu in Ethiopia and the late Neto in Angola).

Currently, the East German domination of internal security in Third World countries is giving the Soviets unprecedented control over Third World leaders. Much more active than their Western counterparts, the East Germans have taken the lead in penetrating and controlling the upper echelons of several Third World governments. Presently, the East German State Security Service (SSD) has advisors in Angola, Ethiopia, Mozambique, South Yemen, and Libya. The East Germans have been particularly useful in training bodyguards, advising both military and civilian intelligence agencies, and in establishing secret police networks. While the East Germans are consequently in an ideal position to prevent coups and assassinations, all their activities have not been defensive. In countries where the leadership is suspected of anti-Soviet feelings and no pro-Moscow "progressive" party exists, the East Germans have been actively urging the creation of such a party or covertly making contacts with opposition groups that might provide more "correct" leadership in the future (Croan 1980). By protecting and threatening a leader at the same time, the East Germans have made it clear that the survival of the regime is in their hands, giving them enormous power over that regime's decisions.

To see how the Soviets have increased their control over Third World leaders, one need only look at their use of East Germans and Cubans in Ethiopia. Having brought the Soviets into his country to cope with a set of pressing crises, Mengistu found himself $2 billion in debt to the Russians and saddled with an increasingly unpopular presence of some 15,000 Cuban troops as well as several thousand Soviet and East German advisors. With the most dangerous threats to his survival overcome, Mengistu must be under considerable pressure to emulate Anwar Sadat and expel the Soviets and their allies, repudiate the debt, and perhaps even turn to the United States for assistance. It will probably never be known, however, whether Mengistu wishes to follow this course of action. Surrounded by Cuban bodyguards and with both his regular and secret police forces under East German control, Mengistu (or a successor) is unlikely ever to risk this course of action

Mengistu is not unique in his fear of the Soviets. Across the Red Sea from Ethiopia in South Yemen, the Soviets have clearly demonstrated the will and capability to use threats in molding regimes to their liking. The Russians began their campaign by signing a ten-year military agreement with South Yemeni President Salim Ali Rubay in 1972. When Rubay showed signs of becoming too close to pro-American Saudi Arabia, the Soviets (according to many observers), along with the East Germans and Cubans, assisted in 1979 in Rubay's overthrow and execution, replacing him with a dedicated Marxist, Abdul Fattah Ismail. When Ismail, however, proved uncooperative in the Russian attempt to develop closer ties with North Yemen (in the wake of an ineffective American effort to provide security assistance), the Soviets reportedly helped to depose him. Understandably, the latest South Yemeni leader, Nasser Muhammad, has gone to great lengths to demonstrate loyalty to the Russians.

Soviet actions in South Yemen, coupled with Soviet behavior in Afghanistan (where the Russians set a new standard by personally executing a Third World leader after failing to overthrow him) have left a chill among the regimes in the Third World. The fact that the Russians have been invited into any country at all reflects the desperation many of these leaders must feel. Under these conditions, the United States must demonstrate to these leaders that they can now rid themselves of Soviet involvement without suffering the fate of their predecessors.

LESS THAN VITAL THIRD
WORLD COUNTRIES

Before policy suggestions can be made to improve the American position in the Third World, the necessity for concern in this area must be considered. After all, for the countries that matter most (such as Saudi Arabia) the United States will probably overcome any bureaucratic or other constraints to insure the survival of pro-American regimes. If the Soviets wish to extend their influence to the rest of the world, they should be permitted to do so, especially since experience has demonstrated that any such gains might very well be short-lived.

In response, a few brief points: first, many countries in the Third World (such as Zaire), though not vital to the United States, contain needed raw materials. If they fell under hostile control, Western economic and national security interests would suffer even if, in the long run, alternative sources of supplies could be developed. Second, countries which in themselves are not important to the United States may border on countries which are. They are therefore in a position to undermine their neighbor's security either through an armed invasion or internal subversion (both of which are made much more difficult—and sometimes impossible—for Third World countries when there is no common frontier). It is clear that the United States has no vital interests in North Yemen, but that country's defection to the Soviets could have a profound impact on Saudi Arabia.

Moreover, if the Soviets can maintain influence in enough countries they will be able to control regional security to the point where anti-Soviet governments and alignments toward the West will become a thing of the past. Nor can the United States evade its responsibilities by relying on the expectation that the Soviets will eventually be forced out of the countries in which they have become involved. The Soviet Union was eventually expelled from Egypt, but only after a period of twenty years during which time their influence severely complicated American policy in the Middle East. How complacent could the United States be about a twenty-year Russian presence in Saudi Arabia? Furthermore, as suggested earlier, the Soviets have begun to learn from their mistakes. Forcing them and their proxies out of Third World countries will be increasingly difficult in the future both for the United States and the Third World countries themselves. Finally, there exists a moral factor. Since there is a bipolar world (in terms of military power), for the United States simply to concede most of the countries to Soviet domination because of lack of direct interest would be a cowardly and, in the end, a disastrous policy.

POLICY RECOMMENDATIONS

The key to American success in the Third World lies in the adoption of policies for the protection of leaders which bolster those areas where the United States is weak (relative to the Soviet Union) while exploiting those areas where the Russians have the disadvantage. The former requires new American policies to guard better against short-term military threats and coups d'etat. The latter demands that the United States, in certain situations, utilize indigenous insurgents to challenge Soviet long-term military assistance capabilities.

In the area of general military assistance there is much the United States can do to enhance its effectiveness in the Third World, particularly in relation to less than vital countries. The arms transfer process must be drastically streamlined to eliminate many of the time-consuming and irrelevant checks. To enable Third World nationals to use the arms once they arrive, the United States should develop expanded and more rapid training programs, especially in those relatively simple weapons that often decide Third World conflicts. These training programs should also strive to adapt as much as possible to local conditions rather than merely duplicating the American experience.

Similarly, in order to meet the specific defense needs of the Third world it would be advisable to encourage (rather than inhibit) the production of arms designed solely for export. Light tanks, relatively simple jet aircraft (such as the F-5 series), portable antitank and antiaircraft weapons, and easy-to-maintain transport vehicles (including jeeps, trucks, and armored personnel carriers) should all be emphasized. The largely moribund grant-aid program should be revived for those countries deserving of support but who lack the funds to purchase enough to meet their defense needs. Finally, special attention ought to be focused on those countries which depend on the United States for assistance and are forced to confront Soviet supplied adversaries.

For countries previously in the Soviet sphere of influence that turn to the United States in the midst of a real or potential conflict, providing rapid military assistance without direct American intervention requires additional efforts. In those situations where proxy troops are not employed by the Soviets, the United States must concentrate on bolstering the strength of its new clients through the infusion of large amounts of arms. Since it is likely that there would not be sufficient time to assimilate American weaponry no matter how quickly it is transferred, the United States must provide familiar Soviet arms, which can be accomplished in two basic ways. First, the United States must develop contingency arrangements with friendly Third World countries that either produce Soviet arms (for example, the People's Republic of China and possibly India) or have large stocks of arms from an earlier relationship with the Soviet Union but must now depend on the United States for military assistance (for instance, Somalia, Sudan, and Egypt). Second, the United States should explore the possibilities of producing spare parts for some of the more sophisticated Soviet weaponry (such as tanks and aircraft) or developing the expertise to retrofit American parts into Soviet equipment. Given the paucity of spare parts Soviet clients are allowed to maintain, this proposal could be an inexpensive way for the United States to provide protection for its clients during the dangerous transition period as well as alleviating the need for large-scale arms transfers once the crisis is passed.

Once Soviet-backed proxy troops are deployed against a regime the United States chooses to support, the problems of supplying effective military assistance (especially but not exclusively if the regime had previously relied on the Soviets for support) are made even more difficult. Clearly, countries which are fortunate enough to be of vital interest to the United States (such as Saudi Arabia and Israel) or countries which remain important concerns of their former colonial powers (such as Djibouti and Zaire) can count on direct Western assistance. Yet, for all the other Third World countries, dependence on direct military intervention from the West is foolhardy at best. This Western restraint, though understandable, severely cripples the ability of the United States to affect intrawar outcomes especially when one of the sides has achieved superiority through the direct intervention of skilled foreign troops. Unless the United States can devise a credible response (that is, one not requiring American intervention of combat forces) to counter Soviet-backed proxy threats against regimes friendly to the United States, these threats are likely to continue while the number of leaders entrusting their security to the United States diminish.

An adequate American response to the Soviet proxy threat involves several dimensions. The United States must first exert greater efforts to secure the services of its own proxies. Although the United States (with its relatively loose relationship with its military clients) will probably not be able to match Soviet successes in this area, it is far from being totally impotent. The United States can apply increased political and economic pressure on pro-Western countries to act militarily either in a regional role (for instance, Egypt in the Middle East) or in a more general anti-Soviet context (South Korea might be available for these types of contingencies). American allies in Europe should be encouraged and assisted to combat instability and Soviet encroachments in a manner similar to the Franco-American cooperation in Zaire.

Where proxy intervention threatens important American interests and pro-Western forces are unavailable, the United States should consider direct actions against the proxies themselves or an explicit policy of linkage. Direct action would take the form of a blockade or other efforts designed to disrupt the logistical base supporting the proxy intervention. A policy of linkage would attempt to punish the Soviets for actions taken on the regional level (where they are strong) in areas where the United States does not operate from a position of weakness. This is not to suggest that every Cuban or East German advisor should provoke trade sanctions or be allowed to undermine strategic arms limitations talks. What it does mean is that the Soviets must realize that they cannot drastically change the character of regional conflicts through the introduction of tens of thousands of foreign troops without expecting some sort of meaningful American response. While these policies of direct action and linkage will not in themselves remove the threats to leaders where Soviet proxies are already ensconced, they would raise the costs of future interventions and thus deter actions that might have been carried out if there were no fear of retribution.

In order to provide leaders with greater protection against coups, the United States must first do more to improve its ability to collect, analyze, and act on information concerning the internal political dynamics of Third World countries. This will require an enhancement of American foreign and covert intelligence capabilities, particularly in the neglected area of human (as opposed to technical) intelligence. Furthermore, to avoid Iranian-type surprises, greater cooperation with allied intelligence agencies must also be emphasized.

Once the strengths and weaknesses of a given regime within its own country are understood, the United States can adopt the policies necessary to preserve American interests. In those situations where a close identification with the United States is likely to exacerbate threats against the leadership (as in Saudi Arabia), the United States should act to lessen its public ties to the regime while continuing to maintain strong private links. For countries in which the opposition to the leadership draws on social unrest (as in El Salvador), the United States must apply pressure to insure that reforms are undertaken to broaden the leadership's support and allow for nonthreatening channels of dissent.

In those cases where the leadership in question is of extreme importance to the United States and where its probable successors are likely to be hostile to American interests, the United States should have the willingness and capability to foil or reverse coups d'etat. For less than vital countries the United States can have prearranged plans with allies or pro-Western regimes in the area of conflict for rapid transport of loyalist or proxy troops to defend friendly governments. That Third World countries can defend their neighbors has already been demonstrated on several occasions. Examples include the Libyan and Egyptian role in helping to reverse a Communist-inspired coup against President Numeiry of the Sudan in 1971 and Senegal's rescue of Gambian President Dawda Kairaba Jawara from a leftist coup in 1981.

Competing factions of the military of Third World countries should be identified in advance so that in the event of a military coup, the United States would be able to alert indigenous troops to restore order. The efficacy of this type of policy was demonstrated when an American warning to Haile Selassie helped the emperor to use his army and air force to quell an attempted coup d'etat by the Ethiopian Imperial Guard in 1960. For vital countries (such as Saudi Arabia) the United States must be prepared to project American elite troops quickly into the capital (or wherever the disturbance is taking place) to eliminate any antigovernment action. The much-discussed Rapid Deployment Force should be trained to deal with these types of contingencies rather than focusing too greatly on the more remote possibility of direct Russian intervention. In any event, for both vital and nonvital countries, reversing coups d'etat requires speed more than numbers or armor. It is better to move a battalion of U.S. (or proxy) troops in a matter of hours than an armored division in a matter of weeks.

It is also critical that any type of anticoup action carry with it some basis of legitimacy. It must be clear to the country from which the armed force originates and to the country which is the object of the action that the intervention has come about only in response to a request made by some member of the existing government. As such, high-ranking individuals other than the leader himself (who might be incapacitated) that would be sympathetic to an intervention of this type must be identified in advance. Contingency plans should then be established to make certain that a request for American assistance can be carried out.

Despite all of these proposals designed to protect pro-American leaders, the United States should also be prepared for the times when such a policy becomes untenable. As American support for the Shah demonstrated, it is not in the interests of the United States to cling to a leader whose hold on power is clearly at an end. To prepare for such eventualities the United States should maintain contacts with opposition groups if for no other reason than to gauge accurately the depths of any existing antigovernment sentiment. It would also be advisable for the United States to establish links with lower ranking officers (most coups begin with or are supported by the military) to avoid the "leapfrogging" of junior personnel to power over the heads of their pro-American superiors (as occurred in Libya and Ethiopia). If in the end it becomes clear that the position of an American-supported leader is no longer viable, the United States should seek an accommodation with the forces likely to emerge (or already have emerged) triumphant, providing that they are acceptable. This latter recommendation should not, however, interfere with the United States offering political asylum to any leadership that it has given its backing.

Perhaps the most intractable task facing the United States is helping protect Third World leaders from assassination. The difficulty of this task is vividly illustrated by 1981's two near-assassinations of the Pope and President Reagan and the tragic murder of President Sadat. In some cases, protecting Third World leaders might best be accomplished through an emulation of the Soviet "cocoon" policy whereby American proxy personnel would perform the roles now played by Cuban and East Germans. Such a development, however, is clearly unacceptable to many Third World leaders. The United States can work to mitigate the danger of assassination by sharing its (hopefully) improved intelligence information with friendly regimes and by continuing to offer security training. Beyond that, the responsibility for guarding against assassination must remain with the Third World regime itself.

Finally, the United States should not be content with simply reactive or defensive measures. Just as the Soviets have contributed to the undermining of pro-American regimes in the Third World, so should the United States, in certain cases, exacerbate the problems besetting Soviet-installed regimes. This does not mean that the United States should become directly involved in the overthrowing of hostile leaders. Such a policy (through fear of American threats) might well drive more regimes into the Soviet sphere of influence than it would successfully replace. In those situations, however, where indigenous armed rebellion exists against a regime placed in power by the Russians (as in Ethiopia) or against the Soviets themselves (as in Afghanistan), the transfer of arms to the rebels by the United States or an ally should actively be considered. Such a policy would both raise the costs of Soviet (or proxy) intervention (especially when one considers Soviet weaknesses in supplying support and services), thus deterring future efforts and help to establish pro-American regimes by persuading existing leaders (or their successors) that a pro-Soviet alignment is not in their interests.

These recommendations are not a substitute for effective long-term policies. Even if the United States succeeds in preserving the tenure of friendly leaders it must still grapple with fundamental problems such as determining which regimes are worthy of its support, the amount and type of assistance to be provided, and the manner in which it responds and adapts to changes in the Third World. As important as these considerations are, however, they cannot exist in isolation from ongoing developments and needs. If the United States fails to provide for the short-term survival of actual and prospective pro-American leaders in the Third World, all the long-term planning and good intentions will not be doing them—or the United States—any good.

REFERENCES

Central Intelligence Agency. 1978a. *Handbook of Economic Statistics* (October):71–73.
___ . 1978b. *Arms Flows to LDCs: U.S.-Soviet Comparisons, 1974–1977* (November):ii–5.

_____ . 1979. *Communist Aid Activities in Non-Communist Less Developed Countries, 1978* (September):13.

_____ . 1980. *Handbook of Economic Statistics* (October):72, 87, 102, 107.

Croan, Melvin. 1980. "A New Afrika Korps?" *The Washington Quarterly* 3, no. 1 (Winter):31.

David, Steven. 1979. "Realignment in the Horn: The Soviet Advantage." *International Security*, 4, no. 2 (Fall):69–90.

Department of Defense. 1977. *Annual Defense Department Report,* FY 1978. (Washington, D.C.: Government Printing Office).

_____ . 1979. *Annual Defense Department Report,* FY 1980. (Washington, D.C.: Government Printing Office).

Heikal, Mohamed. 1975. *The Road to Ramadan.* New York: Quadrangle.

Huntington, Samuel. 1970. "Social and Institutional Dynamics of One Party Systems." In *Authoritarian Politics in Modern Society: The Dynamics of Established One-Party Systems,* edited by Samuel Huntington and Clement Moore, pp. 26, 28. New York: Basic Books.

New York Times. 1978. February 26.

International Institute for Strategic Studies. 1978. *Strategic Survey, 1977.* London: IISS.

U.S. Congress. 1981. Report for the House Subcommittee on International Security and Scientific Affairs, Committee on Foreign Affairs. *Changing Perspectives on U.S. Arms Transfer Policy.* 97th Cong., 1st Sess. Washington, D.C.: Government Printing Office.

8 WASHINGTON, MOSCOW, AND THIRD WORLD CONFLICT IN THE 1980S

Bruce D. Porter

As the 1970s progressed, the problem of Soviet military involvement in Third World conflicts rose steadily in priority on the U.S. foreign policy agenda. The USSR attempted—by means of arms shipments, military advisers, and sometimes troops—to influence the course of at least eight local conflicts during the decade: the Indo-Pakistani war, the October war, the war in Vietnam, the Angolan civil war, the Ogaden war, the intra-Communist clashes in Indochina (Vietnam's invasion of Cambodia and China's incursion into Vietnam), South Yemen's brief clash with Yemen, and the civil war in Afghanistan. The USSR had been involved militarily in local conflicts before, of course, but the magnitude, scope, and apparent success of its efforts in the 1970s were perhaps without precedent.

In the 1950s and 1960s the Kremlin's involvement in local conflicts, though often noisy, generally took place on a modest scale with respect to the actual quantities of military equipment delivered to clients at war. The exceptions were the arms delivered to Korea and Vietnam, and in those two cases the Soviet Union took care to maintain a safe enough distance from the actual vortex of conflict as to make a collision with the United States a fairly remote possibility. Though Moscow prior to 1969 transferred massive quantities of arms to Egypt, Syria, Indonesia, and India, and lesser volumes to over twenty additional nations, the shipments usually preceded or followed any actual outbreak of hostilities; the USSR displayed its penchant for caution by refraining from large-scale arms shipments to regimes concurrently embroiled in conflict, particularly non-Communist regimes, and by minimizing the direct participation of Soviet personnel in combat or combat support. Commencing with the War of Attrition (1969–70), the Soviet Union's historical restraint in this regard eroded markedly. In that conflict, over 10,000 Soviet military advisers engaged in a wide range of combat support; Soviet soldiers flew fighter missions and manned surface to air missiles (SAM) installations; and Moscow transferred thousands of tons of weaponry to the Arabs. It was the USSR's first massive military effort on behalf of a non-Communist client at war since its effort to support the Kuomintang in the 1920s. Events in the decade following the War of Attrition proved that it was not an anomaly. The 1970s witnessed three massive Soviet air- and sealifts of arms to client regimes at war, the deployment in combat of over 40,000 Soviet-armed Cuban troops in Africa, and the outright invasion and occupation of a Third World country by the USSR—all phenomena unheard of during the Cold War.

The USSR's military activities in the Third World were a cause for growing concern on the part of the Nixon, Ford, and Carter Administrations; their concern derived not only from the quantum leap in the magnitude and boldness of the effort but also from the simple reality that Moscow was more successful at the game than it had been in earlier decades. Though the War of Attrition ground to a halt in 1970 in a tactical defeat for the Arabs, during the remainder of the decade not a single Third World ally of the USSR suffered a *military* defeat—five of the conflicts listed above ended in a military victory for the Soviet-backed side; two ended in stalemate; one, the Afghan civil war, is still disputed. Moscow deserves only partial credit for the military successes of its Third World allies, of course, since indigenous and regional factors also weighed heavily in the outcome of each conflict, but the cumulative effect of a series of Soviet-backed military victories was to engender perceptions both in the West and in the Third World of rising Soviet power and momentum.

The picture appears less bleak when it is remembered that the military successes of Soviet allies in the Third World did not always mean a favorable diplomatic outcome for Moscow. Though the USSR managed to salvage from the Yom Kippur War a military stalemate and a moral victory for the Arab side, it experienced soon afterward a rapid and virtually total loss of influence in Egypt. Soviet military assistance to Ethiopia triggered Siad Barre's expulsion of nearly 2,000 Russian advisers from Somalia in November 1977 and meant the loss of the largest Soviet military base outside the boundaries of the Warsaw Pact. The invasion of Afghanistan may ultimately preserve Communist rule in Kabul, but the USSR incurred high costs in terms of its relations with the Moslem world and with the West.

Undeniably the Soviet Union suffered a number of considerable setbacks in the 1970s, and any discussion of Soviet foreign policy during the decade needs to recognize this. Its achievements were substantial, nevertheless, particularly in comparison with its foreign policy performance in the Third World in earlier decades. Pakistan, an important Asian ally of both China and the United States was dismembered by the Indo-Pakistani war; the United States suffered a deeply demoralizing defeat in Indochina and shortly later endured the embarrassing fiasco of the Angolan crisis; Ethiopia, a former U.S. ally and influential African nation, became a virtual Soviet satellite; the Pol Pot regime, allied with China, was toppled by Hanoi; Soviet troops moved 500 miles nearer the Persian Gulf. The series of pro-Soviet regime changes that began with the fall of Saigon was particularly notable: between 1975 and 1980, seven pro-Soviet Communist or radical leftist regimes came to power by armed force, most of them as the result of civil wars or coups in which Soviet-supplied weaponry was prominently involved.

The events of the decade were also propitious for the USSR in another sense: they contributed to the growing disillusionment of many Third World leaders with the United States, convinced a number of those leaders that the future of the world lay with the East rather than with the West, and in this manner paved the way for close Soviet ties to several previously aloof African and Asian states. In the long run, these somewhat immeasurable effects may prove to be of considerable significance. It is true, perhaps, that the entry of such weak and underdeveloped countries as Angola, Ethiopia, Cambodia, and Afghanistan into the Soviet "camp" does not amount to more than a minor shift in the global balance, not even if their collective weight in world affairs is considered. But widespread perceptions of Soviet strength and American weakness affect the decisionmaking of hundreds of statesmen and diplomats around the world—and not in a manner favorable to U.S. interests. It would be self-delusion on the part of the West to suppose that a cumulative series of setbacks is without significance.

As the 1970s progressed, the Soviet Union found it difficult to maintain the untenable position of seeking normal and even cooperative relations with the Western powers while at the same time supporting the maximalist demands of the most implacable anti-Western regimes with military aid and diplomatic succor. Inevitably, concern that the Russians were running rampant in the Third World served to erode public support for detente in the United States, solidified support for increased military spending, and hastened the momentum of the Sino-American rapprochement. During the Yom Kippur War and again during the Angolan crisis, Henry Kissinger warned that Moscow's actions imperilled the entire Soviet-American relationship and undermined the prospects for a stable international order. Shortly after the Ogaden conflict, Dmitri K. Simes (1978:54) observed that "the new pattern of Soviet imperial gunboat diplomacy threatens to modify the rules of the international game." By 1979 Robert Legvold (1979: 755) could write that turmoil in the Third World had overwhelmed all other considerations in the superpower rivalry "save the growth and increased projection of Soviet military power whose menace it serves to accentuate." President Carter's State-of-the-Union address in January 1980, shortly following the invasion of Afghanistan, identified "the steady growth and increased projection of Soviet military power beyond its own borders" as one of three principal challenges facing the United States.

The challenge of shaping an effective U.S. policy toward Soviet military involvement in the Third World will undoubtedly remain a paramount task of American diplomacy in the 1980s. This chapter addresses that task. It will first evaluate the causes underlying the USSR's extraordinary activism in Third World conflicts in the 1970s; second, it will analyze the failures and successes of the United States in coping with the problem of Soviet advances into the Third World since 1945; finally, it will set forth a number of general principles upon which a possibly effective policy might be based.

Before proceeding, a double caveat is in order. First, though there was a rising trend of Soviet military involvement in the Third World during the 1970s, the USSR was not an actor, and certainly not a principal actor, in every Third World conflict that took place. A number of local conflicts during the decade, as well as during earlier decades, passed without any significant involvement by either Moscow or Washington. For the most part, the Kremlin was prudent in choosing to become involved only in those conflicts where the USSR had considerable tactical and strategic advantages and where the probability of a confrontation with the United States was small. Second, it would be erroneous to suppose that the Soviet Union is in some way able to instigate local conflicts and then orchestrate their unfolding. Though the USSR occasionally has armed and all but outright encouraged clients to resort to hostilities, as it apparently did in the Indo-Pakistani war of 1970–71, it can only do so successfully when the already existing pressures toward conflict are enormous. The USSR has also attempted on occasion, not always with success, to restrain overeager clients: its efforts to pressure Egypt and Syria into an early cease-fire during the October War is an example. But perhaps the most typical scenario is when the Soviet Union simply exploits or seeks to influence the course of a conflict that breaks out independently of Soviet or U.S. pressures. The Kremlin is opportunistic, not onmiscient; tenacious, but far from omnipotent.

Yet if it is fallacious to disregard the manifest limitations of Soviet power, it is equally spurious to deny that there has been an upsurge in the last decade in Soviet interventionary behavior or to assert that the USSR's military adventures in the Third World pose no serious problem for the United States and its allies. The problem exists, and it has become serious. Were the United States simply to allow the Soviet Union unchallenged latitude of action throughout the Third World, untoward consequences would follow: a sharp decline in U.S. influence abroad, and the wholesale defection of numerous Third World regimes to the security afforded by alliance with Moscow. The United States has little choice but to contest in some manner Soviet military initiatives in the Third World; the real challenge is to shape policies that can cope with Soviet efforts effectively while still maintaining the general peace.

A PERSPECTIVE ON THE SEVENTIES

Four historical trends converged in the 1970s to bring about an upsurge in Soviet military involvement in the Third World. In ascending order of significance, they were as follows: (1) The USSR's achievement of a large and survivable second-strike nuclear capability; (2) advances in Soviet mobility forces; (3) the rising confidence of the Soviet leadership; and (4) the post-Vietnam isolationist retreat of the United States. None of these factors alone was decisive, but their cumulative effect was profound.

First, the Soviet Union achieved a large and survivable second-strike nuclear capability. From 1945 until the mid- or late 1960s, Washington enjoyed meaningful superiority over Moscow in strategic nuclear weapons. The crux of this superiority lay in the U.S. capability to destroy, with a first strike, Soviet nuclear delivery vehicles in sufficient number to blunt the effect of any all-out retaliatory strike. Though Moscow would have retained enough residual forces to damage U.S. interests seriously, it could have retaliated only at the risk of inviting the wholesale destruction of its cities; any calculation of the ultimate outcome undoubtedly counseled prudence to the Kremlin. Stated differently, the risks and potential costs of escalation to the nuclear level were higher for the USSR during this period than for the United States.

America's nuclear superiority exerted a tacit but pervasive influence on diplomatic and military developments around the world. It counterbalanced the Soviet advantage in conventional ground forces in Europe, and it deterred Moscow from making too overt challenges to U.S. interests in the Third World. The latter consequence came about because of the risks of escalation implicit in any crisis or local conflict in which both the United States and the USSR were involved. Washington's nuclear advantage was by no means a tractable instrument. It could not prevent the USSR from putting pressure on Berlin, nor could it prevent it from indirectly and cautiously supporting revolutionary movements around the world. Above all, it was an insufficient factor in the total equation to guarantee diplomatic and political outcomes favorable to the West when other factors were missing.[1] But logically it must have resulted in a dampening effect on Soviet assertiveness and latitude of action in the Third World and elsewhere.

As the 1960s progressed, the political advantages conferred upon the United States by its nuclear superiority began to erode in consequence of the USSR's build-up of its sea-based nuclear forces, the several-fold expansion of its intercontinental ballistic missile (ICBM) forces, and the hardening of its missile silos. Robert McNamara in January 1968 declared that the USSR "had achieved, and most likely will maintain over the foreseeable future, an actual and credible second strike capability . . . " (*Statement Before the Senate Armed Services Committee on the FY 1969–73 Defense Program and the 1969 Defense Budget* 1968:46–47). That same year the Soviet Union deployed for the first time a medium-range ballistic missile (the SS-N-6) aboard a nuclear-powered submarine; there followed the rapid deployment of nuclear-powered submarines with medium- and (in 1974) long-range missiles. The existence of this fleet made the security of the Soviet second strike force virtually unassailable throughout the 1970s. Long before the U.S. Minuteman force became significantly vulnerable to a Soviet first strike, Soviet ICBM and submarine launched ballistic missile (SLBM) *invulnerability* had radically altered the nuclear equation: by greatly reducing the utility of an American first strike, it lowered the threshold of risk for Moscow in local conflicts. In effect, the Soviet achievement of a secure second-strike force gave the USSR a kind of protective umbrella behind which it could exploit its conventional advantages and its ties with revolutionary regimes and parties in the Third World.

Soviet theorists readily recognized the consequences of what was happening. One Soviet scholar, V.V. Zhurkin, in a work on U.S. behavior in local crises and conflicts, asserts that as a result of the Soviet attainment of nuclear parity, "the hopes of the USA for employing nuclear blackmail as a means of obtaining its goals in international crises were exploded" (Zhurkin 1975:49). Other Soviet writers have identified the year 1970—when the USSR is said to have achieved nuclear parity—as the beginning of a new phase in international relations, one more favorable to the achievement of Soviet aims.[2] It seems to be no accident that the USSR's more openly offensive approach toward conflict and revolution in the Third World after 1970 correlated with its achievement of effective nuclear parity. By itself alone, the shift from imbalance to parity would not have sufficed to make possible a more activist Soviet foreign policy, but it was a necessary condition and it was coupled with other even more significant developments.

Second, the Soviets made advances in mobility or interventionary forces. A global diplomacy cannot be conducted without the requisite military capabilities to support and sustain distant initiatives. Grouped under the rubric "mobility forces," such capabilities include naval combat power, sealift capacity, airlift capacity, and distant assault forces (both amphibious and airborne). It is sometimes said that the USSR lacked the capability to project military power much beyond its borders prior to the 1970s. This is only partially correct. As early as the Spanish Civil War (1936–38) the Kremlin managed to muster sufficient sealift to furnish the Loyalist forces with massive quantities of weaponry, and this capacity grew substantially in the fifties and sixties (Ackley 1977:39; *Understanding Soviet Naval Developments* 1975:298). What Moscow lacked was the airlift capacity required for rapid and versatile responses, assault forces adequate for direct military intervention outside the Soviet bloc, and the naval combat power essential for extending political influence overseas and for discouraging foreign interference in distant military operations.

The Soviet Union's drive to expand its mobility forces was in full swing by the end of Khrushchev's decade in power; it continued with accelerated momentum under Brezhnev. The growth in naval combat power was particularly dramatic: from 1961 to 1979 the USSR deployed three new classes of escort ships, five classes of destroyer or antisubmarine warfare (ASW) vessels, four classes of cruisers, and two classes of small carriers; the total number of new, large warships deployed was over 200. In effect, the Soviet Union constructed almost an entire blue-water navy in two decades, an achievement in some ways reminiscent of Imperial Germany's naval build-up prior to World War I. The USSR established a permanent, albeit small, naval presence in the Mediterranean and Indian oceans for the first time, and in 1964 inaugurated an extensive, ongoing program of port visits by Soviet warships to Third World countries (Kelly 1977; Mcc-Gwire et al. 1975). The Soviet fleet also began to play a significant diplomatic and deterrent role in local crises and conflicts.[3]

In sealift, though the USSR already possessed adequate capacity for most military contingencies, the dead-weight tonnage of the Soviet maritime fleet more than doubled from 1965 to 1979, and its logistical competence improved considerably. Moscow also made rapid strides in airlift: the aggregate lift capacity of the Soviet Military Transport Aviation (VTA) in millions of ton-miles grew from 11.4 in 1965 to 26.4 in 1977; it is still increasing steadily because of continuing deployment of new Il-76 transport planes (Berman 1978:36; Borgart 1979:948–950). The ratio of long-range to short-range transports in VTA also rose significantly during this period.

In the area of assault forces, the USSR further strengthened and refined its most potent strike force, namely the eight well-equipped airborne divisions placed under a special directorate in the Ministry of Defense. The range to which this force can be projected is still limited by available air transport, but within a roughly 2,000-mile radius of Soviet-controlled airfields, the USSR can probably match any airborne deployment by the United States, except in Europe. The utility of the airborne divisions for influencing the course of local conflicts or for intervening directly abroad has been demonstrated in the past. All seven divisions were placed on alert during the October War, a move that did much to influence U.S. decisionmaking during the crisis; the 105th airborne guards division spearheaded the Soviet move into Afghanistan, and airborne forces also played a key role in the Soviet intervention in Czechoslovakia in 1968. Progress in amphibious assault capabilities has been much more moderate: the USSR reactivated the "naval infantry" (marines) in 1964, and it has since grown to about 15,000 troops (compared with roughly 180,000 U.S. Marines). The USSR also procured three new classes of tank landing ships between 1962 and 1979, including the modern and well-armed *Ivan Rogov* class, deployment of which continues (*Defense Daily* 1980:118, *Jane's Fighting Ships 1979–80* 1979:548–550; *Strategic Survey* 1979:45).

Though the Soviet Union in some respects might have been considered a superpower following its recovery from World War II, it did not become a truly global power until the 1970s, when these investments began to yield significant fruit. The USSR's growing military "reach" greatly facilitated its massive interventions in the October War, the Angolan civil war, the Ogaden war, and the civil war in Afghanistan. While interventions on that order might have been conceivable in the sixties, they would have taken place at relatively inhibited speeds, and with much higher risks and more formidable logistical difficulties.

Despite impressive advances, by 1980 the USSR's overall standing with respect to mobility forces remained clearly inferior to the United States. It had attained nuclear parity, but not nuclear superiority. Therefore, though the growing military power of the USSR was an important factor in and a precondition of its growing involvement in Third World disputes, it alone cannot explain why Moscow, more often than not, dominated the United States diplomatically in Third World crises from 1970–80. In order to understand what happened, it is necessary to consider two additional elements of a more political nature.

Third, the confidence of the Soviet leadership increased. In the United States it has become customary to speak of the "lessons of Vietnam," a phrase that usually connotes the declining utility of military power in the modern world. Often overlooked is the fact that the Soviet leadership also learned lessons from Vietnam and from other local conflicts in the 1970s—lessons not about the limitations of military power, but about its manifest political utility. The Politburo learned that military power—indirectly employed by means of arms shipments—*can* help sustain a client regime and that involvement in a local conflict *can* yield significant political and strategic benefits. Since 1975 Soviet commentators have referred to the fall of Saigon and to the victory of the Popular Movement for the Liberation of Angola (MPLA) in Angola shortly thereafter as together constituting a crucial turning point in postwar history, a turn toward Soviet ascendancy.

Throughout the 1970s Soviet leaders and spokesmen repeatedly stressed that the overall balance of forces in the world was shifting in favor of the socialist bloc, that "a fundamental restructuring" of international relations was underway.[4] Regarding Soviet advances in the Third World during the decade, A. Iskenderov wrote in December 1978:

> . . . one thing is indisputable: on the whole the national liberation movement is on the ascent. . . . This is confirmed by the historic victories of the heroic Vietnamese people, the emergence in the course of revolutionary struggle of progressive states like Angola, Mozambique, Guinea-Bissau, and the Cape Verde Islands, the successful course of the revolution in Ethiopia, the revolution in Afghanistan and other revolutionary changes in Asia and Africa (Iskenderov 1978:73).

Boris Ponomarev of the Central Committee Secretariat observed in January 1980 that the past decade had been marked by the continuing unfolding and deepening of the national liberation process and by the erosion of capitalist strength. He added to Iskenderov's list of successes the overthrow of the Pol Pot regime in Cambodia, the Iranian revolution, and the rising revolutionary ferment in Latin America. Echoing Gromyko's words at the 24th Party Congress, Ponomarev declared that the strength of the socialist community had reached such proportions that no serious international problem would or could be resolved without its cooperation (Ponomarev 1980:11).

The growing self-assurance of the top Soviet leadership flowed both from the reality of the changing military balance and from the decade's succession of military victories by Soviet-backed client regimes in the Third World. A kind of self-feeding mechanism was in operation—each successful intervention increased the assurance and decisiveness with which the Kremlin acted in the next crisis. Confidence in turn contributed to successful implementation.

The invasion of Afghanistan demonstrated the newfound confidence of the Soviet leadership perhaps more than any other event of the decade. Attempts by some Western analysts to portray it as an act of Soviet desperation are unconvincing. The Kremlin acted swiftly and decisively, pursuing its purposes without apparent hesitation even after the full extent of the international uproar became evident. The significance of the move is underscored by an anecdote Chiang Kai-shek tells about a meeting with Lenin in the early twenties. Sun Yat-sen had sent Chiang to Moscow to seek Soviet backing for the Kuomintang's struggle for power in China. Lenin readily agreed to supply the Nationalists with ammunition, arms, provisions, instructors, and advisers, but he laid down a firm caveat: absolutely no Russian soldiers would engage in combat. Lenin explained that following the Red Army's disastrous losses in the Polish campaign of 1920, he had issued a new directive regarding the future policy of world revolution. It ruled that Soviet Russia should render the utmost material and moral support to wars of national liberation, but "should never again employ Soviet troops in direct participation" (Chiang Kai-shek 1957:22).

Although Soviet pilots flew combat missions in the War of Attrition and Soviet advisers regularly undertook a broad variety of combat support missions, it is remarkable that during the six decades following the Red Army's debacle on the Vistula in 1920, regular Soviet ground troops did not once engage in combat in the Third World. When Moscow intervened in local conflicts, it did so with arms shipments and advisers, and with the help of Cuban troops, but never with Soviet troops. The invasion of Afghanistan marked the crossing of a historic threshold. It is inconceivable that a regime that had conducted its foreign policy steadfastly according to the Leninist principle of retreating where weak and advancing only where victory was assured would have gone into Afghanistan without a high measure of confidence in the ultimate outcome and in the reality of a new world military and political balance.

Fourth, post-Vietnam neo-isolationism developed in the United States. Moscow's growing military power and rising confidence only made feasible what was ultimately made possible by the drift and uncertainty of U.S. foreign policy after Vietnam. Postwar history suggests that the Soviet leadership is finely attuned to shifts and nuances in U.S. foreign policy and to the high risks associated with actions that might arouse Washington to a military response; it was only natural that Moscow take advantage of the opportunities opened to it by America's turn inward in the 1970s.

Already by 1970, the seeming interminability of the war in Vietnam had evoked an unprecedented degree of isolationist sentiment among influential circles in the United States. Pressures to end the war quickly were tremendous and contributed in part to the "siege" mentality of the Nixon White House. Nevertheless, from 1970 to 1975, Washington persisted in conducting a foreign policy that seriously attempted, by means of massive arms shipments (Vietnam, the Yom Kippur war) or even the threat of force (the Indo-Pakistani war), to deter or delimit Soviet military activities in the Third World. The fall of Saigon in April 1975 deepened the isolationist mood of the nation, affecting even many who had supported the fundamental purposes of the war effort. The collapse of the South seemed to confirm the claims of those who had declared that the war effort was futile and that U.S. military power could not prevent an inevitable Communist revolution in South Vietnam. From then until the end of the decade, the United States retreated at least partly into the role of a spectator, instead of an actor, in the international system.

The depth of the U.S. plunge into what has been termed "neo-isolationism" revealed itself plainly only six months after Saigon fell, at the time of the Angolan crisis. The Columbia novelist Gabriel Garcia Marquez, a confidant of Fidel Castro, claims that prior to making a major commitment of troops to Angola, the Cuban cabinet made a "rapid analysis" of whether or not the United States would intervene openly. They concluded that the fall of Saigon, as well as the weakening of the presidency in the Watergate affair, made a major intervention by Washington unthinkable.[5] The Kremlin possibly made a similar assessment. The Cuban analysis was vindicated on December 19, 1975, when the Senate voted fifty-four to twenty-two in favor of the "Tunney amendment" to a defense appropriations bill, cutting off all American aid to Angolan nationalist groups and effectively ending a small CIA operation in support of the National Front for the Liberation of Angola (FNLA) and the National Union for the Total Independence of Angola (UNITA). Though the wisdom of the Ford Administration's decision to undertake the operation in the first place is very questionable, it is doubtful the USSR would have dared to become involved on such a massive scale—thus violating many of the unwritten rules of Soviet-American relations—without a high degree of confidence that it would not face a confrontation with the United States.

The Ogaden war in 1977–78 was the first time in postwar history that the Soviet Union undertook a large-scale military operation outside Eastern Europe without the United States becoming involved militarily. America's neo-isolationism persisted throughout the decade and may have been the principal reason the Soviet leadership so readily abandoned its traditional prudence with respect to the use of military instruments abroad. Adam Ulam observed in 1978 that "no Soviet move or ruse has undercut the effectiveness of U.S. foreign policy as much as what the Americans have done to themselves in the wake of Vietnam and Watergate" (Ulam 1978:567).

VIEW FOR THE EIGHTIES

The first two of the four elements just discussed are almost certain to persist well into the 1980s; the outlook for the third and fourth is slightly more uncertain.

Barring revolutionary technological developments in the West, the Soviet Union will not lose its long-sought status of nuclear parity at any time during the decade. The vulnerability of its land-based forces may increase somewhat after the U.S. MX and Trident II missiles are deployed, but its basic nuclear umbrella—a secure second-strike force—will remain intact, much of it under the oceans. The credibility of either power's launching a first strike against the other will be quite low, unless circumstances arise where one side concluded that the cost of a general war is warranted or where one side miscalculates the intentions of the other. The strategic nuclear balance, therefore, will exert no more of an inhibiting influence on Soviet behavior in the Third World during the 1980s than it did in the 1970s; conventional forces, particularly mobility forces, will hence be enhanced in importance.

Moscow will continue efforts to expand and improve its mobility forces, seeking to close further the gap that now exists between its own capability to project power and that of Washington. It may even strive to attain a kind of "parity" in this area to match its earlier achievement of strategic parity. Admiral Gorshkov's announcement in December 1979 that the USSR's first nuclear-powered, large-deck attack carrier was under construction indicates the seriousness of the Soviet effort; some Western analysts had argued that the USSR would never build heavy carriers because of their high cost, increasing vulnerability, and low utility in defending a traditional land power (see, for example, Herrick 1968:155). The principal value of the new carrier or carriers will be in projecting Soviet political influence and military power overseas. The new aircraft carrier is only the most dramatic product of an intensive ship-building program that seems to portend a decade of increasing strength and assertiveness on the part of the Soviet fleet. As of 1980, the USSR was constructing four new classes of nuclear-powered cruisers, including a number of 32,000-ton battle cruisers with heavy guns for shore bombardment; such guns are of little utility against a modern, missile-equipped fleet, but they might have a telling impact in certain local crises, even if only passively deployed. The USSR is also constructing the new *Berezina*-class of heavily-armed, 40,000-ton logistics craft apparently designed for replenishing warships on the high seas; this should reduce somewhat the navy's dependence on foreign port facilities. The most telling indicator of Moscow's naval ambitions, however, may be the large capital investments apparently being made in the expansion and refurbishing of shipyards, a policy suggesting that Soviet naval construction is slated to accelerate in the 1980s as the USSR bids to close the gap in the area of its most manifest military inferiority (Middleton 1979).

Soviet air transport capabilities will also expand substantially during the decade, as a result of continuing deployments of the II-76 long-range transport and of a new plane being developed, the An-40, expected to have a larger capacity than the American C-5 (Borgart 1979:948–950). This growing airlift capacity will directly enhance the combat strength of the Soviet airborne divisions; amphibious assault capabilities will also improve as further deployments of the new *Ivan Rogov* tank landing ship continue.

Thus, as the decade progresses, Moscow's overall capability to sustain distant military operations will increase steadily and significantly. Whether or not its relative capability vis-a-vis the United States will also increase depends, of course, on what measures are taken by Washington. Current efforts being made suggest that the Soviet leaders would like to narrow the U.S. lead, though they may well never seek to achieve parity in mobility forces simply because their military requirements are so different than those of the United States. The relative balance in this category of weaponry, however, is probably less important than the fact that Soviet capabilities are absolutely expanding.

In turning now to the third category discussed earlier—that of the Soviet leadership's increasing confidence—the picture of what lies ahead becomes more obscured. To some extent, the newfound confidence of the Kremlin's leaders is based on what Soviet ideologists might call "objective factors," namely, the changing military balance. Viewed in historical perspective, however, Russia's present confidence in foreign affairs is a fairly new phenomenon, and it may well be quite fragile. There exists the possibility that the USSR will become bogged down and politically chastened in Afghanistan, Poland, or elsewhere. It is also thinkable that a succession struggle or pressing economic troubles might place a damper on the Soviet Union's recent activism abroad. A series of diplomatic reversals or bungled military interventions abroad might also cause the Soviet leadership to turn inward for a period of internal reform and development, in much the same way as it did in the late 1920s. Certainly U.S. policymakers would do well to keep in mind the possibility that appropriate diplomatic steps might, in the right circumstances, encourage a certain reassertion of prudence and caution on the part of the Soviet leadership.

The United States, however, cannot *rely* on the 1980s to bring any turnabout in Soviet attitudes or activism, not even if the war in Afghanistan continues interminably or if the USSR's troubled economy stagnates even further. Internal difficulties can have the effect of encouraging foreign policy activism, as desperate leaders undertake foreign initiatives in the hope either of enhancing their own political power and standing at home or in an effort to unite a fragmented polity. An internal succession struggle following Brezhnev's death or retirement might lead to an extended pause in Soviet endeavors abroad, or it too might lead to greater activism—Khrushchev's rise to power resulted simultaneously in gestures of rapprochement to the West and in a much more vigorous policy of wooing Third World regimes away from the former colonial powers by means of economic and military aid; the transition to Brezhnev took place abruptly and without evident crisis, yet Soviet foreign policy became somewhat more hard-line and activist as a result, particularly with respect to supporting wars of national liberation in the Third World. The United States cannot afford to stake its own security on the assumption of yet unevidenced internal developments in the USSR leading to a new Soviet moderation abroad; the West will be fortunate enough if the historical pull of centuries of Russian military inferiority and diplomatic caution suffices to render Soviet foreign policy no more belligerent or activist than it is now.

Assuming that the Soviet leaders continue to act with a measure of self-assurance in their foreign affairs, the foregoing three elements alone point toward a decade of heavy Soviet involvement in local conflicts, one likely to be all too reminiscent of the latter 1970s. It seems almost certain that the USSR will continue to arm local clients and will seek to take advantage of any hostilities that may occur if political and strategic gains seem attainable. Moscow will probably continue to exploit revolutionary tendencies in the Third World, seek to establish itself more firmly as the "natural ally" of leftist regimes, and strive to undermine the stability and security of countries friendly to the United States. Quite possibly further massive air- and sealifts of Soviet arms to Third world regimes will take place, and the troops of the Third World allies of the USSR may again be deployed in combat in a manner that will serve Soviet interests. The relative contribution of Cuba to the Soviet effort in the Third World will probably decline, however, at least as far as Havana's military contribution is concerned. This is because Castro has had up to 40,000 troops in Angola and Ethiopia alone, as well as a few thousand in other countries, and he cannot keep sending more abroad indefinitely. Perhaps other "proxies"—Ethiopian, South Yemeni, Vietnamese, or even East German troops—will take their place. Since the USSR has crossed the threshold of employing its own troops in combat in the Third World, there may be a somewhat greater probability that Soviet soldiers will be sent abroad again in the 1980s. The Kremlin is likely to use this particular instrument with great caution and, due to logistical limitations, only in regions near to the USSR.

In the face of such eventualities, the future direction of U.S. foreign policy becomes a critical variable. Of the four elements that contributed to Soviet success in the Third World during the 1970s, this one is most under American control and most subject to change by the decisions and leadership of American statesmen. The United States cannot control the outbreak of local conflicts or determine the course of events in the Third World, any more than the Soviet Union can, nor can Washington prevent Moscow from providing military assistance to client regimes that seek it. To state these limitations is but to acknowledge the verities of international diplomacy. But if the United States does not control Third World events, it can influence them, and sometimes decisively. If it cannot prevent the USSR from arming client states in peacetime, it can perhaps dissuade, discourage, or deter it from shipping weapons to clients actually at war or on the brink of war. It can affect the costs and benefits of Soviet actions, and influence the military and political outcome of local conflicts. Certainly many of Moscow's interventions in the 1970s and at least some of the resulting military and political successes would have occurred even if the United States had responded with perfect acumen, but U.S. isolationism and the consequent failure of the White House to formulate an effective policy toward the problem contributed to its acuteness.

By the end of the 1970s, growing concern about Soviet interventions abroad had begun to stir the United States from its isolationist langour; the hostage crisis in Iran, the occupation of Afghanistan, and the presidential campaign in 1980 gave impetus to this turnabout. This swing of the pendulum back toward internationlism is likely to continue for a few years at least, but its direction is as yet ill-defined. It may amount only to a revival of the policies and strategy of the fifties and sixties, colored by a new era when the balance of military forces between East and West has shifted so much. If Washington's former policies for coping with the Soviet challenge in the Third World failed during an era of unquestionable U.S. superiority, they are likely to fail in an era when the military balance is far less favorable to the United States.

PAST POLICIES

New policies are clearly needed; the best point of departure may be to consider the fate of the old. From the late 1940s until roughly 1971, the United States attempted to counter Soviet advances in the Third World by a policy that consisted primarily of three closely linked elements: containment, limited war, and alliance-building. The latter two elements were essentially instruments for achieving the more fundamental aim of containment.

Containment as a cornerstone of U.S. foreign policy began to take shape as early as 1947 with the promulgation of the Truman Doctrine and the announcement of the Marshall Plan. The goal of containment was to forestall the establishment of additional Communist regimes, and, in the words of George Kennan, to resist Soviet advances "by the adroit and vigilant application of counterforce at a series of constantly shifting geographical and political points" ("X" 1947: 576). Though the policy of containment initially developed in response to the postwar instability of Western Europe and though its principal aim was the containment of Soviet advances in Europe, its application to other parts of the world was portended by the U.S.-Soviet dispute in 1946 over the presence of Soviet troops in Iran. The fall of Peking to a Chinese Communist army in 1949 and North Korea's attack on the South the following year served to broaden the scope of U.S. concern over the advance of Communist rule and led to the extension of containment into the Third World.

Limited war was not the only instrument implied by Kennan's term "counterforce," but it soon became the cutting edge of the policy of containment, and around it a whole body of strategic thinking grew up. American policymakers and strategists turned to the concept of limited war for two principal reasons. First, the unparalleled destructiveness of nuclear weapons made total war unthinkable except in the most drastic of situations. If war were to make any kind of political sense, it had to be limited. Second, limited war was an attempt to tailor the defense of the West to the nature of the challenge it faced. The Soviet Union's advances into the Third World took place in piecemeal fashion—by low-level and localized war, by indirect intervention, by the use of surrogate forces, by subversion and propaganda. In accordance with the classic Bolshevik approach to political struggle, developed by Lenin and refined by his successors, each Soviet advance was deliberately incremental, always well short of a *casus beli.* Moscow thereby deflated the military superiority of its adversaries by making it difficult for them to justify bringing that superiority to bear at any given point of conflict. There seemed to be only one way around this dilemma: resisting incremental advances by incremental defenses—thus, limited war.

In 1950, Truman's decision to commit American troops, under nominal U.N. aegis, to the defense of South Korea, solemnized the first marriage of limited war and containment. The results were ambiguous, neither vindicating nor discrediting the policy. On the one hand, the Communist threat to South Korea's independence was indeed contained, and Truman did manage, barely, to keep the war limited in both aims and methods. Robert Osgood wrote, "One can hardly overestimate the importance of the United States' achievement in containing the Communist attack on South Korea without precipitating total war. By this achievement, the nation went a long way toward demonstrating that it could successfully resist direct military aggression locally by limited war . . . '' (Osgood 1957:178). On the other hand, the traditional preference of Americans for "all or nothing" wars created strong public pressures to withdraw entirely or to escalate both aims and methods. Limited war proved tremendously unpopular and divisive; in the end Washington reduced its bottom-line war aims to containment at the Thirty-eighth parallel only because it was forced to do so by Peking's entry into the war with a million men. Limiting the war in Korea entailed high costs, including the sacking of a five-star general and the longest retreat in U.S. military history. In the end, status quo ante at the price of 40,000 lives seemed a pyrrhic victory to many Americans.

In the MacArthur hearings conducted by the Senate on the administration's performance in the war, the government defended the new course of U.S. policy by guising it in cautious language and familiar rhetoric. It did not openly advocate limited war, but simply stressed the overriding necessity of avoiding total war over a single peninsula in Asia. The word "containment" surfaced only once in the hearings, but great stress was laid on the concept that unchecked aggression would lead to further aggression. The lessons of Munich and the principle of containment are not the same, but the former proved an effective means of intellectually defending the latter. Though the Democrats lost the election in 1952, partly as a consequence of Korea, the war did much to establish the course of U.S. policy toward Communist advances in the Third World for the following two decades.

The Republican platform of 1952 called containment "a negative, futile and immoral policy" ("Republican Campaign Platform" 1952). John Foster Dulles argued that the United States would be driven into bankruptcy and exhaustion if it reacted to local Communist aggression by military resistance all around the world. Hoping to infuse U.S. foreign policy with a more positive purpose, Eisenhower and Dulles declared that the spread of freedom—and the ultimate liberation of the Communist states—should be the central goal of the nation's policy. But the new administration soon learned that the logic which had led to containment and a policy of limited war was not so easily circumnavigated. Liberation implied either aggressive local wars against vulnerable Communist states or the encouragement of internal revolution inside the Soviet bloc. The former was too dangerous, while the latter appeared futile. Liberation became a mere ideal; containment remained the policy.

Dulles advocated replacing the concept of limited war with a policy of "massive retaliation"—a kind of superdeterrence in which the United States would respond to even minor and indirect Communist aggression in the Third World by massive nuclear strikes against the Soviet Union or China or both. As quoted in the *New York Herald Tribune,* he declared, "The only way to stop prospective aggressors is to convince them in advance that if they commit aggression, they will be subjected to retaliatory blows so costly that their aggression will not be a profitable operation."[6] Secretary of the Air Force Donald Quarles, two years later in 1956, stated the policy more bluntly: "If it were obvious that limited aggressions would be met with the full force of atomic weapons, I do not believe such aggression would occur" (Quarles 1956). The concept of massive retaliation, which the Eisenhower Administration was forced constantly to qualify and redefine, was an attempt to squeeze more out of the principle of deterrence than was there to be had. Herbert Leuthy accurately called it a "lame compromise between the crusading spirit and the spirit of budgetary economy" (Leuthy 1955:459). Nuclear superiority conferred certain advantages on the U.S.—it was a factor the Soviets always had to take into account—but it did not give Washington the power to dictate the outcome of every political event in every part of the world. The policy lacked credibility, and, in fact, the administration never pursued it to its logical conclusion.

The Republicans' disavowal of containment and of limited war notwithstanding, Eisenhower and Dulles demonstrated in 1958 that in a crunch they, too, would pursue a policy that bordered on containment by means of limited military action. Confronted with a civil war in Lebanon that appeared to be instigated partly by Nasser and concerned about the USSR's increasing assertiveness in the Middle East, the United States landed nearly 15,000 marines at Beirut to keep order until the political situation resolved itself. The action was over in less than four months, with ambiguous results: the action demonstrated to Nasser that there were limits to how far he could press against Western interests, and it revealed the emptiness of Soviet threats and promises to intervene on behalf of the Arabs. The political costs were high, however, and it soon became evident that the intervention had done little to alter the fundamental instability and rising nationalist fervor of the Middle Eastern countries.

Though the Eisenhower Administration failed to develop a suitable alternative to containment or to limited war, its uneasiness with the latter concept did affect its policy toward conflict in the Third World. The administration moved quickly to settle the war in Korea; it refused to support France and Britain in the Suez war; and it refrained from air strikes in support of the beleaguered French garrison at Dien Bien Phu for fear that it would lead to U.S. participation in another Asian ground war—on which Eisenhower had commented, "I cannot conceive of a greater tragedy" (Donovan 1956:263). And though Dulles ostensibly abhorred the notion of containment, he set about with some verve to forge an alliance system in Asia and the Middle East, the patent intent of which was to contain Communist advances. In September 1954 the Southeast Asian Treaty Organization (SEATO) came into being with the signing of the Manila Pact; it was followed by the Baghdad Pact (CENTO), the ANZUS pact with Australia and New Zealand, and by mutual security pacts signed bilaterally with Japan, the Philippines, and Taiwan. This alliance system was largely in place by 1960, which would have been a remarkable achievement were it not for the fact that it crumbled only slightly less rapidly than it arose. Only a few months afer the Baghdad Pact was signed, the Soviet Union signed a large arms agreement with Egypt, proving how easily the U.S. alliance ring could be leap-frogged. Obviously something more than a colored band on the map, representing a handful of paper treaties, would be required to contain a tenacious and ambitious superpower. Two years later the Kassem coup in Iraq left a gaping hole in CENTO, though fragments of that alliance struggled on for some time. SEATO lasted considerably longer, but ultimately disintegrated—at least in its center—with the fall of Indochina to Communist armies. By 1975 the U.S. alliance system outside Europe was reduced to a series of bilateral treaties, mostly with developed countries such as Australia and Japan, and to remnants of the past multilateral structures.

The necessary preconditions for successful alliance construction simply did not exist in most of the Third World. NATO, by far the most successful of U.S. alliances, endured because it both reinforced and was built upon conditions of internal stability in the West European countries; other U.S. alliances collapsed because their success was dependent on the survival of highly fragile regimes beset by turbulence and unable to contribute much to their own defense. The system amounted in practice to a disguised set of unilateral American guarantees and thus condemned Washington to the endless and unpromising task of propping up dozens of unstable regimes in order to maintain its credibility as an ally. In short, the U.S. alliance system in the Third World was built on shifting sands, hardly a propitious foundation for constructing an edifice of credibility or of containment. The idea was slow to die, however, and it enjoyed a brief renaissance under the Nixon Administration.

As for limited war, it was revived as the predominent instrument of containment under the Democratic administrations of John F. Kennedy and Lyndon B. Johnson. Kennedy, in his first State-of-the-Union address, declared that world domination remained the ultimate ambition of the Communists. "Our task is to convince them that aggression and subversion will not be profitable routes to pursue these ends" (*Public Papers of The Presidents: John F. Kennedy 1961* 1962:23). The administration took immediate measures to reinforce the armed forces, both nuclear and conventional, and Secretary of Defense Robert McNamara pressed Kennedy to work for more balanced forces capable of coping with limited and local contingencies around the world. It was believed that the reliance on massive retaliation had atrophied the nation's capacity for flexible conventional responses. On March 28, 1961, the president urged Congress to appropriate funds for creating more versatile mobility forces "to prevent the steady erosion of the free world through limited war. . . . Any potential aggressor must know that our response will be suitable, swift and effective" (*Public Papers of the Presidents: John F. Kennedy 1961* 1962:231–232). Containment and limited war were back in vogue.

The French experience in Algeria and Indochina had convinced many that guerilla warfare and popular revolution, backed by Moscow and Peking, posed the principal threat to U.S. allies in the Third World. "Counterinsurgency," as a school of thought and a bureaucratic preoccupation, blossomed. Yet despite the flurry of activity and the administration's open enthusiasm about proving to Khrushchev that he could not win "wars of national liberation," Kennedy proved wary when it came to actually committing American soldiers to fight in the Third World. When the Pathet Lao threatened to overrun Laos, Kennedy seriously considered dispatching U.S. troops but changed his mind when he learned that as many as 250,000 might be needed. Instead, the United States grudgingly agreed to participate in a Geneva Conference that eventually neutralized Laos under a coalition government. The president viewed with skepticism the Taylor-Rostow recommendations of 1961 on sending 8-10,000 troops to Vietnam, believing it would be the wedge to a much larger commitment. But as the Diem regime weakened, the United States in 1962 began sending hundreds of additional advisers, specialists in counterinsurgency training, and helicopter combat and support personnel; by the time of Kennedy's assassination, roughly 15,000 American military personnel were in Vietnam. Still, barely 100 Americans had been killed—the United States had a presence in Vietnam; it did not yet have a major war.

The pursuit of containment by means of limited war reached its zenith—and eventually also its nadir—under Lyndon Johnson. Though Johnson had declared publicly in the 1964 campaign that American boys should not do the fighting for Asian boys, he presided over the massive U.S. build-up in Vietnam that began in 1965. That same year Moscow stepped up its own military shipments to the North, principally in order not to be outbid by Peking in winning influence with Hanoi, but perhaps also seeking a chance to humiliate Washington. Throughout the war the USSR provided Hanoi the vast bulk of its weaponry in what eventually became the largest military aid effort ever undertaken by the Soviet Union in the Third World ("National Security Council Memorandum No. 1" 1972).[7]

In April 1965 Johnson ordered U.S. Marines to land in the Dominican Republic, then torn by civil war, ostensibly to protect American lives, but actually because "We don't expect to sit here on our rocking chairs with hands folded and let the Communists set up any government in the Western Hemisphere" (quoted in Stebbins 1966:87). The Dominican intervention was reminiscent of the intervention in Lebanon seven years earlier—both were limited military actions undertaken to contain "Communist" advances, though in neither instance was Moscow involved in a significant degree. Both actions succeeded in their immediate aim of reestablishing civil order, and it is also conceivable that they averted situations that might have eventually been exploited by the Kremlin, but the diplomatic losses that resulted probably exceeded the benefits. Certainly the USSR lost little in either case.

Vietnam proved the rock against which the doctrines of containment and limited war were broken. Washington's manifest aim-containment meant that no serious consideration was ever made of liberating the North or even of invading it with massive force. U.S. conduct of the war was limited in the most classic sense: the White House and its political appointees in the Pentagon controlled the military's actions even to the point of reviewing in detail tactical operations and specific bombing missions; hundreds of restrictions were placed on the military in order to minimize civilian casualties, reduce the odds of escalation, and avoid threatening the People's Republic of China. Yet by 1968 the magnitude of the burden the nation had assumed was appallingly apparent. Over 500,000 American troops, 28 tactical fighter squadrons, 3,000 helicopters, and a massive bombing campaign had failed to end the war. The limited settlement sought by the United States was nowhere in sight; the nation at home was badly divided; the costs of the war were leading to huge deficits and high rates of inflation; American prestige in much of the world was declining. Though the security of the Saigon regime had improved somewhat, its continuing survival depended on the indefinite occupation of the South by U.S. troops.

The Nixon Administration continued to pursue the war for nearly four years, but it did so while unilaterally and steadily withdrawing American troops, and while searching for a more effective approach to the Communist challenge in the Third World. For all practical purposes, containment and limited war had met their demise by 1969, when the new administration entered office. The search for new doctrines preoccupied U.S. policymakers and thinkers throughout the 1970s.

THE FAILURE OF CONTAINMENT AND LIMITED WAR

Before considering the evolution of U.S. policy in the 1970s, it is important to consider why the doctrine of containment and the tactic of limited war ultimately failed.

First, containment overextended U.S. resources. Kennedy declared in his Inaugural Address: "Let every nation know, whether it wishes us well or ill, that we shall pay any price, bear any burden, meet any hardship, oppose any foe to assure the survival and the success of liberty" (*Public Papers of the Presidents: John F. Kennedy 1961* 1962:1). The context makes it clear that Kennedy was referring to freedom around the world, not just at home. His pronouncement was idealistic and altruistic, but wholly unrealistic. Its universal pursuit might well have meant the rapid erosion of U.S. resources and strength, and ultimately thereby the compromising of the nation's own security. Vietnam dramatized this possibility—the United States expended over $100 billion, sacrificed over 50,000 lives, and heavily mortgaged the national economy in order to defend a regime that could not defend itself. Though the intent was laudable, the end sought was plainly not worth the price required. Obviously it is not possible for America to place a price on its own security—and at times the security of other nations may be closely related—but costs must bear some proportionate relation to ends sought.

Second, the tactic of limited war suffered from what might be termed "the dilemma of blood." American presidents did not realize until it was too late what far-reaching transformations would take place in domestic opinion and politics after substantial numbers of Americans had been killed in combat. Though the attitude of Americans toward economic and military assistance programs tends to be one of generosity or benign indifference, a very different dynamic occurs once blood is shed. Americans deeply believe that the sacrifice of lives is only justified when the waging of a war will defend their nation's own security and prevent even more blood from being shed. There is an understandable reluctance to pay the ultimate price for less than ultimate goals. This reluctance leads to the almost paradoxical result that once large numbers of American soldiers are killed, even in a limited war, Americans do not want to contemplate any other outcome than victory. Cutting losses and retreating becomes highly difficult. To the very end of the war in Vietnam, polls showed that a majority of Americans favored pursuing an outright military victory over the North. It is doubtful that by 1968 any administration could have ditched South Vietnam outright and survived politically.

The experience of World War II illustrated that the American people can be aroused to astonishing heights of unity and determination when they are convinced that their own security is threatened by an aggressor who will continue expanding unless checked. Korea showed that they will, with much reluctance and deep misgivings, support a limited war when told by their leaders that even indirect aggression by the Communist giants, if unchecked, would lead to further aggression. Vietnam proved how limited the latter impulse is when the aggression is distant, indirect, and prolonged. The successful conduct of an internationally oriented American diplomacy requires a high degree of domestic consensus, far surpassing a mere majority; to flout the national tendency to see only those wars as justified where the security of the nation or of nationals abroad is directly threatened is to invite national disunity and to court foreign policy disaster. This is particularly true if conscripts are employed in combat. The Munich analogy was never convincing in the cases of Korea and Vietnam because the only nation that could then directly threaten American or even European security was the Soviet Union, and it was not the first-line aggressor in either war. It sent arms, not troops.

Finally, both policies, applied in tandem, suffered from an acute philosophical schizophrenia. For two decades the United States attempted to pursue two contradictory visions of world order—one based on deeply held ideals of democracy and freedom, the other founded upon U.S. military superiority and political hegemony. The problem was that neither vision was practically attainable: a great many nations in the Third World lack the necessary internal conditions for democratic or free government, and aiding them cannot be justified on that basis; on the other hand, the United States does not possess the overwhelming military superiority and political influence necessary to impose its own settlement on every dispute in the world. Yet U.S. leaders from Truman to Johnson, with varying degrees of commitment, sought both to advance democratic ideals in the Third World and to settle Third World disputes by means of U.S. power. The result was an odd mixture of *Idealpolitik* and *Realpolitik*. Because U.S. policymakers lacked a clear conception of what kind of world order would favor the nation's interests, and of how to get there, U.S. foreign policy tended to be vaguely idealistic in conception but negative in practice, essentially a set of ad hoc reactions to Soviet initiatives. This made U.S. diplomacy hostage, in a sense, to decisions made in the Kremlin—it lost its flexibility, creativity, and sense of self-control. A policy that defended a world order based on more limited principles than democracy and freedom, one which espoused a less negative principle than anti-Communism, and one which employed military force much more judiciously might have been more successful both in preserving the strength and unity of the free democracies and in preventing the spread of Communism by violence or otherwise.

THE PALLIATIVES OF THE SEVENTIES

In the 1970s, the United States attempted to piece together some kind of new policy for coping with the Communist—increasingly seen as the Soviet—threat to the Third World. One such effort began well before the war in Vietnam had ended, when President Nixon in a background briefing on the Island of Guam, en route to the Philippines, articulated a set of principles that became known as the Guam or Nixon doctrine. He formally articulated the doctrine in his Vietnam speech of November 3, 1969, and in his Foreign Policy Report of February 18, 1970. It asserted that the United States would continue to keep all its treaty commitments, but that in the event of aggression against an American ally by any source other than a nuclear power, "We shall look to the nation directly threatened to assume the primary responsibility for providing the manpower for its defense." Washington's role in such cases would be the furnishing of economic and military assistance, not the dispatching of combat troops. Nations too weak to defend themselves alone would obtain security by entering into regional alliances buttressed by U.S. aid and diplomatic support.

The Nixon Doctrine was a logical consequence of the national experience in Vietnam, a retreat from the former American commitment to pursue containment by means of limited war, but not a retreat from containment per se. It did not overcome all the problems of the old policy, but it did solve the dilemma inherent in calling on Americans to sacrifice their lives for Third World regimes. Its aims were within the reach of American power and resources, and it did not suffer from excessive idealism or philosophical ambition. In many respects, it was a revival of the alliance-building approach undertaken by the Republicans in the 1950s. The Nixon Doctrine failed, however, to define what the United States would do if indigenous defenses and regional alliances both collapsed before a determined Communist offensive. In the decade since Dulles, no one has yet discovered how to build an effective alliance on the shifting sands of Third World instability, turbulence, and change. The doctrine never really acquired the substance or widespread acceptance necessary to endure as a pillar of American foreign policy, and in the end it became a victim of the very war that spawned it. The collapse of Saigon four years after Nixon's Guam declaration seemed to demonstrate, on the one hand, that some Third World allies simply could not survive without American combat support; on the other hand, it deepened the isolationist sentiment in the United States to the point that offering *any* type of military aid to foreign regimes at war met considerable resistance at home.

The Nixon Doctrine ushered in a transitional period in U.S. foreign policy. The diplomacy of the Kissinger years reflected this change. Many elements of containment survived, and limited war, though phased out in Vietnam, was not ruled out. The Nixon Administration responded to the Indo-Pakistani war and the Jordanian crisis by deploying military forces in a manner that seemed to threaten intervention; it undertook a massive airlift and ordered a general military alert during the Yom Kippur War. Under Gerald Ford, the United States attempted to provide emergency assistance to Saigon when the final North Vietnamese offensive began in 1974–75, and it initiated a small program of military aid to the Angolan nationalists opposing the MPLA in 1975—in both cases, its efforts were cut short by congressional fiat. In retrospect, Kissinger's efforts to shape a coherent post-Vietnam diplomacy appear as a rearguard action—an attempt to salvage a minimum consensus on the traditional aims of American foreign policy, while trying to forge the tools with which to pursue diplomacy in a new era.

The concept of linkage was one of the tactics developed in order to shore up the weakened international position of the United States vis-a-vis the USSR. Kissinger was the most ardent proponent and practitioner of the tactic, which in its application to the Third World amounted to an effort to delimit Soviet interventionary behavior by the offering of rewards and the administration of penalties in other diplomatic arenas.

A certain degree of linkage is inevitable in diplomacy, since it is not possible to compartmentalize every issue area. Even the Carter Administration, which disavowed the concept of linkage, acknowledged that in some cases public opinion created pressures that amounted to linkage. But linkage is fundamentally a tactic of weakness, its open employment an admission of inability to influence diplomatic developments more directly. Being a tactic of the weaker side, linkage suffers from several problems. It posits a relatively high level of cooperativeness between the United States and the USSR, for only when the superpowers are intertwined by a multistranded web of agreements, commitments, and negotiations does the United States possess sufficient leverage over Moscow to reward or penalize its international behavior. The frosty aloofness that characterized most of the postwar era offered few prospects for linkage. The United States was unwilling to reward the USSR much of anything and there was little short of severing diplomatic relations or going to war that it could do to penalize it. Before linkage could operate, the level of Soviet-American cooperation had to be raised; detente, in other words, was a prerequisite to linkage. Unfortunately, the very time when a policy of linkage might prove most useful is when U.S.-Soviet relations are at a low ebb.

If the currency of linkage is weak to begin with, it also depreciates rapidly when once employed. This was demonstrated by the U.S. reaction to the occupation of Afghanistan. The grain embargo, the Olympic boycott, the temporary shelving of SALT II, and the cooling off of exchange in all areas amounted to the most determined employment of linkage the United States had ever engaged in, but it did not succeed in pressuring the Soviets out of Afghanistan, and once all the cards were played, there was little else left to play. The superpower relationship was back at the bottom line, with military action perhaps the only convincing form of "linkage" left.

Kissinger himself never employed linkage in the negative sense quite so forcefully, nor did he achieve much success in applying it more positively to win Soviet restraint in the Middle East, Indochina, or Angola. Nor did Kissinger and Nixon (or Ford) ever succeed in formulating a more general policy for coping with the Soviet challenge in the Third World, one that could avoid the pitfalls inherent in containment and limited war. The Republicans improvised, very adroitly at times, yet their improvisations did not long outlast their tenure in office.

Jimmy Carter entered office with a coterie of foreign policy advisors, many of whom had drawn certain maximalist conclusions from Vietnam—lessons about the limits of military power, the intractability of the Third World, and the futility of containment. The administration declared its intent to downplay the Soviet-American relationship and to shed inordinate fears about Communism. In essence, it abandoned containment—or what was left of it—as a doctrine, and it all but ruled out limited war. Some vestiges of alliance-building and of the Nixon Doctrine survived in the administration's attempt to court "regional influentials," but the fall of the Shah—long considered the most successful case of a strong regional ally of the United States—virtually put an end to Washington's serious alliance-building in the Third World. Instead, the administration sought to promote long-term stability by means of economic aid programs and to cultivate good will by displaying American restraint and restoring America's moral prestige around the world. It purported to be sensitive to nationalist aspirations. The administration promulgated a human rights policy intended to infuse American diplomacy with a more positive purpose, overcoming the negativism and reactiveness inherent in containment. It was argued that in the long term these policies would serve to prevent or to undercut Soviet gains in the Third World far better than past policies had done.

This did not prove to be the case. By 1980 the Carter administration was in a state of unacknowledged retreat, reduced to a series of panicky, ad hoc reactions to Soviet moves and general chaos in the Third World. The USSR had intervened massively in the Horn of Africa, with Ethiopia becoming a virtual satellite state; it had supported Vietnam's occupation of Cambodia, engineered coups in both Yemens, and backed South Yemen's attack on Yemen; it had invaded and occupied Afghanistan with 100,000 troops. The Iranian revolution and the Sandinistas' triumph in Nicaragua, though not attributable to Soviet involvement, seemed to open further opportunities for Moscow to exploit. Human rights, good will, long-term programs, and moral prestige—while undeniably admirable per se—proved impotent before the very short-term reality of Third World revolutions, coups, and conflicts.

The architects of the Carter administration's new approach were critical of the idea that the United States could effect change in the Third World by military means, yet they set out with near-proselytizing zeal to transform the very nature of politics in the Third World by nonmilitary means. Their ultimate aims were in some respects as maximalist as those declared by Kennedy in 1961. Though they purported to respect the nationalist aspirations and self-determination of developing nations, the human rights program in its more extreme forms often took an unrealistically black-and-white view of what was attainable in the Third World. Many Third World regimes friendly to the United States were offended by the campaign, which they saw as a violation of their national sovereignty. It was perhaps naive to assume that the United States faced a choice between democratic and dictatorial regimes in the Third World; in many cases, the unfortunate choice was between pro-American and anti-American dictatorships. Under Carter, the United States ceased acting as the policeman of the world; it assumed the only slightly more felicitous role of schoolmarm.

By the final year of his presidency, Carter appeared to have abandoned, for all practical purposes, many of the assumptions with which he entered office. Yet no new doctrine, policy, or clear vision was advanced to replace them. U.S. foreign policy functioned in a void, confused in its purposes, incoherent and inconstant in its application, miscellaneous in its methods. The need for new approaches was starkly evident.

PRINCIPLES FOR THE FUTURE

The United States could perhaps restore a measure of coherence and confidence to its diplomacy in the Third World and vis-a-vis the Soviet Union by the consistent application of three general principles: a commitment to sovereignty; a proportionality of means employed to ends sought; and the primacy of national security, narrowly defined. The remainder of this chapter will elaborate what is meant by these three principles and will discuss their practical application and likely consequences.

First, sovereignty. The presence of a powerful, revolutionary state such as the Soviet Union within the global system constitutes a latent threat to the sovereignty and survival of every non-Communist regime in the world (not to mention "revisionist" Communist regimes such as the PRC). It virtually compels the United States to conduct an internationalist diplomacy, for if it did not do so, Moscow would dominate the world order and dictate the terms of its evolution. But the fact that U.S. foreign policy is doomed to be internationalist does not mean that it is doomed to be interventionist—the inherent, tremendous difficulties in attempting to influence the domestic affairs of foreign countries or the course of foreign conflicts by the unilateral exercise of American military power have already been discussed. The United States might well fare better as an international actor if it exerted its influence and power toward the end of promoting and defending an international order based on national sovereignty. This is a positive end that can be pursued principally by measures short of committing American troops to combat.

A U.S. commitment to sovereignty is proposed on the grounds that it is a superior and more achievable principle of international order than military hegemony, universal democracy, or simple anti-Communism. Since at least 1648, when the Peace of Westphalia was signed, national sovereignty has been the one principle of world order that has worked for any length of time. Every successful postwar restoration of international stability has been based upon it, and nothing better has yet been found to replace it. A great power, particularly a conservative power with a stake in the contemporary order, such as the United States, can enhance its own security by defending the universality of the principle. Sovereignty, as used here, does not necessarily mean "self-determination of peoples," a principle that can open the door to endless irrendentism and strife; it means simply "self-determination of states," a narrower and more practical concept. The United States would act with surer purpose and greater coherence in the world if it consistently defended the norm of sovereignty, in the Third World and elsewhere. It could pursue this end with foreign policy instruments tailored to suit the nature and magnitude of specific threats to sovereignty, as well as the extent of U.S. ties to threatened states.

The Soviet Union, from its inception, posed a formidable challenge to the traditional international system based on state sovereignty. Marxism-Leninism denies that sovereignty is a legitimate basis for any state; the USSR ultimately seeks to supplant national sovereignty with ideology—the legitimizing principle of a new international order. Though Moscow for tactical purposes purports to support the principle of noninterference, the whole thrust of its foreign policy is to erode and undermine any regime not compatible with its ideological conceptions. For this reason an American commitment to the defense of sovereignty would have the simultaneous, though secondary, effect of countering Soviet advances.

Sovereignty is a norm which must be defended in all parts of the globe, if at all: the following pages, however, focus on the application of the policy in the Third World. Developing countries face a wide range of threats to their national sovereignty, but they are least able to cope by themselves with those threats that originate with a major power such as the Soviet Union—threats that range from Soviet-backed coups and insurgency to outright Soviet invasion. In order to establish a credible claim as a defender of the sovereignty of states in the Third World, the United States would have to concern itself also with threats that did not originate with Moscow, and it would have to moderate those of its own economic and military policies that plainly constitute encroachments on the sovereignty of developing nations. Then, by assisting Third World regimes to defend their sovereignty against threats originating with the USSR, the United States could strengthen its political standing in the Third World, exert a stabilizing influence on international events, and simultaneously inhibit the USSR's more reckless attempts to advance in the Third World.

First, the United States would consistently and constantly affirm its support of sovereignty and noninterference in every international forum and at every diplomatic opportunity. This would take the form of a sustained moral and verbal offensive. The USSR has made tremendous gains in the Third World since the mid-fifties by emphasizing its opposition to colonialism and imperialism; with the colonial era passed and the Soviet threat to the Third World regimes on the rise, the United States can reverse the tables and gain significant political advantage by establishing its commitment to sovereignty. Washington must make it clear that it can accept political change, but only as long as it is not dictated nor manipulated by outside powers; it should continually assure developing regimes, even those unfriendly to the United States, that it strictly opposes interference in their internal affairs. This will place the United States in a position to denounce Soviet interventionary activities on the grounds that they are "imperialistic," "blatant interferences in internal affairs," and the like. The rhetoric of anti-Communism does not impress most Third World leaders; the rhetoric of sovereignty has universal appeal.

Second, a commitment by the United States to supporting and defending the principle of sovereignty would require an approach to the issue of human rights considerably more sensitive and skillful than the campaign conducted by the Carter Administration. Though the moral concerns reflected in that program were wholly laudable, its practical implementation was too often an unnecessary affront to the nationalist sensibilities of the Third World regimes. Certainly it is appropriate, indeed virtually imperative, for America to articulate and advance high political and moral values in its international relations; a great power that does not stand for something higher than its own narrow self-interest will not long remain great in its own eyes or in the eyes of the world's people. On the other hand, the United States lives and acts in a diverse and often morally complex international environment; it cannot fall prey to the illusion that democracy lends itself to being imposed on the Third World, or the Communist world, by diplomatic pressures. The extent to which a given regime honors human rights should significantly affect the substance of U.S. relations with that regime, but human rights ought not to be given a peculiar precedence outweighing all other considerations, such as traditional ties, common security interests, and the necessity of shoring up local and regional stability during periods of crisis and threat. There exists an unavoidable tension between the principle of sovereignty and the norm of human rights in that neither can be pushed to its logical extreme without violating the other. The tension between the two can only be resolved by treating foreign regimes on a case-by-case basis, mindful both of the importance of good bilateral relationships and of the United States' broader foreign policy purposes. Certainly quiet diplomacy should always be first attempted when questions of human rights are raised with foreign governments, but if it fails after reasonable time and effort, there will be instances when the United States will want to voice its concerns loudly, unmistakably, and with full moral force. A commitment to and recognition of the principle of sovereignty requires sensitivity and realism, but it does not mean that the United States need abandon other equally important principles or ever condone repression and brutality.

Third, the United States should refrain from every form of activity intended to encourage or support opposition to any regime that enjoys broad international recognition. Covert operations aimed at affecting regime changes ought particularly to be avoided. It is difficult to point to any enduring and concrete foreign policy gains the United States had made by clandestine or even open support of opposition forces in peacetime; the sometimes-celebrated return of the Shah of Iran to his throne in 1953 quite possibly might have occurred without U.S. assistance, which was only one of many factors involved. On the other hand, Washington ought not to hesitate in publicizing and condemning confirmed instances of the Soviet Union's seeking to subvert or weaken foreign regimes. The USSR's claim that it has the right to support "wars of national liberation" against illegitimate (that is, "imperialist"-backed) regimes should be rejected as fradulent, since Moscow invariably labels every local conflict in which it chooses to become involved a war of national liberation no matter how patently expedient its motive for involvement.

These general policy recomendations no doubt would require considerable statesmanship to implement, and the effort would have to be tenacious in order to yield fruit. Yet the most difficult challenge would be assisting specific regimes to defend themselves against specific threats to their sovereignty. Before discussing that, however, a number of possible arguments against a U.S. commitment to sovereignty deserve mention.

First, it will be argued that there will be cases when the United States will want to intervene and therefore will violate the principle of sovereignty. In fact, such instances should be very rare and ought only to occur when the U.S. security is profoundly threatened. Since the genuine and clear-cut defense of one's own security is easily justified both at home and abroad, and since it can itself be viewed as a special case of the defense of national sovereignty (in this case, one's own), this is less of a problem than it first appears. Such cases will be examined in a later section.

A second argument against a U.S. commitment to sovereignty might be that our past record makes it impossible for the nation to establish a credible commitment. This argument is not so much unsound as largely irrelevant, since *any* significant change in the direction of the nation's foreign policy would require a certain amount of departure from the past. Unless a reversion to pre-Vietnam policies or a continuation of post-Vietnam nonpolicies is desired, there is no way around this dilemma. The task of statesmanship is to learn from past mistakes and to advance.

Finally, some may argue that sovereignty is an anachronism in the contemporary world, one soon to die amid flames of postcolonial border-scrambling in Africa, resource wars in the Middle East, and revolution in Asia. Whether or not the nation-state will prove as short-lived as all that remains to be seen, but two facts hold nonetheless: no workable alternative to national sovereignty as an international ordering principle has yet been found, and every regime, however revolutionary or irredentist its policies may be, is always eager to affirm the principle as far as its own territory and integrity are concerned. It is not easy to get around the principle of sovereignty, however much it is criticized.

A policy of defending the sovereignty of states in the Third World, if pursued with appropriate and proportionate instruments, would be a manageable commitment: it should not lead to an overextension of U.S. resources and power. The general principle is realistic, and at the same time defensible to critics on both the right and the left in America. By adopting such a policy, the United States would not abdicate its internationalist role, but would reestablish it on a new basis, more practically and philosophically sound than that of the past policies. The policy would have considerable appeal to friendly Third World regimes in that it is compatible with their nationalist aspiration and desire for self-determination; as such it would enhance the nation's political position among nonaligned countries as well.

COPING WITH THREATS TO SOVEREIGNTY
IN THE THIRD WORLD

Third World regimes face numerous threats to their sovereignty, the vast majority of which arise from their bordering neighbors or nearby regional powers. There are at least three types of threat that originate wholly or partly with the Soviet Union: direct Soviet aggression; aggression by another state, backed by Soviet arms; internal challenges—revolution, insurgency, and coup—that are precipitated by or supported by Moscow. One key to a successful U.S. policy may be the second principle mentioned earlier of the proportionality of means to ends. U.S. responses should be carefully tailored to the nature and magnitude of the threat in question. Namely, U.S. troops to deter or meet Soviet troops, U.S. arms to meet Soviet arms, and U.S. diplomatic and economic support to counteract Soviet-backed internal threats. This principle is best illustrated by examining each of the three categories in turn:

Category 1: direct Soviet aggression.   Morally and politically, the proper role for U.S. forces in the contemporary world, particularly ground troops, is to deter—and, if necessary, to resist with force—*direct* Soviet aggression against weaker countries. The Munich analogy comes to life once Soviet troops begin crossing borders, for the United States is the only power in the world capable of providing an adequate counter to the USSR in such instances.

The number of Third World countries within effective striking range of the USSR's conventional forces is quite small. Because Moscow does not possess sufficient mobility forces to sustain a conventional offensive far beyond its borders, the only feasible direction for an outright Soviet attack against Third World countries in the 1980s will be in the direction of the Persian Gulf and Arabian Peninsula. Soviet conventional forces can directly threaten the following developing countries: Pakistan, Iran, Iraq, Saudi Arabia, Jordan, Syria, Israel, Egypt, the Yemens, and the smaller states of the Arabian peninsula. (India is also in reach of Soviet forces, but its size and close ties with Moscow make Soviet aggression against it a remote possibility.) Pakistan and Iran face the most immediate and probable threat. The odds may be quite small of a direct Soviet attack against any of these countries, but the invasion of Afghanistan, the apparent growing confidence of the Soviet leadership, and the vital interests at stake force the United States not to overlook the possibility.

U.S. policy must emphasize deterrence. If Washington deploys forces in a manner that renders credibility to the possibility of a U.S. military response, it is very doubtful that Moscow will risk open aggression and superpower confrontation. The essence of Leninist politics has always been only to advance where the opposition is weak and victory assured; this will probably remain true in the 1980s. Successful deterrence requires political resolution even more than military capability, though both are important. In the case of Afghanistan, which for decades had leaned toward Moscow even in its neutrality, the failure of the United States to protest forcefully the Soviet-backed coup that brought Taraki to power in April 1978, and to register its continuing concern thereafter, may have bolstered the Kremlin's confidence that it could invade Afghanistan with impunity. Once the USSR's preparations for an invasion became apparent, a division of U.S. airborne troops moved to within striking range of the country; and air and naval forces deployed so as to make a U.S. military response appear possible, coupled with ambiguous warnings, might possibly have deterred the USSR from invading Afghanistan in force. Had Moscow gone ahead anyway, such an action would not necessarily have obligated the United States to fight in order to maintain credibility, because the diplomatic warnings could have been veiled and short of commitment. What was lacking all along was the political will to contend with the USSR's takeover of Afghanistan from its first inception—rather than only after a full-scale invasion was launched.

The question of whether or not to fight if deterrence fails is profoundly difficult. It would have to be resolved partly on the basis of whether or not the United States could win the contest over the immediate issue—or at least force a stalemate and negotiations. Military defeat would accomplish nothing and might lead either to pressures for dangerous escalation or to national humiliation and a further retreat into isolationism. For this reason, U.S. troops should never be deployed merely as a "tripwire" in the Third World country that is likely to be attacked, not even for purposes of deterrence, unless Washington has the means and will to back them up with additional conventional forces if they are challenged. "Plate-glass deterrence" is pointless and dangerous. Unless it can be reinforced conventionally, a tripwire that fails can have only four outcomes: destruction of the tripwire force, Dunkirk, a nuclear response, or a presidential decision to put the nation on a war footing and prepare for a long-term struggle. The first two are disastrous; the nuclear response over a

Third World issue is not credible; and the decision to prepare for war is extremely dangerous in the nuclear age and does nothing to resolve the immediate issue.

Of course, acquiescence is hardly a useful response either. It would therefore seem imperative that the United States greatly improve its capabilities for responding militarily in the Persian Gulf region. Because Washington ought not to draw down its forces in Europe or elsewhere to defend the region, this means that some expansion in the size of the nation's conventional forces is essential. Because the purpose of deploying American troops in the region is principally to provide a counterweight to Soviet power, U.S. forces stationed in or designated for the Indian Ocean should be structured and armed so as to be able to meet—and thereby deter—the Soviet airborne and mechanized forces they might face in combat. Because of the Soviet Union's geographical proximity and the advantage it would have in utilizing internal supply lines, it would be virtually impossible for the United States to prevent a sustained and massive Soviet offensive from eventually overrunning the region, but the Soviet leadership would be most unlikely to mount such an effort if it risked confrontation and serious resistance from the United States. U.S. forces in the region should be large and strong enough to prevent a Soviet fait accompli from occurring before negotiations on terminating conflict could begin.

This would require the capability to deploy rapidly large numbers of jet fighter and fighter-bombers, as well as a mobile ground force more heavily armored than present plans for a Rapid Deployment Force call for. The Soviet geographical advantage could be reduced somewhat by the pre-positioning of tanks and tank landing ships in the region. Serious consideration might also be given to assigning a permanent naval task force to the Arabian Sea with at least some of its vessels deploying tactical nuclear missiles for deterrent purposes. In order not to compromise the political standing and sense of sovereignty of pro-American regimes in the region, U.S. deployments and facilities should be reasonably discreet, and generous financial compensation should be made for any facilities that must be leased from Third World countries.

Category 2: Aggression by one Third World country against another, with Soviet assistance.

Such cases arose frequently in the 1970s: the Indo-Pakistani war, the October War, Vietnam's invasion of Cambodia, and South Yemen's attack on Yemen. The general approach proposed for defending sovereignty in such instances would be to employ diplomatic and military measures *short* of sending American troops. There exists a broad spectrum of such instruments, listed here in ascending order of forcefulness: diplomatic expressions of support for the defending side and denunciations of the attacking side and of the Soviet Union; United Nations resolutions; offers of mediation; diplomatic efforts to encourage military support from countries in the region whose security is affected by the conflicts; shipments of nonlethal military equipment; shipments of arms and ammunition; the passive, but communicative, deployment of U.S. naval forces; the passive, but threatening, deployment of U.S. tactical air forces (where access to friendly air bases permit). The utility of passively deploying American naval forces deserves particular emphasis. Until the Iranian crisis, this instrument was largely neglected by the Carter Administration, but its purposes are manyfold: to deter the attacker or cause him to turn back for fear of U.S. intervention, to discourage greater Soviet involvement, to hedge against the possibility of escalation, to signal the seriousness of the U.S. commitment to the beleaguered state. Since Vietnam, Washington too often has assumed that the choice was between fighting and doing nothing militarily. The middle course of deploying forces, but not committing them to combat, can sometimes be an enormously useful diplomatic tool. The Soviet Union, for one, has employed it with great skill in recent years.

The decision as to which of the foregoing measures to use would depend on the magnitude of the threat and on the extent of American interests in the defending country. If the regime under attack is Communist, or anti-American, then U.S. support of its sovereignty would in most cases be confined to the diplomatic level. If the state in question has been genuinely neutral or pro-American, then as many of these measures as necessary should be undertaken in its support. However, if the threat can be handled largely by the country's own armed forces, U.S. arms shipments should be sized roughly to replacement levels, and the United States should not deploy military forces passively. Massive arms shipments and passive deployments should be reserved for situations of profound threat. In such circumstances a rapid U.S. response is essential for both military and political reasons. The efficacy of decisive responses was demonstrated by the Carter Administration's shipment of nearly $400 million worth of arms to Yemen in 1979 when it was attacked by South Yemen. Though the actual volume of arms was excessive, the action contributed to a rapid solution of the conflict. To facilitate early responses, the president's authority to order arms shipments and cut through bureaucratic tape might be broadened and an early warning system be set up within the National Security Council, with links to the Pentagon and intelligence services, to trace Soviet arms shipments and provide the White House with early forecasts of incipient conflicts and of states likely to be in need of assistance. Military assistance offered prior to a conflict, by averting hostilities entirely, may be more effective than aid granted during a conflict.

Category 3: internally-based threats with Soviet involvement. Such threats range from coups to rural insurgencies to urban revolution. The general rule in the case of internal threats to sovereignty is that the United States would not employ its own armed forces but would seek to strengthen the existing regime by means of a broad spectrum of measures: economic assistance, private and public expressions of confidence, high-level visits, diplomatic support in international forums and in bilateral contacts, arms shipments, military consultations and training. Again, as in Category 2, the United States would feel no obligation to provide material support to anti-American regimes, but even in such cases it would oppose foreign intervention at the diplomatic level.

Washington would relentlessly publicize any existing links between the internal opposition forces and the Soviet Union—both to discredit the nationalist credentials of the opposition and to establish the justification for U.S. support of the reigning government. The task of actually subduing an internal revolution, insurgency, or coup, however, would rest with the regime being challenged. In order to govern with confidence, a regime must prove to itself, to its opposition, and to the world that it can maintain control at home without foreign troops.

The United States must avoid two cardinal errors in political strategy when dealing with regimes that face serious internal opposition. First, even if the State Department becomes convinced that a given regime must implement certain reforms to survive, Washington should not press this course too strongly on the government when its troubles are at their height. Reforms made under pressure from the opposition may only be viewed as a sign of weakness and could encourage the rebellion. If anything, the government in question should be encouraged to overcome any immediate threat posed by the insurgency or revolution first, and then to announce a program of reforms so as to win popular support and undercut the rebellion's future appeal. The United States should also avoid the serious error of second-guessing that the opposition's victory is inevitable and abandoning the existing regime in the hope of winning favor with the new regime after it comes to power. Aside from creating a self-fulfilling prophecy, such an approach will likely result only in contempt for the United States, while winning it nothing with the new regime. The cases of Iran and Nicaragua, though not examples of Soviet-inspired revolution, illustrate the general principle. The time to seek reconciliation with a new government is several months after it comes to power, at the earliest.

Coups pose a special problem, because the element of surprise makes it difficult to support the existing regime with conventional measures. The first goal of U.S. policy should be to preempt such coups by assisting crucial Third World regimes with intelligence information. Any Soviet involvement in coup attempts is certain to be covert—confined principally to encouraging the intrigue, providing financing and small arms, and assuring the conspirators of political support and diplomatic recognition. Accordingly, the U.S. role would not be to break up an impending coup directly—by covert or other means—but simply to provide a second source of information and warning to a friendly government.

ENSURING NATIONAL SECURITY

Are there any interstate conflicts or civil wars in the Third World in which the United States should intervene with combat troops, even if the USSR confines its own involvement to arms shipments and diplomatic support? Should Washington ever send U.S. troops to fight against the armies of Third World countries?

Perhaps these questions may best be decided on the basis of the third principle advanced earlier: the primacy of national security, narrowly defined. The first priority of U.S. foreign policy must be the safeguarding of the nation's security in the most fundamental sense, meaning the defense of its territory, its population, its citizens living abroad, and is tangible possessions overseas. A second legitimate use of U.S. military force would be to help defend those few regimes abroad whose collapse would seriously impair the long-term capacity of the United States to defend itself. These are perhaps the only uses fully compatible with America's values and sense of purpose in the world. The principal reason American troops are in Europe is because the fall of Western Europe to Soviet power would substantially lessen the United States' long-term prospects for survival; a similar criterion ought to determine whether or not U.S. soldiers be sent to fight in the Third World. In order to ensure its own national security, it is important that the United States not risk or deplete its armed forces in pursuing secondary political ends or marginal strategic gains in the Third World.

It is possible, of course, to see in virtually every form of Third World instability or conflict an incipient threat to U.S. security. A sufficiently paranoic prescience will see threats—and grounds for intervention—almost everywhere. But in fact, there is no regime in the Third World that can mount a plausible military threat to U.S. territorial security, and there are only a handful of regimes whose collapse would significantly lessen U.S. prospects for national survival. Certainly the United States should conduct a vigorously internationalistic diplomacy—tenaciously defending its interests, supporting its friends, and seeking to influence the course of diplomatic events around the world—but the actual dispatch of soldiers to fight abroad should be a step reserved for grave threats of a magnitude sufficient to elicit a high degree of national unity and a deeply felt national commitment to achieving military and political success.

The most clear-cut examples of Third World regimes critical to U.S. security are those of Saudi Arabia and Mexico. If either regime were threatened by anti-American forces—externally or internally based, with or without Soviet support—the United States would probably have little choice but to attempt to prevent its collapse by the use of armed force. In the case of Mexico, fortunately, there are no apparent threats to the present regime, but Saudi Arabia's situation is somewhat more precarious. Though the political situation there may be calm on the surface, the royal family is in many respects an anachronism whose ruling authority is likely to face challenges from a variety of internal forces in the coming decade—forces unleashed by the very modernization which oil wealth has brought with it. Saudi Arabia is also situated in a highly volatile region and could well face some form of external attack during the decade. Since U.S. and Western security virtually demand that Saudi Arabia be governed by a pro-Western regime, there is a not insignificant probability that Washington may have to send troops to the peninsula sometime in the next several years. Certainly even in this instance other measures should be attempted first, but an urgent threat may well require immediate U.S. military action.

Aside from Saudi Arabia and Mexico, there are a number of other regimes in the Third World which the United States might have to consider defending with U.S. troops, depending on the circumstances surrounding the threat to their survival. It is obviously impossible to lay out in advance a simple set of criteria on which such a decision might be based, but a president would have to consider the overall global position of the United States, its capacity to engage successfully in a local conflict, the extent to which Soviet arms were a principal factor in enabling the opposing forces to mount a military challenge to a given regime, and the degree of popular support and political stability possessed by the threatened regime. Two examples that come to mind are Israel and South Korea, where considerations of historical loyalty and traditional American commitments might compel a president to take direct military action in their defense if and after all other measures proved inadequate.

Certainly the United States should not get involved in any war it is not prepared to win—not in the moralistic sense implied by total victory or unconditional surrender, but simply in the sense of avoiding defeat on the battlefield and achieving a political and diplomatic outcome favorable to U.S. and Western interests. And before committing forces, the question might well be asked: Will it be worth the price, even if it costs ten times what we estimate it will cost? If the president concludes that the fall of a given regime is simply unacceptable and plainly unavoidable without American combat support, the White House should commit American troops rapidly and massively, with the goal of achieving victory as quickly as possible. Gradual escalation is militarily, politically, and diplomatically unsound. Washington can reduce the odds of superpower confrontation by communicating to Moscow, the attacking state or forces, and all concerned parties, that its principal war aim is restoration of the status quo ante, meaning the survival and territorial integrity of the state under siege. The U.S. involvement should be justified to the world not in geopolitical terms, but as the defense of the Third World country against outside aggression or internal subversion.

It is important that a national and congressional consensus on entering the conflict and on the aims of U.S. involvement exist or be created prior to committing U.S. troops. This is the task of inspired presidential leadership, without which U.S. foreign policy is certain to founder in any event. In order to prevent the erosion of that consensus in a lengthy conflict, however, it may be wise to structure U.S. forces in the Third World as a Special Expeditionary Force for which only professional soldiers and volunteers were eligible. Reserve forces and conscripts, if a draft were in effect, would then be used at home, in Europe, or to man overseas bases outside the area of combat. Such a division within the military is not ideal, but it would do much to alleviate the "dilemma of blood" discussed earlier. Such a Special Expeditionary Force would not be a permanent entity within the military, nor would it be the same entity as the Rapid Deployment Force, though it might draw from the latter. It would be a special command set up temporarily for the purpose of undertaking a specific mission in the Third World. The Marine Corps would provide the majority of troops for the force, with one or two all-volunteer divisions from the regular Army designated to join the force if needed. Once the war aim is achieved, the bulk of U.S. troops should be withdrawn as quickly as feasible, though a residual force might be left long enough for sense of stability to be established in the immediate region.

If a friendly regime in the Third World were toppled unexpectedly by a coup, direct American intervention would probably be both justified and successful only when certain conditions applied: the coup is either clearly Soviet-inspired or clearly of an anti-American and anti-Western character; the survival of the regime in question is *crucial* to U.S. interests (again, the primacy of national security, narrowly defined); the coup does not reflect widespread, popular opposition to the government; sufficient elements of the toppled regime survive the coup to invite U.S. assistance and to continue a struggle of some kind within their country. Saudi Arabia and certain of the smaller oil states in the Persian Gulf may be the only states that will fulfill these requirements in the near future. If it takes place at all, U.S. intervention should be overt. The Marine Corps or other elite forces should be employed, since there will be no time to establish a special command; the operation should take place within days—hours, if possible—of the coup. The goal would be to enable the surviving elements of the former regime to reassert their authority, following which American withdrawal should take place. Only very rarely will the United States want to consider intervening against an attempted coup, but in such circumstances speed and decisiveness are critical.

The deployment of U.S. troops in combat, even on a small scale, ought to be seen as a highly extraordinary step, not as a routine policy instrument. Sending soldiers into battle inevitably places a vastly greater measure of the nation's prestige, resources, will, and moral commitment on the line than any other less drastic action; it is a crucial threshold, the crossing of which is justified only by overriding considerations of national security. By recognizing the significance of that threshold, the United States may succeed in pursuing a strongly internationalistic foreign policy and an influential role in world affairs without vacillating between the twin extremes of interventionism and isolationism.

CONCLUSIONS

U.S. foreign policy, it is widely agreed, is undergoing a period of flux and evolution; the debate over underlying principles and concrete policies has perhaps never been more intense. The vast subject of international security in the world is inevitably a major focus of the debate, and among the questions central to the discussion are those dealing with the Soviet-American rivalry in the Third World. This chapter has concentrated on what is perhaps the most critical dimension of that rivalry: local conflict and revolution. The discussion, however, has unavoidably touched on many other aspects of U.S. diplomacy, for policy prescriptions can only take on their full meaning within the framework of an entire and integral foreign policy. It is at that more general level that a new American consensus, and a more effective American diplomacy, must ultimately be rebuilt.

In conclusion, let it simply be observed that the nation's most urgent need in its foreign policy—whether in the Third World or elsewhere—is a restoration of national confidence, sense of purpose, and esprit de corps. Although the nation suffered a cumulative series of small setbacks during the 1970s, some of them as the result of superior Soviet diplomacy, the events of the decade did not even come close to irretrievably compromising U.S. security or even U.S. standing in the Third World. It is pointless and self-defeating to dwell on the past mistakes of American diplomacy; it is imperative to realize that the United States possesses numerous advantages over the Soviet Union and other potential adversaries, not the least of which is its free and democratic system of government that still appeals powerfully to the peoples of the world. The United States would do well to shed the self-effacement and neo-isolationism of the post-Vietnam period— never forgetting the lessons of that war, but also not focusing on them near-sightedly—for only a purposeful and resolute American diplomacy will be capable of meeting successfully the challenges that lie ahead in the 1980s.

NOTES

1. Blechman and Kaplan (1979) argue that the strategic weapons balance did not influence the outcome of crisis incidents in which both the United States and the Soviet Union were involved. The argument is based principally on a statistical breakdown of the *outcome* of incidents that occurred during various eras of the strategic balance; the study, however, does not (and perhaps could not) separate out all the other factors that came to bear in each situation, nor is it possible to measure or know how many times the USSR refrained from taking action (that is, times when no incident occurred) precisely because of its leaders' perceptions of the strategic balance.

2. See, for example, Trofimenko 1972:7; 1976:15; Georgiev and Kolosev 1973:13.

3. An extensive study of the diplomatic role played in recent years by Soviet fleet is edited by Dismukes (1979).

4. For numerous examples of this, see Mitchell (1978:366–390).

5. This was reported in the *Washington Post,* 12 January 1977, and it was an excerpt in translation from the original by Marquez (1977: 6–15).

6. See also Dulles' address at the Council on Foreign Relations 12 January 1954 (Dulles 1954).

7. This memorandum is available in *Congressional Record,* May 10, 1972. See in particular pages 16779 to 16782, which suggest that neither Hanoi nor the Viet Cong ever suffered a crippling attrition in the rate of equipment being received from China and the Soviet Union, during the period up to 1969. The vast bulk of the equipment was Soviet.

REFERENCES

Ackley, Richard. 1977. "The Merchant Fleet." In *Soviet Naval Influence: Domestic and Foreign Dimensions,* edited by Michael MccGwire and John McDonnel, p. 298. New York: Praeger.

Berman, Robert P. 1978. *Soviet Air Power in Transition.* Washington, D.C.: The Brookings Institution.

Blechman, Barry M., and Stephen S. Kaplan. 1979. *Force Without War: U.S. Armed Forces as a Political Instrument.* Washington, D.C.: The Brookings Institution.

Borgart, Peter. 1979. "The Soviet Transport Air Force." *International Defense Review,* no. 6:948–950.

Defense Daily. 1980. (March 21):118.

Department of State Bulletin (DOSB). 1973. 69 (October 29):528.

———. 1976. 62 (February 23):209.

Dismukes, Bradford, ed. 1979. *Soviet Naval Diplomacy.* London: Pergamon Press.

Donovan, Robert J. 1956. *Eisenhower: The Inside Story.* New York: Harper & Brothers.

Dulles, John Foster. 1954. "Address at the Council on Foreign Relations, January 12, 1954." *Department of State Bulletin* 30 (January 25):107–110.

Chiang Kai-shek. 1957. *Soviet Russia in China: A Summing-up at Seventy.* New York: Farrar, Strauss & Cudahy.

Georgiev, K.M., and M.O. Kolosev. 1973. "Sovetsko-amerikanskie otnosheniia na novom etape." *SShA* (March):13.

Herrick, Robert Waring. 1968. *Soviet Naval Strategy.* Annapolis: U.S. Naval Institute.

Iskenderov, A. 1978. "Edinstvo trex revolyutsionykh potokov—vazheishaya predposylka sokhraneniya i uprocheniya mira." *Mezhdunarodnaya zhizn* (November):73.

Jane's Fighting Ships 1979–80. 1979. New York: Franklin Watts.

Kelly, Anne M. 1977. "Port Visits and the 'Internationalist Mission' of the Soviet Navy." In *Soviet Naval Influence: Domestic and Foreign Dimensions,* edited by Michael MccGwire and John McDonnel, pp. 510–529. New York: Praeger.

Leuthy, Herbert. 1955. *France Against Herself.* New York: Praeger.

Legvold, Robert. 1979. "The Super Rivals: Conflict in the Third World." *Foreign Affairs* 57 (Spring):755.

MccGwire, Michael, and others. 1975. *Soviet Naval Policy: Objectives and Restraints.* New York: Praeger.

Mitchell, R. Judson. 1978. "A New Brezhnev Doctrine: The Restructuring of International Relations." *World Politics* 30 (April):366–390.

"National Security Council Memorandum No. 1." 1972. *Congressional Record* (May 10).

Osgood, Robert Endicott. 1957. *Limited War: The Challenge to American Strategy.* Chicago: University of Chicago Press.

Ponomarev, Boris. 1980. "Neodolimost osvoboditelnovo dvizhenia." *Kommunist* 1173 (January):11.

Presidential Documents. 1980. (January 28):195.

Public Papers of the Presidents: John F. Kennedy 1961. 1962. Washington, D.C.: U.S. Government Printing Office.

Marquez, Gabriel Marquez. 1977. "Cuba en Angola: Operacion Carlota." *Proceso* (January):6–15.

Middleton, Drew. 1979. *New York Times* (December 10, 17).

Quarles, Donald. 1956. "Testimony Before a Congressional Committee." *New York Times* (August 5).

"Republican Campaign Platform." 1952. *New York Times* (July 11).

Simes, Dmitri K. 1978. "Detente, Russian Style." *Foreign Policy,* no. 32 (Fall):54.

Statement Before the Senate Armed Services Committee on the FY 1969–73 Defense Program and the 1969 Defense Budget. 1968. (January 22): 46–47.

Stebbins, Richard P. 1966. *The United States in World Affairs, 1965.* New York: Evanston.

Strategic Survey. 1979. London: International Institute for Strategic Studies.

Trofimenko, G.A. 1972. "Sovetsko-amerikanskie soglasheniya ob ogranichenii strategicheskikh vooruzhenii." *SShA* (September):7.

———. 1976. "Vneshnyaya politika SShA v 70-e gody: deklaratsii i praktika." *SShA* (December):15.

Ulam, Adam. 1978. "U.S.-Soviet Relations: Unhappy Coexistence." *Foreign Affairs: America and the World 1978* (Year-end issue):567.

Understanding Soviet Naval Developments. 1975. Washington, D.C.: Office of the Chief of Naval Operations.

"X." 1947. "The Sources of Soviet Conduct." *Foreign Affairs* (July):576.

Zhurkin, V.V. 1975. *SShA i mezhdunarodno-politicheskiye krizisy.* Moscow: Nauka.

9 ENERGY SECURITY STRATEGY

Joseph S. Nye

Acute energy vulnerability constitutes a clear and present danger to the security of individual nations and to the international order. Half the oil in world trade comes from the Persian Gulf, one of the world's most politically unstable areas, and, despite the current glut, its loss for just a year could stagger the world economy, gravely damaging both the United States, its allies, and less developed countries.

Since the end of World War II, American military strategy has focused on the defense of Europe and Japan, the two greatest concentrations of economic power in the world outside the United States and the Soviet Union. Their prosperity and alliance with the United States has been central to the postwar balance of power. Now energy security problems not only pose a new threat to that prosperity; they also inject a new type of tension into the alliances. The source of threat lies not in Europe or East Asia, but in the Middle East, outside the scope of the formal alliance frameworks. Our allies are more vulnerable than are we. Not only are they more dependent on imported oil as an energy source but 70 percent of Europe's and 77 percent of Japan's oil imports come from the Middle East, in contrast to 32 percent for the United States (Department of Defense 1980).[1] The

This article draws in part from the author's introduction to David Deese and Joseph Nye, eds., *Energy and Security*, published by Ballinger Publishing Company in December 1980.

necessary policy responses go beyond military measures; they involve the conflict-filled areas of domestic economic and energy policies where coordination is particularly difficult for democracies. There is a real danger of disarray in a crisis, as well as divergence in the efforts to avoid crisis. Indeed, different energy vulnerabilities among the Western nations present better opportunities than do direct military threats for the Soviets and other countries to disrupt the Western alliance.

Nor has the United States done very well at home. The experience of the Arab oil embargo of 1973 did not save us from making mistakes when the Iranian revolution curtailed production in 1979. The oil lost in the first half of 1979 amounted to only a few percent of the world total, yet inadequate preparations and panic responses produced both gasoline lines and a 130 percent price increase. Many of the government actions taken after 1973 actually made the situation worse. This was partly because of public unwillingness to see rising prices benefitting some Americans while penalizing others. Adjusting to higher energy prices is painful, and democratic politics are concerned with equity in the sharing of burdens. Yet domestic squabbling over the sharing of the pain produced policies that made the overall burden grow. American dependence on oil imports increased 25 percent between 1973 and 1979, and our overall energy security situation worsened. We *talked* the high rhetoric of energy security, but our actions belied the words. If we are to avoid repeating such mistakes, we need clearer strategy for dealing with energy as a security problem.

DEFINITION AND DAMAGES

Devising a strategy and thinking about energy as a security problem is not as simple as it first seems. Determining the adequacy of energy security is "a complex judgment" (*The Oil Import Question* 1970:21). So is any judgment about security. Security is a matter of degree, and how much insurance one needs in order to feel secure is a function of the probability of the threatening event and the magnitude of the damage. Damages can be defined narrowly in terms of survival or broadly in terms of a whole range of values including welfare, independence, status, and power. We generally speak of national security as the absence of threat to a broad range of values in addition to survival. Indeed, some national security policies, such as our possession of nuclear weapons, may increase the risk to simple survival in order to deter threats to our other values. Simply defined, energy security is the absence of threat of damange to our country from disruptions originating in the supply or price of energy.[2] Energy security is only part of national security; in some circumstances we would risk energy supplies for other values in the broad context of national security.

Energy security is also a matter of degree, and the degree cannot be measured only in terms of imports. In some cases, it may not be too difficult or expensive to alter the policy framework of import dependence. In situations of vulnerability, however, we are liable to high costs that cannot be escaped without incurring similarly high costs. In other words, degrees of vulnerability are judged by the costs of interruption even after taking measures to alleviate the situation.[3]

In the case of most commodities, we accept the benefits that accompany sensitivity to world prices while insuring against the vulnerability costs of interruption by maintaining stockpiles and reserve capacity. Our degree of vulnerability depends not only on the level of imports but also upon the other instruments and policies available. At a given level of oil imports, we are vulnerable to the extent that the level is too high to be handled by remedial measures (such as stockpiles, additional production measures, and emergency demand restraint) at modest levels of cost. Unfortunately, our current level of imports and the current low levels of our stockpiles and emergency procedures do indeed leave the United States highly vulnerable in its dependence on oil imports.

Energy insecurity may damage our foreign policy as well as our domestic society. All too often, costs are defined solely in domestic terms, and the connections between domestic and foreign policy adjustments are ignored. This is something like looking at the domestic effects of the military budget while ignoring the foreign policy objectives the military is designed to advance. Moreover, there are often hard trade-offs between domestic and foreign policy adjustments. A country may adjust its preferred foreign policy position in order to avoid domestic adjustment. In the 1973 oil crisis, a clear example was Japan's decision to develop a Middle East policy different from that of the United States in order to earn transfer from the Arab list of unfriendly nations to their list of friendly nations (Juster 1979). Conversely, certain foreign policy positions such as our support for Israel make the energy supply less secure.

The domestic costs to the U.S. economy of world oil supply interruptions are likely to be extremely high. For example, a 1980 Department of Energy study gave the numbers shown in table 9-1.

Clearly the numbers are enormous, approaching a quarter of the Gross National Product (GNP) or the scale of a 1930's Great Depression in the extreme case. The costs to the rest of the world would be even greater. By another estimate, a nine-million-barrel-per-day cutback of Saudi oil for a year would cut U.S. GNP 6.6 percent, European GNP 8.8 percent, and Japanese GNP 9.5 percent. The loss of all Persian Gulf oil would raise the figures to 17.6 percent for the United States, 23.3 percent for Europe, and 27.3 percent for Japan (Rowen and Weyant 1980).

Of course, such estimates are only rough approximations; altering the assumptions behind the economic models used to produce them can alter the predictions considerably. Even if the numbers were too high by a factor of two or more, it is clear that the domestic costs of major supply interruptions are enormous, and we and our allies ought to make major efforts to avoid them.

The dilemma is that such efforts to escape domestic costs may do great damage to our foreign policy. Tensions may arise in our alliances with Europe and Japan which reflect the relative rather than absolute levels of vulnerability. Europeans, for example, might wish to respond positively to Soviet offers to hold conferences to discuss or guarantee supplies of Persian Gulf oil, while the United States would argue that such steps would legitimize a Soviet presence in the Gulf and would unnecessarily increase Soviet influence over the North American Treaty Organization's (NATO) economic lifeline. Failure to maintain alliance cohesion on such an issue could weaken deterrence and our ability to avoid crises. Tensions have already arisen over the Arab-Israeli conflict, with our allies preferring a position more accommodating to the Arabs. While the idea of trading Israeli interests for a "guaranteed" oil supply would be a mistaken energy security

Table 9-1. Costs to U.S. Economy of World Oil Supply Interruptions for One Year.

Size (in millions of barrels a day)	3mbd	10mbd	20mbd
Cost:	$84 billion	$323 billion	$686 billion

Source: Department of Energy (1980).

policy (putting too many eggs in a Persian Gulf basket that would remain fragile) as well as bad alliance policy, there are more subtle aspects of the balance which can lead to friction with our NATO allies. Other sources of foreign policy difficulty include the temptation to trade sensitive nuclear technology for oil supplies—witness Italy's relations with Iraq—and the problems of managing the world economy as well as preserving stability in crucial countries (such as Turkey) when prices rise precipitously. These foreign policy costs are not susceptible to numerical statement, but their magnitude can be judged by imagining the resources in the defense and aid budgets which we would spend to avoid them if such spending could avoid them.

These foreign policy problems are exacerbated by the fact that different countries fear different types of damages. We can further divide the costs to domestic society into direct damage and economic damage. Economic damage of the sort just discussed is mediated by price rises and is composed of wealth transfers to producer countries, economic inefficiency from misallocation of resources, and the difficulties of managing an economy which simultaneously suffers the depressing effects of the equivalent of a large excise tax and as well as its inflationary effect on prices. Direct damage to society, on the other hand, includes threats to life, health, or public order when energy is not available at any price. In the long term, these damages may also show up as price-mediated economic costs, but in the short run, they cause quite different political anxieties. They are more closely related to the narrow survival definition of security and raise different political and moral issues. Moreover, they are felt by different countries in different ways.

Compare the United States and Japan. Japan is four times more dependent on energy imports (88 percent versus 22 percent); more dependent on oil (75 percent of total energy versus 50 percent); and more dependent on Persian Gulf sources (78 percent versus 30 percent). It is not surprising that Japan feels greater anxiety about direct damage than does the United States, just as the United States, as a global power and alliance leader, is more concerned about damage to foreign policy than is Japan. The differences among countries increase the difficulties in devising a strategy for energy security that includes foreign policy consideration. But an energy security strategy that ignored our allies' energy priorities would be inconsistent with our overall national security strategy.

U.S. POLICIES AND ENERGY SECURITY

Ostensibly, the United States has always considered energy as a security problem. In reality, however, our policies have focused more heavily on price and economic effects than on the security dimensions of the issue. During the two decades before 1973, the main preoccupation of American energy policy was with the glut of inexpensive oil on world markets. World oil production increased steadily, despite political perturbations. The problem of Persian Gulf oil was that its low cost posed a problem to higher priced American domestic producers. Moreover, U.S. antitrust actions and the entry of new independent firms into the international market prevented the major companies from effective collusion to raise prices.

Faced with rising import levels, a cabinet advisory committee recommended in 1955 that voluntary measures be followed to maintain the existing ratio of imports to domestic production. Intensified voluntary restraints were recommended in 1957, and in March 1959 President Eisenhower instituted mandatory quotas to keep oil imports at roughly 12 percent (with regional and product exceptions). While the import quota program had an explicit national security goal, its real political roots were in trade protectionism. As a security measure, the program was a failure, for it stimulated artificially high production levels that eroded domestic reserves, rather than creating stockpiles and spare capacity.

In 1970, a cabinet task force recommended the gradual elimination of the quotas on the grounds that they did little for national security while imposing high prices on our economy. Ironically, this occurred at the same time that U.S. domestic oil production was peaking at 11.2 million barrels a day (mbd). By 1973 imports had risen to 30 percent of oil consumption. U.S. spare capacity of 4 mbd in 1960 had represented 44 percent of U.S. demand and 21 percent of Free World demand. By 1970, U.S. spare capacity of 1 mbd had declined to 8 percent of U.S. demand and less than 3 percent of Free World demand (Department of Energy 1980). Thus, U.S. policy before 1973 ostensibly focused on security but in reality was concerned about price, although the concern was to protect rather than merely to lower prices in the domestic market. Nonetheless, during the 1960s, the price of oil dropped by 10 percent relative to other goods, and consumption rose by 5.4 percent per year in the late 1960s (McKie 1975:74).

The U.S. was ill prepared for the 1973 Arab oil embargo. Under tightening market conditions in the early 1970s, the government had attempted to play a conciliating role in bargaining between OPEC countries and major companies, but it did little diplomatically or in energy policy to prepare effectively for an embargo. During the embargo, the U.S. government encouraged oil companies in their efforts to equalize the burden, stepped up its Middle East diplomacy, and took the lead in organizing the International Energy Agency (IEA). Domestically, a Federal Energy Administration (FEA) was established to administer a system of oil price controls and direct allocation of oil among refiners which did little to improve the situation and actually made it worse. Public attitudes tended to blame the Nixon Administration and the oil companies for the crisis (McKie 1975:85).

Between 1974 and 1979, the official goal of U.S. energy policy was to reduce dependence on imported oil. In November 1973, President Nixon's "Project Independence" had set an unrealistic goal of eliminating imports by 1980. A year later, the FEA realized the fallacy of focusing on import levels alone (which could always be reduced by stopping economic growth), and set a more realistic objective of reducing vulnerability to disruptions. In 1975, the Energy Policy and Conservation Act provided for a Strategic Petroleum Reserve. Unfortunately, however, policy continued to focus on prices. The system of domestic price controls actually subsidized oil imports whose higher prices were blended in with the lower prices of controlled domestic oil. Vulnerability increased as imports rose from 6 mbd in 1974 to 8 mbd in 1978, and there were delays in filling the reserve.

Our international strategy kept energy policy and overall political-military strategy on largely separate tracks (Nau 1978). Energy strategy rested on the expected economic effects of the enormous 1973 price increase in stimulating the new supply, restraining demand, and eventually reducing the real price of imports. Many policymakers agreed with Milton Friedman that OPEC would erode in the glut that would follow a ten-dollar oil price. At one point, for example, U.S. diplomacy in IEA was focused on establishing a seven-dollar floor price so that the expected cheaper oil would not destroy incentives for investing in long-term energy alternatives.

To an extent, the strategy worked. Energy efficiency in industry improved 10 percent from 1973 to 1977; and the real oil price dropped by 25 percent from 1976 to 1978. But ironically, the price gains were more than wiped out by the aftermath of the Iranian events in 1979. In the meantime, the lower prices had perverse effects on political will and consumer demand restraint, and the increased imports of Persian Gulf oil exacerbated the energy security situation.

The focus on price rather than security contributed to the divisive nature of the political debate over energy in the United States. In April 1977, when President Carter announced his first energy plan which eventually led to relaxing price controls on natural gas and increased incentives for conservation, the general public did not believe his statement that a more stringent energy policy was the "moral equivalent of war." In the oil glut of 1978, conventional wisdom and congressional opinion felt little sense of urgency. It was widely expected that Saudi Arabia could be persuaded to increase production to 16 mbd in the 1980s, and that tightness in markets would be a problem for the 1990s.

There was little urgency in filling the SPR, and it contained only 92 million barrels (about 12 days' imports) early in 1979. When interruptions accompanied the Iranian revolution, we again were ill prepared.

The Iranian events dramatized the fragility of the political assumptions behind the previous American energy strategy. Relying on economic forces plus gentle pressure on fragile Persian Gulf governments for ever-increasing levels of production might help on price in the near term, but it increased vulnerability over the longer run. The most important policy change after the Iran crisis was the April 1979 decision for phased decontrol of oil prices which President Reagan speeded up early in 1981. The United States agreed at the 1979 Tokyo Summit to hold future oil imports to a ceiling of 8.5 mbd, and President Carter set a goal of cutting oil imports in half by 1990 while maintaining a growing economy. Other post-Iran initiatives included a synthetic fuels program to be prompted by a synthetic fuel corporation and subsidies for conservation.

Unfortunately, energy projections are notoriously unreliable. According to Koreisha and Stobaugh's review of energy models, "The major studies since 1973 have given us predictions about the U.S. energy situation that have been consistently more optimistic than the reality has proved to be, especially in regard to energy supplies" (Koreisha and Stobaugh 1979:235). On the other hand, government projections of energy demand have been consistently too high and drifted downward over the decade. A similar trend is found in company demand projections. In 1973 Exxon projected 1985 Free World demand at the equivalent of 163 mbd of oil; by 1977 this was lowered to 130, and in 1980 it was further reduced to 118 (Brown and Kahn 1980:68; Marshall 1980:1353).

One reason for difficulty in projection and for the downward trend in demand forecasts has been slackening GNP growth rates. Another reason is uncertainty about how responsive demand will be to changes in price. Given the unprecedented levels to which prices have recently risen, historical data about the price elasticity of demand at lower prices may be quite misleading as an indicator of the future. Over the decade, ratios of energy to GNP have tended to decline among industrial countries, but they also oscillate widely. The summit leaders at Venice in 1980 set a target of .6 in energy to GNP ratio by 1990, indicating that growth could increase without proportionate energy demand increases. Nonetheless, the Summit statement is a target, not a prediction.

The supply side is even harder to project because it depends more heavily on political factors than does demand. For example, political and environmental factors have tended to undercut projections of nuclear and coal supply. The largest supply factor will continue to be oil, particularly the rate of OPEC production which represents about half of the Free World consumption. In the early 1970s, it was common to find bouyant projections of OPEC production in the range of 40 to 60 mbd in the 1980s. The original Saudi Arabian development plan called for raising production to a level of 20 mbd. By 1977, the CIA and the private Workshop on Alternative Energy Strategies were projecting OPEC supply would fail to satisfy demand by the early to mid-80s.

A 1979 comparison of eight major government, international organization, and private company forecasts made between 1977 and 1979 found that most of their estimates for OPEC production fell between 30-35 mbd for 1980; 33-39 mbd for 1985, and 36-46 mbd for 1990 (Missner 1979). As recently as May 1979, the IEA forecasted OPEC production at 38 mbd or higher in 1990; in 1980 this figure was reduced to 30 mbd. Actual OPEC production in 1981 was under 20 mbd.

The current conventional wisdom is that oil markets will be slack in the 1980s. It is widely believed that the oil glut has removed the threat. Some observers even see the prospect of the collapse of OPEC (for example, see Singer 1981-82:115-121).

William Brown and Herman Kahn argue, for example, that "it is likely that in the not too distant future we will be witnessing major oil gluts, tumbling OPEC prices, and sharply reduced OPEC shipments. . . . Barring wars, insurrections, or replays of the Iran debacle in other countries, there is no reason to expect endless increases in oil prices" (Brown and Kahn 1980:67–68). But to bar the role of accidents or political disruptions is to miss the central problem of the changing international energy situation. It was such political events that produced the enormous price spikes of 1973 and 1979. And it is such political events which pose the central and unpredictable problems of the future. Essentially, one cannot understand the changing nature of the international energy situation unless one sees it in a broad international political context.

THE DECLINE OF THE
INTERNATIONAL OIL REGIME

International economic transactions occur within a set of governing arrangments that are often taken for granted. When generally accepted rules, norms, or procedures exist in a given issue area, we speak of an international regime governing the issue. (Depending on the degree of elaboration and acceptance of the norms or procedures, there may be only a quasi-regime or no regime at all [Keohane and Nye 1977]). Regimes generally reflect the power of states at the time of the regime formation, and they tend to erode or change as the structure of power changes in general or in the specific issue area. What has happened in oil over the past decade is that a quasi-regime has eroded and has not been replaced.

In 1970, world oil was still governed by and large by a loose international regime that might be termed "guided laissez-faire." It had two essential components. First, price and production decisions were made mostly by major international oil companies for essentially their own commercial reasons. Second, the major powers (particularly the United States and Britain) occasionally intervened diplomatically to guarantee access for companies and generally oversee the process. Thus, for example, the United States had pressed diplomatically to assure access to Middle Eastern oil in 1943; again in 1950, to assure access and favorable tax treatment of the companies in Saudi Arabia; and in 1954, to assume a broadened access to renewed flows of the Iranian oil that had been boycotted by the companies during nationalization by Mossadegh. With a few exceptions, these governing arrangements were stable and generally accepted. There seemed to be no real alternative.

One result of the regime was that oil prices and production levels tended to reflect supply-and-demand conditions in major consumer countries rather than the expected long-term scarcity value or political considerations in producing countries. As low-cost Middle East oil became more plentiful in the postwar period, most of the difference in value between its low cost of production and the high cost of alternative sources of energy went to consumers who enjoyed low and declining oil prices.

A second result of the regime was that the United States' (and other countries') energy security policy could maintain a low profile. Even Europeans and Japanese with a longer tradition of thinking about oil as a security problem were lulled into deliberately increasing their dependence on Middle East oil. Basically, supply was assured by efficient operations of the companies under a Pax Americana that involved only an occasional diplomatic assurance of access, or antitrust measures to insure a modicum of effective competition.

The changes in the regime by the end of the 1970s were dramatic. Prices and production levels were being set by producer governments rather than international companies, and for political as well as commercial motives. Such decisions were difficult to predict and did not follow a stable or recognizable set of international rules. Producer rather than consumer countries were capturing a large part of the difference between the low costs of production and the higher costs of alternative replacements for Middle East oil. The companies were increasingly constrained by governments at both ends of their pipelines, and their assured access to crude oil under predictable long-term contracts diminished. Moreover, guarantees of access and oversight of price and production decisions had become widely regarded as absolute sovereign prerogatives of producer governments rather than the major Western powers.

Why did such a remarkable change occur over the course of a decade? Basically because of longer term trends in the underlying structure of power, both in general political-military terms as well as in the oil area itself. In the overall political structure, Western dominance of the producing countries declined with decolonization. In 1960, six of the thirteen present OPEC members were colonies or protectorates, and the key straits of Hormuz, Aden, and Malacca were under European control. The rise of nationalism in the producer countries also made the Western intervention more controversial and more costly—witness the events in Iran in 1953 compared with 1979.

More specifically, a turning point occurred with the British withdrawal of its military presence from the Persian Gulf in 1971. At the same time, the Vietnam war insured that the United States would neither replace the British as it had in the Eastern Mediterranean in 1947 nor fully counter the increasing military capabilities of the Soviet Union. Instead, the United States sought to fill the power vacuum in the Gulf by building up the Shah of Iran as the local leviathan. This allowed policing of the Gulf "without any American resources" (Kissinger 1979:1264). At least in budget terms, it seemed that we were buying energy security on the cheap. The fall of the Shah damaged American energy security policy by more ways than through the loss of Iranian oil!

In addition to these general political changes, there were important changes in the structure of power in the oil issue area. A key turning point was the loss of the American surplus after 1971, when our production peaked and our dependence on imports began to increase. The United States lost the spare capacity that it had called upon to supply its allies in the face of political interruptions at the time of the Suez crisis in 1956 and the June war in 1967. The power to balance the market in a time of crisis passed from the United States to OPEC, particularly Saudi Arabia.

A second important change was in the relative power of the companies and the producer governments. Consistent with long-standing patterns in the relations between transnational corporations and less developed countries, original bargains became obsolescent and contracts "renegotiable" as the host countries gradually developed their indigenous capabilities. This trend was accelerated by the entry of new independent oil firms into the world oil markets in the 1950s and '60s. Eager to gain access to crude oil, their competition with the established majors increased the options and enhanced the bargaining power of the producer-country governments.

Initially, the increased production by the new transnationals had the effect of forcing the price of oil down, and producer governments tried to maintain revenue levels by increasing production. Ironically, in 1959, the United States reacted to the falling prices by imposing protectionist quotas that exacerbated the problem of glut in world markets, increased the resentment of producer governments, and contributed to the creation of OPEC. (But it was not until the oil market tightened for other reasons that OPEC proved effective in raising prices.)

Chronologically, the changes in the 1970s occurred in three major steps, with political events acting as key catalysts in the political-economy education of the producer countries.

At the beginning of the decade, the closing of the Suez Canal and destruction of a pipeline across Syria had tightened the tanker situation. This allowed the new revolutionary regime in Libya to capitalize on its geographical location and the weak position of the independent companies to extract a price rise. This in turn triggered a similar demand upon the majors by the Persian Gulf producers. Eager for political harmony, the U.S. government sent a representative but did not support the companies in the critical meeting at Teheran in 1971 (Sampson 1975). Essentially, the Middle East producers learned they could press the companies with threats of nationalization and shutdown without incurring serious penalties from the Western powers.

The second step was larger. In the context of the U.S. resupply of Israel in the October 1973 Arab-Israeli war, the Arab producers instituted a 25 percent cutback in production. Even before the cutback, the OPEC governments had decided on a 70 percent price increase that reflected tightening markets as U.S. imports increased. But the embargo created a scarcity and panic in world markets which drove prices for marginal quantities to extraordinary levels, and allowed Iran to lead the other OPEC states in a 400 percent increase over prewar prices (Penrose 1975:50). Essentially the political catalyst of the war taught the producers the value of cutbacks and indicated that the long-run price of oil might be much higher than they expected.

This lesson was reinforced by the third step—the Iranian revolution in 1979—which showed that even uncoordinated curtailments could have large effects on price. In addition, the experience of the Shah led some producers to conclude that production cutbacks sometimes make domestic-political as well as economic sense.

The result is that control over prices, production, and—to an increasing extent—distribution channels has largely passed to OPEC countries. Historically, OPEC price increases have generally reflected market tightness more than their accompanying political rhetoric would imply, but models of OPEC countries behaving as economic maximizers are too simple. While economics can tell us a lot about demand in energy markets, it tells us only part of the story about supply in a world of sovereign states. Production decisions are made on a national basis and often reflect domestic political conflicts and decisions about matters as diverse as development plans, desirable social trends, and how to cope with external events. For example, following the Camp David signatures in 1979, Saudi Arabia's political decision to reduce production to 8.5 mbd in April contributed greatly to the market's turbulence. Earlier it had helped to make up the missing Iranian oil, but the Saudi cutback shook assumptions about future production levels and contributed to the panic buildup of stocks in a tight market that drove prices to record levels (See Stobaugh and Yergin 1980 and also Nissen 1980).

Moreover, production decisions are affected by prior investments in capacity that may reflect internal political conditions of years ago. It appears that Saudi slowness in developing capacity a few years ago may have been designed to avoid pressure for higher production from the United States which would have been embarrassing in inter-Arab politics and could have stimulated transnational terrorist attacks. The result was that the 1979 cutbacks by Iran and by smaller producers (who were traditionally price-followers) occurred in a relatively tight market where revenues actually increase as production declines. Current reported Saudi efforts to increase capacity toward 12 mbd might be interpreted as an effort to regain its position of power within oil markets. But we do not fully know the determinants of Saudi behavior. Revenue needs and foreign policy positions provide clues, but it may be that oil production decisions really reflect shifts in internal royal family coalitions in which the guiding principle is to minimize the sense of domestic and international political pressure and threat felt by the royal family.

Nor can one be certain about the domestic politics of other producing states. Reserves and revenue needs provide clues but only part of the political story. One would expect Mexican production, for example, to increase on that basis. But rates of increase will reflect internal politics. Mexicans worry that too-rapid growth of oil exports will create inflation and a high-priced industrial structure unable to export and unable to meet their employment problem. Similar political arguments over economically and socially desirable production levels occur in such developed allies as Norway and Britain.

Even if projections of a continuing glut prove correct, a softer market would not remove the danger of production cutbacks due to revolutions, accidents, or sabotage which are beyond the producer's control. If consumers again ignore the political fact that the old regime has collapsed and that a large part of oil production decisions are out of the control of the consumer governments, we may be condemned to repeating the costly 1970s cycle of disruption's raising prices; high prices causing a temporary glut; and then renewed crisis and severely disruptive price increases. Faced with risk and uncertainty in production decisions, it behooves us to be skeptical about all projections and to carry considerable insurance.

In summary, the loose regime that governed oil broke down in the 1970s for a complex series of reasons related to shifts of power in both the overall structure and in the oil issue area and catalytic political events. It did not break down because of the formation of OPEC or market forces alone. The prospect of recreating a more satisfactory regime to us remains questionable as long as the structure of overall power and market power in oil remain as unfavorable to consumers as they now appear and as long as internal politics in key producer countries are unstable or unclear. The result is a world of political uncertainty with unpredictable prices, renegotiable contracts, and the lurking threat of disruptive interruptions.

Simple reliance on market forces is not an adequate policy for energy security. It was widely believed that in the period after 1973, government measures at home and market forces abroad would solve our energy problems. To some extent, they will, but they are a necessary rather than a sufficient condition. Indeed one might argue that part of our past energy security problem stemmed from an underreliance on economists' remedies domestically, but an overreliance on them internationally. On the contrary, thinking about energy as a security problem requires attention to the broader political context of the oil issue area. But thinking in political strategic terms also requires economic as well as political sensitivity. Many of the proffered political solutions lack both qualities.

POLITICAL PANACEAS

A recurrent problem in thinking about energy security is the temptation to be done with the problem by imagining that there is some easy way to solve it. A variety of political panaceas have been suggested over the past decade. Proposals have been made to invade the oil fields, break OPEC, nationalize the oil companies, set up a new international organization, and so forth. Not one solution is realistic.

Some only divert our attention, but others suggest elements for the real job of integrating a broad range of domestic and foreign policy instruments for a long-term strategy.

1. Political-Military Coercion.   Given the political limits of the international market, some analysts have urged a political-military response of taking over Persian Gulf oil fields (see, for example, Tucker 1975). They argue that the global (and national) costs of continued acquiesence to cartel price rises are so high that they merit a change in our frame of reference, and justify military intervention and "internationalization" of Persian Gulf oil resources.

The political and economic costs of such a remedy, however, are likely to be extremely high. The risk of destroying the oil infrastructure through fighting or sabotage could *create* a major costly disruption which an energy security policy is supposed to avert.

The prospects are great that saboteurs would be successful. A perimeter around only the Saudi core oil fields would encompass 10,000 square miles, twice the size of Connecticut. Within that area more than 1,000 miles of pipe depend on two dozen pumping stations, half a dozen power packs for propulsion, and a few loading facilities (Congressional Research Service 1975). Some 60 percent of Persian Gulf exports pass through these ports and are controlled by eight critical pump sites (Levy 1980). Many of the giant valves and pumps are custom-built equipment not easily or quickly repairable.

The Persian Gulf is 8,000 miles from the United States. Logistics would be difficult, particularly if allies and local friendly states did not share our political goals. One airborn division at full strength would be insufficient. An amphibious marine division would take at least two weeks to arrive. "Chances that U.S. assault forces could achieve surprise are close to zero" (Congressional Research Service 1975). Success would depend on slight damage to the key installations and Soviet abstinence from armed countermeasures directly or elsewhere in the region. Even small failures would be costly (Collins and Clyde 1979). The chances are great that an effort to seize the oil fields would be like shooting ourselves in both feet by bringing about a several-hundred-billion-dollar interruption as well as Soviet intervention in the region.

Moreover, there is little prospect for developing broad international legitimacy for what would be characterized as a new colonial occupation, with resultant disruptions of our foreign policy elsewhere. Unless the situation approaches what Kissinger termed "strangulation," it is uncertain how much public support abroad or at home would be maintained for such an occupation, particularly if less questionable alternatives such as demand restraint had not been fully implemented first. How many lives spent are worth how many minutes in gasoline lines saved?

While this option is not a promising policy under foreseeable circumstances, it does call attention to more modest components of military policy in oil strategy. An enhanced defense posture in the Middle East is a very good energy investment. Our ability to deter Soviet intervention and to quickly help protect those who ask for our assistance provide important assets in the complex diplomacy of oil. But force is not a sufficient strategy.

2. "Break OPEC."   While military coercion is likely to be too costly, some analysts have felt that efforts to break OPEC are appropriate given the enormous gap between the cost of producing Persian Gulf oil and what they see as its artificial cartel maintained price. A variety of schemes have been suggested ranging from food export embargoes to governmental purchasing in sealed bid auctions ("Alternatives to Dealing with OPEC" 1979).

There are several problems with this approach. OPEC as an organization is not the sole cause of high prices. *Cheap* oil is scarce and concentrated in a few states, while alternatives to oil are expensive and take time to produce. Producers have learned the benefits of oligopolist pricing and limiting production; successful oligopoly behavior does not necessarily require organization. Moreover, OPEC as an organization has never succeeded in controlling production rates. That is in the sovereign control of producer states.

Saudi Arabia is the key country because it can finance its development plan by producing 6 mbd, giving it a discretionary capability of 4 to 5 mbd. During much of 1981, Saudi Arabia produced more than its stated 8.5 mbd target and sold its oil for less than its OPEC partners until it brought them into line with Saudi price policy. The Saudis produced more than their revenue needs in order to dampen their partner's price rises. Saudi behavior was affected both by its long-term economic interest and by the politics of its several economic and security interdependences with the West.

While we might benefit from a natural erosion of OPEC, efforts to "break OPEC" that exacerbate the U.S.-Saudi relationship would be costly in foreign policy as well as energy security grounds. Efforts to embargo or limit food shipments would fail in the face of alternative sources of food supplies, but might well trigger expensive retaliation. In addition, efforts to break OPEC would almost certainly cause friction with our European allies and Japan who feel too vulnerable to engage in such economic brinksmanship.

3. International Collective Bargaining.
One can imagine a smooth long-term transition from cheap oil to more expensive energy alternatives that would benefit both consumers and producers. Give the long lead times for alternatives and the opportunities for price gouging in conditions of political uncertainty, the current price of oil may often be pushed higher than the long-term price. This could reduce long-term producer revenues; create uncertainty for their development planning; and by destabilizing the world economy, threaten the value of their new investments. Politically, a stable world economy enhances the security of producers who depend on an unprovoked and reliable West. It also reduces the economic sources of political instability in the oil-importing, developing countries. A consumer-producer dialogue might help nations to shift their focus to these potential long-term joint gains.[4]

Such a dialogue might seek two- or three-year intergovernmental agreements to stabilize the oil market. For example, OPEC and IEA countries would agree on production targets and consumption limits (at first separately, and then in joint bargaining) which would allow for modest real price rises over the decade. A band of prices might be established for the duration of the agreement. OPEC countries would agree to maintain sufficient spare capacity to increase production if a shortfall of production from any subgroup of producers threatened to push prices outside the band. They would cut production (or agree to permit consumers to increase demand above the agreed limits) if prices threatened to fall through the bottom of the band. Additional inducements might be needed to assure adequate production levels. For example, consumers might offer indexing of assets and assurances of assistance and market access for the new OPEC industries. Special credit or aid provisions might be agreed upon for oil-importing, developing countries; some such countries could be included in bargaining sessions.

The number of problems and questions that have to be solved should make us cautious about embarking on such a course: *Could we keep the agenda focused on energy*? Given the politics of the Middle East and the strong bargaining position of the producers, we might find ourselves unable to keep certain awkward political issues off the table. If other developing countries participate, we might find ourselves replaying sterile North-South debates, but with much higher stakes than in the United Nations. We need to be sure we can control the Pandora's Box effect before we start down the path to serious international collective bargaining.

Is a reasonable bargain likely? Economic interests diverge among OPEC surplus producers who lean toward conservation and high absorbers interested in maximizing revenues. Would OPEC countries be able to agree to a bargain that meant higher production and lower prices than the market would otherwise determine? Or would the process of collective bargaining help OPEC to pull its act together but at a higher price?

Does OPEC have sufficient cohesion to make a bargain stick? So far OPEC countries have been unwilling to limit their separate sovereign control over production decisions concerning the resources that is their major source of power. They compete for power within the oil arena, and they reserve the right to use oil as a weapon in wider political games. Given the politics of oil and the domestic instability of many OPEC governments, how credible is an OPEC promise to increase production if a future shortfall has political ramifications?

Would the benefits exceed the costs? Basically consumers would gain a formal framework for debating production (and price) decisions that are now entirely in OPEC hands (except insofar as bilateral diplomacy has an effect). What is it worth paying for such a framework? OPEC cohesion for collective bargaining may be achieved at higher prices than would otherwise be the case. Special instruments such as indexing may prove very costly, particularly if the precedent spreads. Add the risks just outlined, and the benefits of a formal collective bargaining framework look slimmer than the costs.

This is not to argue that conversations with producer states are not useful, or that restoration of an international regime is not a worthy long-term goal. Various bilateral and multilateral discussions are essential. But the time is not ripe for fruitful collective bargaining when power is so imbalanced. Efforts to reconstruct a satisfactory regime under current circumstances are unlikely to be fruitful unless they are part of a larger strategy to enhance energy security.

STEPS IN THE RIGHT DIRECTION

Painful though it was, the United States learned some useful lessons from the interruption of Iranian supply. In April 1979, we began the decontrol of domestic oil prices and learned the folly of putting too many eggs in the Persian Gulf basket. In addition, the shock of the Shah's fall plus the Soviet invasion of Afghanistan led to steps to repair our military posture in the area.

We still have a long way to go. Even with decontrol, oil industry sources project declines in domestic oil production levels during the 1980s. Moreover, even if the United States is successful, our allies will remain vulnerable. A successful strategy will have to focus on deterring and preventing interruptions and alleviating their damage in the short term while reducing our vulnerability over the decade. This will require a better integration of political-military policy, domestic energy policy, and international energy policy than we have achieved at home or in our alliance relations in the past. The diversity of the inventory of instruments appropriate to different tasks and situations is illustrated in table 9–2.

Political-Military Measures.   The United States is vital to the security of the conservative states in the Persian Gulf, and this is a key card in the larger diplomacy of energy security. Proposals for neutralization of the area ignore the geographical reality of the Soviet Union's presence on the border of the area some 600 miles from the oil fields (see Wohlstetter 1980). At the same time, projections of Soviet domestic energy shortfalls may have been somewhat exaggerated, and a direct Soviet move to capture the oil fields is not the most probable event.[5] The fact that the Soviet Union is not the only threat to stability in the region complicates the appropriate military posture. For example, one can rank threats to Persian Gulf oil on an ascending scale of the military response required: (1) terrorist sabotage of key loading facilities; (2) civil or interstate wars which destroy production capacity; (3) Soviet proxy takeover of an oil-producing state; and (4) Soviet airborne or tank-led invasion. Yet the prominent military posture most effective in dealing with the Soviet threat may actually increase the probability of the indigenous threats (see Carnegie Endowment Panel on U.S. Security and the Future of Arms Control 1981).

Not surprisingly, this mixture of threats has led to local ambivalence about the U.S. military role. As the Saudis sometimes put it,

Table 9-2. Inventory of Policy Instruments and Scenarios.

	I. "Bargained Extortions"		II. "Chaotic Interruptions"	
	Domestic Policy	Foreign Policy	Domestic Policy	Foreign Policy
Deter and prevent Actions	Demand restraint	Military posture		Military posture
	Strategic reserve	Diplomacy		Diplomacy
	Private stocks	Diversify sources		
		Import restraints		
Defend flows				Intelligence
				Military assistance
				Intervention
Restore flows		Foreign policy Concessions	Stock surplus equipment	Repair capacity
				Airlift capacity
		Interventions if "strangulation"		
Alleviate effects	Strategic reserves	IEQ sharing plan		
	Private stocks	Coordinate stocks		
	Emergency procedures	Coordinate demand restraint	Same alleviation measures	
	Disruption tariff or taxes			
	Surge capacity			

they want a U.S. presence, but just over the horizon. This situation requires a subtle mixture of significant naval presence backed up by prepositioning of equipment in places like Diego Garcia, combined with conditional basing rights closer to the area. It also involves sharing of intelligence, development of rapid repair capacity, and technical assistance. In some instances, a divison of labor with our allies makes political sense. The military card must be played with neither too heavy nor too light a hand.

Also important is our mediatory role in regional conflicts which could escalate to destructive wars in the area. The most important of these is the Arab-Israeli dispute. Because the 1973 oil embargo was related to the October 1973 war, it is sometimes assumed that resolution of this conflict is synonymous with solution of the energy security problem. The loss of 6 mbd from Iran at the end of 1978 should have destroyed this myth. The Arab-Israeli conflict is not the sole source of instability and threats to oil. What a resolution would do is remove one of the incentives to terrorism and extortion, and one of the important inhibitions to more forward military basing in the Gulf. A solution of the Arab-Israeli conflict would help ameliorate but not solve our energy security problem. There are good and sufficient reasons in addition to energy—for example, the prospect of eventual nuclear proliferation in the Middle East—for seriously attempting to solve the problem now.

Domestic Energy Policy

Next to continuing decontrol of energy prices, the most important step to be taken in domestic energy policy is building up public and private reserves. Our ability to reduce our dependence on imports (at an acceptable level of costs) is limited in the short run, but we can build stocks to reduce the degree of vulnerability that imports entail. Congress legislated the strategic petroleum reserve (SPR) in 1975. By 1980, it was scheduled to hold 500 million barrels or sixty days of imports. Through a combination of administrative problems and Saudi unhappiness about filling the SPR, it reached only one-fifth of that target. In 1981, the Reagan Administration took advantage of the soft market to more than double the SPR to 230 million barrels. But there is still a long way to go, and budgetary constraints may slow the necessary expansion of capacity. Fortunately, private stocks were built to high levels in the aftermath of the Iran crisis, and that helped to buffer the effects of the Iran-Iraq War. Policy measures should be developed to encourage holding of high levels of private stocks of oil and gas, and to plan for an SPR disbursal by auction early in a crisis.

A second priority is putting in place robust emergency procedures that can reduce panic and pressure on the central political institutions (which may have to deal simultaneously with other security dimensions of crisis). Government allocation and rationing is not likely to meet the need. There is good reason to believe that government allocation made the 1974 and the 1979 shortages *worse*, and that the administration of a rationing plan for 150 million vehicles would take at least six months to begin to work smoothly (if by then) and would generate widespread political conflicts. A standby emergency tax with rebates on witholding taxes (to minimize fiscal drag and inflationary effect) would be a more flexible instrument with fewer demands on the administrative and political process.[6] The Reagan Administration has not made clear what its emergency plans would be.

Third in priority is demand reduction measures to reduce dependence over time. The decontrol of gas and oil prices provides signals for energy efficiency throughout the economy as well as incentives for increased production. Legislated efficiency standards for automobiles and buildings and subsidies to encourage conservation also help to stimulate appropriate investment decisions. A further measure would include an oil import fee or a gasoline tax.

Economic considerations such as inflation and unemployment effects set limits on the rapidity of import reduction. After all, a large enough depression would cut imports, but the cure would be worse than the disease. Economists differ about the appropriate rate and level of import reduction, but the correct direction is clear.

Fourth are measures to increase domestic alternatives to imported oil. As noted earlier, such measures contribute only modestly to insurance against vulnerability in the short run, but they are important components of the strategy to reduce dependence over the longer term.

International Energy Policy.   Given the flexibility of world oil markets, there is no way to isolate the effects of our actions from those of other major consumer nations. The seven summit nations consume about three-quarters of world oil. Their agreement on import ceiling targets at Tokyo in 1979 signalled an end to the previous path of ever-increasing Western dependence, but ceilings are not a sufficient international energy policy. Ceilings designed for normal times are irrelevant in a disruption; international emergency measures are needed.

The most important measures in an emergency are release of stockpile oil and emergency taxes (or tariffs). These two measures help to moderate the precipitous price rise that will occur and limit the transfer of wealth to foreign producers. Prices will rise in a crisis, but we can affect the extent and direction that the money goes. We can keep some of the money by taxing ourselves before OPEC does it for us. Cooperation on these measures with other consumer nations multiplies their effect. Alternatively, if we apply them and others do not, the others get the benefit of our stockpiling and demand restraint for free.

IEA members have agreed to hold ninety days of imports in public and private stocks. Most countries now slightly exceed this level, and it would make sense to try to raise the agreed level permanently. Agreements on tariffs or taxes will be harder to reach, but their economic merit makes them worth discussing.

We could also try to get some agreement on panic buying in disrupted markets of the sort that caused such precipitous price rises in 1979. We might start with an agreement among the summit countries or simply with Japan since the United States and Japan represent 50 percent of world oil imports. It is worth noting that Japan's 1979 panic-buying in spot markets which the United States criticized reflected her 99 percent dependence on imported oil and the cutback of deliveries by the majors when they lost their Iranian (and other) sources of crude oil.

Any agreement on restraint in disrupted markets will require assurances that remaining supplies will be shared. The IEA emergency sharing plan is important and would be effective under many conditions, but it requires a 7 percent shortfall before taking effect. Maximum overall shortfalls in 1979 were more in the order of 3 or 4 percent, and some of the ensuing doubling of price could have been avoided by better procedures. The IEA secretariat has the power to call an emergency ministerial meeting when it finds market disruption. But further steps would be needed to make it easier to arrange informal multilateral or bilateral agreements on sharing short of the 7 percent trigger. Some such arrangments would be a necessary precondition for effective restraint in disrupted markets. Although such steps may be politically difficult, the alternative is that we share the remaining oil anyway through competitive bidding, reaching the same outcome at higher prices and with a shaken alliance.

While our allies are the other major consumers in world markets, they are not the only countries about which we are concerned. Less developed countries import only about 10 percent of world oil, but what appears to be small numbers to us can present very large problems for them. There are several steps we can take to help. First, we should use international forums to press for assistance to help them cope with oil price rises. Second, we can support International Monetary Fund (IMF) loans to back up the private banking system in financing the deficits. Third, we can avoid making their situation worse through depressing our demand for their goods and closing our markets to their exports. Finally, through bilateral assistance and through the World Bank, we can support the development of conventional and new energy sources in those countries. While such sources cannot provide an instant panacea, every drop helps.[7] In the context of our broader energy and security interests, these steps to help developing countries are also steps that help ourselves.

Obviously, there are difficult issues and nuances in blending domestic, military, and diplomatic measures in a successful energy security strategy. We must avoid bogging down in acrimonious, domestic, distributional disputes or diverting our attention to spurious, international, quick fixes rather than focusing on the hard work of integrating the instruments at hand into a realistic energy security strategy. Only then, as we deal ourselves a hand with better cards in it, can we look ahead to the prospects of re-creating an equitable international regime for international energy issues. Whether such a regime can be recreated during the decade is an open question. Certainly, there is a long-run common interest, and ideally one can think of collective energy security as a worthy goal. But we are now a long way from the structure of power and control of political issues that would make possible the re-creation of a stable and equitable international oil regime.

CONCLUSION

The energy crises of the 1970s provide important lessons for formulating American strategy. After easily defeating an oil embargo in 1967, the impact of the 1973 embargo came as a shock. Many analysts concluded that we were entering a new era of economic power based on raw materials. Even a traditional realist like Hans Morgenthau wrote of "an historically unprecedented divorcement" of military power from economic and political power resulting from "the monopolistic or quasi-monopolistic control of raw materials" (Morgenthau 1974). In fact, the lessons of '73 were more limited than that. Oil, not all commodities, provided an effective power instrument for reasons just mentioned. But that instrument was limited. The oil weapon raised the Middle East issue to the top of the U.S. agenda; given the interdependence between the United States and Saudi Arabia, it was not played in a way that would force a dramatic policy reversal.

The real lesson of the oil crises for analysis and strategy is the importance of integrating economic, political, and military factors, and instruments—both domestic and international. As Albert Wohlstetter writes, "Our plans, at least since World War II, have always recognized the crucial wartime importance of gulf oil. However, we have centered less attention on the damage the West would incur from hostile political control of the oil it required during peacetime. . . ." (1980:136). During the 1960s our system of quotas was described as a security measure but was really a response to domestic economic pressures. In the 1970s we used price controls to shelter our domestic market from international price increases and wound up increasing our dependence. Internationally, we placed too much faith in the conventional economist's wisdom that high prices would solve the oil problem. At the same time, we launched diplomatic initiatives like Indian Ocean arms control which we failed to relate to our growing dependence on Persian Gulf oil and to the complex interplay of oil and military security in the diplomacy of that region.

On the other hand, as was just shown, realist critics like Tucker also failed to understand properly the role of force in energy strategy. Force alone is not a sufficient strategy. In 1976, Robert Keohane and I argued that asymmetrical interdependence is a source of power, whether it is military, economic vulnerability, or economic sensitivity. "It must be kept in mind furthermore, that military power dominates economic power. . . . Yet exercising more dominant forms of power brings higher costs. Thus, relative to cost, there is no guarantee that military means will be more effective than economic ones to achieve a given purpose" (Keohane and Nye 1977:17). We developed models of power based on different forms of interdependence, including a model that extends realist analysis by applying it to economic issues. Some critics have taken us to task for having "grossly expanded the *scope* or focus of realist theory. . . . Realism is an inappropriate theoretical perspective for analyzing issues stemming from interdependence, as realists themselves would readily admit" (Michalak 1979).[8] But that is exactly the problem: 1973 and its aftermath was not Morgenthau's "divorcement" of military, economic, and political power, but a perfect illustration of their complex interweaving.

As long as analysts insist on a false dichotomy between realism and economic interdependence, their strategic visions will oscillate between over- and underreliance on the role of force rather than the relevant task of integrating force with other policy instruments into an effective strategy. As Michalak concedes, "*Power and Interdependence* has punctured this simplistic bifurcation by showing the ubiquity of politics across the whole range of international issues" (1979:150). The approach to a strategy for energy and security outlined here illustrates the problems of power and interdependence in a case which will continue to threaten us over the coming decade. At

ENERGY SECURITY STRATEGY   327

least with the right strategic conception, we can better cope with the threat.

NOTES

1. "The first danger comes from the heavy European dependence on OPEC oil and the possibility that its supply could be disrupted" (Department of Defense 1980:46).
2. This definition is consistent but more general than others offered by Willrich (1975:67): ". . . the assurance of sufficient energy supplies to permit the national economy to function in a politically acceptable manner"; or Deese (1979–80:140): ". . . a high probability that (a nation) will have adequate energy supplies . . . at affordable prices."
3. See the discussion in Keohane and Nye (1977), Chapter 1.
4. For a recent proposal, see Smart (1980) and *North-South* (1980).
5. See Marshall Goldman's (1980) critique of CIA estimates in "Communist Countries."
6. This point and other proposals are developed in detail by Alm and Hogan (1980).
7. But Walter Levy cautions, "Even in the unlikely case that within the next 10 to 15 years massive new discoveries should be made, comparable to those in the Middle East, it would take perhaps some 10 additional years before they could be fully developed" (1980:1014).
8. Earlier, David Baldwin (1979) took us to task for exaggerating the effectiveness of force. Robert Art made the opposite criticism in "To What Ends Military Power" (1980a), but he subsequently (1980b) admitted that he misrepresented our argument.

REFERENCES

"Alternatives to Dealing with OPEC." 1979. Hearings before a Subcommittee of the Committee on Government Operations, House of Representatives, June 20 and 21.
Art, Robert. 1980a. "To What Ends Military Power?" *International Security* (Spring):3–35.
———. 1980b. "Letters." *International Security* (Fall):187–190.
Baldwin, David. 1979. "Power Analysis and World Politics." *World Politics* 31 (January):161–194.
Brown, William, and Herman Kahn. 1980. "Why OPEC Is Vulnerable." *Fortune* 102, no. 1 (July 14):66–69.
Carnegie Endowment Panel on U.S. Security and the Future of Arms Control. 1981. *Assessing the Balance: Defense Spending and Conventional Forces.* Washington, D.C.: Carnegie Endowment.

Collins, John, and Mark Clyde. 1979. "Petroleum Imports from the Persian Gulf: Use of U.S. Armed Forces to Ensure Supplies," Congressional Research Service Issues Paper IB79046, July.

Congressional Research Service. 1975. *Oil Fields As Military Objectives.* Washington, D.C.: U.S. Government Printing Office.

Deese, David. 1979–80. "Energy, Economics, Politics and Security." *International Security* 4 (Winter):140–153.

Department of Defense. 1980. *Annual Report, Fiscal Year 1981.* Washington, D.C.: U.S. Government Printing Office.

Department of Energy. 1980. "The Energy Problem: Costs and Policy Options." Staff Working Paper.

Goldman, Marshall. 1980. "Communist Countries." In *Energy and Security*, edited by David Deese and Joseph Nye. Cambridge, Mass.: Ballinger Publishing Company.

Hogan, William. 1980. "Import Management and Oil Emergencies." In *Energy and Security*, edited by David Deese and Joseph Nye. Cambridge, Mass.: Ballinger Publishing Company.

Juster, Kenneth. 1977. "Foreign Policy-Making During the Oil Crisis." *The Japan Interpreter* 11 (Winter).

Keohane, Robert, and Joseph Nye. 1977. *Power and Interdependence.* Boston: Little, Brown.

Kissinger, Henry. 1979. *The White House Years.* New York: Little, Brown.

Koreisha, Sergio, and Robert Stobaugh. 1979. "Limits to Models." In *Energy Future*, edited by Robert Stobaugh and Daniel Yergin, pp. 235–265. New York: Random House.

Levy, Walter. 1980. "Oil and the Decline of the West." *Foreign Affairs* 58 (Summer):999–1015.

Marshall, Eliot. 1980. "Energy Forecasts: Sinking to New Lows." *Science* 208 (June 20):1353.

McKie, James. 1975. "The United States." *Daedalus* 104 (Fall):73–90.

Michalak, Stanley J., Jr. 1979. "Theoretical Perspectives for Understanding International Interdependence." *World Politics* 32 (October):136–150.

Missner, Susan. 1979. "A Comparison of Energy Forecasts, 1977–79." Stanford University International Energy Program. Mimeo.

Morgenthau, Hans J. 1974. "The New Diplomacy of Movement." *Encounter* (August).

Nau, Henry R. 1978. "Continuity and Change in U.S. Foreign Energy Policy." *Policy Studies Journal* (Autumn):121–132.

––––––. 1979. "U.S.-Japan Relations in the 1973–74 Energy Crisis: Bilateral Confrontation and Multilateral Cooperation." Unpublished manuscript, George Washington University.

Nissen, David. 1980. "OPEC Oil Pricing." Chase Manhattan Bank. Unpublished paper.

North-South. 1980. Report of the Brandt Commission. Cambridge, Mass.

Penrose, Edith. 1975. "The Development of Crisis." *Daedalus* 104 (Fall): 39-57.

Rowen, Henry, and John Weyant. 1980. "The Problem of Security of Supply of Persian Gulf Oil: Analysis and a Proposed Strategy." Mimeo.

Sampson, Anthony. 1975. *The Seven Sisters*. New York: Viking Press.

Singer, S. Fred. 1981-82. "An End to OPEC? Bet on the Market." *Foreign Policy* (Winter):115-121.

Smart, Ian. 1980. "Communicating with the Oil Exporters: The Old Dialogue and the New." *Trialogue* (Winter):22-29.

Stobaugh, Robert, and Daniel Yergin. 1980. "Energy: An Emergency Telescoped." *Foreign Affairs* 58, no. 3:563-595.

The Oil Import Question. 1970. Washington, D.C.: U.S. Government Printing Office.

Tucker, Robert. 1975. "Oil: The Issue of American Intervention." *Commentary* (January):21-31.

Willrich, Mason. 1975. *Energy and World Politics*. New York: Free Press.

Wohlstetter, Albert. 1980. "Half-Wars and Half-Policies in the Persian Gulf." In *From Weakness to Strength*, edited by Scott Thompson. San Francisco: Institute for Contemporary Studies.

INDEX

Military power equation (total), 194
Military power
 limitations of, 262
 political utility of, 262
Military power, Soviet, 13–14
 compared to U.S., 1, 12
 capabilities of, 6, 10–11, 15, 259
 expansion of, 2, 10, 255–256
Military power, U.S.
 decline in, 1
 factors undermining, 217
 limits of, 281
 necessary rebuilding of, 2–3, 49
 previous nuclear preeminence,
  3, 264
Military psychology, 186–187, 194–
 195, 198
Military readiness, 12, 84, 186,
 217, 219
Military spending
 Soviet, increased, 1–2
 U.S., 2, 256
Military success
 contributing factors of, 185–
  186, 194
 numerical measures of, 183
Military superiority, 240
 Soviet deflation of enemy's,
  270
 U.S. lack of, 278
Military tactics, 173
 combined arms, 182
 necessary improvement of, 198
 problems of, 165
 single weapon, 182
Military technology, 173, 180, 186,
 193–225
 design variety, 196
 narrowing of quality gap, 207
 revolutionary advances in, 195–
  196
 Soviet quantitative advantage,
  196

U.S. reliance on material quality,
 197–206
 See also Technological research
  and development
 wartime primacy of, 172
Military thought, schools of, 165,
 172–173
Military training, 198, 241, 248,
 292
Ministry of Defense, Soviet, 260
Minuteman missile, 70, 141, 152–
 153, 168, 179, 259
Minuteman III, 96n, 121
"Missile gap," 70, 113
"Mobility forces," 259–261, 265–
 266
 Soviet compared to American,
  257, 259, 261, 288
 U.S., 274
Model J aircraft, 209
Model K aircraft, 209
Model L aircraft, 209
Mongolia
 Chinese threat to, 27
 Soviet ties with, 4, 19–21
Moorer, Admiral Thomas, 94n
Morgenthau, Hans, 325–326
Morocco, 44, 236–237
Moslem rebels, threat in the Phil-
 ippines, 236
Mossadegh, 310
Mozambique
 revolutionary struggle of, 262
 SSD advisors in, 243
MPLA. See Popular Movement
 for the Liberation of Angola
Muhammad, Nasser, 244
Multiple independently targetable
 reentry vehicles (MIRVs), 96,
 121, 125, 144–145
Munich Conference (1938), 27,
 278, 288
Mutual assured destruction (MAD),

ABOUT THE EDITOR

Samuel P. Huntington is Clarence Dillon Professor of International Affairs and director of the Center for International Affairs at Harvard University. During 1977–78 he served at the White House as coordinator of security planning for the National Security Council. He was a founder and co-editor (1970–77) of the journal, *Foreign Policy*. Among his books are *The Soldier and the State* (1957), *The Common Defense* (1961), *Political Order in Changing Societies* (1968), and *American Politics: The Promise of Disharmony* (1981).

ABOUT THE CONTRIBUTORS

Richard K. Betts, senior fellow at the Brookings Institution, has taught at Harvard, Columbia, and Johns Hopkins. He is the author of *Soldiers, Statesmen, and Cold War Crises*, and editor of *Cruise Missiles: Technology, Strategy, Politics*.

Eliot Cohen is an assistant professor in the Government Department at Harvard University, where he received his B.A. and Ph.D. degrees. He is the author of *Commandos and Politicans: Elite Military Units in Modern Democracies*, and has written for *Foreign Policy, Commentary, The Public Interest*, and other journals. He is currently completing a book on military manpower policy.

Steven R. David received a Master's degree from Stanford University in East Asian Studies in 1973 and a Ph.D. in political science from Harvard University in 1980. In 1980–81 he was a post-doctoral fellow at the Center for International Affairs. Dr. David is presently an assistant professor of political science at Johns Hopkins University where he is working on a book dealing with Third World security needs.

Aaron L. Friedberg is a graduate student in government at Harvard University. In 1979 he was a consultant to the National Security Council and since that time has also worked as a consultant to the Department of Defense.

Michael I. Handel is senior lecturer in international relations at Hebrew University. He received his Ph.D. from Harvard University and has recently been a research associate at the Harvard Center for International Affairs and at the MIT Center for International Studies. He is the author of *Weak States in the International System* and *The Diplomacy of Surprise: Hitler, Nixon, Sadat.*

Joseph S. Nye is a professor of government at Harvard University. He was a deputy to the under secretary of state from 1977 to 1979. He is co-editor of *Energy and Security* (Ballinger, 1981), and he publishes articles in many professional journals, as well as in *The New York Times Book Review.*

Bruce D. Porter received his Ph.D. from Harvard and was a post-doctoral fellow at the Center for International Affairs in 1979–80, where his chapter was largely researched and written. He is now a senior research analyst of Soviet foreign affairs at RFE/RL, Inc., Munich, West Germany.

Stephen P. Rosen received his Ph.D. from Harvard University in 1979, where he was a member of the National Security Studies Program at the Center for International Affairs. He is presently working for the Office of the Secretary of Defense in Washington.